British Art and the First World War, 1914–1924

The First World War is usually believed to have had a catastrophic effect on British art, killing artists and movements and creating a mood of belligerent philistinism around the nation. In this book, however, James Fox paints a very different picture of artistic life in wartime Britain. Drawing on a wide range of sources, he examines the cultural activities of largely forgotten individuals and institutions, as well as the press and the government, in order to shed new light on art's unusual role in a nation at war. He argues that the conflict's artistic consequences, though initially disruptive, were ultimately and enduringly productive. He reveals how the war effort helped forge a much closer relationship between the British public and their art – a relationship that informed the country's cultural agenda well into the 1920s.

JAMES FOX is a Fellow of Gonville and Caius College, University of Cambridge.

Studies in the Social and Cultural History of Modern Warfare

In recent years the field of modern history has been enriched by the exploration of two parallel histories. These are the social and cultural history of armed conflict, and the impact of military events on social and cultural history.

Studies in the Social and Cultural History of Modern Warfare presents the fruits of this growing area of research, reflecting both the colonization of military history by cultural historians and the reciprocal interest of military historians in social and cultural history, to the benefit of both. The series offers the latest scholarship in European and non-European events from the 1850s to the present day.

This is book 43 in the series, and a full list of titles in the series can be found at: www.cambridge.org/modernwarfare

BRITISH ART AND THE FIRST WORLD WAR, 1914–1924

JAMES FOX
Gonville and Caius College, University of Cambridge

CAMBRIDGE
UNIVERSITY PRESS

CAMBRIDGE
UNIVERSITY PRESS

University Printing House, Cambridge CB2 8BS, United Kingdom

Cambridge University Press is part of the University of Cambridge.

It furthers the University's mission by disseminating knowledge in the pursuit of education, learning and research at the highest international levels of excellence.

www.cambridge.org
Information on this title: www.cambridge.org/9781107105874

First published 2015

Printed in the United Kingdom by TJ International Ltd. Padstow Cornwall

A catalogue record for this publication is available from the British Library

Library of Congress Cataloguing in Publication data
Fox, James, 1982–
British art and the First World War, 1914–1924 / James Fox (Gonville and Caius College, University of Cambridge).
pages cm. – (Studies in the social and cultural history of modern warfare)
Includes bibliographical references and index.
ISBN 978-1-107-10587-4 (hardback)
1. World War, 1914–1918–Art and the war. 2. World War, 1914–1918–Social aspects–Great Britain. 3. Art, British–20th century. 4. Artists–Great Britain–History–20th century. 5. Art and society–Great Britain–History–20th century. 6. Great Britain–Intellectual life–20th century. I. Title.
N9155.G7F69 2015
709.41'0904–dc23 2015010003

ISBN 978-1-107-10587-4 Hardback

CONTENTS

PLATES

Colour plates can be found between pages 116 and 117.

FIGURES

ACKNOWLEDGEMENTS

I have been working on this book intermittently since I began my doctoral thesis in October 2006. The project thus possesses the dubious honour of lasting twice as long as the war it chronicles. And yet it would not have been possible at all without the advice, support and assistance that I have been fortunate enough to receive over the last eight years. My gratitude must first go to my supervisor Duncan Robinson, who agreed to take me on as his PhD student in the first place. I am grateful to other colleagues at the University of Cambridge, particularly Jean Michel Massing, whose wisdom and friendship have proved invaluable throughout. I have also received advice from a legion of scholars in the field who have made the time to offer suggestions that helped shape (and reshape) this volume. Grace Brockington, Michael Walsh, Maria Tippett and David Peters Corbett have been especially charitable.

This project relied heavily on primary sources, and thus on the competence and benevolence of their custodians: my thanks go to Simon Fenwick at the Royal Watercolour Society; Mark Pomeroy at the Royal Academy; Monica Grose-Hodge at the Art-Workers' Guild; Emmanuel Minne at the Royal Society of British Sculptors; Emma Pearce at Winsor & Newton; Alan Crookham at the National Gallery; and to the staff at the Artists' General Benevolent Institution and the Professional Classes Aid Council, who opened their offices to me. I must single out Sandra de Laszlo and Caroline Corbeau at the De László Foundation in London for particular praise: they allowed me to pore over Philip de László's remarkable papers (many of which were uncatalogued at the time), and met my every request with generosity, enthusiasm and efficiency.

It goes without saying that this book would never have happened were it not for the support I received from various institutions in Britain and beyond. I am grateful to the Arts & Humanities Research Council, who funded my doctoral studies; to Churchill College, Cambridge, who gave me a base from which to work following the completion of my PhD; to the Yale Center for British Art, where a visiting scholarship allowed me to undertake further research in the autumn of 2010; to Hawthornden Castle for granting me an invaluable month of undisturbed writing time; and above all to Gonville and Caius College, Cambridge, whose generous four-year Research Fellowship gave me the necessary space to transform my doctoral thesis into the (very different) book that exists today.

Some of the material here has appeared in other places before. Parts of Chapter 2 were published as '"Traitor Painters": Artists and Espionage in the First World War, 1914–1918', *British Art Journal* 10 (Spring 2009); and as '"Fiddling While Rome is Burning": Hostility to Art during the First World War, 1914–1918', *Visual Culture in Britain* 10 (Spring 2010). Material that was published as 'Conflict and Consolation: British Art and the First World War, 1914–1919', *Art History* 36 (September 2013), pp. 810–33, reappears here in Chapter 5 and I am grateful to the Association of Art Historians for granting me permission to reproduce it. I must also thank the team at Cambridge University Press who converted my shabby manuscript into such an elegant volume. Michael Watson was a pleasure to work with; Christopher Feeney was a superb copy editor; Rosalyn Scott was a model of efficiency; and my anonymous readers scrutinized the text with diligence and insight – and saved me from embarrassment at several points. And last but emphatically not least I must express my gratitude to the series editor Jay Winter. An exceptional historian whose vast output is as terrifying as it is inspiring, Jay's support has meant a very great deal to me. It is a pleasure and an honour to be published in the wonderful series that he edits.

Finally, I must thank my friends and my family: to Jessica Berenbeim, Tom Stammers and Kirty Topiwala for advising on (and tolerating) the banalities of 'writing up'; to my grandfather for offering me a quiet space in Cyprus in which I was able to write this book's introduction and conclusion; to my obsessively tidy mother, who somehow endured a dining-table littered with library books and laptop leads for the best part of eight years; and of course to my brother Josh, who – though I never tell him – is my greatest inspiration.

INTRODUCTION

On 4 August 1914 large crowds gathered in London's principal public spaces to celebrate – or in some cases denounce – the imminent outbreak of the European war. In Trafalgar Square the maffickers' chants were so loud that according to at least one eye-witness they were still echoing some twenty minutes after they had been sung.[1] Trafalgar Square was certainly an appropriate venue for such martial proceedings: conceived to commemorate Britain's victory in the Napoleonic wars a century earlier, it was arguably the nation's most belligerent political arena. The space, after all, was populated by military statuary, and surrounded by buildings that proclaimed the country's imperial might. One of those buildings, however, was the National Gallery. Devoted to beauty, peace and a common European spirit as expressed through the continent's art, the institution had for decades occupied an uneasy relationship with its bellicose surroundings.[2] But as the war crowds ambushed its steps and transformed them into makeshift grandstands for their demonstrations, the future of that relationship seemed unusually uncertain.

For the many commentators who spent the late summer of 1914 speculating on art's likely place in the society that was about to be forged on the anvil of war, the scenes in Trafalgar Square might have suggested a number of possibilities. Pessimists might have seen the crowd's submersion of the National Gallery as a worrying sign that the delicate world of art was going to be crushed by waves of philistine 'war fury'.[3] Optimists, on the other hand, may well have interpreted the public's decision to gather *there*, on the steps of a *museum*, as heralding a new alliance between art and society – a return of the long-estranged cultural domain into the heart of heroic human affairs. But there were others who surely noticed that in the face of those marauding crowds, indeed throughout the momentous events of early August, the National Gallery's doors had remained locked.[4] The realists among them might have concluded that despite superficial appearances, artistic life and public life would remain as obstinately discrete as they had been before the war.

Before 1914 art had indeed played a relatively minor role in British public life. At the outbreak of war the art world was admittedly large – it consisted of thousands of artists, dealers, organizations, museums and critics that were proliferating by the day – but its public reach and official recognition remained limited.[5] Exhibition attendances were small and static; arts coverage in the national press was sporadic at best and negligible at worst; and the government's support for art was inferior to that which was provided in comparable European countries. Moreover, if this British indifference to visual art was famously longstanding (the artist and critic Roger Fry described it as 'pathological'), it had if anything been emboldened in the decades before the war.[6] From the 1870s and 1880s onwards, progressive artists and aesthetes had repeatedly challenged the philistinism of popular and official taste, and by 1914 the most advanced artistic trends were dismissive of, if not altogether hostile to, the larger public.[7] This had alienated the public yet further, and thus widened the gap between the British art world and mainstream society. By the outbreak of war the two spheres seemed all but irreconcilable, and many concluded that the only satisfactory solution was a policy of mutual disregard.[8]

Many members of the art world hoped that the outbreak of war would not end the cultural independence that they believed was a condition of aesthetic purity. In the first war issue of the *Burlington Magazine* – a major journal which more than any other represented this world-view – a brief 'special notice' declared its editor's intentions:

> In the face of the present international situation, we must expect that for a time interest in art and the history of art is likely to give place to more violent claims on the attention of the public. We feel it to be none the less of the utmost importance, at such a time, to keep alive those disinterested activities which are the distinguishing mark of civilization. Even though the appeal that art makes is feebler than the more pressing demands of self-preservation, it is more persistent and more enduring.[9]

The *Burlington Magazine*, in other words, proposed that as wartime society ignored art, so art should ignore wartime society. It certainly upheld its part of the bargain – at least initially. The pages that followed featured essays about Rembrandt and Petrus Christus, the portraits of Michelangelo, the stylistic development of central Italian medals, and an extended discussion of a newly discovered head of Constantine the Great – but they made hardly any reference to the ongoing conflagration.

Most people, however, believed that the art world could no longer insulate itself from its immediate context, and the optimists among them believed that the war might actually be *good* for art. As it happened, the conflict helped end the biggest pre-war threat to artworks – the suffragettes – with an amnesty, and on 20 August the National Gallery reopened to the public for the first time since May.[10] Inside, visitors would have seen in Uccello's *Battle of San Romano*, in war pictures by van Huchtenburgh, Weier and Wouwermans and in a set of newly acquired Napoleonic battle paintings by Vernet, centuries of proof that great art and great wars were two sides of the same coin. Meanwhile, critics assembled grand art-historical trajectories – from the origins of art 'where artist and warrior were one', through ancient battle reliefs, the military works of Leonardo and Michelangelo and the modern war paintings of West, Goya and Verestchagin – to confirm that, as one declared, 'never does genius flourish as it flourishes in times of disaster'.[11] Most of these essays relied heavily on a passage in George Moore's *Modern Painting*, from 1893:

> The Greek sculptors came after Salamis and Marathon; the Italian renaissance came when Italy was distracted with revolution and was divided into opposing states ... Art came upon Holland after heroic wars in which the Dutchmen vehemently asserted their nationhood ... Art came upon England when England was most adventurous, after the victories of Marlborough. Art came upon France after the great revolution, after the victories of Marengo and Austerlitz, after the burning of Moscow.[12]

All, however, including Moore, were ultimately informed by John Ruskin's 1865 exposition of a 'creative and foundational war' in *The Crown of Wild Olive*, which – if ever forgotten – was now being seared into public consciousness by a patriotic press:

> All the pure and noble arts of peace are founded on war ... There is no great art possible to a nation but that which is based on battle ... As peace is established or extended in Europe, the arts decline ... All the great nations learned their truth of word, and strength of thought, in war; that they were nourished in war, and wasted by peace; taught by war, and deceived by peace; trained by war, and betrayed by peace – in a word, that they were born in war, and expired in peace.[13]

At the core of Ruskin's formulation and all those who reiterated it lay the abiding conviction that, for all its concomitant hardships, war was an invaluable source of artistic inspiration. This widespread belief not only persuaded artists to enlist in order to 'strengthen their art by physical and moral courage and ... adventure, risk and daring';[14] it also convinced cultural commentators that 'a true Renaissance of Art might be brought about under the stress of a noble and all-pervading emotion'.[15]

The nature of this renaissance predictably depended on each prognosticator's aesthetic predispositions. Reactionaries like A. C. R. Carter (editor of *The Year's Art*) maintained that the conflict would obliterate the noxious currents of modernist experiment that had been gathering force in the years before the war. He wrote: 'It will sweep away cant and insincerity, the slip-shod and the shirk, above all the fumbling worship of strange gods in the mad camps of the mungo inventors of epileptic distortion and fungoid colour.'[16] Radicals conversely believed that it would finally scuttle the moribund traditions that had stifled cultural progress for decades: the English painter C. R. W. Nevinson famously declared that the war would represent a 'violent incentive to Futurism' because there was 'no beauty except in strife, and no masterpiece without aggressiveness'.[17] Reactionaries and radicals nevertheless concurred that whether it was a 'sovereign disinfectant', a 'cleansing purge' or a 'purifying fire', the war would ultimately be a remedial cultural force.[18] 'The medicine is severe', concluded one contemporary, 'but we have no fear of its destroying the body along with the pimples.'[19]

Not everyone, however, was convinced that the war would leave the body unscathed. And thus while optimistic commentators assembled historical surveys to demonstrate that war and art were age-old allies, pessimists composed alternative narratives to prove that they were age-old adversaries. In one of these essays, the director of the National Gallery himself, C. J. Holmes, reminded his readers of the looting and destruction that had gone hand in hand with conflict for centuries. Holmes cited the theft of artworks in Spain and Italy under Napoleon as well as the Franco-British ruination of Peking's Summer Palace during the Opium Wars with China in 1860. He had no reason to think matters would be different this time round:

> War is no longer waged with arrows and lances, or tardy muskets, but carried on both on earth and in the air with high explosives that blow to atoms all that they strike, and strike haphazard from afar. We have thus no guarantee whatever that this struggle between the enlightened or Christian nations of Europe will not be just as destructive to fine things as the wars waged by the barbarous conquerors of the past whom we are accustomed to execrate.[20]

It wasn't long before Holmes was vindicated. Although the Hague Peace Conference of 1907 had legislated that cultural institutions should be spared from all future violence, they became collateral damage before even a month of fighting was out.[21] On 25 August 1914 German forces sacked the town of Louvain and destroyed numerous cultural treasures there including the University Library and its 230,000 books, 800 incunabula and 950 manuscripts.[22] In the following weeks numerous architectural masterpieces – including Reims cathedral – were damaged or destroyed, and there were even reports of widespread looting of art collections, at least one instance of which was allegedly perpetrated by the German Crown Prince.[23]

Other pessimists felt that the war's threats to art were not simply physical. Some were concerned that the conflict would make an already philistine community even more unsympathetic to 'high' culture. In a September 1914 essay called 'Art after Armageddon', one commentator surveyed these bleak visions of the future:

> In the press of conflict we find out what we really value, and it is usually assumed that art of every kind will be one of the first things we shall do without. We are shown the picture of a relapse into barbarism: a world fighting for existence, the necessities of life – a few of the coarser luxuries retained, the refinements of existence despised. How is it possible, we are, moreover, asked, for the artist to concentrate his mind on the pursuit of his ideal at a moment of acute anxiety, and with tales of carnage on every hand?[24]

Others were more concerned about the war's economic ramifications. Lawrence Haward, who became the first director of the Manchester Art Gallery in 1914, remarked that 'when the money and the energy of a nation are devoted to the prosecution of a war, little may be left for the enjoyment of what is unhappily regarded too often as a luxury'. He concluded:

> There is no reason for supposing that the present war will differ from others in its effects and will give birth to masterpieces as some are expecting it to do. It is much more likely to nip them in the bud by bringing about conditions unfavourable to the artist and his work and by killing those who might have produced them.[25]

A hundred years after the events of 1914, scholars seem as compulsively drawn to grand diagnoses of the First World War's cultural consequences as had been their predecessors. Moreover, their discussions still break down along surprisingly similar lines: they continue to debate whether the conflict's effects were constructive, destructive, progressive or regressive in nature, and how broad and lasting those changes ultimately were.[26] Most, however, have sided with the pessimists of 1914 and concluded that the war was ultimately detrimental to art. The clearest evidence for this conclusion has been biographical. Over the last few decades, art historians have exhaustively recounted the experiences of the many young artists whose peacetime careers were cut short when they went to the front; how the horrific events they witnessed undermined their creative confidence, altered their stylistic trajectories and challenged the viability of artistic representation itself; how their professional integrity was compromised by official employment and propagandism; and how a number of them – including Henri Gaudier-Brzeska, Umberto Boccioni, Raymond Duchamp-Villon and Franz Marc – perished in battle and never fulfilled their potential.[27]

These personal tragedies are often seen as part of a much broader cultural setback: one that Benjamin Buchloh has called the 'collapse of the modernist paradigm' and others have termed the *rappel à l'ordre*.[28] Before the war, modernist movements and avant-garde factions were beginning to flourish in almost every country in Europe. These groupings, however, depended on specific social conditions that were largely obliterated by the conflict. Cubism in France, Expressionism in Germany, Futurism in Italy and Vorticism in Britain consequently saw their members dispersed, their audiences distracted and their fragile markets dissipated.[29] This process was particularly damaging in Britain. Vorticism had only antedated the war by a matter of months, and British modernism in general was not established enough to survive the conflict intact. Many British artists simply abandoned the progressive styles with which they had flirted before the war, and most never returned to them. Art historians have traditionally seen this as a disappointing, if not disastrous, development: the war, they have concluded, ended a promisingly radical moment in British art and produced in its aftermath an insular and reactionary period characterized by 'stagnation', 'uncertainty' and 'retreat'.[30]

The *rappel à l'ordre*, however, was not quite as definitive as that. More recently, scholars have shown that cultural experimentation did survive the conflict in one way or another, whether it took the form of a 'pacifist modernism' or an 'adaptive revisionism'.[31] Moreover, art historians have claimed that for all the aesthetic failures that came with so much official employment, the nation's best war art (by the likes of Paul and John Nash, Stanley Spencer, C. R. W. Nevinson, Wyndham Lewis and David Bomberg among others) represents some of the finest modern British paintings of the century – as formally inventive as they were politically uncompromising.[32] Nevertheless, the pessimism that inflects more general evaluations of the war continues to inform conclusions about its art. Despite the more nuanced interpretations of recent years, there remains an overwhelming sense that, to quote Bomberg, the conflict was ultimately 'bad news for art'.[33] Art historians still largely believe that the years 1914 to 1918 destroyed more than they created; that they were inhospitable rather than conducive to serious cultural activity; and that, when plotting a larger story of British art, the war years are better seen as an end than a beginning.

Art historians, however, are by no means alone in evaluating the war's impact on visual culture. Over the last three decades historians have become increasingly interested in the conflict's artistic and intellectual consequences. Indeed, according to Jay Winter, cultural historians now represent 'the pioneering sector of research on the Great War'.[34] Winter himself, Annette Becker, Antoine Prost and many other cultural historians have repeatedly explored wartime painting and sculpture, but all of them have interpreted those art forms (along with other kinds of cultural output like graffiti, toys, postcards, photographs and public memorials) through the wider lens of '*culture de guerre*': what Winter and Prost have neatly defined as 'the mental furniture men and women draw on to make sense of their world at war'.[35] In this book I have endeavoured to incorporate some of the approaches adopted by cultural historians – their willingness to move between different forms and registers of cultural production and experience; their examination of art in light of its social and psychological functions – to advance a new argument about the relationship between British art and the First World War.

In this book I will argue that the war's artistic consequences, though initially disruptive, were ultimately, and enduringly, productive. Between 1914 and 1918 the conflict created an unusual set of social, political and cultural conditions. These conditions facilitated a change in the relationship between British society and its art. As 'total war' tightened its grip on all aspects of national life, the self-contained sphere that the art world had previously inhabited became unsustainable, and artists and their institutions found themselves operating within society as a whole. Though challenging at first, these new circumstances eventually brought art into a more symbiotic union with national life than it had perhaps ever experienced before. Under pressure to prove that it was not an enemy of the war effort, the art world self-mobilized to raise morale and recruit, to inform and entertain, to console and commemorate, and of course to fight. As the art world reached out to the country, the country in turn reached out to art. Britain's government, its press, its civic institutions and its public all began to use artworks precisely in order to deal with the unusual conditions of war. These developments produced in Britain a more social art as well as a more artistic society – and I believe that they informed the country's cultural agenda well into the 1920s.

In order to reach these broader cultural conclusions I will expand the parameters that have hitherto circumscribed art-historical accounts of the war. Art historians have traditionally focused their attentions on three areas: the experiences of young male soldier-artists; the government's propaganda campaign with its official war artists' schemes; and the fate of modernism after 1914. While all three areas are of undeniable importance, they are hardly representative of wider artistic developments. Not every artist went to the front, and very few were modernists or employed as official war artists. This book does not ignore those exceptional cases, but it does seek to place them in their appropriate context alongside the amateur watercolourists, popular illustrators, jobbing portraitists, provincial engravers, old Academicians and memorial sculptors who have hitherto been neglected but were just as much affected by the conflict. Moreover, all of them became extremely popular with wartime audiences; they are thus of crucial importance to comprehending how the country came to understand the war through art, and understand art through war.

Since I am interested more in art's social status and function than in its aesthetic qualities, my understanding of art for the purpose of this study is informed by sociological research. For some years, sociologists have interpreted art as a social activity. They have shown how it is produced by networks of individuals and organizations that collaborate to produce, exhibit, distribute, consume, commission and discuss objects that they – and we – understand as artworks. Sociologists and philosophers have called these conglomerations 'art worlds', defining them as 'institutions' that are just as real as any other feature of social life.[36] Using this definition, I will examine the constellation of people, organizations and practices that constituted the art world in wartime Britain. In addition to the obvious focus on artists and their work, I will discuss the experiences of collectors, dealers, curators, administrators, critics, publishers and scholars; I will analyse the activities of museums, galleries, artists' organizations, art schools and art-related businesses; and I will consistently relate both those individuals and those institutions to government policies, public discourses and private gestures in order to discern how the social position and reputation of the art world was altered by the conflict.

This book comprises six chapters that extend from the outbreak of war in 1914 to the opening of the British Empire Exhibition ten years later. Although I claim that art was ultimately invigorated by the war, my first two chapters describe how its initial experiences were far from promising. Chapter 1 focuses on the war's material consequences. Drawing on the financial records of auction houses, art collectors, art dealers, exhibiting societies and finally artists, it shows how the conflict produced a series of commercial disruptions that brought the art world very close to collapse. In the first six months of war the art market all but vanished; art institutions ceased to function; and artists were paralyzed by a shortage of material resources that were increasingly commandeered by the state. As a result, many artists changed careers and many arts organizations disappeared. Those that survived were left with little choice but to compete with the war effort and the rest of society for the same resources. I argue that this was not only futile; it created a situation in which artistic needs and national needs came to be at odds with each other.

This was just one part of the problem. In Chapter 2, I turn from war's quantifiable effects on the business of art to its less quantifiable, but equally potent, effects on the perceptions of art. Using all kinds of public and private discourses – from academic theories to popular novels, from official legislation to unofficial gossip – I show how the war initially poisoned social perceptions of art and artists. No longer understood as a self-contained activity that could either be evaluated on its own merits or altogether ignored, art from 1914 was instead judged through the prism of the war effort. Artistic activities came to be considered trivial, unethical and unpatriotic distractions from the needs of the country, and artists were regularly identified as profiteers rather than patriots and as shirkers rather than soldiers. Moreover, as the final section of the chapter – which focuses on public fears of espionage – makes clear, artists were very often believed to be genuine enemies of the state. In every case, art was constructed as an unacceptable activity within a society at war.[37]

It was, paradoxically, as a result of these almost unanswerable criticisms that the art world began to find an answer. Chapter 3 shows how from about 1915 many individuals and institutions within the art world began to rethink their social purpose in order to prove that they could in fact play a role in national life. I describe how critics, scholars and exhibiting societies reconceived paintings and sculptures as the embodiments of national identity; how the art market restructured itself around the acceptable face of charity while museums devoted themselves to propaganda and public information; and how artists gave up their peacetime careers, rallying the home front with posters and calibrating the front line with reconnaissance and camouflage. The art world, in short, transformed itself from a private peacetime institution into a public wartime institution. In the process, it not only secured its wartime survival; it may also have laid important foundations for a new and more central role in post-war Britain.

As the unique conditions of war encouraged the art world to reach out to the public, so they encouraged the public to reach out to art. In Chapters 4 and 5 I show how, somewhat surprisingly, the conflict created a set of voracious social demands for images. Chapter 4 describes how 'war fever' caused civilians to take an unprecedented interest in anything that represented the realities of the front line. Images were widely believed to be the most vivid, accessible and reliable ways of doing this. While photographs and films became the most prolific sources of these war pictures, the graphic arts were not left behind. Concentrating on the hugely popular output of the pictorial press, I demonstrate how artists produced images of war that were arguably more useful, more powerful and often more popular than those made by their photographic counterparts. In doing so, they secured vast new audiences for their work, and proved themselves to be so integral to the mediation of the war that from 1916 the government itself began to employ them as official war artists.

The nation's sudden demand for images was not just driven by the desire to experience the war; it was also motivated by the need to escape and overcome the war. Like its precursor, Chapter 5 explores a wide and demotic range of visual material that was hugely popular with the wartime public but has since been largely neglected. It describes how the many pastoral landscapes exhibited at the Royal Academy and Royal Watercolour Society after 1914 were embraced by those who yearned for nostalgic escapism; how the commissioning of posthumous portraits helped grieving families cope with the premature deaths of their loved ones; and how a boom in amateur sketching – as well as being an early experiment with art therapy – enabled soldiers to come to terms with the traumas of the front line. In all of these cases, the war had not only brought entirely new audiences to art; it had lent their engagement with artworks a pressing emotional importance: not a matter of aesthetic curiosity but psychological survival.[38]

If the unusual conditions of war had transformed the reputation, function and importance of art, my final chapter shows how those changes were very much sustained in the conflict's aftermath. Focusing on the five years between the Armistice of 1919 and the British Empire Exhibition of 1924, I survey the state of the arts in a nation that was itself attempting to rebuild. I explore artists' participation in the construction of memorials around the country, and the proliferation of largely forgotten artistic organizations like the Arts League of Service; I trace the development of increasingly sympathetic governmental attitudes towards art and art education; and I investigate an unusually reconciliatory mood within the art world itself, both between modern artists and traditional institutions and between fine art and popular design. Taken together, the art of the post-war period was productive, collaborative, civic-minded and socially engaged, and I conclude that this promising cultural landscape was one of the many long-term products of the First World War.

If this brief summary seems to paint a complex and even contradictory picture, that is only because the war's cultural consequences were themselves complex and contradictory. The conflict created obstacles and opportunities simultaneously; it demolished cultural reputations and audiences precisely as it built them. For this reason, this book should not be read as a strictly linear path through the period. It may be the case that the war's most acute artistic hardships (described in Chapters 1 and 2) were felt at its beginning; that the art world only started to mobilize (as described in Chapter 3) in its middle; and that war pictures and peace pictures (described in Chapters 4 and 5) were at their most socially influential towards its end. However, all of these themes overlapped and coexisted throughout the war years. One thing, however, seems clear: by 1924 British art was more conscious of society and British society more conscious of art than they had been a decade earlier.

1 THE OUTBREAK OF WAR AND THE BUSINESS OF ART

At the beginning of August 1914 politicians and businessmen alike were optimistic about the opportunities that war would bring. Both believed that unabated commercial activity would help Britain defeat Germany by capturing her trade.[1] A policy of 'business as usual' – which in the early months of the war was endlessly extolled in newspapers, trades journals and government speeches – thus seemed to represent a felicitous combination of profit and patriotism, in which both business and the business of war would become mutually reinforcing aspects of national success. As the weeks progressed, however, these predictions were proved emphatically incorrect. Precisely as the virtues of 'business as usual' were being praised, the nation's conventional business patterns were falling apart. Amid the uncertain political landscape Britain's banks ceased to lend money, its traders ceased to speculate and its public – gripped as they were by the unfolding events of the conflict – changed their consumption habits altogether.[2] These developments had severe consequences for the country's businesses: indeed, by September nine out of ten firms had suffered as a result of the conflict.[3]

British art was not insulated from the financial dislocation that affected the country's other businesses. It was, after all, a business as well, and like others it thrived only in favourable economic conditions. Art historians have traditionally neglected these commercial imperatives of art. Those who have studied the war have generally focused on individual experiences, intellectual epiphanies and stylistic reorientations. Yet by ignoring the institutions that surrounded those individuals, the markets that mediated their work and the social conditions that gave rise to their creations, they have often failed to explore what were surely the conflict's most striking artistic consequences. The outbreak of war had a catastrophic impact on the established institutions and practices of art: it affected buyers, auction houses, dealers, museums, exhibiting societies and arts charities just as much as it affected artists; and its material effects were, if anything, more damaging than the aesthetic consequences that have hitherto received more attention.

This chapter will use Howard Becker's concept of an 'art world' – a 'social system' that involves collaboration between artists, businesses, organizations and audiences – to reach a wider, and more social, understanding of British art after 1914. It will argue that in the first half of the war, the conflict did not just inhibit the art world's ability to function; it changed the relationship between the art world and British society. Becker has written that art worlds have 'intimate and extensive relationships with the worlds from which they try to distinguish themselves. They share sources of supply with those other worlds, recruit personnel from them, adopt ideas that originate in them, and compete with them for audiences and financial support.'[4] With the onset of total war, however, the terms of those relationships were changed. As the war effort monopolized British social life, the art world's space within it was threatened. Artists and art institutions were forced to compete with the rest of society for resources that previously they had shared. As a result, they contributed to a scenario in which artistic needs and national needs came to be at odds with one another.

Art sales

The first signs of political crisis are typically expressed in the market. This was certainly the case in 1914, when the famed art boom of the pre-war years actually expired in the early summer. In part, the art market had become a victim of its own buoyancy: the inflated prices at the big sales of 1911, 1912 and 1913 had left dealers full of overpriced stock.[5] Nevertheless, the international uncertainty that followed the assassination of Archduke Ferdinand in Sarajevo on 28 June 1914 had a decisive impact on market confidence. Political anxieties militated against the international transactions that had contributed to the pre-war boom; and with income unpredictable and credit unobtainable many buyers withdrew from the market until stability returned. The few who had purchased at *ante-bellum* prices found themselves in serious difficulties. Hugh Lane had bought pictures for a pre-war premium at the Grenfell sale just two days before Ferdinand's assassination and was subsequently unable to obtain the cash to cover his outlay. By late July he was on the verge of a hitherto unthinkable bankruptcy.[6]

Britain finally declared war on Germany at 11 p.m. on Tuesday, 4 August, more than a month after the events in Sarajevo. Its entry into the conflict only confirmed the art market's concerns. In the following weeks and months buyers were all but absent from the salerooms, and sellers too, as A. C. R. Carter observed in *The Year's Art*, 'showed a natural diffidence' in submitting their possessions to auction for fear that they would fetch disappointing prices.[7] Faced with the crisis, Christie's, Sotheby's and other major auction houses (including Manson & Woods, Knight, Frank & Rutley, Robinson & Fisher, Foster's, Phillips', Neal's and Wilkinson & Hodge) all decided to cancel their winter sales season. The majority did not reopen for business for at least six more months.[8] It was a remarkable development. Indeed, W. T. Whitley in the *Burlington Magazine* believed that the cessation of sales by virtually all the major auction houses was 'without precedent' in the entire history of the British art market.[9]

As far as the auctioneers were concerned, 1915 showed little improvement. Christie's did not receive a single object for conventional sale in the whole year, and the firm even considered permanent closure.[10] Sotheby's, meanwhile, did recommence business in the spring but listed twenty-eight sales in all, compared with 108 in 1913 – although it could probably not have coped with more given its war-induced staff shortages.[11] The clearest indication, however, of the collapsing market for art is found in the 1,400-guinea threshold – a prestigious price that only the most valuable artworks secured. In 1913, eighty-five pictures had made 1,400 guineas or more in British auctions; in 1915, that number had plummeted to four.[12] This staggering statistic was partly due to the absence of high-quality pictures offered for sale at the start of the conflict. However, it also reflected a wider collapse in the monetary value of art. Indeed, the depreciation of paintings in 1915 was so noteworthy that even the pictorial press took note: one cartoon in *Punch* (Figure 1.1) depicted an auctioneer trying to sell an elegantly framed picture with the line '"What! No advance on three shillings? Why, *the picture by itself* is worth that!"'[13]

The plummeting value of artworks had a simple cause: after the outbreak of war, very few people were buying them. It is true that Britain had never been famed for its art collectors. In 1915 Wyndham Lewis had written that it was 'almost alone amongst the countries of Europe' in not having produced a community of people who were willing to 'spend a few hundred pounds a year less on petrol or social pyrotechnics, and buy pictures'.[14] Nevertheless, the few collectors who had purchased artworks before the war now found themselves distinctly less able to do so. War conditions reduced the number of 'the rich' (those classed as being worth £10,000 or more) in Britain by more than two-thirds (from 4,000 to just 1,300).[15] The art market was particularly affected by this development because the social groups from which it traditionally drew its buyers – the landed aristocracy and the metropolitan middle classes – were the principal sufferers from the wartime economy.

The wealth of the aristocracy had in fact been declining since the agricultural depression of the mid nineteenth century.[16] The war accelerated its demise. Aristocrats felt the increased burden of taxation – particularly through death duties, which doubled to 40 per cent during the conflict – but their main concern

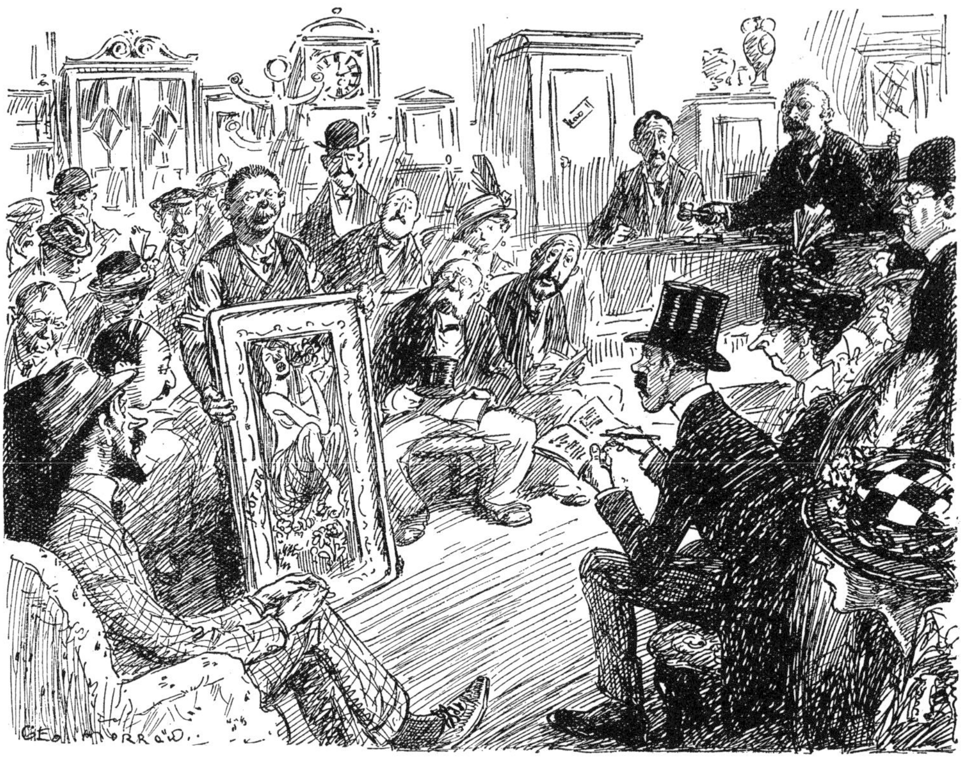

Auctioneer (reproachfully). "WHAT! NO ADVANCE ON THREE SHILLINGS? WHY, *THE PICTURE BY ITSELF* IS WORTH THAT!"

Figure 1.1 George Morrow, 'Cartoon', *Punch* (22 September 1915).

was the decimation of their usual sources of unearned income. Amid the uncertainty of the markets their investments depreciated by an average of 40 per cent, while the 1915 Rent Restriction Act caused the income from their estates to fall precisely as the cost of managing them increased.[17] It is no surprise then, that few aristocrats seriously considered expanding their collections during the war. In fact, the very opposite was the case. In a letter to *The Times*, Lord Knaresborough wrote that 'country gentlemen' were being forced 'to sell their most cherished possessions in the way of pictures of their ancestors, old furniture, silver and whatever works of art they may have, in order to keep their heads above water'.[18] From the middle of 1915 Britain's impoverished aristocracy unleashed on the country a 'superabundance' of estate sales.[19] Indeed, in the first few years of the war this was the only business on which auction houses seemed able to rely.

The collecting habits of the middle classes were similarly undermined as the government's fiscal policies became increasingly punitive. Six incremental tax hikes caused their standard income tax rate to rise from 5.8 per cent to 30 per cent. By the end of the war they were also liable to pay supertax, which was levied on well-paid professionals at up to 52 per cent.[20] Businessmen, meanwhile, saw inflation (220 per cent by the end of the war) and indirect duties increase their overheads, and Excess Profits Duty – which from September 1915 charged 50 per cent on profits exceeding pre-war norms – eat into their incomes. Hew Strachan has estimated that taken together, the wealthiest members of the middle classes – and surely those who were most likely to invest in expensive luxuries like art – could potentially have faced a combined tax burden of 77 per cent.[21] It was for this reason that in some quarters the middle classes came to be known as the 'new poor'.[22] The war had diminished, and often obliterated, their disposable income. They were forced to economize in order to make ends meet, and extravagances like art and antiques were the very first outlays to be abandoned.

Individuals were not the only acquirers of art objects to witness their spending power evaporate. Before the conflict museums had boasted modest collecting capacities (the National Gallery, for instance, had received an annual purchase grant of £5,000 from the government that if unspent, had to be returned), but they had nonetheless been able to expand their collections in wise and often impressive ways.[23] However, in November 1914 the first war budget suspended all such purchase grants – though the British Museum retained a modest sum for the continued acquisition of books not secured under the Copyright Act.[24] Museums' difficulties were further damaged by the fact that their other sources of funding (savings, investments and donations) were similarly affected by the war economy. Since 1908 the National Art-Collections Fund – a charitable body that had been formed to assist museums in the acquisition of artworks – had been extremely helpful in this regard. But it too suffered as a result of the war. In the first year of the conflict almost 10 per cent of its paying members resigned; its income from subscriptions and donations plummeted; and it could distribute only half of what it had done in the previous year.[25]

Museums, in fact, were so concerned about the war's impact on their collecting policies that some contemplated extreme measures. In 1916 the trustees of the National Gallery drafted a bill that requested the power to sell off the over-represented parts of its collection in order to raise funds for new works by artists who were under-represented. 'It is not a "war emergency" measure', explained Lord D'Abernon in Parliament, 'but it is a measure of which the urgency has been greatly increased by economic changes resulting from the war.'[26] The National Gallery Bill was almost universally condemned: MPs described it as a 'monstrous proposition' that would transform the 'permanent resting-place of the nation's pictures' into 'an occasional auction mart'.[27] The bill was abandoned at the end of 1916, and it now seems little more than a wartime curiosity. Nevertheless, it clearly expresses the degree to which the conflict had transformed thinking about art. After the outbreak of war money seemed more finite than before. Collectors of all kinds had to make difficult decisions and painful sacrifices, and art was often the victim of them.

Art dealers

The widespread inhibition of art buying inevitably affected the firms who depended on selling it. In February 1915 the *Fine Art Trade Journal* carried out a nationwide survey of art dealers' experiences in the first six months of the war. Its results were unequivocal: all dealers selling all kinds of art objects in every part of the country were in 'complete agreement' that the biggest problem they faced was the disappearance of custom. In Manchester, a firm's trade was down 75 per cent; in the West Country, dealers reported a 'serious diminution of business'; in Bradford, the war had allegedly 'killed all good work, such as gilding and the sale of engravings of any value'; in Oldham, one dealer revealed that 'in the first month [of the war] nothing was done at all, and very little has been done since'; in Portsmouth, a firm's regular customers had departed for naval service; and for a dealer in Newcastle there was quite simply 'no fine art business' at all.[28]

These commercial hardships were not limited to minor provincial firms. The Grosvenor Gallery in London's Bond Street was one of the most distinguished dealerships in Britain, yet according to its director's letter-books it too struggled in the wake of the war. Like other establishments, the Grosvenor recorded an immediate decrease in sales, and at the beginning of 1915 Francis Howard filed for reduced tax liability 'on account of the depreciation of the value of business resulting from the conditions of war'.[29] As the year progressed, Howard was unable to pay his expenses and faced a deficit of £600.[30] He abandoned exhibition plans for the year ahead and even attempted to dispense with his lease.[31] However, his inability to find a tenant compelled the gallery to continue operating through 1916, where it posted a record loss on trading of £1,000.[32] The Grosvenor Gallery somehow survived the war years, but it did not recover from them. In December 1919 the institution – which had previously been an 'essential element in London's artistic life' – closed its doors forever.[33]

Many dealers did not last as long as the Grosvenor Gallery. In South Kensington alone, in just one week in November 1914, no less than fifteen art and antiques firms apparently ceased trading.[34] Throughout the war, newspapers carried bankruptcy notices of small provincial traders like E. L. Airey in Blackburn and F. W. Miller in Fakenham all the way up to internationally renowned dealers like Raphael Bialogowski of the English Fine Art Co. and Alexander Tooth of

Tooth & Sons.[35] Some dealers decided that it was better to change business than go out of business. Concluding that fine art had become 'taboo', Messrs Phillips & MacConnal of Liverpool abandoned picture sales and launched instead into the retail of ladies' millinery.[36] Others simply abandoned Britain. Within three weeks of the outbreak of war, the Duveen brothers – perhaps the most powerful impresarios in Britain's Old Masters market before the war – decided to close their Bond Street base and move to the United States, where the taste for luxuries was undiminished.[37]

If the Duveens' departure was a major setback to Britain's market in Old Masters, the nation's market for contemporary art suffered in similar ways. The conflict saw the end of the Grafton, Stafford, Doré, New, Sackville and Marlborough galleries; closures that had a great – and hitherto underestimated – impact on the development of British art. These establishments, after all, had done more than any others to introduce the country to modern painting. The Grafton Galleries had hosted Roger Fry's seminal show 'Manet and the Post-Impressionists' in 1910; the Stafford Gallery had exhibited paintings by Cézanne and Gauguin in 1911 and pictures by Picasso the following year; the Doré, Sackville and Marlborough galleries showed Futurist work in 1912, 1913 and 1914; and the Doré also hosted the first Vorticist exhibition in 1915.[38] With the disappearance of these firms it not only became significantly harder to see and buy modern art in Britain; it reduced the already limited opportunities for progressive British artists to exhibit.

These retrogressive artistic developments were not just brought about by galleries' closures. The few progressive dealerships that stayed open during the war (like the Leicester, Goupil and Chenil galleries) altered their business models. They soon realized that any dealer who continued to display work by largely unknown artists experimenting with modernist form would be committing a brand of commercial suicide. As a consequence, they withdrew financial support from their less commercial artists and largely abandoned the high-risk strategy of one-man shows in favour of topical exhibitions that were more likely to catch the attention of a distracted and impoverished public.[39] These decisions are entirely understandable. The war had created uncertain commercial conditions and all businesses had to be willing to change if they wished to survive. In this industry, however, those decisions had serious cultural consequences. Indeed, it is this author's contention that they were just as instrumental in the wartime collapse of modernism as were the aesthetic decisions made by artists on the front line.

Dealers' artistic choices made little difference to their fate because the war's most challenging problems were not aesthetically selective. As the conflict went on the cost of rent, insurance, electricity bills and raw materials increased exponentially. Early shop closing legislation and a restricted lighting ordnance made it 'more and more difficult [for retailers] to attract customers by their window displays' and all but impossible to remain open for London's after-work patrons.[40] Yet it was not just patrons who were disappearing: the art trade's workforce was, too. By 1915 the Fine Art Trade Guild already reported that 300 of its 700 members were on national service. This number included twenty from Maple's art department, sixteen from Agnew's, six from the Fine Art Society, two from Colnaghi and all four partner-brothers from W. C. Price & Co.[41] Many of these individuals had been integral members of such businesses for decades. When the Edinburgh-based Doig, Wilson & Wheatley lost nine of its employees to war work, it lost with them a combined service of 365 years.[42]

It would be invidious to claim that the problems faced by Britain's art dealers were unique; all kinds of businesses suffered in similar ways. Nevertheless, art dealers were especially susceptible to such commercial difficulties. Unlike many other trades, they simply could not increase prices to cover their inflated expenses. Their goods, after all, were not necessities, and if they became more expensive they would simply not be bought. The art dealer's singular dilemma was neatly summarized by the *Fine Art Trade Journal* in January 1916: 'Rates, taxes, wages, carriage, packing; all his expenses are "up", yet his sales are down – often badly so – and, unlike the butcher or baker, he cannot raise prices.'[43] Dealers, however, were not the only members of the art world to occupy the crucial mid-ground between art and business, between artists and their audiences. Considerably more powerful were the country's exhibiting societies.

Exhibiting societies

Exhibiting societies were arguably the oldest and most influential institutions in the British art world. From as early as the mid eighteenth century, organizations associated with every form, medium, style, genre and gender of artistic endeavour had been crucial to the structure and status of the discipline. Their influence had only increased in the decades before the war – a period that the artist Walter Crane had dubbed 'the age of societies'.[44] By 1914 these institutions still very much dictated the practices and products of British art. Their exhibitions regulated the production, display and consumption of a vast quantity of artistic output; their schools trained many of the nation's aspiring artists and thus informed prevailing approaches to style and technique; and their unique ability to bring together artists, collectors, dealers and critics was instrumental in generating a metropolitan art world as well as in shaping public taste.[45]

The primary aim of these art societies – which were themselves run by artists – was to bring together artists. They usually provided a range of facilities (libraries, function rooms, studios) and events (lectures, dinners, balls) in order to do so. Indeed, they depended on a large and active membership – and the income that derived from it – for their existence. However, the initial effect of the war was to draw artists away from the art world, and away from each other. Art historians have already shown how Vorticism (itself a kind of exhibiting society) disintegrated under the centrifugal effects of the conflict, leaving the poet Ezra Pound to memorably complain that he was 'the only person of interest left in the art world, London'.[46] Yet this process was not confined to the avant-garde: reactionary and progressive groups alike suffered comparable crises of membership.

The principal cause of these membership crises was national service. Not a single society was untouched by the nation's call for men. Predictably, the younger groups were the hardest hit. The Allied Artists' Association – whose democratic, jury-free composition was alone in offering exhibiting opportunities to unproven artists – lost 200 members to the war – including its artists' committee chairman Henri Gaudier-Brzeska, its secretary, two members of its management committee and ultimately its talismanic president Frank Rutter.[47] The Junior Art-Workers' Guild represented even younger individuals, and a year into the war it had lost so many members to the armed forces that it considered a temporary suspension of business.[48] Nevertheless, the less youthful societies suffered, too. The Royal Society of Painters in Water-Colours, whose average member was almost fifty-nine years old, received regular letters of resignation from associates who had taken on national obligations.[49]

These absences had serious financial implications. Membership subscriptions were fundamental to organizations' survival, yet societies could clearly not continue to demand fees from enlistees. All of them dutifully waived subscription charges for serving members. Yet even that issue raised profound questions about the role of such institutions: should societies prioritize themselves or the artists they represented? Should they waive subscription fees for all in order to help their suffering members, even if it was at the risk of their own bankruptcy? Soon after the outbreak of war the Royal Watercolour Society did precisely this.[50] Others decided differently. Desperately indebted, both the Art-Workers' Guild and the Royal Institute for Oil-Painters appealed to their members for additional contributions, as well as donations of money, pictures and other assets. It will come as no surprise that with members often experiencing financial difficulties themselves these appeals were rarely successful.[51]

Members' absences did not only have financial consequences. Many societies found that they no longer had enough associates to transact business. A large number of trustees did not wish to waste valuable time in meetings, and for those based outside of London the restrictions on train travel (as well as the increasing fears of zeppelin raids) were further disincentives to attending them. This severely affected the Royal Society of British Artists: before the war its general meetings had been attended by an average of sixty members; in 1915 that number had plummeted to fifteen; and at times they were cancelled because no more than three members appeared.[52] Incidents like these are not surprising: with money scarce, travel difficult and priorities changed, it was entirely understandable that artists should choose to put themselves before their societies.

Declining memberships most gravely affected what these organizations were principally supposed to deliver: regular, and profitable, exhibitions. The result, after 1914, was the opposite. Indeed, at the beginning of the war societies were unsure whether to stage them at all: '"To be or not to be"', wrote the *Western Press* in November 1914, 'is the question which those responsible for organising art exhibitions are asking themselves.'[53] Most exhibiting societies erred on the side of 'not to be', and cancelled their autumn and winter programmes. Their decisions were partly political – a deference to the importance of the times – but they were also financial. In August 1914 the Royal Institute of Oil-Painters sent a circular poll to its members on the matter. It read: 'Under the distressing circumstances at present existing, if we open to the public we shall inevitably have to meet a very heavy loss … If we close the Galleries, we shall save a considerable portion of the loss – probably over £100.' Its respondents were overwhelmingly opposed to the prospect of a winter exhibition.[54] These decisions were not lost on the public. By the spring of 1915 the absence of shows was such that many art-lovers feared London would go the same way as Paris, where art exhibitions were allegedly 'as rare as char-a-bancs'.[55]

It was an absence, however, that would not last long. Many exhibition societies realized that indefinite prorogation would result in a disappearance of income earned through commissions (usually between 10 and 12½ per cent) and the resignation of yet more members. From the middle of 1915, then, most societies that could hold exhibitions did hold exhibitions. The results, however, were invariably poor. Contemporary reviews suggest that the two principal criteria by which exhibitions' success was measured – quantity and quality – were conspicuous by their absence. The dispersal of members caused shows to shrink in size: the Allied Artists' Association's 1916 exhibition, for instance, hung 465 pictures, compared to approximately 3,000 in its pre-war days.[56] It also influenced the quality of the shows, because there was less new work to display. Some groups had to resort to retrospective exhibitions, repeat showings or small displays from their permanent collections. This did not fool the critics: societies were repeatedly criticized for failing to live up to their pre-war standards.

Times were particularly hard for groups that had taken bold aesthetic stances before the war. The London Group, which had been formed in 1913 as the most modern exhibiting body in the country, saw its hard-earned radicalism evaporate as its younger Vorticist members disappeared from London on various forms of national service. At its third show in November 1915, half of its elected members (including David Bomberg, Wyndham Lewis and Edward Wadsworth) were unable to contribute. To sustain the group through the war, compromise was required: at its next exhibition the committee invited ten non-members to exhibit, including older and more conservative painters (like Walter Sickert and Nina Hamnett), in order to fill the Goupil Gallery's walls. The resulting show displayed a marked transformation in the group's original aesthetic: a retreat from hard-edged abstraction to figurative post-impressionism.[57] The war, in short, had quietly dismantled the London Group: it had forced realignments and coalitions that would not have been made before 1914, and had resulted in creative compromise. Here, once again, is evidence that the collapse of the avant-garde in wartime Britain was driven just as much by the art world as it was by individual artists. In exhibiting societies, as in art galleries, modernism had simply ceased to be commercially feasible.

If exhibiting societies were divided by their cultural values, they were united in their failure to sell work. Not a single organization increased, or even maintained, its sales figures after 1914, and most of them recorded precipitous declines. This was not lost on observers. Reviewing a 1915 exhibition at the Royal Watercolour Society, one journalist noted that 'instead of about half of the works having found purchasers by the second day, as is usual, one sees a lamentably sparse sprinkling of little "sold" labels next to the pictures'.[58] The show, as the society's annual reports revealed, had actually sold less than a sixth of what it had sold at the corresponding exhibition two years earlier. In fact, between 1913 and 1915 the Royal Watercolour Society's overall picture sales had dropped by two-thirds, its revenue from commissions, admissions and catalogues had fallen comparably and its total income from exhibitions had halved.[59] The pattern was repeated across the whole of Britain: in Wales, the Royal Cambrian Society was so desperate to boost sales that it placed a sign outside its gallery that read 'Offers for Pictures'.[60]

With revenues down, many societies spent the war years on the verge of financial ruin, and a not insignificant number disappeared as a result. Even otherwise wealthy institutions were forced to confront their growing deficits. In March 1915 the Royal Academy of Arts formed a Committee of Ways and Means in order to deal 'with the whole system of income and expenditure, with the object of securing a satisfactory balance'.[61] The committee recommended a cancellation of all social events (*soirées*, banquets and balls); a reduction in the number and size of publications; a closure of the Royal Academy's schools; and general economies regarding hanging, postage, salaries, electricity, gas and sundries.[62] All were subsequently implemented, but they were evidently not enough. The Royal Academy made a loss of £2,000 in 1915, and was forced to withdraw funds from its savings in order to cover the shortfall.[63] Unavoidable as they were, these kinds of decisions were extremely dangerous: as soon as organizations began to plunder their own assets (which had often been amassed over very many decades), their futures became precarious.

Many organizations' most valuable assets were their premises – which were often grand properties in central London. The war, however, turned those assets into liabilities. This was not only because the costs of electricity, gas and insurance rose prohibitively; it was also the result of the increased threat posed by aerial attacks. In late 1914 most institutions reluctantly obtained anti-aircraft insurance – an expense that had never before entered their account books.[64] The Royal Academy was also required to secure additional insurance for thirty-two 'works of national importance' in its collection, including Michelangelo's only sculpture in Britain, a cartoon by Leonardo and paintings by Reynolds, Hogarth and Gainsborough. The works were removed to a government safe deposit box under the General Post Office, and stayed there for the remainder of the war.[65] Aerial attacks themselves were not infrequent. In September 1915 a Zeppelin bomb fell in the garden of Queen Square and damaged the Art-Workers' Guild's headquarters; in October 1917 the Royal Watercolour Society's roof in Pall Mall was smashed by shrapnel;[66] and at 8.57 p.m. on 24 September 1917 a bomb fell directly on to gallery IX in Burlington House, breaking windows and destroying a number of casts. Fortunately the Royal Academy's earlier decision to insure itself against such risks resulted in a successful claim of almost £5,000 for repairs.[67]

Organizations did not only face the risk of damage to their premises; they also risked losing them. At the beginning of the war, the Royal Academy offered parts of Burlington House to war workers. Over the next four years five galleries, the architecture room, lecture room and refreshment room had been occupied by the United Arts Force; other galleries were used for postal censorship; several studios housed a dazzle camouflage team; and some rooms had been employed to manufacture army uniforms.[68] As the government's need for office space in central London increased, many other arts institutions were commandeered: the National Portrait Gallery in Trafalgar Square was taken over by the War Separation Allowances Department; the Tate Gallery at Millbank became the headquarters of the Ministry of Pensions; and the famous Egyptian gallery in the British Museum was appropriated by the Register of Friendly Societies.[69] These takeovers are vivid examples of the way that the art world was threatened, invaded and ultimately consumed by the expanding reach of the war effort as well as the increasing power of the state.

The state's power over independent exhibiting societies remained limited, but it could do what it liked with museums. Britain's public museums cost the treasury approximately £300,000 a year.[70] This had been a negligible sum in peacetime, but the conflict necessitated such a vast increase in national expenditure that the government soon looked to make savings. In 1915 it officially dropped its policy of 'business as usual' and appointed a committee to cut costs. The Retrenchment Committee's eventual report drew up a vast schedule of economies. One of them required that 'all museums, galleries &c, should be closed to the public forthwith and placed at the disposal of the Government'.[71] It was estimated that the measure would have numerous benefits: it would free up museum employees and premises for national service; it would save the exchequer approximately £26,000 a year; and it also would be, so the committee believed, a 'valuable object lesson in economy' that would set an example in belt-tightening to the whole country.[72]

The Retrenchment Committee's proposal was not well received. Indeed, doubts even surrounded its estimated financial benefits. It was calculated that the annual saving effected by the closure of all national museums equated to merely 1 per cent of the cost of a single day's fighting.[73] In February 1916 the Museums' Association led an official protest against the scheme that was backed by virtually the entire British art world. The government, however, was unmoved. In response to the artists, art critics, arts organizations and exhibiting societies that had united to make a case for the museums, the Prime Minister said:

> But, gentlemen, we are at war. That is the governing consideration at this moment. It takes the first place, and must take the first place ... We must accept as one of the conditions of war and of our ability to prosecute the war to a successful and triumphant conclusion these discomforts and limitations upon the ordinary opportunities and amenities and indeed valuable developments both of our social and of our literary and artistic life.[74]

H. H. Asquith's argument was extremely revealing, because it clearly described the new relationship between art and the war effort. For Asquith, it was no longer possible for art and war, for the art world and the wider world, to coexist. The times had changed, resources were limited, and difficult decisions had to be made. The government as well as the public were faced with a straightforward choice between the survival of art and the survival of the nation, and to Asquith at least, it was very clear which of those two came first.

Asquith's binary formulation was certainly confirmed by the experience of exhibiting societies. Since the eighteenth century their power to shape the art world, as well as the wider world, had rarely been challenged. The war, however, had reminded them of the ease with which they could be discarded by the public, the government and even the artists they represented. When in January 1917 the architect and metalworker Henry Wilson was sworn in as the new master of the Art-Workers' Guild, he confessed to his colleagues: 'I have sometimes wondered ... whether all artistic societies ... are to be regarded as encysted, reactionary, retrogressive developments in a body which has no use for us, from which body to-day we are being rightly removed by the surgery of war.'[75] His analysis was not inaccurate: this section has shown that under the social and commercial pressures of war, the institutions that typically exploited the connections between artists and the public, between artworks and the market, were extremely fragile. This next section, however, will show that Britain's artists were no less vulnerable.

Artists

Artists do not, of course, operate in vacuums. Sociologists and social historians of art have consistently argued that their activities are dependent on the institutions and practices of the art world, as well as the social and financial conditions in which that art world operates. For Howard Becker, 'the creating artist works with a network of suppliers of materials, distributors of art works, fellow artists, and with critics, theorists and audiences. These contributing individuals and organizations ... gives artists the opportunity and means to make art.'[76] Claims like this are now widely accepted, yet their implications are still absent from most art-historical accounts of the war. These accounts continue to limit artists' experiences of the conflict to an issue of styles and sensibilities. However, by reconceiving artists as a social group and art-making as a social practice, this section will argue that the war's most violent effects on artists were the most material.

Contemporaries predicted that artists would struggle from the start. Within days of the war's outbreak, many declared that the conflict's dislocation of business would purge the profession of the many 'lesser' artists who had proliferated in the pre-war prosperity.[77] However, as the months progressed it became clear that the conflict was not just helpfully dismissing the weaker artists; it was seriously undermining the foundations of the whole profession. Journalists wrote that 'no class of professional workers' was 'suffering more acutely', had been 'more severely hit', and was feeling 'the sharp edge of privation more quickly';[78] aid councils declared that 'the ARTISTIC PROFESSIONS were the HARDEST HIT of all';[79] and even the Board of Trade reported that artists were 'among the worst hit of the professional classes'.[80]

Artists' principal problems, of course, were financial. They, like auction houses, dealers and exhibiting societies, had been affected by the collapsing market for luxury goods. The ubiquity of artists' distress was particularly apparent to the Artists' General Benevolent Institution, which provided assistance to struggling members of the profession. Its applicants' book is filled with sentences like 'difficulties directly attributable to war', and 'hardship due entirely to war'.[81] Painters referred to the 'impossibility of selling pictures', the 'stoppage of all sales' and the 'near total-closure of international markets for art goods'; illustrators complained that 'no illustrated books had been published since the war'; stained-glass window designers wrote of a 'total paralysis of all work'; printmakers reported a 'cessation of demand for important engravings'; and sculptors bemoaned the 'total disappearance of major public projects'.[82]

The Artists' General Benevolent Institution was principally designed to help Britain's less established artists, but their more distinguished counterparts were similarly challenged by the unhelpful commercial conditions. Even the two most celebrated society portraitists of the period saw their more lucrative commissions dwindle to almost nothing. Philip de László's studio files reveal patrons cancelling ('I do not think that I ought to permit myself the luxury at present'), postponing ('You will understand how very busy my life is just now. Munitions give me *no* time') or requesting 'war discounts' on existing commissions ('I cannot afford to pay full before the War prices').[83] In William Orpen's studio books, meanwhile, amounts of £500 and £700 were struck out, and brief notes – 'off because of war', 'not paid because of war' and even 'returned because of war' – were scrawled over the details of dozens of projects. Both artists saw their incomes decline precipitously. In 1913, Orpen had turned over £8,509; by the middle of the war that figure had dropped to £500.[84]

Artists who sold through art-world intermediaries found their situation was even worse. Unlike established studio artists, they were entirely dependent for sales on exhibitions mounted by art societies and dealers. This chapter has already described how, panicked by the disappearance of buyers, both such institutions were reluctant to incur the costs required to stage them. When they did, their representatives frequently pressurized artists to reduce their asking prices in order to boost the chance of sales. These price cuts were not ideal for the intermediaries – their commission, after all, was a percentage of total sales – but they were significantly more damaging for artists. It was reported that in August 1914 some oil painters had slashed their rates from the previous month by as much as 75 per cent.[85] Even the most modest of pictures did not escape the depreciation. The Royal Watercolour Society's statistics reveal that a small watercolour that had fetched £40 in the summer of 1914 was worth just £16 a year later.[86]

When the depreciation or disappearance of revenue from art sales was combined with across-the-board increases in the cost of living, it is not surprising that all but the most fortunate artists were driven to the brink of ruin. Indeed, a brief survey of even the period's most famous names is revealing: Jacob Epstein doubted he would even 'pull through the summer' of 1914;[87] Mark Gertler described his position as 'really terrible' ('I haven't a penny to my own and no prospects of earning any');[88] his teacher from the Slade, Henry Tonks, was anticipating 'starvation';[89] Augustus John was on the verge of bankruptcy;[90] while of the Vorticists, Fredrick Etchells was 'destitute', Wyndham Lewis was debt-ridden and William Roberts found money 'conspicuous by its absence'.[91] It was worse at the other end of the spectrum. By November 1915 one unknown and unemployed draughtsman was in prison for not paying his council rates.[92]

A not insignificant number of artists ended up appealing for benevolence. The Professional Classes War Relief Council reported that more than 500 artists and craftsmen applied for financial assistance in the first year of the war. By the end of 1915 they represented at least 8.8 per cent of the thousands of wartime claimants – second only to musicians at 9 per cent.[93] The Artists' General Benevolent Institution, whose applicants' book has already been mentioned, received a similar surge in applications. Between 1913 and 1915 its number nearly trebled, and in the latter year the institution distributed almost £10,000.[94] Nevertheless, as hardships proliferated it became increasingly difficult for charities to meet the demand. The Artists' General Benevolent Institution was forced to introduce certain qualitative criteria to filter the many applications. Artists' pictorial submissions were ranked from one down to five and assistance then allocated based on their rating. The evaluations were evidently not aesthetically progressive: David Bomberg's near-abstract submissions did not even merit a mark; they were categorized as 'inadmissible specimens' and he was refused aid.[95]

Bomberg's misfortune raises an important issue about the war's cultural consequences. Art historians have long claimed that artists rejected avant-garde styles for intellectual or ethical reasons. For Frances Spalding, 'the widespread destruction in Europe suggested that their own destruction of long-standing traditions in art had been, in some way, callous and inhuman ... Artists felt a need for a return to order.'[96] The information presented here suggests that such need might equally have been motivated by more pragmatic considerations. Faced with the increasing conservatism of dealers, a diminution in buyers and a general decrease in liquidity, all kinds of artists – not only avant-gardists – were under pressure to abandon ambitious or experimental projects in favour of more commercially viable output. Mark Gertler – who before the war had forged a highly idiosyncratic style – expressed this dilemma in a 1916 letter to Lytton Strachey:

> I hate with all my being the idea that money should be so able to influence my freedom. It is terrible to think that the more interesting my work becomes, the more difficult it becomes to sell it and to live! I only ask of life to be allowed to paint, to be allowed to dip deeper and deeper into the wonderful mysteries of art. But if one has no money the purity of one's art studies are spoilt, because one can't help thinking of what the stupid buyers would like, as one must live. That is my trouble. To be a good artist one must have an income ... The starving artist in the garret is a thing of the past. To paint good pictures one must have a comfortable studio and good food ... Let no person come and tell me that poverty is good for an artist! If an artist is poor he simply has to please.[97]

This process did not only involve a migration from the experimental to the conventional. It often entailed a move away from fine art altogether. Women – whose status as serious artists in 1914 was far from secure – were particularly vulnerable. Faced by difficult commercial conditions, a not inconsiderable number of female artists drifted into the applied arts, and many who had started the war making paintings, prints and sculptures ended it in the more lucrative – if less aesthetically adventurous – businesses of toy-making, clothes designing and interior decoration.[98]

Commercial considerations were not the only determinants of artists' output; practical factors played a similarly decisive role. Before the war, most art materials had been imported from Germany.[99] From August 1914 that supply was discontinued. A number of German pigments, like alkali blues and lead white, became all but unobtainable.[100] Pencils, too, which had traditionally been manufactured in Bavaria or Austria, ceased to appear in shops, and forced Winsor & Newton (Britain's leading art materials firm) to devise its own alternative: the 'Winton'.[101] Items did not have to originate in enemy nations to become scarce. William Orpen complained that he could not find his favoured Belgian canvas after German troops 'knocked out' the factory that produced it: 'I am perfectly willing to pay quite a sum of money to get this canvas on the market again and would make a lot of use of it. I cannot find any canvas at all like it at present. I also know several well known British artists who would certainly give big orders for it.'[102]

Where artists were able to obtain their desired materials, the sudden scarcity caused price rises. By the end of 1915 ink houses reported that synthetic blues had risen by 200 per cent, red lakes by 125 per cent, whites and ultramarines by 75 per cent, while copper and tin had doubled in price.[103] In that same period, paper had more than quadrupled in cost, with one journal joking that printers should use gold leaf instead 'because paper was dearer'.[104] Winsor & Newton dispatched circulars to inform retailers of increased wholesale prices, and artists became so angered by the hikes that some companies had to publicly defend themselves against allegations of profiteering:

> Hog-hair brushes are very dear because there are a few or practically none of British manufacture to be had owing to the scarcity of the raw material which was formerly imported, while the foreign brushes are very expensive. With regard to colours … the prices of our oil and water colours remained at a pre-war standard … [but] cost of labour … has risen enormously. Owing to the great demand of the Government for all kinds of flax and cotton, canvas, both of good and school qualities, has risen enormously in price, but this was a matter quite beyond our power to alter, and as prices of raw cloth advanced so we were obliged to advance ours. Our catalogue would compare favourably with that of any other manufacturer in any other trade.[105]

These developments may all sound rather banal; they are certainly far removed from the more familiar narratives of trauma in the trenches. Nevertheless, these quotidian factors were arguably just as important as those front-line epiphanies in shaping the art that ultimately emerged from the conflict. After all, even a timeless and transcendent war picture can only be produced with the materials that are available to its maker.

Supply difficulties were exacerbated by the war effort itself. The copper, tin and lead on which sculptors and engravers depended, as well as the mercury from which vermilion was made, were needed to produce ammunitions, while green pigments were required to dye uniforms khaki. Munitions firms purchased both of them in bulk long before they reached art retailers' shelves. Government controls made materials yet harder to obtain. The Paper Restrictions Order confined most painters and draughtsmen to working with small quantities of high-cost, low-quality paper.[106] Sculptors meanwhile were hampered by the Ministry of Munitions' decision to release only 10 per cent of the nation's metal supply to civilians.[107] In 1915 the Ministry formed a Priority Department to distribute such materials appropriately. Its advisers created four levels of need: 'Direct War Work', 'Indirect War Work', 'Necessary Work' and 'Non-Essential Work'. Art, unsurprisingly, fell into the final category, and sculptors received nowhere near the quantity of materials they required.[108]

Britain's competition for resources was not limited to money and materials: arguably the most valuable resource of all was men. Keith Grieves has written that the organization and mobilization of the country's workforce was a 'key factor in the conduct of the nation's war effort'.[109] As part of this process, it was crucial that all able men migrated from 'non-essential' work to 'essential' work. Although the government did not introduce conscription until 1916, men of all ages had been under pressure to perform some kind of national service from the start of the conflict. Artists had quickly obliged. Indeed, one of the very first volunteer corps to be formed during the war was the United Arts Force – a Home Defence Unit composed entirely of artists, musicians, actors, architects and writers who were generally too old to enlist in the armed forces. By the end of October 1914 it boasted 1,600 members. Among them were some of Britain's most distinguished artists, including Edward Poynter, William Nicholson, John Lavery and George Frampton. The United Arts Force subsequently underwent a number of different iterations, but eventually became an official auxiliary branch of the army, where it undertook important home-guard duties.[110]

If ineligible artists volunteered for home-front duties, eligible artists enlisted with the armed forces. There is, however, considerable doubt about exactly how many did so. Although, for instance, the 14,000-strong Artists' Rifles regiment is assumed to have been dominated by patriotic painters and sculptors, some sources suggest that they were actually 'conspicuous by their absence', and when Adrian Hill enlisted in November 1914 he believed himself to have been the first professional artist to join.[111] The art world's rolls of honour are rather more helpful: *The Studio* recorded more than 500, and the Imperial Arts League more than 600, artists serving with the forces by the end of 1915.[112] These lists were not comprehensive, but neither were they particularly long, considering that the 1911 Census counted almost 17,000 active artists in Britain.[113] More impressive are the figures that relate to aspiring artists. According to art-school registers, the outbreak of war comprehensively dispersed Britain's art-student population. If the Slade had been the most influential art school in the years before 1914, its golden age was abruptly ended by the conflict. Of its 200 male students, 135 joined the armed forces.[114]

Once at the front, most of these men found that military service was largely incompatible with artistic activity. On and even behind the front line, materials were hard to obtain, time was in short supply and working conditions were far from ideal. In his recent book *A Terrible Beauty*, Paul Gough has described how artists who tried to continue producing pictures encountered a constellation of practical obstacles – from worrying altercations with vigilant military authorities to the more modest concerns of keeping hands warm and paper dry.[115] A number of artists found that such practical impediments outlasted the war. The painter Harold Earnshaw had his painting arm amputated in 1916 after an injury sustained at the Somme. He admirably trained himself to paint with his left hand but eventually died, aged fifty-one, from complications associated with his wounds.[116] Likewise, in 1914 James Bateman was a highly promising young sculptor, having that year won a prestigious scholarship to the Royal College of Art. He sustained serious injuries while serving and was forced to give up sculpture in favour of the less physically demanding act of painting.[117]

The most permanent impediment to artists' careers, of course, was death. We do not know exactly how many artists perished in the Great War, although several distinguished figures (Henri Gaudier-Brzeska, Gerard Chowne, Henri Doucet, Isaac Rosenberg, Henry Samuel Teed) were among their number. Nevertheless, a perusal of British art-school registers makes salutary reading. At the Royal Academy, the pages are poignantly littered with the words 'Killed in Action', 'Killed in the Great War' and simply 'Dead' next to its students' names.[118] The Royal Academy archive also possesses a particularly moving letter from a young student called Charles Gordon Paramore. As he enlisted in September 1914 he wrote: 'So it's all off with the old life ... I am looking forward to the great time when this damned war will be over. I think people will be far happier and contented than ever they were before.' It is moving because Paramore died exactly a year later, the very first officer killed at the Battle of Loos.[119]

***

When in 1933 the critic Frank Rutter reflected on the cultural impact of the Great War, his analysis was unequivocal: 'Art is creative. War is destructive. It can do nothing for artists but kill them.'[120] Rutter was referring to the many painters and sculptors who had lost their lives in the conflict. Yet his phrasing revealed more than that. Rutter was articulating a conviction that art and war were fundamentally incompatible. This chapter has shown that initially his sentiment was supported by the facts. By focusing on the social and economic realities of art, I have shown how in 1914 and 1915 the business of war was emphatically at odds with the business of art. As the war tightened its grip on all aspects of national life, the discrete realm that art had previously inhabited was challenged, invaded and undermined. The consequences, at least at the start of the war, were catastrophic: the art market collapsed, artists' organizations ceased to function and artists were paralyzed by a series of commercial and practical problems that had a decisive impact on their art.

Yet this antagonism went further: in a diminished and homogenized national community the art world was repeatedly forced to compete with the war effort for the same social terrain. Conflicts that had been unnecessary or even unthinkable before 1914 were now fought over almost every single issue. They centred on whether money should be spent on art or saved for war; whether material resources go to luxuries or munitions; whether cultural institutions remain open or be commandeered by the government; and ultimately whether men live and work as artists or fight and die as soldiers. In each of these small but frequent skirmishes, art became not only an adversary to the war effort; it became an adversary to British society. Yet this was only part of the story. As the conflict undermined art's material foundations, it also undermined its intellectual foundations. The next chapter will show how, in the hyper-politicized climate of war, art and artists came to be understood as active and dangerous enemies of Britain's wartime survival.

2 PERCEPTIONS OF ART

We have seen how the outbreak of war severely damaged the British art world. The conflict created a cocktail of social, political and financial problems that placed the cultural sphere under intense pressure from the start. Denied the money, men and materials on which its existence depended, the business of art repeatedly came close to collapsing. If conditions were not hard enough as they were, these concrete material difficulties were complemented and exacerbated by a set of cultural problems that were no less detrimental. The war gave rise to a set of discourses that fundamentally changed public perceptions of both art and artists. These perceptions may not have carried the quantifiable footprint of lost buyers, commandeered premises and vanished materials. Yet perceptions can be just as important as realities. Indeed, the French cultural historian Roger Chartier has argued that social representations – what he called the 'social imaginary' – are themselves 'constituents of social reality'.[1] And they are never more real, never more potent, than in wartime.

It has been said that a principal feature of 'total war' is the 'refraction of the everyday'. Maureen Healey has written that during the First World War many social practices that had previously been considered private or sub-political were 'refracted through the medium, or lens, of war', and were reinterpreted accordingly.[2] This chapter explores how the unfolding events of the conflict 'refracted' perceptions of art. It examines how an initially overriding obsession with the war diminished the nation's receptivity to aesthetic experience, and made the arts seem more trivial than before. It shows how in a climate of collective hardship and self-sacrifice, art came to be seen as antithetical to the war effort. And it describes how with social identities subjected to unprecedented scrutiny, artists as a group were reconceived as shirkers, outsiders and ultimately enemies of the state. In the process, I will argue that the outbreak of war not only weakened but gravely poisoned the relationship between the British people and their art.

'Futile-ism'

In recent years scholars have debunked the traditional accounts of the outbreak of war. They have shown that the notorious 'war enthusiasm' of August 1914 was as much a myth as a reality – and that in all of the combatant nations support for the conflict was nowhere near as widespread or unequivocal as previously had been assumed.[3] However, this did not mean that the outbreak of war failed to affect the mental state of the millions who experienced it. Indeed, contemporary accounts repeatedly referred to its profound psychological reverberations. They described how the events of August 1914 produced in men's and women's brains a mixture of 'shock', 'stupefaction', 'paralysis', 'anxiety' and 'excitement'. They also claimed that the country's obsession with the conflict was so totalizing that all other thoughts were 'knocked away by vital news, public news, private news, pouring out perpetually'.[4] The war, it seemed, monopolized the nation's mental resources in much the same way that it commandeered its material counterparts. This process would have huge effects on all sectors of peacetime life, with acute cultural consequences.

Like other cultural producers, artists were not insulated from the war obsession of 1914.[5] Indeed, an anecdote in a weekly periodical at the end of that year suggests that they were among the most profoundly affected. Three weeks after the outbreak of war, the story went, an English artist was painting a landscape in the hills above his home when he saw a postman cycling back from his round. Shortly afterwards, his wife hurried towards him with a newspaper in her hand. 'Namur', she exclaimed, 'has fallen.' The news was important. Namur was a Belgian fortress town that had stood as one of the last major obstacles to a German invasion of France. Its unexpected collapse was thus of grave strategic significance, and would quite possibly have inaugurated a major new phase in the conflict.[6] The artist absorbed the information. After a moment's reflection, he turned back to the subject of his picture. He scrutinized the landscape he had just lovingly depicted, and then experienced a painful realization: everything he had just painted – and everything he had ever painted before it – was 'wanting if not actually irrelevant'.[7]

This modest story is perhaps too well crafted to be entirely true, yet it nonetheless reveals how the war's unfolding events not only consumed attentions but transformed attitudes, no matter how robustly they had hitherto been held. After all, if we are to believe the account described above, an artist's entire career had all but been extinguished by a single newsflash. His views were by no means unrepresentative. Many artists recorded similar creative crises. Roger Fry experienced a 'terrible lack of confidence' in his art; David Bomberg felt 'the urge was gone' to make pictures; and Stanley Spencer – who found it 'impossible to settle down to work' – asked: 'How could all this be entered into whole-heartedly when war came?'[8] This widespread imaginative impotence often gave way to depression. In the Tate archives is a remarkable series of letters by the landscapist Frederick Milner. They chart a precipitous psychological decline over the war's first six months. In August 1914 Milner like many others recorded an inability to work, his mind being 'full of the serious outlook'.[9] By early 1915, however, his letters were littered with despairing phrases like 'everything is rotten', 'what is the use?' and 'what good anything?'.[10]

These imaginative hardships may have had deeper causes. Throughout the conflict a number of intellectuals claimed that there was a basic mental incompatibility between artists and war. In his seminal *Instincts of the Herd in Peace and War* – which had been conceived a decade before the conflict but was first published as a book in 1916 – the neurosurgeon and social psychologist Wilfred Trotter claimed that the experience of war naturally stimulated what he called the 'herd instincts' in humans. These instincts fostered a psychological as well as social homogeneity that together worked to protect any community under threat.[11] The obverse of this development, however, was that all feelings that were produced by, or helped nourish, individual thoughts correspondingly perished, for they could not feasibly contribute to the morale of the herd. Artists, of course, greatly depended on these 'individual instincts'. Indeed, their originality was normally understood to be an integral component of their value to the community. Trotter's claims, however, cast doubts on the value of the individual in an emphatically collective experience.

In 1914 and 1915 the public did not need to understand the subtleties of group psychology to draw similar conclusions. Faced by the war's historic significance, they came to see all but the most momentous domestic activities as trivial by comparison. Their resulting views on art are best represented by a 'typical' comment made by 'the man on the street', which was printed by *The Studio* in 1915:

> Art is a luxury and a product of peaceful and luxurious times. Its purpose is only to amuse; and necessarily it disappears when people are faced with the serious facts of life and have neither money to spend on luxuries nor time to give to amusement ... Art has had a very good innings, and we have wasted a good deal of time and money on it. For the future we shall have to do without it; it goes the way of most of our other luxuries.[12]

'The man in the street' had admittedly long believed that art was an unnecessary extravagance. Britain was, after all, renowned for its traditionally unsympathetic attitude to the visual arts. The war changed three characteristics of this opinion: first, it politicized the man in the street's previously sub-political prejudices; second, it increased the social influence of his perspective; and third, it seriously weakened the community who might normally have mounted a rebuttal.

The weakness of the pro-art lobby is explained in part by the marginalization of many of the nation's cultural voices. In 1914 and 1915 the conflict commandeered more than three-quarters of all news space in national newspapers, and exhibition reviews and arts essays were among those that disappeared to make room for it.[13] This process was compounded by the curtailment, suspension and cancellation of many influential cultural publications: *The Athenaeum*, which had appeared weekly since 1828, went monthly; the *New Weekly*, which had only been established in March 1914, abandoned its attempt to 'keep ideas alive in the world of action' at the end of the year;[14] *Poetry and Drama* ceased publication in December 1914; Wyndham Lewis's Vorticist organ *Blast* famously failed to continue past its second, truncated issue, in 1915; and Frank Rutter's ambitious plans to release a review called *Arts and Letters* in the autumn of 1914 were 'scotched'.[15]

Given the uncertain commercial conditions that have already been outlined, it was not surprising that arts publications with niche audiences began to disappear. More surprising was the changing timbre of the voices that remained. In the first year of the war even established supporters of the arts took the unprecedented stance of accepting, endorsing and even contributing to the criticisms that had initially been made only by 'philistines'. The distinguished music critic Ernest Newman confessed that 'in the face of the extreme realities of life, art – even to artists and lovers of art ... suddenly took on an almost ludicrous air of insignificance'. He continued:

> In times of crisis one begins to understand the Philistine point of view that art is merely a plaything for the idle hours. [To discuss it seemed] as absurd as for a family to be quarrelling a whole day about the relative merits of the humming of this insect or that in the garden, while inside the house someone was dying in slow agony ... That frame of mind requires a certain ease in life, a certain abstraction from life: and the value of our recent experiences is the proof that artistic emotion cannot exist in the soul at the same time as an overwhelming emotion derived from reality.[16]

Arnold Palmer, critic and editor of the soon-to-be-cancelled *New Weekly*, was somewhat less circumspect:

> It is hardly worth while to utter a plea for the artist ... During the peaceful years we have got into the habit of talking about the artistic needs of the people. Now we shall see that they hardly existed, that there is nothing more than a faint curiosity, which, in times of plenty and prosperity, people allow themselves the luxury of satisfying. The nation sheds art

> like a garment, with an ease and a rapidity which artists, whether they practise or not, will never come to understand. And even those of us who have come to think that we cannot live without some kind of beauty to appreciate are shaken by the cataclysm.[17]

It is impossible to discern whether statements like these were results of a pragmatic attempt to avoid being branded unpatriotic or reflected a genuine change of opinion on the part of their authors. Perhaps it does not matter. What matters is that in the early months of the war public support for the arts had all but disappeared. Through the autumn of 1914 it was not unusual to find previously staunch aesthetes describing picture-making as 'the sport of fools', 'entirely frivolous and futile' or 'mere daubing', while calling artworks 'trivialities' and 'fripperies'.[18] Even Selwyn Image, Slade Professor of Art at the University of Oxford and a passionate believer in the social and spiritual importance of the arts, used his first lecture of the term in November 1914 to remind students of their potentially degrading social consequences: 'Art has her dangers – dangers coming to her from men's frivolity, their absorption in sumptuousness and luxury, their over-attention to trivialities and mere curiosities, their morbid excitement after titillating novelties, their resultant shallowness of judgment and sane appreciation.'[19]

Historians of modernism have already noted similarly deprecating patterns in the discourses that surrounded the avant-garde.[20] Vorticism, for instance, may have generated outrage and excitement in the summer of 1914, but a year later it induced nothing but disdainful *ennui*. One critic wrote:

> Their reputation as amusing creatures and puzzle painters might, in normal conditions, have carried them through another season. But Life decreed that something serious should come to the rescue of a costive world ... In August, to our horror, we were tipped right into things that really mattered. And now, when we have opportunity to look again at those old ingenious notions, our nerves still tingling with the impact of reality, we simply wonder what on earth was up with us that we should ever have been entertained by them.[21]

The author of these comments was the reactionary critic C. H. Collins Baker, who had consistently supported the English pastoral tradition in painting. He had never approved of Vorticism, and would surely have continued to condemn it regardless of the war. The conflict, however, had lent political force to his previously aesthetic objections, and it was those political implications that led modernist commentators to join him in criticizing the avant-garde. Before the war, Alfred Orage's journal the *New Age* had been a liberal forum for progressive cultural discussion. After 1914 it renamed Futurism 'Futile-ism'; described

Vorticism as 'incomparably feeble', Imagist poets as 'idlers, hiding from one reality in pretence of another'; and instructed aesthetes to retire 'into a monastery' or at least adopt the 'monastic gift of silence'.[22] What is notable here is that regardless of their aesthetic predispositions, critics – like the public – were deploying a surprising consistency of terms to attack the arts: terms that carried associations of triviality, futility and feebleness. Moreover, the grammar of this opprobrium was not a unique response to modernism; it was the way by which all non-essential activities were trivialized by war.

The most prevalent derisory metaphors likened artists to entertainers: they were variously referred to as 'monkeys on sticks', 'pretty-pretty babblers', 'purveyors of comic interludes', 'performing dogs' and 'self-advertising mountebanks'.[23] This strand of discourse is extremely revealing, if only because it reflected the view increasingly taken by the authorities. In early April 1916 the Chancellor proposed a new tax on 'tickets for entrance fees charged on amusements, such as theatres, cinemas, football matches, horse races and other similar shows'. He believed the duty would raise almost £22 million per annum by charging ½d on admission fees up to 2d, and rising from there.[24] When the Chancellor was asked in Parliament if art exhibitions would be liable to the duty, his response was unequivocal: 'Exhibitions of pictures, whether by a society or a private individual, will be liable to the tax.'[25] When the proposal was approved later that month, the art world was outraged, and the Royal Academy, together with the Imperial Arts League, prepared a formal deposition outlining the commercial hardships that would result from the 'vexatious and injurious' measure.[26]

More damaging than Entertainments Duty's financial consequences, however, were its ideological associations. As far as government fiscal policy was concerned, art exhibitions were now simply sites of casual amusement, little different from cinema-screenings, football matches and music-hall shows. In a protracted (and mostly unidirectional) correspondence with the Exchequer, the Royal Academy sought to prove that art – at least that which was to be found at its own exhibitions – was more than mere entertainment. It maintained that the finest artworks were capable of 'elevating the minds of ordinary people through the contemplation of beauty'; they imparted 'definite instruction'; and they helped produce in the public a 'strong and permanent taste'.[27] It was a bold defence of the arts, but the Royal Academy waited over five months for a response. On 25 October 1916 a dismissive letter arrived from Custom House announcing that it was 'not satisfied' that art exhibitions were 'entitled to exemption'.[28] The government's decision to uphold its policy was as revealing as it was disappointing. As the first levies started to be collected at exhibitions in 1916, Alfred Baldry in the *Imperial Arts League Journal* wrote: 'After centuries of dreaming about his lofty mission as a moral influence, an historian, or teacher, the artist has been put finally in his proper place among the purveyors of amusement ... Fit only to rank with the other clowns who posture for the amusement of the crowd.'[29]

This is not the place to debate the intellectual validity of the government's stance, nor even the fiscal effectiveness of its measure. What is important here is how, exactly halfway through the war, Entertainments Duty can be viewed as the culmination of a process that had begun back in August 1914. The outbreak of war had transformed perceptions about the social value of art. In light of what were suddenly such momentous times, dominated by life, death and national survival, art was naturally dismissed as a trivial concern – a frivolous sideshow distracting Britons from issues of greater importance. Over the following two years, that sentiment proliferated through British life. It had started when artists privately and often painfully reassessed their own vocation. It was used by 'the man in the street' to vindicate his longstanding concerns about the value of the arts. It was employed and deployed by critics as they consciously tapped into the public mood. And by 1916 it had even forced its way into government policy. Yet these were iterations of art's very mildest criticisms. In another strand of wartime discourse, art was not merely trivial and futile; it was unethical and unpatriotic.

'Fiddling while Rome burns'

The government's approach to Entertainments Duty had ostensibly reflected the much wider view that art was an unnecessary addition to life. However, the very notion of entertainment was considerably more complex than this. The outbreak of war had produced in Britain an ethics of enjoyment. Here, public discourses repeatedly represented 'amusement', 'play' and 'leisure' as antitheses to 'work', 'sacrifice' and 'patriotism': all were unproductive and unethical, and all demonstrated an improper disregard for the suffering of others.[30] Journalists often described indulgence in them as 'fiddling while Rome burns' – a reference to the apocryphal account of Emperor Nero playing his fiddle during the Great Fire of Rome in AD 64.[31] It is important to note that such criticisms were not directed solely at the arts: commentators also rebuked 'lavish feasting' and those who showed 'undue excitement' over sporting events or persisted with 'conspicuous philandering and loud junketing'.[32] In the ethics of enjoyment, however, art was particularly improper, for it could also be condemned as a luxury.

Like many other social activities, domestic consumption was politicized during the war years. A National Savings Committee was established at the start of the conflict to reduce individual spending and divert private liquidities towards the war effort through government bonds, loans and securities. It was a vast campaign: 35,000 local associations, 200,000 volunteers and saturation advertising brought its message to almost every British subject, and 17 million people – a third of the nation's population – subscribed to it.[33] That message dwelled on an important idea, of which the ethics of enjoyment was a part: the so-called 'morality of consumption'.[34] The 'morality of consumption' did not just confer on every financial or material transaction an ethical significance; it turned consumers into a 'civilian army' for whom saving became a duty not unlike the sacrifices that soldiers were performing at the front: 'Let the nation', commanded one National Savings pamphlet, 'place its comforts, its luxuries, its elegances, on a national altar, consecrated by such sacrifices as these men have made.'[35]

Art was one of those luxuries. The National Savings Movement described the continued acquisition of artworks as an activity that was indulged in by selfish, wealthy and 'useless spendthrifts'; it was a 'serious evil', a 'wicked thing' and even, the committee claimed, 'helped the Germans'.[36] These allegations were provocative but effective. Indeed, they probably played as significant a role in the wartime collapse of the art market as the commercial changes that were discussed in Chapter 1. Collectors of luxury objects, who were struggling as it was to raise funds to continue purchasing, now found another reason to desert the art market. In the hysterical social climate generated by the morality of consumption, many feared that to be seen walking down Bond Street, stepping inside expensive shops and emerging with luxury objects in their hands was to risk a highly public reprimand. 'The intensity of the war fervour', wrote one alarmed collector, 'is such that those of us who buy a picture or a piece of bric-à-brac, see a play or indulge in a game of golf, are in danger of being dubbed unpatriotic.'[37]

The notion that art was a luxury and that luxuries were socially degenerative was eventually expressed in public policy. Unlike the entertainments tax, Luxury Duty was never fully implemented. It was, however, a similarly revealing barometer of changed government attitudes. The policy had been inspired by French and German precedents, and proposed a levy on all goods and services that were defined as luxuries. After seventy meetings, 150 interviews and three months of fraught deliberation (in which three members and one sub-committee resigned), the Select Committee on Luxury Duty concluded that 'pictures, paintings, mosaics, drawings, sculptures, statuary, bronzes' would be subject to the duty irrespective of their cost.[38] With that decision art entered an exclusive tax category that included jewellery, perfumes and yachts – all of which were classified as 'unnecessary', 'wasteful' and 'extravagant'.[39] As far as art was concerned, the British schedule was considerably more punitive than its continental counterparts: in France rates were lower, while in Germany artworks were classed as luxuries only if they exceeded a certain price.[40] On the other hand, it was considerably more forgiving of the more typically British preoccupations of sport and pets. The art world immediately detected the discriminatory consequences of traditional British philistinism. Reginald Grundy, editor of *The Connoisseur*, wrote:

> If the English Report is carried into effect, it will be possible for an individual to keep a carriage and pair, or, indeed, as many carriages and pairs as he likes, a harem of prize Angora cats worth £100 or more apiece, a menagerie of wild animals, and an aviary of valuable singing birds, without coming under the tax, while the collector who buys a work of retrospective art of any description would at once be liable.[41]

More concerning than the definition of art as a luxury was the definition of 'Luxury' itself. The Select Committee declared that luxury was at its core a moral problem. The continued purchase of expensive products was a 'form of self-indulgence which shuts a man off from the mass of his fellow-men', 'incompatible with hard work and a useful life', 'demoralising to the individual and the nation' and 'unjustifiable in a community where many lack what is necessary for a civilised existence'.[42]

The Select Committee's criticisms of the social ethics of art were reinforced by the conflict's societal consequences. Social historians have shown that while the war flattened class differences it inflamed class awareness. 'Art' became one of the many sites in which this developing social confrontation was played out.[43] Working-class newspapers like *John Bull* and the *Star* described the arts as symptoms and causes of the rupture between the 'the average decent British citizen' – who was sacrificing his income, pleasure and often his life for the good of the community – and the 'unpatriotic extravagance' of a degenerate metropolitan elite.[44] This concern frequently focused on the issue of profiteering.[45] Patriotic papers wrote of profiteers investing dirty money in expensive artworks, published cartoons of artists tricking the public into buying overpriced pictures of spurious war subjects and frequently reported 'despicable' cases like that of a memorial sculpture firm which had sent advertisements to servicemen's families before they had even died.[46]

Unlike dealers, collectors and other members of the art market, artists were normally able to sidestep criticisms produced by the 'morality of consumption'. They could not, however, evade debates about a 'morality of production'. Supporters may have argued that the artist was 'as important to the state as is the lawyer, the engineer, or even the farmer' but with millions of men enlisting, stay-at-home artists invariably came to be seen as 'slackers', 'idlers', 'workshys' and, above all, 'shirkers' from national duty.[47] One commentator spoke for many when he branded it both 'criminal and disgraceful' for men, and even women, to be employed 'in the production of mediocre pictures while the call is for service of pressing national importance'.[48] As these discourses intensified, the work of the artist was repeatedly contrasted with the work of the soldier, to the distinct disadvantage of the artist: one was selfish, the other selfless; one was useless, the other essential; one disloyal, the other patriotic.

This public image of artists as shirkers was reinforced by an abiding identification of them with effeminacy and homosexuality, and also by several high-profile artists' apparent avoidance of national service.[49] No group seemed to substantiate this prejudice quite like the Bloomsbury Group. Of its members, Duncan Grant, David Garnett and Mark Gertler registered as conscientious objectors; Leonard Woolf, Lytton Strachey and Clive Bell were declared medically unfit; Roger Fry – a Quaker – was too old to fight; and many of them ended up farming at Vanessa Bell's house, Charleston, in lieu of active service. Moreover, they persistently criticized the prevailing jingoism of the war years, and deliberately avoided any such themes in their work. In her recent book, Grace Brockington has argued that this aesthetic disinterest was not an act of solipsistic disregard, but actually an 'active form of pacifist resistance'.[50] This did not, however, deflect criticisms at the time. The Bloomsbury Group was repeatedly condemned for its apparently effete, self-indulgent and unpatriotic behaviour: Wyndham Lewis dismissed its wartime work of 'national importance' as 'pruning trees, planting gooseberry bushes and hay-making, doubtless in large sun bonnets'.[51]

Popular opinion on the issue was most zealously expressed in June 1917 after the modernist sculptor Jacob Epstein – himself a critic of Bloomsbury – was temporarily exempted from military service on the grounds of 'national interests'.[52] The news triggered an avalanche of comment in the press: in the *Evening Standard* the painter Philip Burne-Jones wrote that no artist was 'entirely indispensable at home while his country is engaged in a life-and-death struggle ... Art cannot take precedence over the moral rights of mankind while the issue of civilisation or barbarism is being decided once for all.'[53] G. K. Chesterton questioned the principle that 'because a man is a great artist he should not share the ordinary responsibilities of citizenship ... Real national need is of annihilating superiority to any art.'[54] The *Pall Mall Gazette* inquired: 'Ought the genius have an advantage over the plain man in matters of public duty?'[55] And Collins Baker asked: 'Is art so frail and rare that her ministers should be preserved from ... the more immediate responsibilities of mankind?'[56] Despite their tonal variety, the denunciations of Epstein shared one embittered conviction: that artists considered themselves separate from and superior to the rest of society, and thus exempted from duties that every other subject was obliged to perform.

The assumptions that underpinned these criticisms dated back to long before 1917. In the decades before the war, aestheticism, modernism and the bohemianism associated with both had increased the perceived cleavage between artists and mainstream society. From as early as the 1860s, Britain's leading progressive artists had cultivated a highly public stance against prevailing opinions. The American-born painter James McNeill Whistler routinely ridiculed the Victorian establishment and deliberately confounded the expectations of the art-going public.[57] This aesthetic detachment was further entrenched in the decades that followed, and by coincidence was most passionately codified just months before the outbreak of war, when Clive Bell's book *Art* was published in 1914. In that volume, Bell formulated an idea of a discrete aesthetic sphere within British society, based on a distinction between a cultural elite ('educated persons of extraordinary sensibility') and the wider public. In doing so he not only claimed that artists were special people ('all artists are aristocrats'); he declared that as a result, they did not need to 'bother about the fate of humanity'.[58]

The outbreak of war contaminated the public estrangement on which aesthetes like Bell had insisted. Indeed, throughout the conflict commentators repeatedly singled out 'art for art's sake' and its disciples – particularly 'Jimmy Whistler' – for criticism.[59] What we are seeing here is the discursive counterpart to the developments discussed in Chapter 1. As social and commercial changes were undermining the integrity of a discrete art world in Britain, these cultural discourses were attacking the notion of the discrete aesthetic realm that so often accompanied it. Yet it was more than that. The invocation of the American-born, French-trained and highly controversial figure of Whistler triggered a certain set of public associations: dandyism and charlatanism; the elitist conviction that art was for the few rather than the many; the famous allegation of 'flinging a pot of paint in the public's face'; and, perhaps above all, that baffling, cosmopolitan foreignness.[60] In all, the intention was to represent artists – whether they were exotic aesthetes like Whistler or foreign Jews with German names like Epstein – not as irrelevant figures on the margins of British society, but as inscrutable aliens at its centre.

In his book of the same title, Benedict Anderson famously defined modern nations as 'imagined communities' – societies that existed not through concrete interactions but cultural representations.[61] Anderson and the many who have been influenced by him described how the construction of imagined communities depended in part on a distinction between 'insiders' and 'outsiders'. As Britain imagined its own community after August 1914, it too made these distinctions.[62] Panikos Panayi has described how while the country forged an inclusive model of nationhood, it monitored, demonized and interned thousands of enemy aliens.[63] The art world was extremely susceptible to such a policy. For many years, it had not only been one of the more cosmopolitan sectors of British life; it had also been one of the most German. In 1914 England imported half of all its art materials from Germany; German firms dominated the country's art supply trade;[64] and men with German or Jewish names or origins were among the country's most famous artists (Walter Sickert, Jacob Epstein, Mark Gertler), dealers (Asher Wertheimer) and collectors (Julius Wernher).[65] Together, they could very easily suggest that the British art world was in fact a hub of enemy alien activity: a cluster of 'outsiders' residing at the nation's core.

These suspicions inflected wartime interpretations of art around Europe. Kenneth Silver, for instance, has shown how nationalistic rhetoric profoundly affected the Parisian avant-garde.[66] In Britain, rearguard critics repeatedly likened modernism to a Germanic virus that was compromising the integrity of English civilization.[67] When the London Group opened its second exhibition of progressive art in March 1915, the normally sober *Times* headlined its review 'Junkerism in art', and claimed that the painters within seemed to 'execute a kind of goose-step'.[68] A few months later, at its third exhibition, Mark Gertler's work was attacked by the *Morning Post* for displaying a 'Hunnish indecency'. Shortly afterwards a member of the public entered the show and appended a label that read 'Made in Germany' to his painting *Creation of Eve*.[69] These developments, as a number of scholars have made clear, were undoubtedly part of a specifically anti-modernist discourse. However, this section has shown that they were also part of a much broader set of discourses that sought to portray all artists as outsiders.

This section has described how certain patterns of wartime discourse represented art and artists not just as distractions from the war effort, but as enemies to it. As the war politicized all kinds of social groups and activities, art came to be interpreted as a politically unacceptable endeavour. This was both a development from the milder forms of criticism already discussed, and an inversion of them. If the first strand of discourse dismissed art as a triviality, the second was convinced of the opposite. It configured art as a practice with so many dangerous social implications that it could potentially have a decisive impact on the outcome of the war. Things, however, were to get worse for artists. A final cluster of wartime discourses emerged, in tandem with government legislation, which seemed to render explicit many of the latent suspicions about artists' alien origins and suspicious identities. In this bundle of perceptions, artists were not simply fiddling while Rome was burning; they were fanning the flames.

'Traitor' painters

In August 1914 long-held concerns about the presence of secret agents in Britain erupted into an epidemic of 'spy mania'. Espionage had been a highly marketable subject for more than a decade, with the writers William Le Queux and Erskine Childers writing successful novels on the theme and spy films attracting ever-expanding audiences.[70] As peacetime curiosity gave way to wartime paranoia, Le Queux, like others, amplified these public concerns into highly profitable hysteria. In his book *German Spies in England* (which was reprinted six times in three weeks following its February 1915 publication), Le Queux declared that: 'Among us here in Great Britain ... are men – hundreds of them – who are daily, nay hourly, plotting our downfall.'[71] Vague but also comprehensive, these unverifiable claims had the power to transform any innocent citizen into a potentially nefarious spy. In the witch-hunt that followed, all social groups became objects of suspicion. Nevertheless, contemporary sources suggest that among the people most regularly suspected of espionage were artists.

This unlikely identification stemmed in part from contemporary understandings of espionage techniques. At the beginning of the war several semi-official sources stressed the role that pictorial codes played in the communication of covert information. Robert Baden-Powell, who had served at length in the British army, described in detail how spies would pose as artists in order to produce these codes unsuspected. He revealed that many English agents on the continent were using such disguises, confessed that he had done so himself and even printed a series of plans disguised as artists' sketches in order to prove his point (Figure 2.1).[72] Le Queux also maintained that spies usually 'received thorough instruction in sketching' and reiterated Baden-Powell's explication of the pictorial code technique.[73] The method was even discussed, in some depth, by the popular press. On 7 October 1914 the *Illustrated War News* published a feature (Figure 2.2) in which two adjacent landscapes – one loose and tonal; the other schematic and topographical – illustrated how a plan could masquerade as a sketch and its producer pose as an artist:

> The illustration on the first of these two pages ... shows an apparently innocent drawing of a landscape made by a spy. Were he caught with it in his possession, he might pose with comparative safety as an artist who had been sketching for his own amusement ... In point of fact, however, his sketch would have been made in accordance with a secret pictorial code known to the Government in whose interest he was spying ... The landscape, received by the spy's Government, is read in accordance with the code, and the result is a plan. In this code a windmill, for example, would represent a lighthouse; a plantation of trees, a fort; a single farmhouse or cottage, a group of buildings; a group of houses, a town; a church, Admiralty offices or a Town Hall; double lines (ostensibly roads), railways tracks, and so on.[74]

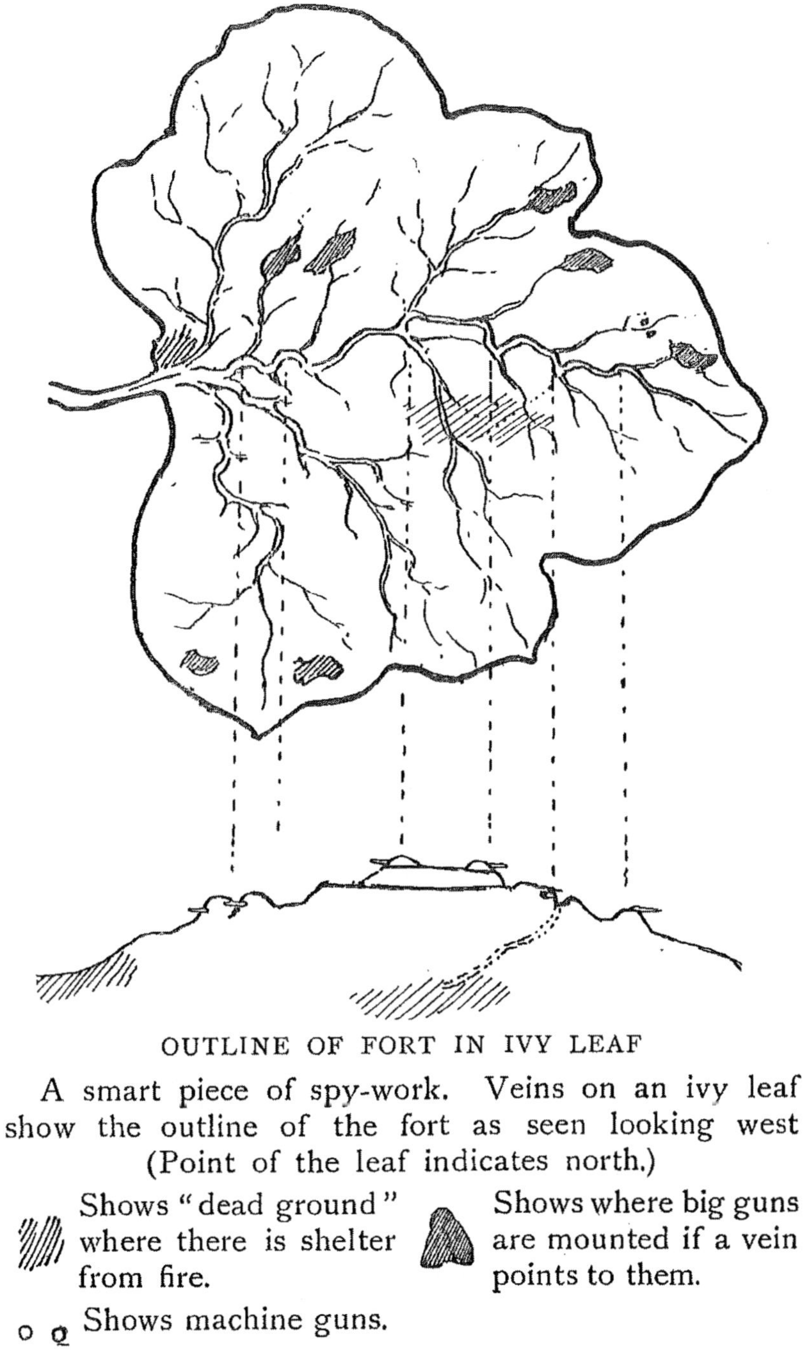

Figure 2.1 Robert Baden-Powell, 'Plans of Forts disguised as a sketch of a stained glass window', reproduced in Robert Baden-Powell, *My Adventures as a Spy* (1915).

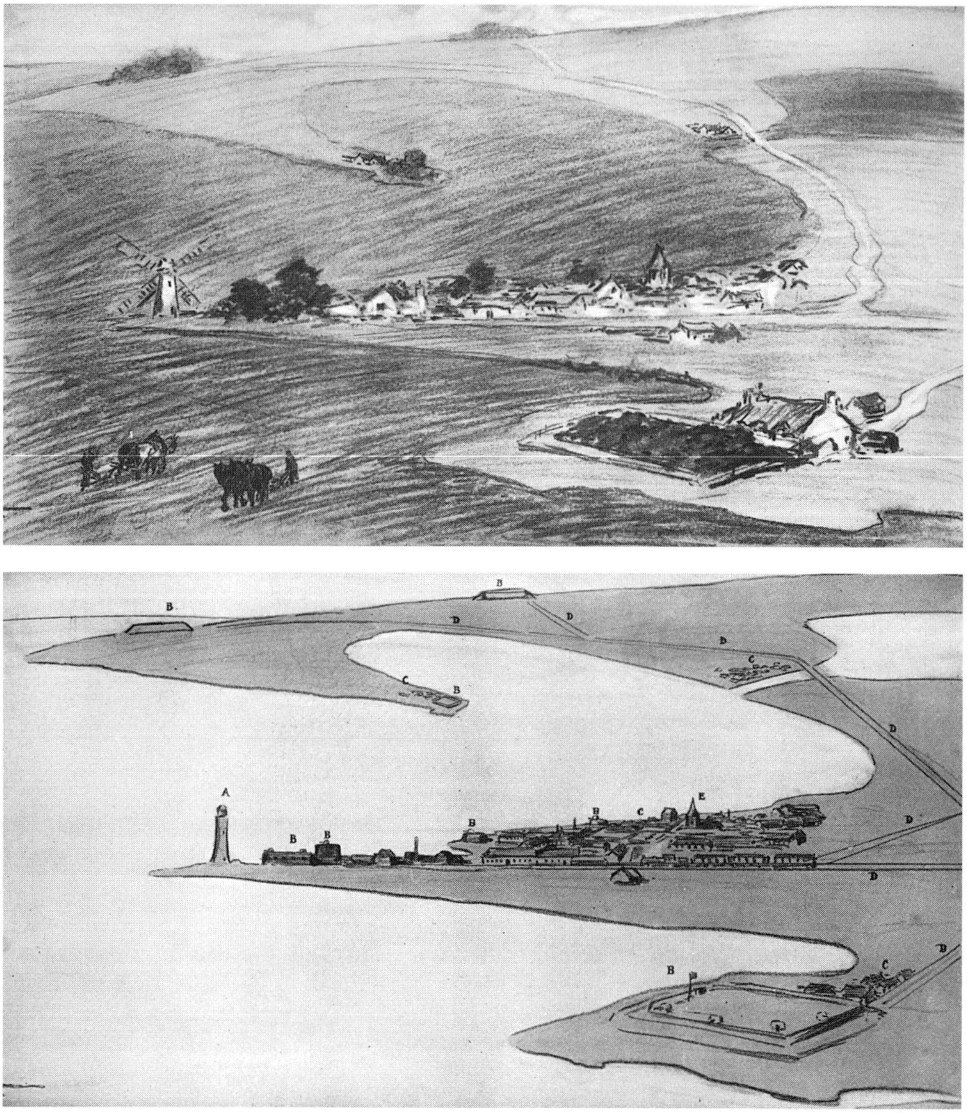

Figure 2.2 'An Apparently Innocent Landscape', *Illustrated War News* (7 October 1914).

If these were not the most reliable accounts of espionage techniques, they nonetheless had far-reaching implications. I have already described how the war transformed perceptions of the various practices associated with the art world. Here, however, it was the artwork itself that was being reassessed. The pictorial image, which might previously have been interpreted merely as an object of beauty, was now a vector of sensitive and potentially threatening information.

Such a realization soon convinced the British authorities that image-making had to be restricted. At the beginning of the war, the government passed the Defence of the Realm Act (DORA). This notorious legislation was designed to safeguard the nation's military, industrial and intellectual resources, and in the process suspended many basic civil liberties that Britons had long considered their birthright.[75] Two of its regulations affected artists. The first was straightforward censorship, and prohibited the production, distribution and sale of any image that seemed 'likely to cause disaffection and alarm'.[76] The other regulation was worded as follows: 'No person shall without the permission of the competent naval or military authority ... make any photograph, sketch, plan, model, or other representation of any naval or military work, or of any dock or harbour, or with intent to assist the enemy, of any other place or thing.'[77] It was a small paragraph that had huge consequences. In effect it made a vast quantity of artistic activity illegal.

With the enforcement of DORA, innumerable British artists were confronted, interrogated and arrested for working out of doors. Among them were John Lavery, Philip Wilson Steer, Augustus John and Laura Knight. The architect and designer Charles Rennie Mackintosh was a particularly unfortunate victim: he spent a night in a police cell, was cross-examined by a local magistrate and was subsequently followed by detectives everywhere he went.[78] The legislation had severe professional ramifications for landscape painters. In Cornwall, which was home to the largest art colonies in the country, the regulation was so strictly enforced that many *pleinairists* found it impossible to work. Artists were so concerned that in September 1915 a group of them (which included Laura Knight, Alfred Munnings and Stanhope Forbes) sent a formal petition to the government. It read: 'The regulation is so worded as to exclude the right of any artists whatever to paint anywhere except inside their studios and houses ... Artists are faced with the prospect of ruin and bankruptcy if the war is of long duration.'[79] The petition was joined by a statement from the Imperial Arts League and a personal appeal to Lord Kitchener from the Royal Academy.[80] The government eventually released a small number of outdoor painting permits to pre-selected artists, but the real damage had been done: DORA had only served to embolden the public's already established suspicion of artists.

From the very beginning of the war civilians had driven rather than followed governmental action on espionage. Indeed, in the conflict's first month they reported some 9,000 (overwhelmingly unfounded) cases to the authorities.[81] When this general paranoia was connected to an older suspicion of bohemians, the press's promulgation of the 'pictorial code' technique and the news of painters' frequent public arrests, it is no surprise that artists joined the leading targets in the British public's witch-hunt. It was for this reason that most artists'

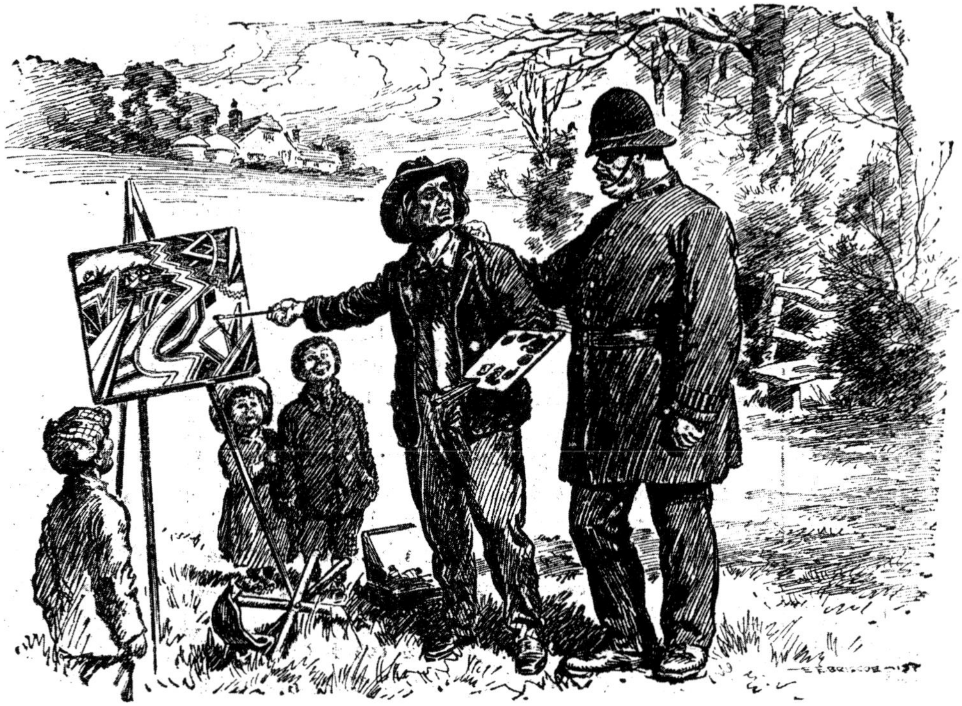

"So vast is Art, so narrow human wit."

Cubist Artist (who is being arrested for espionage by local constable). "MY DEAR MAN, HAVE YOU NO ÆSTHETIC SENSE? CAN'T YOU SEE THAT THIS PICTURE IS AN EMOTIONAL IMPRESSION OF THE INHERENT GLADNESS OF SPRING?"

Constable. "STOW IT, CLARENCE! D'YER THINK I DON'T KNOW A BLOOMIN' PLAN WHEN I SEES ONE?"

Figure 2.3 E. E. Briscoe, 'So vast is art, so narrow human wit', *Punch* (9 June 1915).

altercations originated not from the authorities but rather from 'busy-bodies who see a German spy in every painter'.[82] Newspapers were filled with accounts of artists being arrested by 'posses of villagers', captured by 'natives with specials, pitchforks, dogs' and harassed inside their own homes, and cartoonists even began to ridicule the situation (Figures 2.3 and 2.4).[83] The incidents were so widespread that when the artist Hugh Thomson toured Galloway and Carrick to illustrate a *Highways and Byways* volume, the *Scotsman* newspaper issued a notice to its readers:

> [Thomson] has been subjected to much annoyance and hindered in his work by the 'German spy' craze ... 'The hostile and suspicious attitude which is general' is most uncomfortable. I do not write in order to throw ridicule on those who have thus obstructed an innocent artist who is as

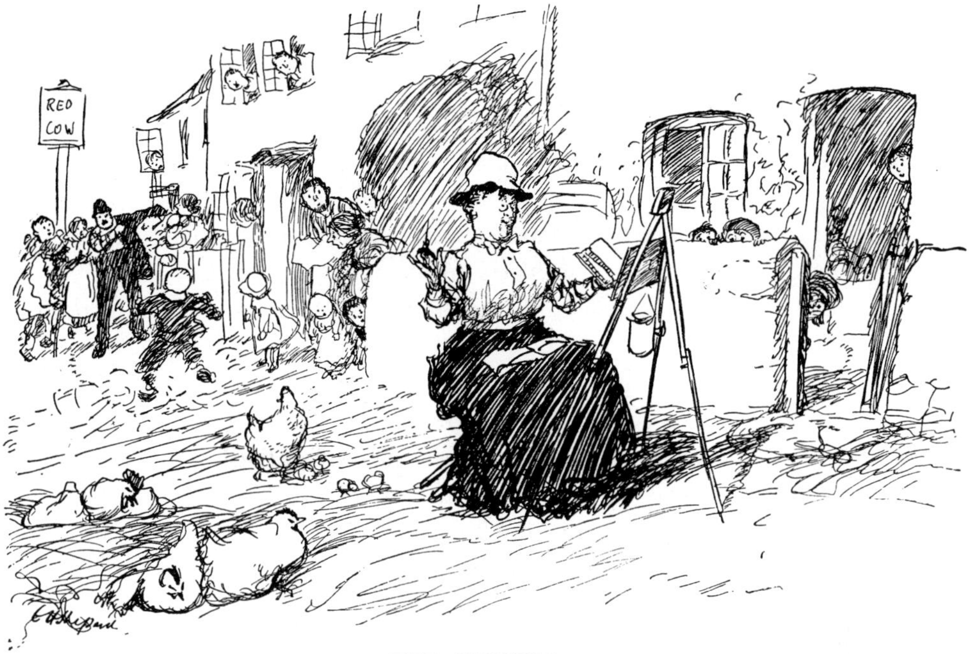

THE SUSPECT.

Figure 2.4 E. H. Shepard, 'The Suspect', *Punch* (9 September 1914).

sound a patriot as anyone can be, but to express hope that in future anyone who detects an unknown gentleman making sketches of old bridges, ruined castles and abbeys, pastoral villages, and bits of pretty scenery may not at once conclude the worst.[84]

At the same time, art journals advised artists how to evade suspicion: 'Keep to districts where [you] are well known, and in which people are used to [your] ways ... When [you] go to strange places and prowl about in what seems to the local idea a suspicious aimless fashion [you] are asking for trouble and [you] must not be surprised if [you] get it.'[85]

Despite the ubiquity of the confrontations, interrogations and arrests, artists were very rarely convicted of espionage.[86] Just one of them was found guilty, and the pictorial code technique was not even his *modus operandi*. Alfred Hagn was a young Norwegian Futurist who before the war had failed to secure any significant remuneration for his paintings. In 1916 he was offered money by two Germans (one of whom was also an artist) to enter Britain posing as a Norwegian journalist and report back to them everything he learned. Hagn arrived in London in October 1916 but was arrested seven months later when his suspicious behaviour led to the discovery of invisible ink in his Bloomsbury hotel room. After confessing, he was convicted in August 1917. The court sentenced him to life imprisonment rather than execution, although his subsequent hunger strike led to his eventual extradition to Norway.[87] Hagn was the only concrete instance of artists' connections to espionage, yet his fate was not the most injurious to their reputations. If any case confirmed the widespread conviction that artists were traitors, it was that of the famous portraitist Philip de László.

Hungarian by birth, Philip de László had become a naturalized British subject immediately following the outbreak of war in 1914. Many considered this proof enough of his duplicity: Le Queux warned his readers that aliens became naturalized 'for the sole purpose of blinding us, and of being afforded opportunities to pursue their nefarious calling'.[88] The fact that de László had undertaken naturalization as recently as he did, and also that his profession entailed mixing privately and at length with the rich and influential, only compounded the suspicions that he was an informant. Debate circulated concerning his status as a British subject, and many argued that he, like other aliens, should be immediately interned. His nationality started to have unfortunate professional consequences: commissions were cancelled, galleries decided that his pictures were no longer welcome at their exhibitions and his membership of several art societies was annulled.[89]

By the middle of 1917 rumours surfaced that de László was a spy, and that summer his wife was misinformed that her husband had been taken to the Tower of London and shot.[90] The rumours, however, were not so far from the truth. For some time de László had been investigated for sending information and money to his family in Hungary. And when, on 17 July 1917, he unwisely offered assistance to an escaped Hungarian prisoner of war, he initiated a chain of events that ultimately led to his arrest, on 21 September. De László was charged with being of 'hostile origin', for corresponding and trading with enemy countries and with rendering assistance to an escaped prisoner of war. The authorities concluded that 'he cannot be regarded as otherwise than a disloyal British subject' and 'a potential danger to the public safety and the Defence of the Realm', and he was ultimately interned under DORA regulation 14b for two years.[91]

The news of de László's arrest was received with great public interest and his face emblazoned the front pages of a number of Sunday newspapers on 23 September.[92] It had several personal implications: a few months into the subsequent academic year, the headmaster of his son's school wrote that he had experienced 'a great deal of trouble with a large number of the parents', before informing him that it would 'be wiser for [his son] Patrick to pass on to a boarding school' when the term was over: 'I need not tell you', he concluded, 'how ashamed I feel at being forced to write in this way, but

I am sure you will understand my position.'[93] His friend the writer Jerome K. Jerome (who himself had adopted the Hungarian middle name Klapka) tried to rally other artists to his defence: 'If we don't help each other no one else has any feeling for us!', he remarked. However, the art world generally refused to offer assistance, and condemned Jerome for even attempting to do so.[94]

The public response quickly turned to confusion and anger. The sustained ambiguity surrounding the case – and the decision to intern de László like an enemy alien rather than try him for treason like the British subject he had become – created a suspicion that he was at the heart of a much larger conspiracy. Newspapers called for the details of the case to be made public, and questions were asked in the House of Commons and the Lords.[95] The patriotic press intensified their campaign against de László. They stressed his foreign origin: that he had been raised to the Austrian nobility in 1912; that he possessed numerous German and Austrian honours; and that he was 'very popular in Berlin and Vienna ... frequently the guest of the Kaiser'.[96] The *People* called him 'The Enemy in our Midst'; the *Evening Standard* considered him one of 'the Most Dangerous Spies' of the war;[97] and *John Bull* dubbed him 'the traitor painter', claiming that his many suspicious activities amounted to 'one of the most amazing cases of enemy perfidy revealed during the war'.[98] On the street, meanwhile, rumours surfaced that he was signalling to Zeppelins with his cigarette lighter in Piccadilly Circus, and at one point demonstrations outside his house had to be dispersed by police.[99]

Importantly, most discourses connected his activities as a spy to his activities as an artist. They cited his pre-war portraits of Kaiser Wilhelm II and the Austro-Hungarian Foreign Minister Leopold von Berchtold as evidence of his intimate association with enemy policy-makers, and argued that his position as effectively a court painter in Britain had proved crucial to his gathering of information. The *Bristol Times* wrote:

> The distinguished character of de László's clientele would have afforded him fine opportunities for obtaining first-class information if he had really been desirous of getting it ... Cabinet Ministers ... are such busy people that they frequently go on working while the artist plies his brush ... King George ... walks about the room and dictates to his Secretaries while he is 'sitting' for his portrait.[100]

And, according to *John Bull*:

> He is a friend of the exalted and the rich; he has painted half of the Cabinet and nine-tenths of Society; he was a welcome guest in the houses

> of the great; he used his position to worm out our military secrets and convey them by letter – nearly fifty of them – to the enemy.[101]

Particular controversy surrounded Lord Curzon, who had apparently sat for de László while a member of the War Cabinet. Curzon was forced to issue a public response to the news: 'I am not aware that there would be anything discreditable in being painted, even in war time, by an eminent artist who had made his home in England for many years, and had become a naturalized British subject.'[102] The next day it was discovered that Curzon had not sat for de László since 1913, but the belief that the artist was extracting information from influential sitters was enduring: in June 1919, after nearly two years' incarceration with no conviction, de László appeared in court to defend himself against the state's decision to revoke his citizenship.[103] In preparation for the case, both legal teams sent questions to his character referees. More than one of those questions asked if he had ever interrogated his subjects about the 'state of the nation' during portrait sittings.[104]

There was a further twist in the de László case. At one point in the proceedings Scotland Yard acquired a letter addressed to him from Geneva, dating back to June 1917. The letter appeared to confirm that de László had indeed been spying for his country of birth. It referred to nearly forty reports that he had made on 'the exact losses of British ships, statistics relating to the critical condition of the mining industry, and views held at Court', and commended him for his most recent work: 'Your report of yesterday confirms what I have said of you for a long time. You have in you the stuff of which diplomats, clever businessmen, and journalists are made. The Report is of the highest importance, and gives a splendid picture of the true situation in England.'[105] On seeing the document, de László was incredulous, and was convinced that it – and others like it – had been 'made up at Scotland Yard' in a massive secret service conspiracy designed to frame him:

> The letter is most clumsily composed by a 3rd rate man and certainly to compromise me here in this country, and I am sorry to say, [it] ... has succeeded. It is so stupidly done, that I can only wonder that any sane and honest man can take it seriously ... I have come to the conclusion that the letter was fabricated.[106]

As far as all subsequent evidence suggests, de László's conclusion was correct.

It is not the place of this book to comment at length on de László's innocence or otherwise, although his ultimate release without charge and the decision to uphold his British nationality in 1919 seem to have been justified. De László's activities were undeniably illegal as far as wartime legislation was concerned, but they were certainly not driven by hostile intentions. Nevertheless, his case – and his eventual 'whitewash' – had captured the public's and the press's imagination, and in the process appeared to corroborate the older and broader suspicions of artists. It had also become a focus for arguments about art's role in wartime class confrontations, and working-class newspapers emphasized how de László was implicated in a secret collusion between an elite, internationalist art world and the 'Society sycophants' for which it catered. In one of its many articles on de László, *John Bull* concluded:

> The case of this Society petted painter is a solemn warning to us to be wary of those in high places who are now ready to whitewash the Hun ... It must make the average decent British citizen sick to see how the fashionable personages hurried to the Law Courts to bolster up the case of this Hungarian traitor who, when it suited him, became naturalised – and, when it suited him, broke and defied the laws of the country whose protection he sought and on whose money he waxed rich.[107]

Following his vindication, de László's career did recover, but for some time he remained a symbol of the art world's allegedly corrupt, elitist and unpatriotic identity. Indeed, for over a decade the term 'Laszloism' was in common usage to describe a high-society criminal absolved of his guilt by powerful allies.[108]

* * *

Philip de László was one of the many victims of the war's social changes. The conflict politicized countless practices and identities that had previously been sub-political, and in the process polarized their societal implications. No longer understood as a discrete activity that could be judged on its own merits, art was reconfigured as an unethical entertainment in the face of unprecedented suffering, a focus for profligacy in a climate of self-denial and an act of 'unprofitable dreaming' when only 'productive labour' was required. Artists, meanwhile, were identified as profiteers rather than patriots, shirkers rather than soldiers, bohemians rather than 'ordinary men' and ultimately traitors to the realm rather than its loyal defenders.[109] In every case, art was understood as a binary opposite to what was valuable and what was commendable. In every case, artists were understood as the 'outsiders' of an imagined community in which only 'insiders' were acceptable.

The first two chapters of this book have shown how the onset of war undermined the position of the arts in British life. The conflict quickly monopolized the material and spiritual resources of the nation. It denied the art world much of the concrete capital on which it had traditionally depended, and it was forced to continually compete with official agencies for men, money and materials. At the same time, it altered the country's mood, giving rise to a set of newly unsympathetic attitudes towards cultural activities. In the process, art was yet further identified as an adversary to the war effort and to public life as a whole. These changing conditions suggested that the precarious relationship between British society and its art was in danger of suffering long-term damage. Nevertheless, many constituents of the art world soon realized that in order to retain, regain or perhaps even increase their relevance amid the conflict, they needed to change themselves and mobilize behind it.

3 THE ARTS MOBILIZE

As we have so far seen, the early part of the war marginalized, impoverished and demonized Britain's art world. Within less than a year of the conflict's start, art was not only struggling to be commercially feasible; its established place in British life was under threat. In a despairing 1915 essay in the *International Journal of Ethics*, Clive Bell expressed a genuine fear that the nation was about to abandon art for ever. 'From every quarter', he claimed, 'comes the same cry – "This is no time for art!"'[1] Nevertheless, it was at this point that the art world finally started to take matters into its own hands. By the beginning of 1915 artists and art institutions had come to two realizations: their own adherence to 'business as usual' was failing, and the war was not going to end quickly. It became clear that if they were to survive the conflict's indefinite hardships they needed to adapt to wartime conditions and prove they were no less patriotic – and no less useful – than the rest of society. Many concluded that the best way to do this was not to compete with the war effort, but to mobilize behind it.

It is now well established that the First World War – like all 'total wars' – was fought as much on the home front as it was on the front line. John Horne has written that after 1914 'all kinds of social groups and institutions mobilized themselves behind the war effort, and in doing so contributed powerfully to a cultural fusion, or at least convergence, in defence of state and nation'.[2] This chapter describes how, amid the many obstacles that it faced, the art world embarked on its own mobilization for war. Exhibiting societies transformed themselves into nationalistic institutions; the art market devoted itself to charitable initiatives; museums became organs of state-issued directives; and artists rallied the home front precisely as they calibrated the front line. As its hitherto private activities took on explicitly public functions, the art world became an increasingly important tool in the waging of the conflict. In the process, it not only neutralized and inverted many of the criticisms that had previously been made of the arts; it went some way towards securing a place for itself in the mainstream of British society.

The nationalization of culture

Parts of the cultural establishment had begun to mobilize in the very first weeks of the war. In September 1914, fifty-two distinguished British writers (including J. M. Barrie, G. K. Chesterton, Arthur Conan Doyle, Thomas Hardy, Rudyard Kipling and H. G. Wells) signed a declaration in *The Times* that endorsed the Allied cause. The initiative had been largely orchestrated by Britain's war propaganda bureau at Wellington House.[3] The wording, however, suggested that the writers had willingly cooperated in order to distance themselves from the German counterparts to whom they were perceived to be too close. 'Many of us', they wrote, 'have dear friends in Germany, many of us regard German culture with the highest respect and gratitude; but we cannot admit that any nation has the right by brute force to impose its culture upon other nations.'[4] The text was extremely revealing: its authors were not just pledging allegiance to Britain; they were claiming that the conflict was fundamentally *about* culture.[5]

The writers in *The Times* were not alone. In the early part of the war many artists and intellectuals situated the conflict within a larger cultural framework that had little to do with reality. A typical example was John Cowper Powys's *The War and Culture*, published at the end of 1914. In that text (which was a rebuttal of the German-born Hugo Munsterberg's book *The War in America*, published earlier that year), Powys argued that the ongoing conflagration was at heart a battle between German *kultur* – a cold, homogenous and state-driven cultural model intent on world domination – and the 'Latin civilization' of France, Britain and Italy that stood in its way.[6] Powys's arguments may seem wholly unconvincing today, but they were repeated so many times during the war that the general public became fluent in the ills of Nietzsche and Wagner.[7] These arguments had other major implications. As soon as Germany's motives for war were understood to be cultural, British cultural life could become as crucial to its defence as the army. Artists, writers and musicians could even claim that their work was integral to the national values for which the war was being fought in the first place.

If British culture was to legitimately proclaim its national credentials, it first had to guarantee its purity. What followed amounted to what Jay Winter has aptly called a *Kulturkampf* over the arts.[8] Scholars have already described how after 1914 universities excluded German professors, orchestras came under pressure to cease playing German music and publishing firms discontinued print-runs of German literature. Yet the nationalization of culture also permeated the visual arts. This process is particularly apparent in the case of the International Society, because the organization had originally been formed on the basis of a 'non-recognition of nationality in Art'.[9] Presided over by figures such as James

McNeill Whistler and Auguste Rodin, and boasting an honorary membership that included Edgar Degas, Gustav Klimt and Adolph Menzel, this association aimed to forge bonds between European and American artists. Only a month into war, however, its council decided to expel all 'enemy aliens' from its register.[10]

The International Society's purge of certain foreign members was replicated throughout the art world. Even ostensibly national organizations like the Royal Society of British Artists found themselves sliding into similarly invidious political terrain. In the Royal Society of British Artists' case, the controversy was ignited when the veteran sculptor George Frampton requested that his name be withdrawn from its list of honorary members because of 'the continued presence in the Society of several natives of enemy countries'.[11] When the management replied that the men he opposed – including Philip de László – were naturalized British subjects, Frampton wrote:

> Your answer to my first letter has certainly given me a great shock, coming as it does from a Royal Society composed of British Artists (?). Your attitude, to my mind, suggests great weakness and a lamentable want of patriotism, and it is quite impossible for me, as a patriotic Englishman, to be associated with a Society that places its interests before the honour and safety of its Country.[12]

A general meeting was called, and the organization's secretary was ultimately compelled to write letters to all 'foreign-sounding' members: 'Your name unfortunately suggests foreign origin', they read, 'and we should be so glad to have proof that you are *quite* English, so that we may be able to support your position.'[13] Those who could not prove their Englishness were asked to voluntarily retire until the war had passed, to defer from using any of the privileges attendant on their membership and to grant permission to have their names deleted from all exhibition catalogues. By the spring of 1915, all such individuals had disappeared from the Royal Society of British Artists' membership list.

George Frampton launched a similar offensive against the Art-Workers' Guild, of which he was a past Master. This time his opprobrium was focused on an individual – Karl Krall, a German-born member who had been a naturalized British subject for over a decade. Brandishing police papers, Frampton exclaimed that 'Krall being of enemy alien birth be asked to resign'.[14] When the Guild defeated his proposal by a vote (seventeen to ten), Frampton himself resigned, asking for his portrait to be removed from the hall and his name erased from all printed matter so that 'future members shall never know that I belonged to a society in which, even during war ... placed the interests of a member of enemy alien birth before those of our own countrymen, and more especially those brave and noble souls who are sacrificing their lives and everything for Right, King & Country'.[15] Krall was so unsettled by the debates that he voluntarily resigned, and asked never to be contacted by the Guild again.[16]

Nationalizing pressures did not just originate from organizations' members. Similar demands were made by proprietors of exhibiting spaces, who were understandably sensitive about how their premises' contents might reflect on them. In 1916 William Marchant, owner of the Goupil Gallery, issued an ultimatum to the London Group, which insisted that 'no enemy aliens, conscientious objectors or sympathisers with the enemy were permitted to exhibit' in his gallery.[17] The Royal Watercolour Society issued a similar reprimand to its own temporary tenants:

> Am much astonished to see that the London Salon of Photography comprises among its exhibits a number of photographs by German and Austrian subjects. Will you allow me to express the opinion that in view of the existing state of affairs, which does not even yet seem to be fully realised in this country, the inclusion of German and Austrian works held in the Galleries of this Society is wholly undesirable.

The Royal Watercolour Society insisted that the committee 'remove all Exhibits by German and Austrian subjects ... at the earliest possible moment'. The London Salon of Photography instantly agreed to the demands.[18]

The nationalization of culture was not confined to Britishness. Indeed, the art of certain other nations became more widely accepted during the war than it had ever been before it. The art of Allied countries in particular was repeatedly used to symbolize the unity of the Triple Entente. The first major example of this came three months into the war when, on 8 November 1914, the distinguished French sculptor Auguste Rodin gave eighteen of his works to the British state (Figure 3.1). His gift came with the following announcement: 'The English and the French are brothers; your soldiers are fighting the side by side with ours. As a little token of my admiration for your heroes, I decided to present the collection to England. That is all.'[19] The bequest – which the *Burlington Magazine* called 'one of the most magnificent gifts which the national museums have ever received' – was interpreted as a powerful symbol of the solidarity between Britain and France.[20] Some could not resist interpreting it further: for *The Times*, the gift was a 'silent answer to all the arrogant German talk about their predominant Kultur'.[21]

Art was found to be a singularly useful way of exemplifying the political fault lines of Europe. It could illustrate national characteristics in legible but subtle ways, and its meanings could be freely interpreted according to the agendas of those deploying them. This approach is best expressed by reference to one

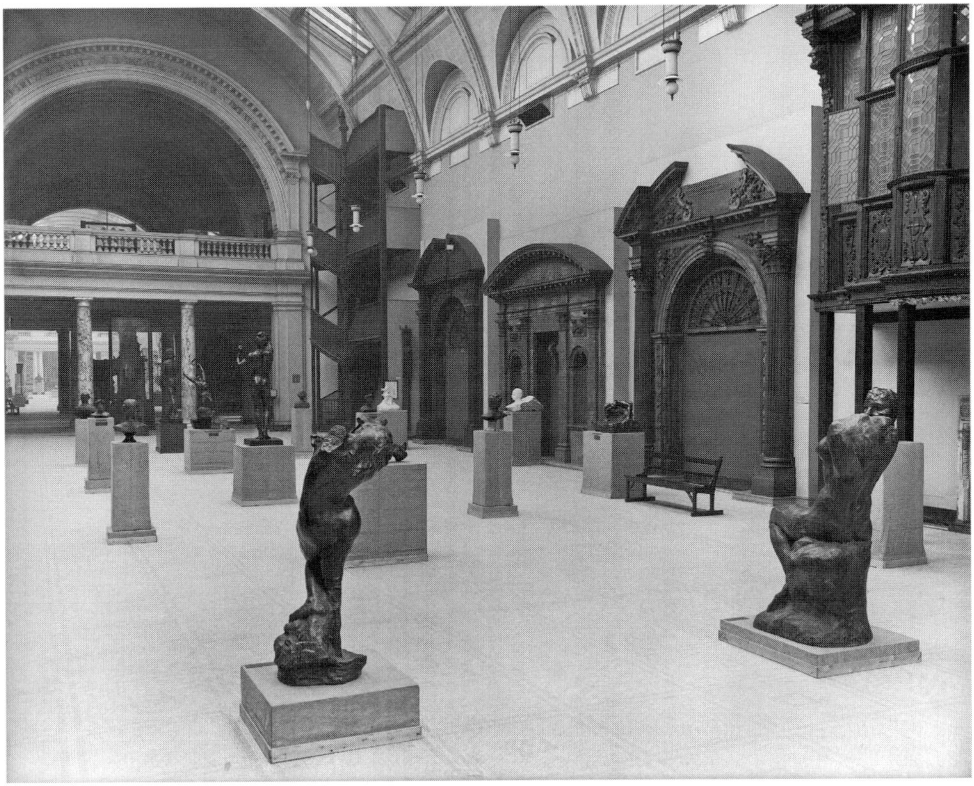

Figure 3.1 Auguste Rodin's sculptures in Gallery 48, Victoria & Albert Museum, November 1914. Photograph. Victoria and Albert Museum.

of Rodin's most talented protégés. In the summer of 1915 a large display of sculptures by the Serbian artist Ivan Meštrović opened in the very same gallery in the Victoria & Albert Museum that had housed the works gifted by Rodin (Figure 3.2). It was, apart from Rodin's display, the first one-man show of a living artist in the museum's history, and in spite of the difficult wartime conditions, it proved to be an unqualified success. The public flocked to the exhibition in their thousands, and the catalogue's sales were so high that it had to be reprinted several times.[22] Critics, meanwhile, were united in approval. One of them hailed the show as 'the most important event' in the London art world since Whistler's memorial exhibition of 1905.[23]

The Meštrović show had actually been stage-managed by a committee of Southern Slav émigrés who were using the exhibition to boost sympathy for the Serbian people and to make the case for a unified Southern Slav state called 'Yugoslavia'. Their propaganda campaign was explicit: in some newspapers the exhibition announcement was printed adjacent to advertisements for the Serbian

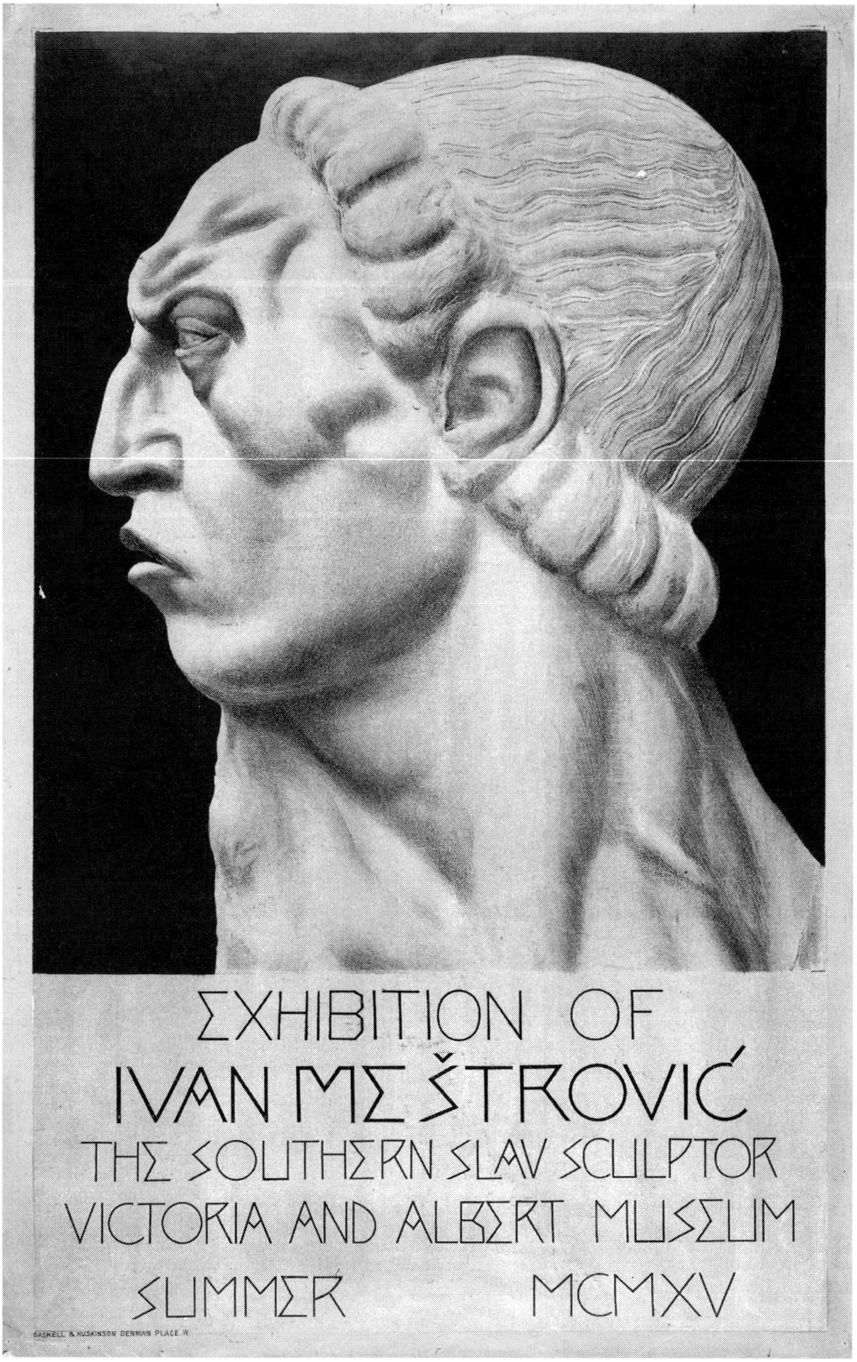

Figure 3.2 'Ivan Meštrović, the Southern Slav Sculptor', 1915. Lithograph poster on paper, 101.2 × 63.2 cm. Victoria & Albert Museum.

Relief Fund, whose headline read: 'Unconquerable Serbia, like our other gallant ally Belgium, has suffered the penalty of withstanding the invaders ... She has fought and beaten back the Austrians: now she has to fight destitution, disease, and starvation ... We plead for your contribution to-day.'[24] The purpose of the show was thus clear. As one observer remarked, it was 'a Southern Slav visiting-card left at the door of England'.[25]

Meštrović's seventy-four exhibits were pregnant with nationalistic motifs: they depicted Serbian military heroes, Kosovan widows, Slavic mythological figures and even a large wooden model of the Temple of Kosovo, which was described in the catalogue as a 'Southern Slav Valhalla'. The catalogue repeatedly portrayed Meštrović as an embodiment of the romance of his homeland. An essay by R. W. Seton-Watson – a founder-member of the Yugoslav Committee – described how the artist had started life as a peasant shepherd boy before emerging, against the odds, as an internationally acclaimed genius. Seton-Watson argued that the sculptures themselves were the 'apotheosis of the Jugoslav idea'. He continued: 'Their native force and virility reveal to us the secret of the Serbian revival, and help us understand the unconquerable spirit which has thrice repelled Austria's "punitive expeditions", and so nobly vindicated Serbia's place in the ranks of the Allies.'[26] It is arguable that only artworks – rich, allusive and silent as they were – could so easily accommodate such a willful act of lobbying.

The nationalistic rhetoric surrounding Ivan Meštrović had not been subtle, but it was swallowed by virtually the entire British press.[27] Critics obediently interpreted the works as unmistakably Serbian – even if they had no previous conceptions about Serbian identity. They drew particular attention to the bold, archaic simplifications of form, the truncation of figures and the extreme characterizations of emotion. The truth, of course, was that Meštrović's work displayed, if anything, a modernist aesthetic of international origin. Yet rather than condemning the sculptures for stylistic cosmopolitanism or a deviation from academic naturalism, most critics endorsed his methods as an authentic expression of Serbian angst.[28] One correspondent wrote: 'Five centuries of Turkish tyranny do not produce drawing-room emotions. What would the feelings of our artists be if the Germans were to set their heels on us for a generation or two? They would break academic bounds.'[29] Responses like these suggest an alternative to traditional statements about modernism and the war. Most scholars have claimed that the conflict increased hostility to modernist methods, as they came to be connected with distinctly un-English values. Here, however, a modernist aesthetic was being embraced precisely because it was foreign.

The reception of the Ivan Meštrović exhibition gives some indication of the war's complex and contradictory impact on the politics of culture. We have seen in Chapter 2 how the politicization of the arts had many damaging consequences for artists and their institutions. This section, however, has shown that the very same process also created much-needed opportunities. Art could be affiliated with the Allied cause just as easily as it could be linked to the enemy's. When this was done effectively the art world benefited accordingly, and exhibitions like Meštrović's – which in normal times would have met either with indifference or condemnation – were now embraced as an invaluable part of the ongoing conflict. But this was only one stage in art's mobilization for war. As the art world attempted to silence the doubters and prove its Allied credentials, it embarked on a set of high-profile initiatives that would assist the war effort in more concrete ways.

Charity work

'The machine of charity in war was as perfect as French .75', wrote A. C. R. Carter, 'and art soon became a bright *vivandière* in the field of voluntary helpfulness.'[30] The art world indeed became one of the country's most proactive centres of wartime charity work. Determined to banish public suspicions of self-indulgence and extravagance, collectors, dealers, auction houses, exhibiting societies and artists devoted themselves to fund-raising with unflagging enthusiasm. They first embarked on this benevolence within only weeks of the war's outbreak. In October the Grafton Galleries devoted the proceeds of its Modern Spanish Art exhibition to the Prince of Wales's recently formed National Relief Fund.[31] At the same time, artists were invited to donate signed and framed works to be sold for the benefit of the organization. Through October and November, hundreds of artists (including twenty-eight Royal Academicians, fifty-six members of the Royal Society of Painter-Etchers and Engravers and thirteen members of the New English Art Club) contributed 414 pictures to the scheme, which eventually raised £2,615.[32]

It was not until the beginning of 1915, however, that the art world started to realize its vast charitable potential. On New Year's Day, the Royal Academy announced that in place of its usual winter exhibition a large show of work by living British artists would be staged later in January. Sales would create a fund whose proceeds would be divided equally between the Red Cross, the Artists' General Benevolent Institution and the contributing artists themselves.[33] The War Relief Exhibition, as it became known, was supported and opened by the King and Queen – who, along with their family and friends, spent more than £410 on pictures during the royal view.[34] Over the subsequent weeks, the show proved to be a not insignificant success: 8,000 members of the public visited the galleries, 167 of the 800 works on display were sold and the exhibition ultimately raised £5,463 in sales.[35]

The Royal Academy's exhibition triggered a stream of charity projects over the course of 1915.[36] By April, philanthropic displays were so ubiquitous that a critic in the *Observer* remarked that there was 'scarcely a gallery in the West End of London that has not held some sort of relief exhibition'.[37] Those responsible for the shows were roundly applauded for their altruism, but the projects rarely made good financial sense. In 1915, Frank Rutter wrote:

> No professions have suffered so acutely from the present state of affairs as those connected with the arts, and yet from none seemingly is more expected. We do not hear of auctioneers, bankers, merchants, and manufacturers giving free, gratis, and for nothing their professional time and labour for various charities ... Actors, artists, musicians, and the like are continually being asked to do this, and unfailingly respond in every appeal. I can only repeat that it is extraordinarily generous, for the artist realises – if the public does not – that each picture sold for the benefit of a charity means a picture the less sold for the benefit of an artist ... If everybody is receiving a quid pro quo, then the artists may fairly complain that they are being exploited and not only for the benefit of charities.[38]

Rutter's warning was ignored. In the patriotic one-upmanship that dictated so much of the period's cultural politics, the art world only intensified its involvement in charitable causes. And undoubtedly its most famous undertaking was the series of Red Cross sales, which commenced later that year.

The British Red Cross had been formed in 1870, and provided aid to wounded soldiers and British prisoners of war. From the start of the conflict, the charity – in conjunction with the Order of St John Ambulance – had asked for subscriptions, but financial donations were not readily forthcoming. Many supporters had instead chosen to give the organization jewels, artworks and other valuable objects. Uncertain how to dispose of these items, the Red Cross approached Christie's in November 1914 in search of advice. The auction house promptly offered its rooms and services free of charge.[39] Christie's decision was not entirely altruistic. As seen earlier in Chapter 1, the company had been closed since the beginning of the war and foresaw few commercial prospects. The Red Cross sale thus presented the directors with an invaluable opportunity to enhance its public profile and boost market confidence precisely as it helped those who were suffering abroad.

The first Red Cross sale opened on 12 April 1915 and ran for twelve days. In that period 1867 lots raised more than £37,000. The Red Cross itself was disappointed with the sum, but in other regards it was a highly successful piece of self-promotion and did much to showcase the patriotism of the British art world.[40] The most noteworthy event occurred on the sale's final day. On 27 April the philanthropist and collector Sir Hugh Lane offered John Singer Sargent (and thus the Red Cross) £10,000 if Sargent were to make a full-length portrait of a yet-to-be-named sitter. Sargent had famously given up making portraits in 1907, but in this case he was unable to refuse. His acceptance was greeted with rapture. The *Daily Telegraph* wrote that 'nothing to equal the auction sensation' had occurred for twenty years.[41] As it happened, Lane died when the *Lusitania* was sunk by German U-boats in May 1915, and was never able to select a sitter. In 1917 his executors asked Sargent to paint President Woodrow Wilson. The eventual portrait acquired its own political associations. In the very same year Woodrow Wilson led the United States into war on the Allied side.

Christie's hosted three more large Red Cross sales over the next three years and in each one, eminent artists – including Augustus John, Philip de László, John Lavery and William Orpen – made generous gifts of blank canvases that were to be painted according to the wishes of the highest bidder. They were a genuine artistic innovation of the war, and some became highly important works. Indeed, *The Year's Art* considered them to include 'some masterpieces of contemporary achievement'.[42] Art made headlines in other ways too. In 1917 Frederick Walker's *The Plough* fetched £5,670 as a result of a contest between Lady Wernher and Morland Agnew ('not for many years has there been such an exciting bout of bidding'), before Lady Wernher – the eventual winner – presented the picture to the nation.[43] Moreover, the sales became increasingly successful as the years went on. The second sale in 1916 raised nearly double what its predecessor had achieved (almost £64,000), the third sale in 1917 raised £71,692 and the final sale in the following year raised £150,000. In total, Christie's handled seven Red Cross sales in various forms during the war, and raised approximately £400,000 for the joint funds of the Red Cross and the Order of St John.[44]

The money, however, was not the most important benefit as far as the art world was concerned. The Red Cross sales were widely covered in the press, and over the course of the war they helped change some public perceptions about the legitimacy of the arts. The sales revealed an elite auction house offering its services for free; a swathe of struggling artists working for no financial remuneration; and a community of wealthy collectors sacrificing their own possessions for the good of those who were less fortunate. As the *Saturday Review* put it:

> These collectors, giving up a treasure to the Red Cross, are parting with something whose value is not in coin. They are cutting a living sentiment out of their lives – something to which they have surrendered a part of themselves ... Its great appeal lies in the very fact of its being an appeal to give up something precious. Had it been an appeal to send subscriptions

> it would not have met with anything like the response. It has made its effect because it has demanded of its supporters that they should surrender the apple of their eye ... Here is a drama of our national dedication – for each of these precious objects which pass from hand to hand, and fall so rapidly to the highest bidder, stands for a private and personal gesture of real sacrifice.[45]

Something significant was happening. The ethics of consumption, discussed in Chapter 2, was being overturned. If the art market had been condemned for being elitist, self-indulgent, profligate and unpatriotic, the charity sales had suggested otherwise. Here, the wealthy were not collecting but dispersing – making personal sacrifices that were not necessarily unlike the sacrifices that others were making for the country; here, artists were not so much painting for the plutocracy as they were for ordinary servicemen; and here, artworks were not conceived as closed, elite objects, but as a currency that reapportioned wealth, a gift that spread goodwill. Luxury, in short, could be as patriotic as it was useful. And it was not the only sector of the art world to prove itself so.

Museums and national service

In August 1914 there were approximately 400 museums in Britain. They varied widely, both in what they displayed and how they were managed.[46] Not all of them exhibited artworks, yet they were probably the most visible cultural institutions in the country. They were also, as Chapter 1 has shown, some of the most severely challenged by war. Museums were faced with huge pressures from the very start of the conflict: publicly funded collections faced budget cuts, the cancellation of purchase grants and the prospect of government-ordered closures; while all museums had to confront a disappearing workforce, declining visitor numbers, increased expenses and growing risks to the safety of their collections. Museums, therefore, found themselves in a particularly perilous position in the first half of the war. It was thus vital that they too reconsidered their social relevance.

If anyone was responsible for thinking through this new sense of purpose, it was F. A. Bather, Director of the British Museum (Natural History) in London (now known as the Natural History Museum). In the first year of the war, Bather wrote a series of influential essays that were published in the Museums' Association's journal and carefully read by the country's curators. In his first essay, 'Museums and National Service', in October 1914, Bather offered a relatively conventional view of the museum's function in wartime, claiming that the institution was best served by continuing to do precisely what it had done in peacetime:

> One of the most useful pieces of work that a museum ... can perform is the arousing of a healthy public spirit. In national, as in individual life, things spiritual are in the long run of more importance than things material ... In time of stern crisis and distressful thoughts, it is well that museums should offer a place of calm retreat, wherein men may be reminded of the steadfast and increasing purpose that runs through the ages, or where they may refresh their hearts and renew their strength in contemplation of that heritage of beauty which it is now the privilege of each one of us to defend ... We too are performing a national service.[47]

If in October 1914 Bather had concluded that museums were places of 'calm retreat', by the summer of 1915 his attitude had very much changed. In July he published an essay called 'Museums and War' in the *Museums' Journal.* It offered an extensive survey of the functions that museums could potentially perform during the conflict:

> First ... we have to arouse the feelings and stiffen the resolve of the nation; each museum must act as a recruiting agent for the army in the field and the army of labour and for all their auxiliary forces. Having effected this, we proceed to instruct the willing hearts and hands in the best methods of accomplishing practical work. All this we must do in our own way, not encroaching on the province of the press or the platform. And the way of the museum is through concrete things: works of art, products of industry, natural objects. Through these it appeals to the eye, and by the arrangement of them to the understanding.[48]

Importantly, Bather instructed his readers (who were largely curators) that if they were to accomplish such goals, they had to abandon their professional principles, put aside concerns surrounding the 'dignity of art' and begin experimenting with methods that would make their exhibits more socially relevant. He concluded: 'Throw away the black cloak of respectability and don the blue overalls or the serviceable khaki!'[49] It may seem a somewhat ludicrous clarion call, but Bather was expressing a fundamentally new vision of the curator as well as the museum.

What, specifically, did Bather have in mind? In order to inspire the public, he proposed that museums stage exhibitions that illustrated glorious moments of British history. Concentration on local regiments could help encourage recruiting, while displays that covered more distant realms could remind Britons of the 'Grandeur of Empire' and the social good that it was doing around the globe. Landscape paintings of 'iconic' national scenes could urge viewers to think: 'How can I help England?', while other exhibits could highlight the cultural and social damage that Germany was wreaking abroad, and thus bear witness to 'his cruelty, his hate, or his determination'.[50] Bather reminded curators that if the message communicated through the displays themselves was too subtle, an accompanying lecture could 'drive home the moral' implicit in them.[51]

Once museums had inspired the public to continue supporting the war, or even to enlist for it, they could then provide an invaluable public information service. Museums, Bather claimed, could instruct the public how to keep themselves and their children healthy, promote economy in the kitchen and 'exercise thrift as a patriotic virtue'.[52] They could also help improve public safety: Bather described how multimedia displays could teach Britons 'how to act under a rain of air-bombs; how to approach and handle an unexploded bomb; how to smother fires caused by thermite bombs or burning fluid; how to meet asphyxiating gases; how to prepare respirators; and a few First Aid hints most likely to be of service'.[53] It was, by any standards, an unorthodox list of objectives as far as museums were concerned. Yet Bather justified his claims:

> This time of trial may be our fiery ordeal, but for every live museum it is also a great opportunity, and the proof of our worth lies in our own hands. Now is the time for each of us to show by his work that a museum is not only a refuge for cloistered learning, but a centre of energising force; not merely a temple of beauty or storehouse of materials for academic science, but an arsenal of tools and weapons, a treasury of vital knowledge, responsive to the pressing call of our country's danger.[54]

Bather's powerful formulation was difficult to ignore. A month after his paper was published, the Museums' Association held a major conference in London, at which the nation's curators debated Bather's strategy. Some of them, like Elijah Howarth of the Sheffield Museums, were not convinced ('museums can do very little in connection with the war, which is entirely outside our province'), but the majority wholeheartedly agreed with Bather.[55] More importantly, the debate suggested to many of them that this was an invaluable opportunity for museums to fundamentally transform their public identity. W. Ruskin Butterfield, director of the Hastings Museum and Library, believed that the war could finally end the popular perception that museums were 'remotely aloof from the serious affairs of men; useful enough on a rainy day for nurse-aids and their small charges; at best places of resort for lovers of antiquity; of nature, and of art'.[56]

Did these new ideas end up being realized? Unfortunately, the government's closure or part-closure of all national museums in London in 1916 makes it difficult to gauge their full effect on the country's most prestigious institutions. Nevertheless, before this point, and afterwards in the provinces, there were signs that museums were indeed making such changes. In the middle of 1915 exhibitions addressed the history of the British armed forces and the damage done by German forces to French and Belgian architecture. Over the following two years, public information displays became increasingly common – and many of them proved as innovative as they were popular. An exhibition in Hull about child welfare and food economy linked artistic exhibits with lectures, film shows, practical demonstrations and even orchestral performances. It was estimated that some 90,000 people – a third of the city's population – attended it.[57]

The success of these exhibitions was such that, in the second half of the war, the government itself started to intervene. By the spring of 1916 Wellington House, the institution behind the government's propaganda campaigns, had established a pictorial propaganda section. The organization often used exhibitions to distribute its message. Indeed, from 1917 it appointed a number of advisers who were experienced in staging such events (including the British Museum's Keeper of Prints and Drawings, Campbell Dodgson; the later Director of the Victoria & Albert Museum, Eric MacLagan; and the gallerist Robert Ross) – a further example of the art world's mobilization behind the war effort. After its inception, the organization sent drawings by Muirhead Bone, the first official war artist, to museums and galleries around the country; it released a series of sixty-six lithographs called 'Britain's Efforts and Ideals', which, beginning at the Fine Art Society in London, toured the nation;[58] and between June 1918 and June 1919 it even organized a substantial display of 'trophies, relics, posters and photographs' that travelled through nine provincial centres, and was seen by as many as 300,000 people.[59]

Museums came to be viewed as so central to national identity during the war that the government even formed its own such institution as a result. In March 1917 the War Cabinet approved the decision to form a National War Museum. They hoped that it would achieve certain propagandistic aims in the short term, but also act as a major memorial to the conflict in the long term. The Imperial War Museum (as it became known) subscribed to the catholicity of approach that Bather had argued was so crucial: paintings, photographs, weaponry, trophies, diaries, personal documents, models, souvenirs and other curiosities were all collected with equal voracity and treated with equal respect. Most importantly, the Imperial War Museum specifically targeted the wider public. In a private memorandum, the institution's first Director, Sir Martin Conway, wrote:

> Such a museum if widely collected and arranged, will be unique in this respect that, alone among museums, it will make a direct appeal to the millions of individuals who have taken part in the war or in war-work of any kind ... When they visit the museum in years to come, they should be able by its aid to revive the memory of their work for the war, and, pointing to some exhibit, to say 'This thing I did.'[60]

The post-war history of the Imperial War Museum is outside the scope of this study, but it is a fitting end to this section. For though the conflict tested museums to breaking point, it also created a number of invaluable opportunities. After the initial disruption caused by the war, many curators were compelled to adjust their practices, aiming their output more directly at national needs and public demands. In the process, museums made significant wartime contributions to British society: raising morale, educating civilians, distributing propaganda and ultimately memorializing the conflict. Like other art-world institutions, museums had planted themselves at the very heart of the war effort, and they had benefited from doing so. The art world's mobilization for war, however, was not confined to institutional activity. If anything, artists and artworks played an even greater part.

Posters

Exhibitions, museum displays and charity sales had done much to promote the causes of both art and war since its outbreak, but their influence had largely been limited to those social groups who chose to attend them. This was emphatically not the case with posters. Posters had been a feature of British public life since the seventeenth century, and had become increasingly intertwined with fine art in the three or four decades before 1914. Many predicted that the continued development of this demotic art would be curtailed by the outbreak of war, yet in reality the opposite was the case. Indeed, one of the conflict's defining cultural features was the unprecedented proliferation of printed images.[61] Between 1914 and 1918 an ever-expanding series of bold and confrontational war posters created on Britain's streets a vertigo of imagery so striking that it made Vorticist innovations seem pedestrian. In one remarkable passage from April 1915, a correspondent described the overall effect in the nation's capital:

> It is impossible, in London at least, to escape the war posters. They grip you everywhere. They assail you from every corner. They take you in the streets and in the trains. They threaten, persuade, cajole, and frighten. Every taxicab cries out at you in forty different sharps and flats, and the only way out of the noise is to get inside. You look on the one hand and you see 'If this caps fits you, join at once'. You look on the other and you are asked what the girls and the grandchildren will think of you if you hold back. Ahead of you Lord Kitchener bars the way with a terrible look and a menacing finger, 'I want *you*'. The eye is subjected to a 'blockade' where everything is contraband but recruiting appeals. Not only is the sight starved of all the normalities, but it is hypnotised by what has taken their place.[62]

Many of the images to which the author referred had been issued by the Parliamentary Recruiting Committee – a cross-party body formed in the first month of the war to incite voluntary enlistment. Between the autumn of 1914 and the autumn of 1915, the Parliamentary Recruiting Committee produced somewhere between 100 and 200 poster designs (which worked out at several new images every week), printing a total of 5.7 million full-sized posters, 550,000 smaller strip-posters 'for use on taxi-cabs and trams and in railway carriages' and 450,000 pictures 'for hanging up in public institutions, offices, shops and houses'.[63] Scholars continue to disagree about the details of the scheme, but they agree that it was probably the largest publicity campaign in the government's history.[64]

The Parliamentary Recruiting Committee's output was not aesthetically distinguished. At least half of its posters were purely typographical, while its pictorial efforts were usually crude and hurried. In fact, the body's only truly memorable image – Alfred Leete's seminal pointing Lord Kitchener ('Your Country Needs You') – had very little to do with its official campaign, having started its life as a front page for *London Opinion* in 1914.[65] Nevertheless, other official bodies did attempt to elevate their output by appropriating works of fine art. This had its precedent in the late nineteenth century, when A. & F. Pears used John Everett Millais's painting *Bubbles* to advertise its soap. In 1917 the National War Savings Committee hijacked a similarly recognizable artwork – Whistler's 1871 portrait of his mother – reproduced it in full colour and then added the legend 'Old age must come … So prepare for it by investing in War Savings Certificates' (Figure 3.3). The committee had hoped that the cultural capital implicit in Whistler's painting would help legitimize its own message. It certainly increased the notoriety of the picture, but vulgarized it in the process: the strident line of text shattered the careful arrangement of shapes and colours in the background. One observer described the poster as 'an act of vandalism … almost as cruel as the firing of a shell into Rheims Cathedral'.[66]

If official poster campaigns were typically characterized by philistinism, private organizations had greater liberty to embark on more inventive initiatives – and major artworks occasionally resulted from them. Frank Pick, the publicity officer at the Underground Electric Railways Company of London, had been exploring the connections between modern art and advertising since 1908. In 1915 he commissioned a number of war posters that have been called 'a real contribution to modern art'.[67] These included Spencer Pryse's *Only Road for an Englishman*, which was if anything too aesthetically sophisticated to be a poster, constructed as it was out of a tonal – and metaphorical – interplay between light and dark. They also included Maurice Greiffenhagen's remarkable *Roll of Honour*, a complex and allusive image that companies could purchase and then

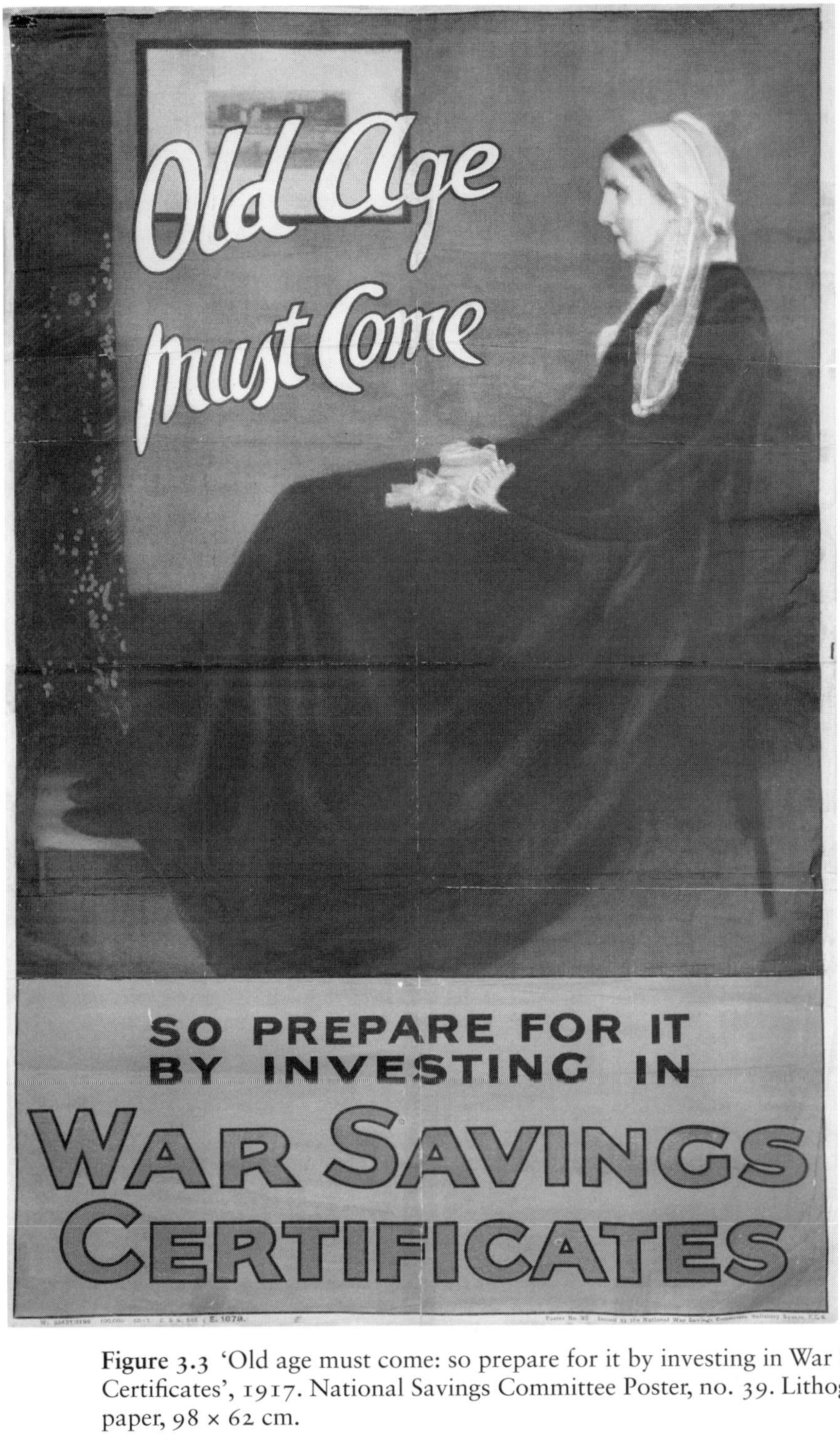

Figure 3.3 'Old age must come: so prepare for it by investing in War Savings Certificates', 1917. National Savings Committee Poster, no. 39. Lithograph on paper, 98 × 62 cm.

add to it the names of staff members who had died in the war. In the following year, Pick commissioned another set of posters, whose function was less to encourage men to enlist as it was to remind serving soldiers of home. His aesthetic ambitions were revealed simply by his choice of artists, which included the distinguished Academicians Charles Sims and George Clausen.

If any fine artist succeeded in making war posters his own, it was Frank Brangwyn. Brangwyn was a versatile image-maker who could effortlessly switch between different registers and media. During the course of the war he is believed to have produced more than eighty designs for posters and prints, including several for Frank Pick. Brangwyn made images for, among others, the National War Savings Committee, the 1914 War Society, the Belgian and Allies' Aid League, the National Institute for the Blind, the *Daily Mail*'s and *Evening Standard*'s Red Cross funds, as well as six recruiting posters for the *Daily Chronicle*. He was even commissioned to design war bond postage stamps for the British Red Cross.[68] Brangwyn rarely charged for these commissions, and thus did much to reinforce the growing realization that some artists were willing to put the war effort before themselves. In 1920, the authors of one book wrote: 'Heaven preserve Mr. Brangwyn from an O.B.E.! But one wonders whether the Government has no suitable reward for one who spared no effort and sacrificed himself and his time and talent in a purely impersonal desire to serve his country.'[69]

Brangwyn was proof that the war could raise artists' profiles if they exploited the vast market for reproducible war images. However, the greatest beneficiary of this process was undoubtedly the illustrator Bert Thomas. Indeed, a contemporary wrote that the conflict had turned Thomas into a once-in-a-generation phenomenon: an artist who was also 'a personality in the eyes of the general public'.[70] Thomas's fame was principally due to his 1914 cartoon *Arf a 'mo', Kaiser!*, which arguably became the war's most famous image, and helped raise £250,000 for the *Weekly Dispatch*'s tobacco fund – considerably more than the first three Red Cross sales combined (Figure 3.4). Thomas's picture subsequently entered every packet of cigarettes sent to the front, and apparently annoyed German forces so much that they prohibited British prisoners of war from smoking.[71] Thomas was later made an official artist for the government's war bonds campaign, and in 1918 he designed a series of war loan posters – one of which was seventy-five feet long and thirty feet high, painted in oils and suspended on scaffolding in front of the National Gallery.[72] It was widely claimed to have been the largest poster ever made in Britain, and one writer wrote that it 'fitted and dignified our strange wartime as gloriously as any priceless Rembrandt lightened the age when it was painted. It was a wonder of Trafalgar Square, and the crowds that massed to see it went away and bought war bonds.'[73] In June 1918 Thomas was awarded an MBE for his contribution to the war effort.

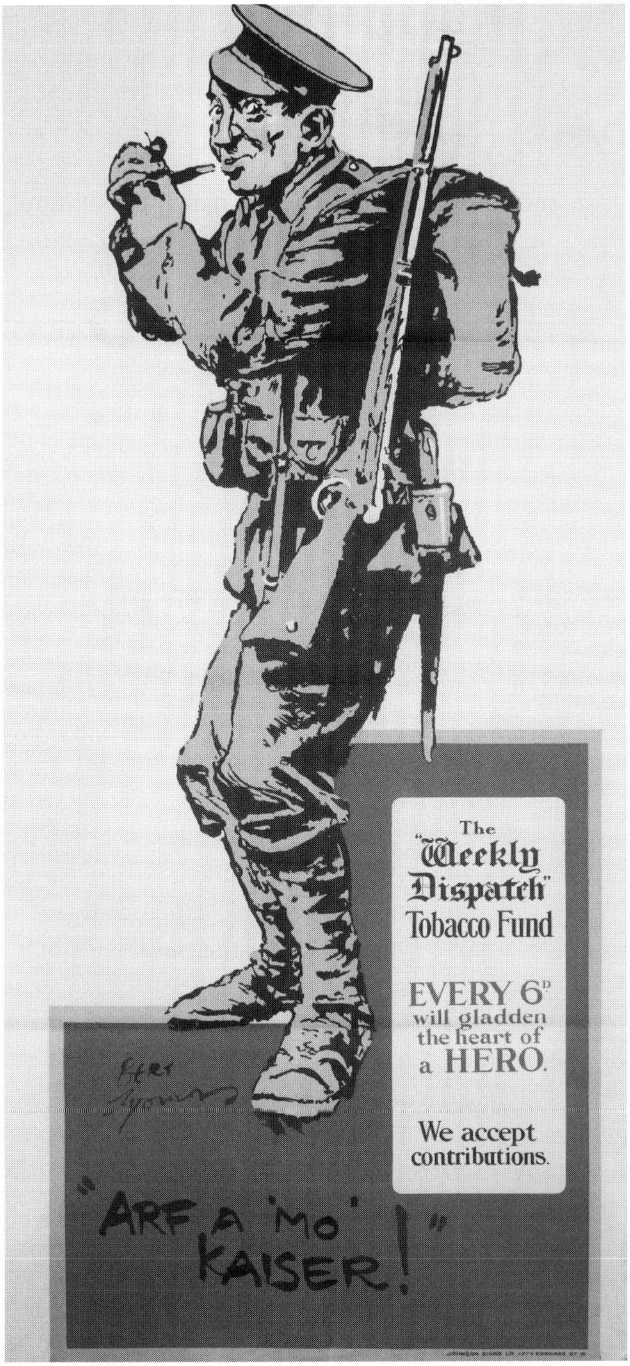

Figure 3.4 Bert Thomas, *Arf a 'mo' Kaiser!*, 1914. Lithograph poster on paper, 153.4 × 70.7 cm. Imperial War Museum.

It is impossible to gauge how successful posters actually were in shaping people's opinions. The government, and the middle classes, widely disapproved of the crassness that characterized most poster campaigns, and the Parliamentary Recruiting Committee's use of the medium was cancelled in the middle of 1915, only a year after it had started.[74] Posters had, however, convinced most people that when designed, distributed and deployed correctly images were uniquely influential in shaping public opinion. In the final year of the war, Victor Branford wrote in *The Athenaeum*:

> Did you desire to stir quiet, home-loving men to go abroad and fight for the liberties of Europe? Or brace delicately nurtured women to go out-of-doors and work for the good of the nation? After logic and exhortation were tried, the artist, with his imaginative presentiment and visual appeal, was discovered to be the best man at these miracles of moral transformation. Did you wish to persuade people to be sparing at meals? In vain you wrote on every wall in large letters: – DON'T WASTE FOOD. But explain the situation to an artist, and he draws a picture of shipwrecked mariners which touches the heart even of the glutton. So we begin to see through artists' eyes the revealing visions of a militant and vital economy instead of listening to the verbalisms and moralizings and marketeerings of a 'peace' and money economy.[75]

Branford had made an important point. He confirmed that artists did not necessarily need to abandon their careers in order to contribute to the war effort; if they mobilized their own peculiar talents, they had the power to mobilize the rest of the nation.

This section has shown how precisely while artworks were being dismissed as irrelevant objects for a wealthy elite, images were reaching the public in potent new ways. Artists were found to possess an unusual ability to recruit, to raise money and to boost morale. Ironically, many of their designs made arguments that had otherwise been used against them: artists had been called shirkers, yet they were encouraging people to enlist; artworks had been called luxuries, yet posters demanded retrenchment; and art had been considered elitist when now it was targeting the masses. Moreover, the war had created a distinctive cultural landscape that necessitated a fluidity between fine art and popular art, as masterpieces became posters, Royal Academicians designed propaganda prints, and commercial illustrators won government contracts. These developments did not simply offer a blueprint for art's place in the war effort; they also suggested a future place for it within British society as a whole. In the meantime, however, the war was still raging. And hundreds if not thousands of artists had little choice but to fight.

At the front

I have already shown in Chapter 1 how on the front line the destructive work of war was nearly always antithetical to the creative work of art. This section, however, will argue that in a number of crucial areas, war-making and image-making were not so far apart. Artists soon discovered that their singular talents were well suited to solving some of the novel military problems of the conflict. And with the increasing support of the authorities, a not insignificant number of them were able to make what was surely art's most concrete contribution to the war.

The war did not look like previous wars. It was vast, diffuse and deadlocked, and when combat occurred it usually took place after dark or at a great distance. Many servicemen remarked that the conflict itself was somehow invisible, or at least smothered in Winston Churchill's 'fog of war'.[76] Amid this perilous obscurity, vision became a crucial tool. If an army could see its enemy and the enemy could not see back, it had already secured a potentially decisive advantage. This situation has led Paul Virilio to claim that the First World War gave birth to the 'logistics of military perception' – a strategic formulation in which the visual mediation of war became more important than the fighting itself.[77] Virilio believed that from 1914 this mediation was not dependent on the human eye – if anything, it rendered that redundant – but on the new visual technologies of photography and cinema. In reality, however, human eyesight very much retained its value, and artists in particular became pivotal figures in the battle for vision. They were widely deployed on the front to see what others could not see, to decipher what others could not decipher, and to disguise what their counterparts were themselves trying to expose. This final section will explore some of the tasks that artists performed, and how they too were able to invert the arguments that had been made against them.

Paul Gough has described how, ever since the establishment of military training academies in the eighteenth century, officers had been taught how to draw – the aim being that in battle, such drawings would help 'neutralise a dangerous terrain and eventually assure mastery over it'.[78] This technique remained official practice during the First World War. Indeed, in 1916 a widely distributed officers' handbook (which was based on the War Office syllabus of training) devoted a whole chapter to military sketching.[79] Nevertheless, the war changed two features of this method: first, its unprecedented indecipherability made the need for observation, reconnaissance and transcription more necessary than before; and second, the vast demographic of the armed forces meant that drawings traditionally made by trained officers were now delegated to volunteers who seemed well suited to such work. The best suited of these volunteers were, of course, artists.

A number of artists consequently undertook military sketching.[80] In the spring of 1916, Len Smith – a private in the army but a commercial illustrator by training – was asked by Brigade Headquarters to make a detailed panorama of enemy trenches near Vimy Ridge. Smith spent four days making sketches while hiding by the German lines under incessant fire ('real, hard risky work'). He then returned to his billet cellar, where, with the light of a single candle, he produced a two-metre-long coloured and annotated panorama. Smith gave the image to his sergeant who in turn took it to headquarters. The following morning, Smith was summoned to a personal interview with the brigadier-general where he received the 'most effusive words of congratulation'. The general commended the panorama for being 'very clearly executed', 'extremely useful' and even 'most artistic'.[81] His final compliment was particularly striking: it was almost as though a squire was praising a landscapist for having made an agreeable portrait of his estate.

Artists did not just chart landscapes from the ground. Harold Wyllie was a distinguished marine artist who was famed for his meticulous attention to detail. One critic claimed that 'it was not until every line had been correctly placed and every curve exactly calculated that he would allow himself actually to begin a painting'.[82] Wyllie's precision was extremely useful in the war, and it was not long before the Royal Flying Corps asked him to become a reconnaissance observer. There, in the back of a Bleriot monoplane, Wyllie took photographs or traced sketches over maps of the front. He often did so under heavy fire.[83] At the end of January 1915 he took one of these drawings to his brigadier-general. The response was extremely positive. According to Wyllie's logbook:

> He was delighted with the information contained in the sketch as it showed some gaps and a parallel being pushed out by the enemy which they did not know of. I was thanked by the general and he said the information was most important and sent some off at once to report to the B.C. 3rd Division General Haldane at Scherpenberg, and to general Moreland commanding 5th Division at St Jean Chapelle. The staff were very interested and general Haldane said he would give orders to have the parallel knocked out at once.[84]

In 1919 Wyllie received an OBE for services to the war effort, and a year later retired from the army as a lieutenant-colonel.

It might be supposed that any draughtsman – or indeed camera – could have done the same job as a professional painter. However, the writings of the French-born artist Paul Maze, who spent time as a scout and front-line draughtsman in the British army, reveal how artists' singular skills were needed to make good intelligence drawings. Much of Maze's reconnaissance was done in the comparative safety of night (which instantly ruled out the use of cameras); the information was gathered through periscopes or rapid peeps above parapets; and his drawings – usually made in charcoal on board – were produced quickly and often under intense pressure.[85] An exceptional visual memory and a fast, confident hand were thus essential. Moreover, it was not a case of recording, as the camera did, simply what was seen. Maze wrote of 'dissecting the ground' with field-glasses and drawing his target 'from every possible angle'; making annotations, optical adjustments and simplifications; imagining himself in German positions; and cross-referencing with other kinds of information.[86] He was, essentially, writing about a synthetic process of scrutiny, distillation, translation and composition – a process that bore an uncanny resemblance to what was taught at art school.

These kinds of correspondences may not seem particularly relevant, but they nonetheless suggest another way by which the wartime criticisms of artists were being overturned. On the home front, artists' powers of scrutiny had been a principal reason for the public suspicion they aroused. 'Traitor painters' were perceived to be capable simply by looking and drawing of exposing the nation's most sensitive military secrets. On the front line, however, it was precisely that scrutinizing gaze that made them so invaluable to the British cause, for they were using those skills to expose the enemy's secrets rather than their own. Furthermore, at the very same time many artists were being employed in another sector of military work that actually involved the concealment of Allied resources. This has since become one of the most famous features of the entire conflict: it was known as camouflage.

Modern military camouflage was invented in the autumn of 1914 by a French portraitist called Lucien-Victor Guirand de Scévola. By November, Guirand de Scévola had formed the first camouflage team, staffed entirely by professional artists, and in February 1915 his unit was formally recognized by the French army.[87] At about the same time, British artists started to lobby their own country to follow suit. On 27 January 1915, the painter and Royal Academician Solomon Solomon wrote a letter to *The Times*, which stated the following: 'Artists, I feel certain, would be only too pleased to place their knowledge and experience at the disposal of the authorities. They discuss these matters among themselves, but so far there is no useful connecting between the makers of the arts of peace and the designers of the munitions of war.'[88] By 1916 Solomon had been put in charge of the first official British camouflage unit. Over the remainder of the conflict, his unit employed artists to design and paint canvases to cover gun pits; to make mock scenery to hide artillery; to produce sniper suits and decoy heads out of *papier-mâché*; and to manufacture observation posts that resembled fake corpses or hollow tree-trunks. It became a vast undertaking: the British camouflage team operated out of several large factories in northern France, and employed hundreds of French women as assistants.

Nevertheless, Britain's major contribution to camouflage was dazzle painting. In 1914 most of Britain's warships and merchant vessels were grey. By 1917, however, the German U-boat campaign was sinking an average of twenty-three British ships a week, and urgent rethinking was needed.[89] At this point Norman Wilkinson, an illustrator and marine painter, wrote to the Admiralty with a solution: 'The proposal is to paint a ship with large patches of strong colour in a carefully thought out pattern and colour scheme, which will so distort the form of the vessel that the chance of successful aim by attacking Submarines will be greatly decreased.'[90] The Admiralty was sympathetic to the idea, and after testing it on HMS *Industry*, ordered fifty ships to be painted by a newly formed dazzle section under Wilkinson (Figure 3.5). Wilkinson's seventeen-person team more resembled a group of artists working on a large commission than a secret naval unit: based in Burlington House, it comprised five male artists, eleven female art students and three model makers, plus ten others (including the Vorticist Edward Wadsworth) to supervise the painting of the ships themselves. Dazzle was appropriated at dizzying speeds: by the following June over 2,300 ships had been painted.[91] Its success, however, remains hard to gauge. A British report from September 1918 suggested that dazzle had little effect, yet in the following month the Admiralty ordered that merchant ships continue to be camouflaged accordingly. The order remained in force until 1937.[92]

Scholars continue to debate the effectiveness of camouflage's various iterations. What matters here, however, is the way that artists used the technique to raise the profile of art itself. Solomon Solomon consistently maintained that camouflage – what he called 'the application of Art to War' – had impeccable artistic credentials.[93] He claimed that only artists could 'fathom the mysteries of a subject which turns on the science of shadows, and on the meaning of subtle tones'; he called camouflaged objects 'ground pictures' with 'post-impressionist patterns'; and he claimed that a great *camoufleur* had to possess the imagination, individuality and inventiveness that were also the hallmarks of a great artist.[94] Solomon even drew parallels between modern *camoufleurs* and the great artists of the past:

> The most advanced and enlightened people of their age in Europe, the Italians of the Renaissance, knew how to value the artist's naturally more than average faculty for visualisation, and entrusted the designing of the fortification of their towns and their arms to the painters and sculptors among them. To walk in the footsteps – *longo intervallo* – of Leonardo da Vinci, Michael Angelo, and Cellini in time of war, makes their humble followers feel proud. They need no other reward.[95]

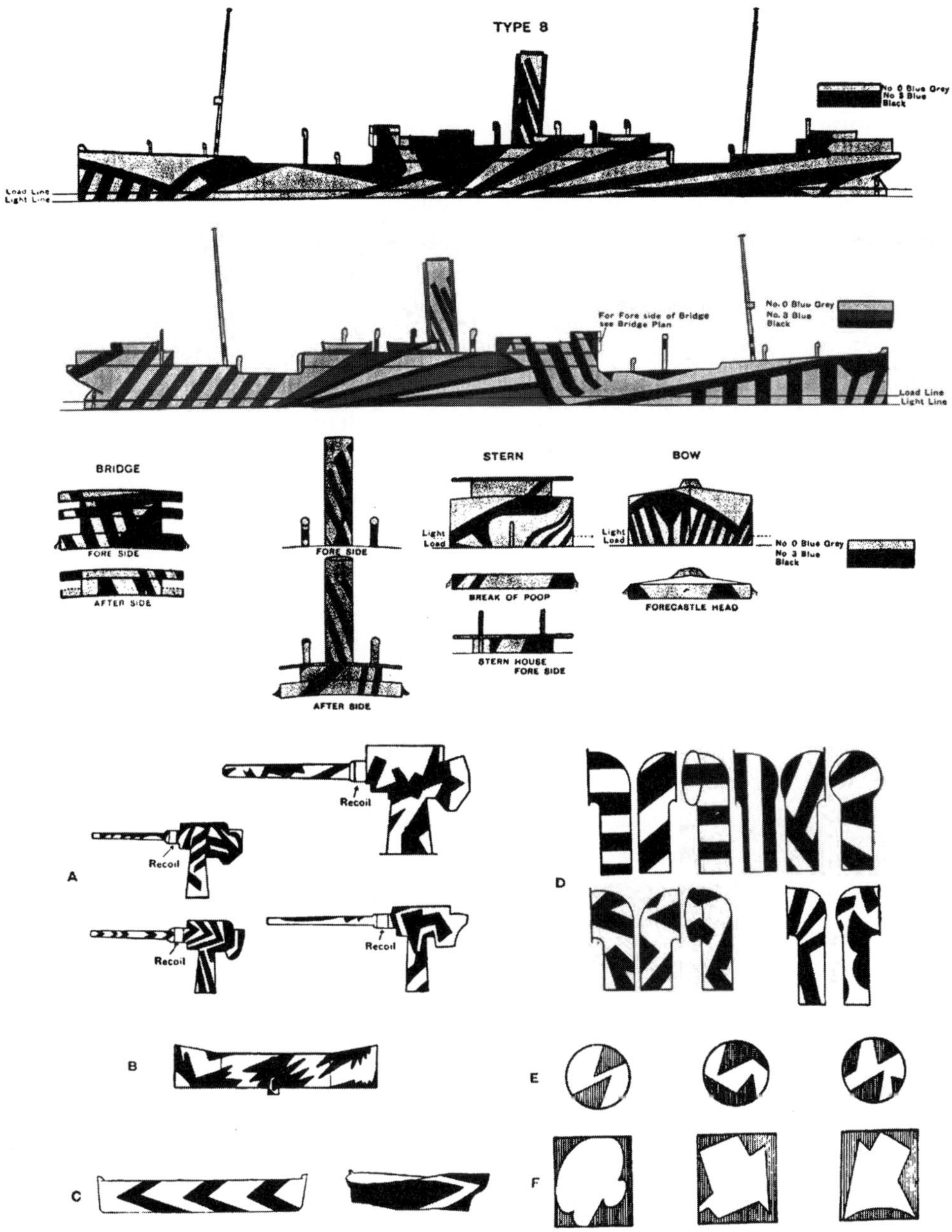

Figure 3.5 Norman Wilkinson, 'Design for Dazzle Camouflage', reproduced in *Encyclopaedia Britannica* (1922).

This established, Solomon made a broader claim: the war had confirmed that fine art was no longer an irrelevant 'side-show' and that it deserved increased support in the future.[96]

Solomon's hope that the military success of camouflage would transform the status of British art may not have been fully realized, but in the war's aftermath camouflage did become something of a cultural phenomenon. Dazzle patterns surfaced in commercial culture, inspiring bathing suits, fashion lines and abstract advertisements that advertised nothing but dazzle itself.[97] Moreover, the British art world wisely laid claim to such innovations. In 1919 the Royal Academy held a major camouflage exhibition, while the Chelsea Arts Ball chose camouflage as its theme. The latter event – which featured a vast dazzled ship painted by Norman Wilkinson himself – was an unprecedentedly bohemian affair, and is a plausible starting point for London's 'roaring twenties'.[98] One might not claim, as Elizabeth Kahn has done, that camouflage was an avant-garde art in itself.[99] Yet it can be argued that it was through camouflage, and particularly through dazzle (which contemporaries described as 'floating cubist paintings' and 'a Futurist's bad dream') that the old and the new could join forces, and that modern art and modern life could better understand each other.[100]

* * *

This chapter has outlined some of the ways that Britain's art world mobilized for the war effort. It has shown how the arts were reconceived as integral components of a wider cultural conflict. It has described how artists' associations purged themselves of enemy aliens so they could proclaim their national credentials, and how artworks were used to reinforce unity between the Allies as well as resolve against the enemy. It has explored how, after a difficult start, art institutions fundamentally rethought their social purpose. The art market restructured its activities around the acceptable face of charity, while museums set aside their aesthetic or intellectual ambitions in favour of propaganda and public information. It has also introduced a point that will be developed in detail over the subsequent two chapters: that image-making itself became central to the war – whether this was through posters that rallied the home front or reconnaissance sketches that calibrated the front line.

Particularly important in this process was the way that these various contributions neutralized or even inverted the wartime criticisms that had otherwise been made of the arts. Art had been dismissed as an irrelevant distraction from the war, and yet here it was reformulated as what the conflict, essentially, was about. Art had been condemned for being suspiciously cosmopolitan, and yet here it was reinvented as a fundamentally British entity. Art had been chastised for being selfish and self-indulgent, and yet the art world now proved to be as generous as any other sector of society, if not more so. Artists were supposed to be shirkers, and yet they designed recruiting posters, volunteered for battle and displayed uncommon courage on the front line. And artists were often believed to be spies, yet here they were using their visual skills to spy on the enemy, to conceal Britain's own armed forces and to help them win the war.

What was taking shape here was an alternative paradigm of art's place in British society. An art world was emerging that, under the vast pressure of war, had briefly been pushed into the margins of British life but was now forcing its way back into the centre. Museums were providing services for the entire public; the art market was funnelling the wealth of the few into the pockets of the many; and artists were applying their skills to posters that would be seen by millions and military artefacts that could potentially save thousands. This new paradigm was admittedly damaging to any lingering hopes for aestheticism (as the 'vandalized' portrait of Whistler's mother so powerfully demonstrated), but this new civic agenda would prove vital to the survival of the arts during the war. Moreover, this was only one side of the relationship. If this chapter has shown how the war encouraged the art world to reach out to the people, the next two chapters will describe how the war encouraged the people to reach out to art.

4 WAR PICTURES: TRUTH, FICTION, FUNCTION

The early chapters of this book have shown how the outbreak of war damaged the public's appetite and respect for traditional forms of art. The conflict, however, had complex and contradictory cultural consequences. It created both obstacles and opportunities in equal measure. And so while the war caused certain forms of culture to be rejected, it caused others to be embraced with unprecedented enthusiasm. In the first half of the conflict this was emphatically the case for any art form that tapped into what I have earlier referred to as 'war fever'. Chapter 2 described how the outbreak of hostilities in 1914 triggered an intense public curiosity in the war itself. That curiosity inflected every sphere and register of cultural life: it caused newspaper circulations to increase exponentially and war-themed books to be published and purchased in their thousands; it inspired countless civilians to start writing and reading war poetry; and it led to a surge of plays, concerts and other theatrical performances that all hoped to satisfy the public's craving for topical entertainment.[1]

War fever's most voracious demands, however, were arguably made of visual culture. The public may well have been obsessed with discussing the war, reading about the war and hearing about the war, but above all they wanted to *see* the war. To civilians the conflict seemed modern, exciting and almost entirely mystifying, and again and again they turned to images to satisfy their curiosity. It would be incorrect to suggest that an aesthetic motivation lay behind these urges. We have already seen that purely aesthetic concerns evaporated as a result of that very same war fever. Moreover, the demands in question were largely indiscriminate: all forms of visual culture, particularly photography and cinema, were implicated in them. Yet they nonetheless had significant artistic consequences. Popular illustrators, Royal Academicians, serving amateurs and official war artists were among the many who produced 'war pictures', and most of them found a large and receptive audience for their wares. This chapter will show how that development revived the popularity of pictorial imagery in Britain and in the process helped transform the social status of art.

Seeing the war

The nineteenth and twentieth centuries are often considered to have been predominantly visual centuries. Indeed, the intellectual historian Martin Jay has called vision 'the master sense' of the entire modern era.[2] It is certainly the case that in the hundred or so years before the First World War, western culture came to be increasingly dominated by the visual. Some commentators were so alarmed by the overwhelming visuality of modern life that they feared all other forms of experience and communication were on the brink of obsolescence. In a provocative 1914 essay called 'Pictures and Words', the poet Charles Leonard Moore wrote:

> In books and magazines the illustrations seem to be getting the upper hand of what is illustrated. Newspapers are becoming a mass of photographs from life with merely a trickle of commenting text. People seem to go through business and games, to perform heroic deeds, to get married or hanged, not for any interest in these things themselves, but simply as an excuse for posing before a camera. And then there are the Moving Pictures![3]

Moore was American, but he was expressing a view that was very much shared on the other side of the Atlantic. At the outbreak of war many British critics were similarly concerned that the public's obsession with novel forms of visual culture would not only eclipse the written word; it also posed a serious threat to their mental capacities.

If such fears now seem to have been overstated, the British people were in 1914 nonetheless surrounded by a disorientating constellation of images, visual experiences and reproductive technologies.[4] Among the most established of these forms was photography. Invented in the 1830s, it had experienced a dramatic change in its status by the turn of the century and had in fact advanced so much that many believed it to be as distinguished an art form as painting and sculpture.[5] If photography was beginning to appeal to an aesthetic elite, it was simultaneously permeating the lives of the populace. In the late nineteenth century a series of technical breakthroughs (which included the rise of the simple portable camera, the gelatin film roll and the commercial processing of prints) meant that a large portion of the public could now afford to make their own photographs.[6] By 1914 there were 350 photographic clubs and societies in the country and somewhere between 10,000 and 20,000 affiliated amateur photographers.[7]

If photography was arguably the most famous medium through which images reached the public in this period, it was not necessarily the most influential. In the 1880s and 1890s the printing industry began to make use of a new reprographic technique. The 'halftone process' simulated continuous tone imagery with a series of black dots arranged at various densities against a white background, and thus enabled printers to reproduce photographs and paintings accurately, inexpensively and simultaneously with text.[8] The halftone process facilitated the mass reproduction of artworks, on posters, cheap prints and postcards, as well as in books and journals. By 1914 journals had even started to reproduce paintings in full colour.[9] These developments had huge cultural consequences, but also inspired considerable debate. Supportive commentators believed that photomechanical reproduction was popularizing fine art and educating the masses, while detractors claimed that it had given rise to a flood of vulgar images – and the vulgar use of images – and had ended up debasing the arts precisely as it made them more widely available.[10]

The halftone process had an even more decisive impact on the press. The technology made it easier and cheaper for newspapers to reproduce images on their pages. It also inspired the expansion of the pictorial press. Illustrated periodicals had of course been a feature of British cultural life for many decades. *Punch* had been thriving since its foundation in 1841; the *Illustrated London News* had been similarly successful since 1842; and *The Graphic* had acquired a large circulation following its creation in 1869.[11] Their reliance, however, on slow and expensive line engravings meant that the quantity and variety of their visual output had been limited. The halftone process removed those limitations, and spawned a new generation of affordable pictorial publications that filled their many pages with vivid reproductions of photographs and paintings. These included *The Sphere*, which was founded in 1900; the *Daily Mirror*, which became an illustrated tabloid in 1904; and the *Daily Sketch*, whose first issue was published in 1909. By 1914 these journals and many others had created in the British public a voracious appetite for topical images that needed to be satisfied on a monthly, weekly or even daily basis.

That appetite was also being satisfied by a medium that was almost exactly the same age as the halftone process: the cinema. In 1914 the cinema was barely two decades old, and was far from universally respected: critics condemned it as cheap and vulgar entertainment for the poor and uneducated, and one that was unlikely to have anything more than temporary appeal. The facts, however, suggested otherwise. With a pricing policy that undercut other forms of popular entertainment (including the theatre and even the music hall), the cinema quickly reached vast audiences. In 1914 there were more than 4,000 cinemas in Britain, and weekly attendances stood at between 7 and 8 million.[12] By the outbreak of war it was without doubt the country's leading form of popular entertainment. In fact, it has been estimated that the public was spending more money on film tickets than on all other forms of commercial entertainment put together.[13]

These figures are further proof that, when the war finally arrived, it met a society whose cultural taste was overwhelmingly visual.

If in August 1914 Britain already possessed an established landscape of visual culture, the outbreak of war nonetheless transformed it. The public's desire to 'see' the conflict had many cultural consequences, the most quantifiable of which were manifested in the press. Virtually every pictorial newspaper in the country saw its sales figures increase through August and September 1914. The appetite for new images from the front was so great that after little more than six months of war, a new generation of illustrated journals like the *Sunday Pictorial* and the *Sunday Herald* (both established in March 1915) came into existence.[14] They both proved to be runaway successes. The first issue of the *Sunday Pictorial* – whose header boasted of 'pages and pages of pictures' – was purchased by more than a million people. Within a year the *Sunday Herald* was also reaching a million readers, while the *Sunday Pictorial* had attained a staggering circulation of almost 2.5 million. Industry commentators confessed that 'the history of journalism reveals no other instance of new papers so quickly stepping into such huge circulations', concluding that both journals 'fit the needs of the moment exactly'.[15] The 'needs of the moment' were clear: to 'see' the war in every way possible.

The nationwide obsession with seeing the front line informed every visual medium. Temporary exhibitions vied with each other to provide the most attention-grabbing visions of war, although surely the most spectacular was the Active Service Exhibition.[16] Organized by the *Daily Mail* for the British Red Cross and opened at the Prince's Skating Club in Knightsbridge in March 1916, the show featured its very own 'miniature battlefield'.[17] This included full-sized trenches (built to an official design by a company of the Grenadier Guards), replete with excavated dug-outs, listening posts, observation stations, firing platforms and barbed-wire entanglements that could be toured by curious visitors. 'To the visitor who explores them', wrote *The Times*, 'things of which he has had perhaps a vague notion, become realities. He understands some of the least of the discomforts which have to be borne by men at the front.'[18] The exhibition proved so popular with the public that the organizers postponed its April closing date and kept it open throughout the summer months.[19]

The phenomenon influenced the fine arts, too. The more enterprising dealers and publishers exploited the public's curiosity through the 'production and sale of subjects which have a patriotic or naval or military interest'.[20] Soon after the outbreak of war they marginalized their normal output in favour of portraits of generals and admirals, battle pictures, patriotic and religious allegories, depictions of ruined Belgian cities, illustrated war maps and other topical postcards, prints and mounted photographs. These items were frequently

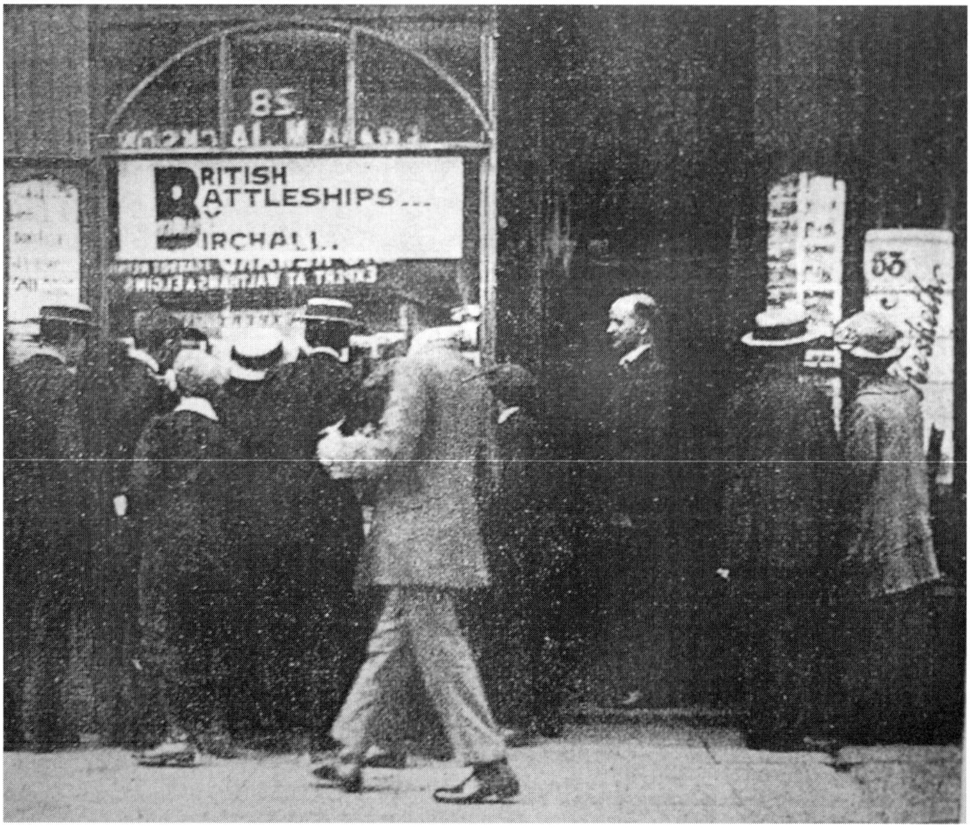

Figure 4.1 'Crowds around a War-Window at R. Jackson & Sons' Moorfield Branch, Liverpool', reproduced in *Fine Art Trade Journal* (September 1914).

exhibited together in shop windows surrounded by union flags and patriotic phrases, with a percentage of their price often being donated to war charities. The 'war-window', as it became known, proved to be an extremely successful commercial device (Figure 4.1).[21] Trade journals wrote that the firms employing it had seen 'large crowds gather round their windows', and according to at least one source, a 'substantial percentage' of those crowds were 'induced to enter and make purchases'.[22]

If the demand for war pictures had created invaluable new audiences in the art market, it had created vast new audiences in the cinema. Indeed, the conflict has not unjustifiably been called the 'seminal event' in the development of the medium.[23] In the first three years of the war, British cinema audiences trebled. By 1917 the nation's 4,500 cinemas sold more than 1 billion tickets, which worked out as 20 million weekly attendances – or every single person in the country attending the cinema at least once a fortnight. In fact, the cinema became such a huge phenomenon in the war years that a government commission was formed solely in order to examine it. Officials came to realize that one of the principal reasons for the medium's 'universal' wartime appeal lay in its ability to visualize the front line for civilians in vivid and dynamic ways.[24] It was not long before they exploited the opportunity for themselves. By the end of 1915 the government produced its first full-length propaganda film, *Britain Prepared*, and in the summer of the following year it released *Battle of the Somme*. The latter arguably became the most successful British film of all time: in 1916 approximately 20 million people paid to see it – the majority of the country's population.[25]

Official war films like *Battle of the Somme* were proof that by 1916 the government had joined the rest of the country in recognizing the undeniable importance of visual culture. This had not always been the case: at the very beginning of the war the government had formed a propaganda bureau at Wellington House in London. Hoping to direct moderate, fact-based propaganda at literate opinion-formers, it had initially concentrated its activities on the written word.[26] By June 1915 Wellington House had printed and circulated 2.5 million books, official publications, pamphlets and speeches in as many as seventeen different languages.[27] But it too came to realize that images could reach and appeal to a much broader audience than could text. In August 1915 Arthur Balfour, First Lord of the Admiralty, confessed that visual media like the cinema 'reached the intelligence of the least intelligent: it required no reading: it touched on no controversial topics: it threw no strain upon the spectator's powers of realisation'.[28] The other obvious advantage of visual propaganda was that it worked equally successfully around the world, and could help shape opinions in communities that did not read English.

The need to exploit and control the many images of war became increasingly 'urgent and pressing' as the conflict developed, and in the spring of 1916 a separate pictorial propaganda section was formed at Wellington House under the direction of Ivor Nicholson.[29] Nicholson's unit managed the production and dissemination of photographs, which he distributed in their thousands both directly to the press and through a number of his own official pictorial publications. One of them was the *War Pictorial*. Printed on the same premises that also produced the *Illustrated London News*, the *War Pictorial* was filled with similarly lavish photogravure images. The journal appeared monthly from 1916. Within a year, it was selling 750,000 copies a month and was being published in eleven different languages.[30] Wellington House, however, did not just distribute its photographs to the pictorial press; it also printed them on to 'lantern slides … cigarette stiffeners, picture postcards, posters, shop-window exhibitions, and in a greatly enlarged form, for exhibition in big cities', and it was sending many of these images around the world.[31]

The principal problem with photographs was one of supply. The Official Press Bureau (which had been formed in August 1914 to gather and censor information before issuing it to the press – as well as to Wellington House) released only a small and inconsistent range of images, which Nicholson considered 'wholly inadequate for presenting some kind of pictorial commentary on the whole war'.[32] The need for more visual material was what helped persuade Wellington House to start employing artists. The various official war artists' schemes are now well known, and have been documented at length elsewhere.[33] They began with the appointment of the draughtsman Muirhead Bone in June 1916. Bone was paid £500 a year to tour the lines (in a chauffeur-driven motorcar) and make drawings of what he saw. More than 200 of his drawings were published later that year in a ten-part book called *The Western Front*, which had a large edition of 30,000 copies. In the introduction, Field Marshal Haig himself emphasized the singular importance of the image:

> It has been said that the portrait and the picture are invaluable aids to the right reading of history. From this point of view I welcome, on behalf of the Army that I have the honour to command, this series of drawings, as a permanent record in pencil of the duties which our soldiers have been called upon to perform, and the quality and manner of its performance.[34]

Over the course of the following year, Wellington House commissioned four more artists (C. R. W. Nevinson, John Lavery, Paul Nash and Eric Kennington) to follow Bone's lead and travel to the battlefields.[35] The work that resulted from those visits was published in 1918 in a four-part edition called *British Artists at the Front*. Their pictures offered the public vivid and colourful insights into the conflict: Nevinson painted bursting shells, secret glimpses into Brigade Headquarters and furtive views from trenches; Lavery painted factories, scenes aboard British battleships and the searchlights of coastal defence units; Nash drew the empty battlefields of Flanders in the aftermath of hostilities; and Kennington focused on everyday life at the front line, such as soldiers enjoying tea between shifts and patients convalescing in hospital wards. All artists, however, sought to satisfy civilians' voracious desire to see aspects of the conflict that were inaccessible, and in many cases unimaginable, to them. This intention was clear from the outset. The very first image of the series was Nevinson's *Banking at 4000 Feet* (Figure 4.2), which captured the artist's point of view in the passenger seat of a fighter plane, his hand grasping the side of the cockpit in panic.[36]

Other schemes followed. In total, government agencies employed, commissioned or bought work from more than 150 artists, and amassed a collection of around 3,000 paintings, drawings and sculptures. These images were not only printed in books; they were distributed to the press, released as portfolios

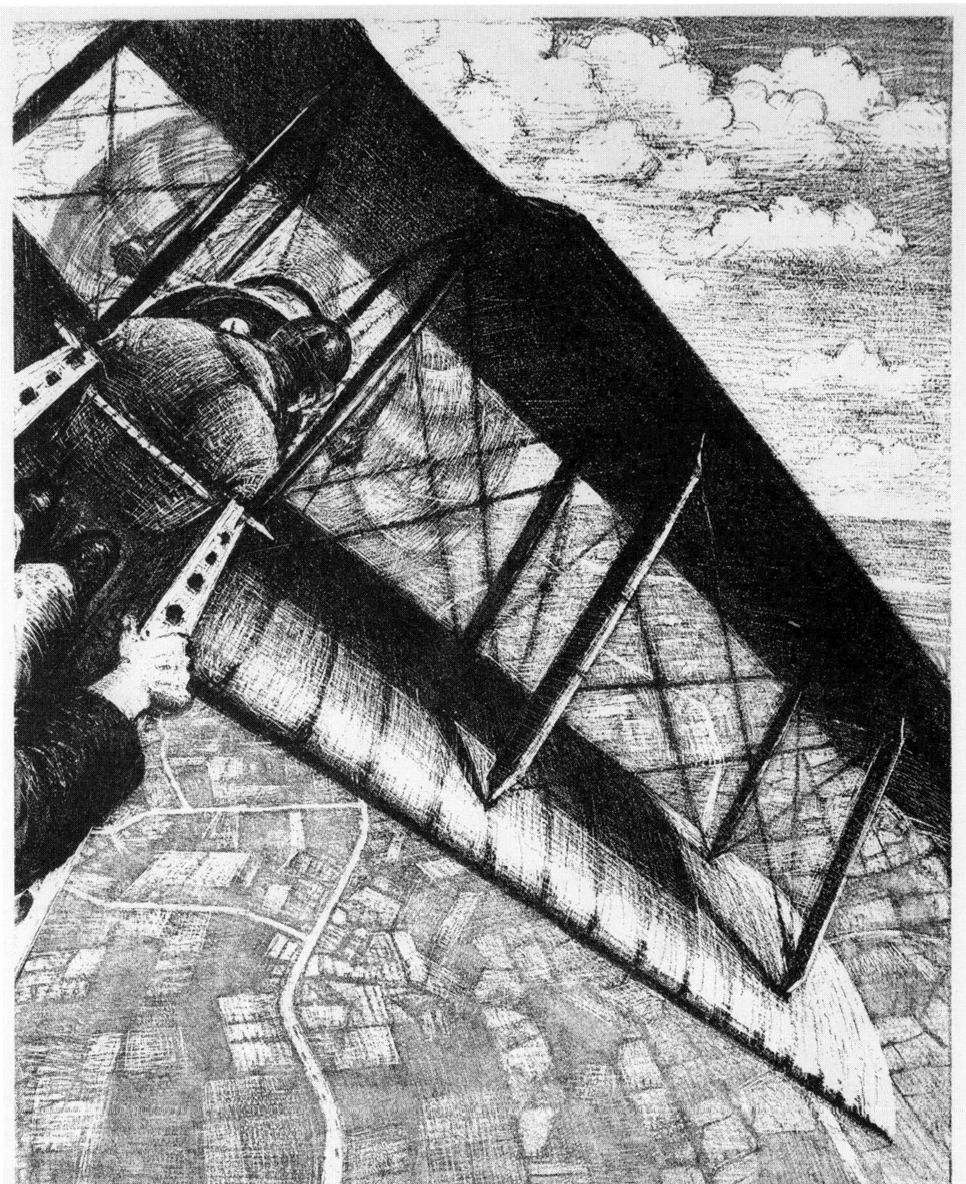

Figure 4.2 C. R. W. Nevinson, *Banking at 4000 Feet*, from *Britain's Efforts and Ideals*, 1917. Lithograph on paper, 40.3 × 31.6 cm. Tate Gallery.

of lithographs, printed as separate plates, postcards and posters for individual distribution and purchase, and exhibited in art galleries around the country. Towards the end of the war and in its aftermath they were displayed in major cultural institutions like the Royal Academy. It was arguably the greatest act of state patronage in modern British history to date, and its significance is hard to overestimate: the official war artists' schemes gave artists the opportunity to paint subjects that were of pressing national importance; they provided an infrastructure that allowed those pictures to be disseminated through many different media platforms; and they encouraged them to produce work that would appeal to an unprecedentedly large and receptive audience.

This first section has briefly described how the nation's response to the war had significant effects on visual culture in Britain. The insatiable demand for vivid images of the conflict brought opportunities for all of the visual media, and photographers, film-makers, journalists, popular illustrators and fine artists of all types duly responded with their own versions of war pictures. In the process, the distinction between the fine arts and the popular arts was eroded, as both came to share the same subjects, the same ambitions and arguably even the same audience. It would, however, be incorrect to assume that no distinctions were made between these very different kinds of war picture. If anything, the war sharpened awareness of the different capacities of different types of images. And for a public that was desperate to know what war was actually like, one issue inflected all such distinctions: the issue of truthfulness. In the next section I will examine war pictures in light of their putative veracity, because these debates had further implications for contemporary perceptions of art.

'War as it is'

Western culture has long been ocularcentric. For centuries, if not millennia, philosophers, scientists and the general public have had faith in the connection between observation and knowledge, between vision and truth.[37] This enduring conviction was one of the principal reasons why the public was so drawn to war pictures from 1914. Ever convinced that 'seeing was believing', they naturally concluded that images possessed an authenticity that was unobtainable through the written word. This sentiment was expressed repeatedly throughout the war. In 1916 one speaker began a lecture on the conflict with the following confession: 'Language utterly fails to describe the glorious feats and magnificent heroisms of the great War, and I find words entirely inadequate to convey more than a faint impression of the greatness and glory of the deeds performed by thousands of men.'[38] He then put up ninety photographic lantern slides of the front to succeed where his words had failed. His choice of medium was no accident: during the war years the majority of people were convinced that photography was the most authentic form of representation. As one writer declared in 1916, its 'superiority over all other forms of graphic record' was all but 'incontestable'.[39]

The faith in photography was grounded primarily in what has become known as 'indexicality'. This idea owed its origins to the philosopher and mathematician Charles Sanders Peirce – who died, coincidentally, in 1914. In his influential theory of semiotics, Peirce made a distinction between three kinds of sign by virtue of their different relations to their objects: some signs – 'icons' – simply looked like their objects (such as a traditional portrait painting); other signs – 'symbols' – were related to their objects by conventions (in the way that a cross symbolizes Christianity); but another group of signs – which Peirce called 'indices' – were connected to their objects 'as a matter of fact'. The index, unlike all other signs, depended on a real causal connection to its referent: storm clouds were an index of impending rain; a weathervane's position was an index of wind direction; and crying was an index of human displeasure.[40] For many people, the photograph could also be called an index. From its beginnings, photography was believed to possess a direct, causal connection to its subjects: the camera, after all, could only record what was actually in front of it. This indexicality became the basis of many theories about the truthfulness of photography. Roland Barthes wrote that the photograph was so indivisibly bound to its subjects that it became nothing less than a 'certificate of presence'.[41] André Bazin was so convinced by photographic realism that he refused even to distinguish between the photograph and its subject matter: 'the photographic image', he concluded, 'is the object itself'.[42]

In recent years, the digital production and manipulation of images has undermined such theorists' confidence in the reliability of photographs.[43] During the war, however, people had no such doubts. Most had little reason to doubt that the 'properly adjusted camera' was anything less than 'completely truthful'.[44] Indeed, when the official film *Battle of the Somme* was released in 1916, almost every critic on record singled out its veracity for praise. The *Manchester Guardian* delighted at witnessing 'the real thing at last'; the *Daily Express* lauded its 'sheer realism'; and the *Daily Mirror* described it as a completely 'true picture'.[45] One journalist who had visited the front even made the staggering confession that the film seemed more real than the war itself.[46] Most importantly, all would have agreed with a critic in *The Times* who claimed that such an accurate vision of the conflict was obtainable 'by no other means'.[47] The irony, of course, is that several scenes in *Battle of the Somme* – including a famous sequence in which a group of soldiers goes over the top under heavy fire – were faked.[48]

If the reliability of photographs and films is now in doubt, it had significant implications for traditional modes of representation at the time. War paintings and illustrations were continually compared to war photographs and films.[49] At first, they were not flattered by the comparison. As 'iconic' rather than 'indexical' images, they could not guarantee the veracity of the events they depicted.

Moreover, the fact that they were hand-made meant that they lacked the dependable objectivity that came with mechanically produced photographs. For these reasons, the latter were believed to be of greater value than the former – the photograph 'worth much more than a sketch by a draughtsman who is trying to produce a pretty picture'.[50] The war, it seemed, was creating the conditions for yet another criticism of art. However, as the art world had combated its other recriminations, so painters, illustrators, their patrons and publishers attempted to neutralize this one. They set out to prove that they could also be legitimate and reliable chroniclers of war. In the process, they proved that traditional forms of art had a crucial role to play in the way the conflict was experienced and understood on the home front.

Artists' principal strategy was to ape the indexical authority of photographic images. This was particularly apparent in the pictorial press, where the pictures commissioned and the manner in which they were displayed indicate an ongoing debt to photography. The *War Pictorial* is one such example. A government-published periodical that hoped to convert a global audience to the Allied cause, it was understandably reluctant to use any image that appeared less than credible. For this reason, when a dearth of appropriate photographs left it with no choice but to enlist illustrations, it deliberately obscured their graphic nature. In a representative image of soldiers going 'over the top' (Figure 4.3), the artist emulated various photographic characteristics: an awkward low viewpoint; abrupt cropping; 'dirty' framing, replete with foreground clutter; a suppression of all stylistic gesturalism; an imitation of focal length differentials; and, of course, the absence of a signature. It is impossible to know exactly how artist and publisher agreed on this aesthetic, but one thing is certain: the *War Pictorial* was forcing 'iconic' images to function in 'indexical' ways.

The strategy was reinforced by captions that encouraged readers to look at paintings as if they were photographs. Kendall Walton has written that photographs encourage, and even require, a special kind of looking. Unlike paintings and drawings, photographs are somehow 'transparent'; we look *through* them, not *at* them.[51] As the war progressed, all kinds of paintings were packaged in order to facilitate this kind of photographic looking. In Wellington House's *British Artists at the Front* series, C. E. Montague's catalogue entries discussed the pictures not as representations of objects but as the very objects they represented. His description of C. R. W. Nevinson's *Inside Brigade Headquarters* is a representative example:

> A typical advanced headquarters in a well-built dug-out. Except in cases of special good fortune, work must be done by candle-light, the air is not

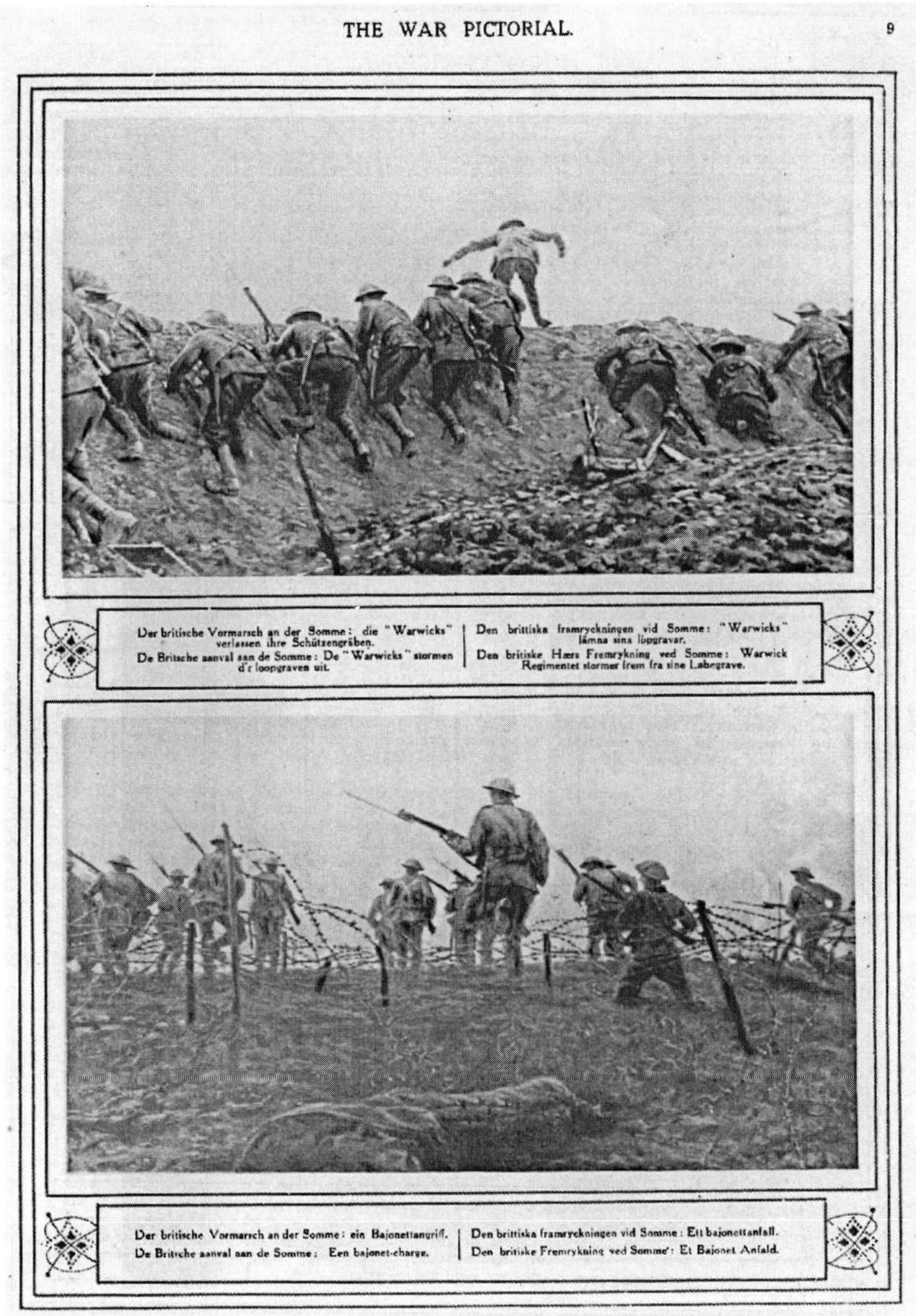

THE WAR PICTORIAL. 9

Der britische Vormarsch an der Somme: die "Warwicks" verlassen ihre Schützengräben.
De Britsche aanval aan de Somme: De "Warwicks" stormen d'r loopgraven uit.

Den brittiska framryckningen vid Somme: "Warwicks" lämna sina löpgravar.
Den britiske Hærs Fremrykning ved Somme: Warwick Regimentet stormer frem fra sine Løbegrave.

Der britische Vormarsch an der Somme: ein Bajonettangriff.
De Britsche aanval aan de Somme: Een bajonet-charge.

Den brittiska framryckningen vid Somme: Ett bajonettanfall.
Den britiske Fremrykning ved Somme: Et Bajonet Anfald.

Figure 4.3 'Over the Top', *War Pictorial* (September 1916).

exhilarating, and you must be careful not to bump your head against the ceiling. A deep dug-out of this kind gives almost perfect shelter, though the sound of any shell bursting near it is curiously loud.[52]

Montague's writing studiously avoided any discussion of the artwork *as* an artwork, focusing exclusively on the nature of its subject matter. In doing so, Nevinson's painting became, like a photograph, a transparent window on to the western front.

Less official sources like *The Graphic*, the *Illustrated War News*, the *War Illustrated* and *The Sphere* also emphasized the indexical quality of their illustrations – although often in different ways. From the beginning of the war they advertised for 'witness images'. *The Graphic* wrote that it would 'pay liberally for any Sketches or Photographs sent either by officers or men at the front ... dealing with striking episodes in the field'.[53] When they did arrive, pictorial journals celebrated them as the products of infallible first-hand authenticity: they were advertised widely and given headlines like 'Real Sketches by Real Soldiers: Reproduced just as they came from the fields of battle in France'; 'Sunday, August 23rd, 1914 – drawn in the trenches'; or 'Facsimile Sketch made during the action by the Commander of one of the British Destroyers'.[54] Even when the illustrations were produced by in-house professionals back in Britain, captions like 'drawn on the spot', 'from direct camera pictures', 'from men who have been there' and 'from notes by an eye-witness' provided confirmation that, like photographs, they were causally connected to the fighting.[55]

Journals continued to publish more finished, professional illustrations, and while they could not reasonably profess that they had been produced under fire at the front, they claimed that these images too were authentic. Of this type, Fortunino Matania's contributions to *The Sphere* were the acme. Contrived and bombastic though these illustrations were, the journal nonetheless 'guaranteed' them as 'a perfectly truthful and accurate presentation' of the war.[56] An account of Matania's working methods suggests that they were doubtless produced with that intention. He visited wounded troops who had witnessed skirmishes, taking with him a map of the battlefield and a box of toy soldiers: 'Bit by bit, with the skill of a cross-examining counsel', Matania extracted information about the event from his subjects:

First of all, the disposition of the troops is settled, by consultation with the wounded Tommy and the manoeuvring of the toy soldiers. Then one comes to questions of detail ... 'How many pillars? Was there one on either side of the door? Any smaller pillars inside the door? What was the rough shape of the opening? Was the door studded with big nails or iron hinges? Did you notice what the handles were like?'[57]

Matania also visited battlefields himself, built a reconstruction trench in his garden at Potters Bar and was even supplied with military equipment by the War Office to ensure that every technical detail was absolutely correct.[58] His resulting illustrations may have possessed neither the directness of photographs nor the emotional authenticity of official war artists' work, but they could certainly claim to possess some kind of basis in fact. Soldiers at least thought so. They were so awed by the 'amazing realism' of his images that he invariably received 'congratulatory letters' from those who 'were present' at the events and were 'absolutely convinced' that he must have been so too.[59]

One of the most common ways to legitimize artists' war pictures was to stress the importance of authorship as a guarantor of veracity, a claim generally denied to photography. The first issue of the *Illustrated War News* in August 1914 proudly announced that its 'special' artists (Frederic Villiers, Sydney Adamson, H. C. Seppings Wright, Julius Price and George Lynch) were 'AT THE FRONT'. It proceeded to establish their pedigrees with portraits and brief biographies that framed them as intrepid British adventurers risking their lives in the 'battle for truth'.[60] Their reports persistently stressed their own perceptual and moral superiority to the impassive transcription of the photographic device: comments would often be appended to sketches that read: 'I saw the devil's work with my own eyes. It was far beyond the reach of a camera.'[61] The resulting representation's truth-content was therefore not vested in the image itself but in the attestation of its creator. It was an important idea. Here the artist was no longer the fallible intermediary; he was the uniquely dependable eyewitness.

The most explicit example of the 'special' artist's function is seen in the representation of the correspondent Frederic Villiers. Villiers consciously cultivated his image as the public's own heroic pair of eyes. His pictorial reports were typically accompanied by a swashbuckling provenance: how their creator had adopted disguises to evade the authorities; furtively gained access to secret locations; and smuggled his evidence back to the home front in defiance of the censor.[62] His portraits were saturated with the iconography of 'the seer': in most he brandishes binoculars like a saintly attribute. In one depiction of a bombardment on the western front Villiers even included himself in the bottom-right corner, observing the action through a periscope (Figure 4.4). In doing so, the image performed a reciprocal authentication. It authenticated Villiers by rendering him present at the front, a reliable proxy for the nation. In turn, that identity authenticated the scene behind, his presence offering a personal guarantee that it had actually taken place. The two, in short, acted as alibis for each other, and the representation was transformed into something approaching a testimony.

The critical framework that surrounded the special correspondent also informed Wellington House's employment and deployment of official artists from

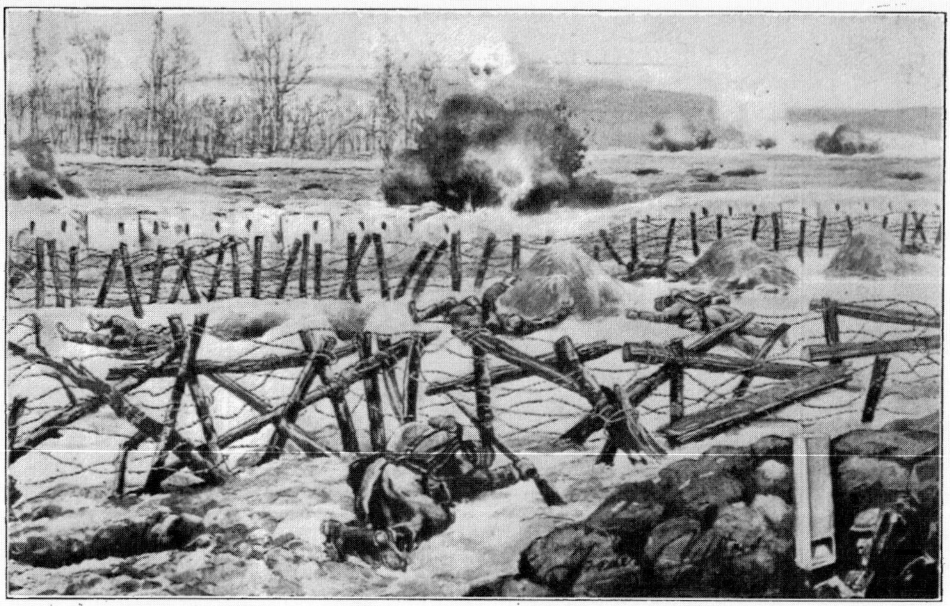

VIEW OF TRENCHES ON WESTERN FRONT, 1914. (PERISCOPE IN LOWER RIGHT-HAND CORNER)

Figure 4.4 Frederic Villiers, 'View of Trenches on the Western Front, 1914', reproduced in Frederic Villiers, *His Five Decades of Adventure* (1921).

1916. It is further proof that the differences between official and popular war art were not as great as is often thought. Like the popular press, official publications introduced their artists with portraits and brief biographies that established their credentials as reliable witnesses. Unlike the popular press, however, this credibility was constructed through the combination of two seemingly incompatible identities. The first democratized the artist and was derived from his social position as a soldier; the second individualized him and was derived from his social position as an artist.[63] The resulting conflation – the 'soldier-artist' – could therefore claim to speak on behalf of all men but with a perspicacity denied to all but a few of them. The 'soldier-artist' also embodied a crucial independence from his official employers. Discussions of Nevinson for instance repeatedly stressed that he was 'uncorrupted', had 'preserved his integrity as an artist' and had 'jealously' guarded his 'own artistic vision'.[64] It was only the social position of the artist, as Sue Malvern has argued, that could embody this credible independence; 'photography, lacking social and cultural status, was unable to fulfill this function'.[65]

The construction of the artist as a visionary intermediary introduced a further set of claims for the truth-content of art – claims that involved a fundamental redefinition of reality itself. A number of commentators maintained that artists had the capacity to discern and communicate a 'deeper truth' than the superficial empiricism of the lens.[66] In an important 1918 essay on Nevinson, J. E. Crawford Flitch wrote:

> Appearance is not reality. Appearance may be observed, but reality, to be known, must be experienced. That is why the report of the official artist has more value than the report of the official photographer. For the camera observes everything and experiences nothing. It is inhumanly impartial and cannot speak the language of the spirit. Concerning the things that we most wish to know it is dumb. We ask for the truth, the whole truth, and it gives us nothing but the facts.[67]

In this formulation the artist and the camera were no longer competing to represent the same reality; they were illustrating qualitatively different realities. As one critic remarked: 'One does not see with the eyes alone, but with the brains and nerves too';[68] thus while the camera might have been able to accurately show how the war looked, only the soldier-artist could reliably represent how it felt. The words of servicemen were then enlisted (as they had been by the popular press) to reinforce such claims. In one (suspiciously vernacular) evaluation of Paul Nash's war paintings, 'Lieutenant John Turner' wrote:

> Show these to any fellow who has inhabited a dug-out. Pass them round any Mess in France or Flanders. Ask the man next to you in hospital in Town what he thinks of them ... You will hear 'Good heavens! – he has got home there right enough'. 'Oh!!! Absolutely it! Sight of it makes you feel queer.'[69]

This infrastructure of commentary was constructing a very different kind of indexicality: one that turned not the image, but the person and the experience that made the image into the true index of the conflict – one that helped produce what Samuel Hynes has called an 'aesthetic of direct experience'.[70]

The 'aesthetic of direct experience' was not available to all artists. The notable feature of this trend is that young and, crucially, progressive soldier-artists were increasingly believed to have secured the monopoly on truth. Indeed, as the conflict unfolded even conservative commentators began to reach this conclusion. If any one event was responsible for convincing them of this, it was Nevinson's one-man show of Cubo-Futurist war pictures at the Leicester Galleries in the autumn of 1916. That seminal exhibition featured some of Nevinson's most enduringly famous war pictures, including *La Patrie* and *Troops Resting*. It attracted a distinguished group of visitors (including Ramsay MacDonald, Arthur Balfour and Winston Churchill) and in its catalogue General Sir Iain Hamilton, one of the most senior figures in the British army, praised the pictures for their 'quality of truth'.[71] In response to the show, hitherto reactionary critics came to agree with him. Clutton-Brock in *The Times* declared that Nevinson's Cubism was 'justified' because its mechanomorphic qualities captured the alienating effects of mechanized warfare.[72] And the *Westminster Gazette* wrote:

> Modern artistic tendencies are extraordinarily well adapted to the pictorial representation of war. Had there been Nevinsons in the world at the time of the Napoleonic wars we should possess fewer pictures of a romantic Emperor on a white charger, or of Grenadiers sleeping picturesquely on the snow; but we should have known a good deal more of what war is like.[73]

Officials, critics and the wider public continued to celebrate the honesty of Nevinson's war pictures for the remainder of the conflict. If the quality of his paintings is widely believed to have deteriorated in the second half of the war, they nonetheless connected progressive methods to the 'aesthetic of direct experience', and forged an unprecedented union between popular opinion, establishment opinion and modern art. In doing so, they contributed to a broader wartime trend. The widespread demand for honest, vivid war pictures was encouraging the British public to look at progressive art with sympathetic eyes, and British commentators to develop a critical framework in which modernist methods could at last be deemed appropriate. This was the beginning of an extremely important wartime process – one that involved modernism being gradually incorporated into mainstream British life – a process that, as Chapter 6 will show, reached its culmination after the end of the war.

Veracity remains central to the evaluation of war pictures. Historians of British art still tend to judge the visual output of the war against its apparent truth-content. Moreover, they continue to claim that the more progressive pictures are generally the most honest. In recent decades, modernist war paintings have been commended for being 'truth-telling' and for articulating a 'rebarbative reality' of combat, while their more traditional counterparts have been condemned as 'risible' and 'reprehensible'.[74] This model is rightfully beginning to be challenged. Veracity may have been – and continues to be – a decisive marker by which artists, publishers, propagandists, critics and subsequently historians have claimed validity for war pictures, but it is a misleading category in the evaluation of war art. The final section of this chapter will argue that war pictures not only regularly deviated from the visible truth; their singular power derived precisely from their ability to do so. And it was by doing so that they were able to secure an invaluable role for themselves in wartime society.

War as it isn't

The First World War posed many challenges to those who sought to represent it. The conflict was fought over vast, diffuse battlefields, often under the cover of darkness; outbursts of combat were unpredictable and infrequent; and the

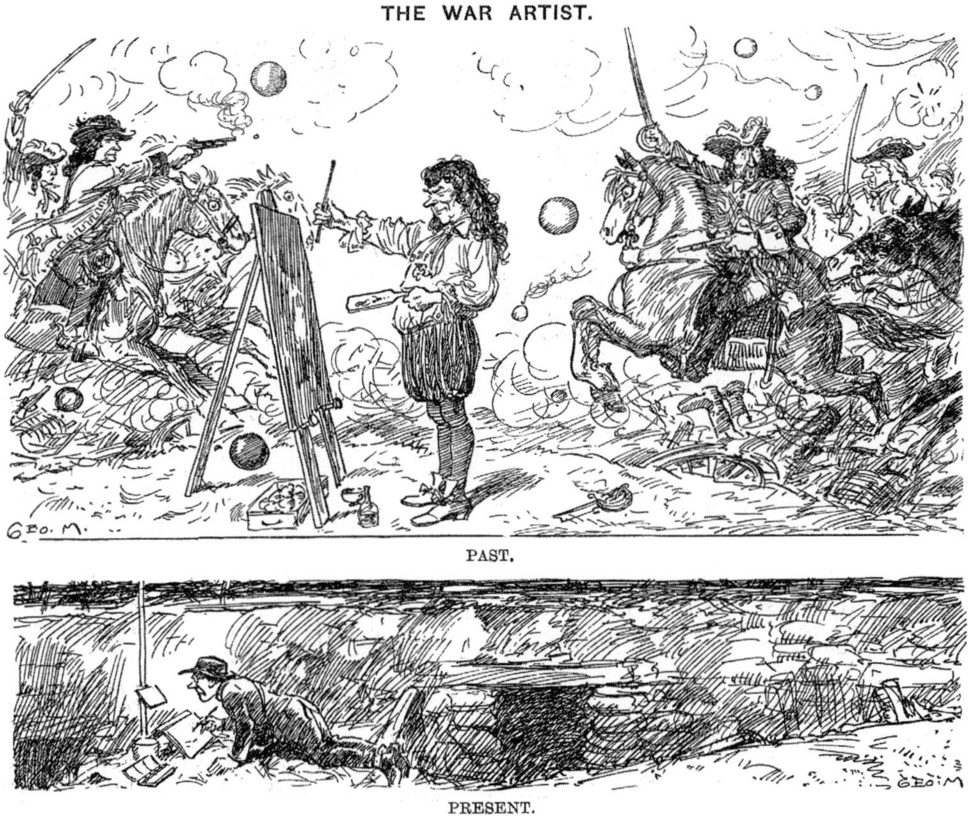

Figure 4.5 George Morrow, 'The War Artist', *Punch* (15 November 1916).

front line was so dangerous and so heavily policed that it was difficult for artists and photographers to gain access to it.[75] Faced by these obstacles, many of them remarked that the conflict seemed all but invisible (Figure 4.5).[76] And if one could not see it, how could one accurately represent it? The resulting 'crisis of representation' affected all of the arts, but photography suffered more than any other medium.[77] Ever dependent on their referents, photographers could only photograph what they were permitted – and able – to see. For this reason the majority of wartime photographs did not show battle itself, but the more accessible (and safer) moments before and after it. Photographers were widely criticized for their largely uneventful output, and many attempted to enrich their images by staging scenes or combining negatives.[78] These efforts, however, met with even greater criticism. They were widely dismissed as 'fakes', and risked undermining the foundation of reliability on which photography had built its wartime reputation.[79]

Artists were under no such constraints. They were free to manipulate, enhance, combine or even invent their sources at will. And yet unlike photographers, their paintings could not reasonably be denounced as fakes. A number of theorists have argued that because paintings do not presuppose an indexical connection to their objects, they can never be seen to betray them. 'A fake painting', Susan Sontag writes, only 'falsifies the history of art', while a fake photograph 'falsifies reality'.[80] When it came to making war pictures, then, artists could take much greater liberties than their photographic counterparts. By exploiting that liberty, they were able to produce war pictures that did more than simply tell the truth: they could make incomprehensible events seem comprehensible; mundane battles seem dramatic; and empty moments appear pregnant with political and poetical meanings. In doing so, they achieved what few photographs could achieve: they reshaped the conflict for civilian consumption.

The more astute contemporaries were aware that artists were not simply filling in the gaps that photographers had left behind (although this was a major reason for their initial employment); they were producing different kinds of representations that performed very different functions. This distinction was even tacitly admitted by journals that otherwise attempted to conflate both forms of imagery: when an advertisement for *The Graphic* read 'Mapped by Morrell – Illustrated by the Camera – Pictured by Artists', its use of the verb 'to picture' suggested that art did not merely 'illustrate' the war like the photograph, but could pictorially reconstruct it.[81] This more conceptual form of image-making was largely unattainable for the photographer. Susan Sontag has written that while photographs are adept at showing us how an object or event looks, they cannot explain how it works. 'Strictly speaking, one never understands anything from a photograph', she writes; 'understanding is based on how [something] functions. And functioning takes place in time, and must be explained in time. Only that which narrates can make us understand.'[82]

The need for understanding was particularly pressing at the start of the war, when a largely ignorant public needed to be educated about the violence occurring in Belgium and the ever-changing positions of the various forces. Artists dutifully made pictures that organized, narrated and clarified the events they depicted. One of the most effective was Philip Dadd's depiction of the German bombardment of Belgian forts Boncelles and Barchon on 5 and 6 August 1914 (Plate 1). This remarkable picture – which was printed in colour so as to capture an 'absolutely lurid – blood-red' sky – was informed by multiple testimonies and then arranged into a legible and chronological account of events. Dadd depicted the bombardment from a fictional high viewpoint above the town of Liège, from which both forts could easily be seen, despite their being many miles apart and in different directions. The picture's expository potential was further assisted by a group of figures in the foreground, one of whom gestures instructively to the narrative unfolding beyond. The gesture made it clear that

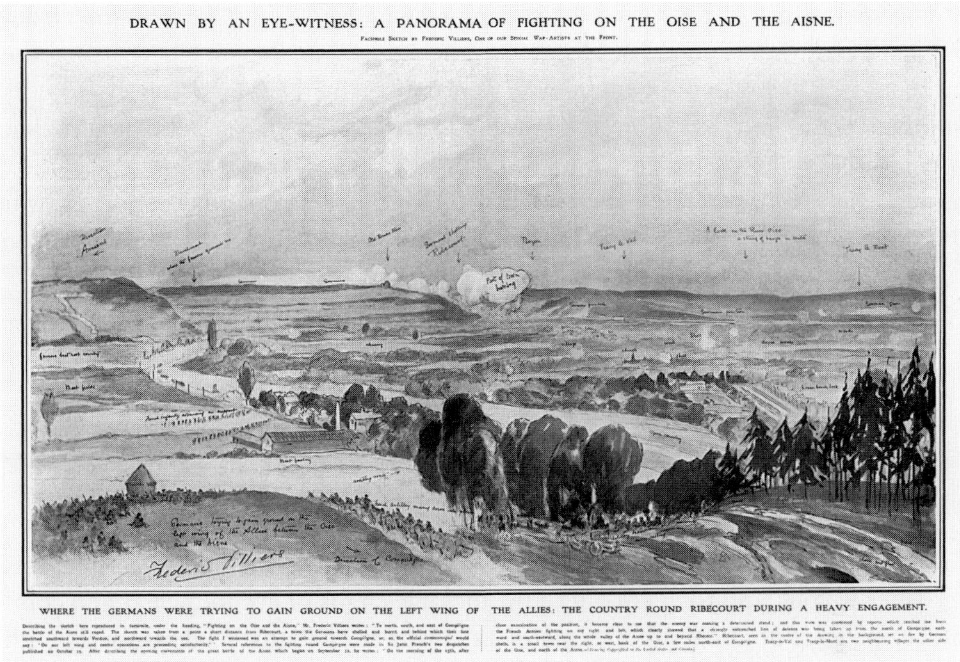

Figure 4.6 Frederic Villiers, 'Panorama', *Illustrated London News* (3 October 1914).

Dadd was not just showing his viewers the bombardment; he was *explaining* it to them.[83]

If the pedagogical nature of war pictures was latent in Dadd's image, it was explicit in others like it. In October 1914 the *Illustrated London News* published Frederic Villiers's four-page pull-out panorama of the Battle of the Aisne, which Villiers had apparently smuggled back from the front in his boots (Figure 4.6). Villiers adopted a similar high viewpoint to Dadd, providing the same omniscient perspective on events. He also, however, included arrows and inscriptions like 'the British are in this direction', 'German and French constantly firing here' and 'German Infantry Entrenched in Woods' in order to explain the positions, movements and tactics of the various forces.[84] Villiers's picture was well received. Indeed, annotated pictures proved so popular with the British public that pictorial journals employed whole teams simply to create them. These multimedia images combined text, illustrations and photographs to explain how Zeppelins, grenades and trenches functioned; how uniforms differed between nations and regiments; and how strategies unfolded on the battlefields. In each of them, however, the artist's image functioned very differently from the photographer's: the former organized, contextualized, interpreted and explicated the whole, while the latter simply illustrated details within that whole.[85]

The expository capacity of artistic representation differs profoundly from Samuel Hynes's 'aesthetic of direct experience'. Here the image was not the intimate visualization of personal experience; its value derived precisely from its ability to transcend that subjectivity and construct a larger, synthetic picture that was indiscernible to any one individual. In this regard, the graphic war picture more closely approximated the traditional print correspondent's report than it did the photograph. As the famous war reporter Philip Gibbs wrote:

> The private soldier and the battalion officer saw the particular spot which he had to defend, knew in his body and soul the intimate detail of his trench, his dugout, the patch of No-Man's Land beyond his parapet, the stink and filth of his own neighbourhood with death, the agony of his wounded pals. But we saw the war in a broader vision, on all parts of the front, in its tremendous mass effects, as well as in particular places of abomination.[86]

Like the traditional correspondent, artists too had the ability to capture this 'broader vision', and to make out of the illegible chaos of events a clear and comprehensible set of images that explained the war to civilians.[87] It was surely with this in mind that when writing about war art in 1919, the critic P. G. Konody paraphrased John Ruskin thus: 'The book of a nation's deeds would be meaningless, or at least indecipherable, without the book of art which supplies the key.'[88]

If it seems that artists deviated from the literal truth only in order to produce a different kind of veracity, this would be incorrect; they very often abandoned the facts altogether. Popular illustrators were regularly commissioned to dress up the unglamorous and attritional conflict in an appealing but largely fictitious theatricality. They produced vivid and diverting images of soldiers going over the top at night, cavalry charges, aerial dogfights, Zeppelins plummeting into the ocean and hand-to-hand combat in no man's land – scenes that, though not necessarily unheard of, were hardly representative of front-line realities.[89] All but the most naïve of contemporaries knew that these images did not show the war as it really was, but this in no way reduced their appeal. After all, as one member of the public remarked: 'Of what value is the literal truth … if it cannot stir the feelings?'[90] Indeed, there is some evidence to suggest that even servicemen themselves preferred melodramatic representations of combat to realistic ones. The *New Statesman* wrote: 'Once they have passed through the horrors of [war], they prefer …to think of it in terms of the romantic and the theatrical.'[91]

When it came to theatrical themes, nothing was more popular than the cavalry charge – even though it occurred very rarely on the western front.[92] Fortunino Matania (*The Sphere*), Richard Caton Woodville (*Illustrated War News* and *Illustrated London News*) and C. M. Sheldon (*War Illustrated*) specialized in

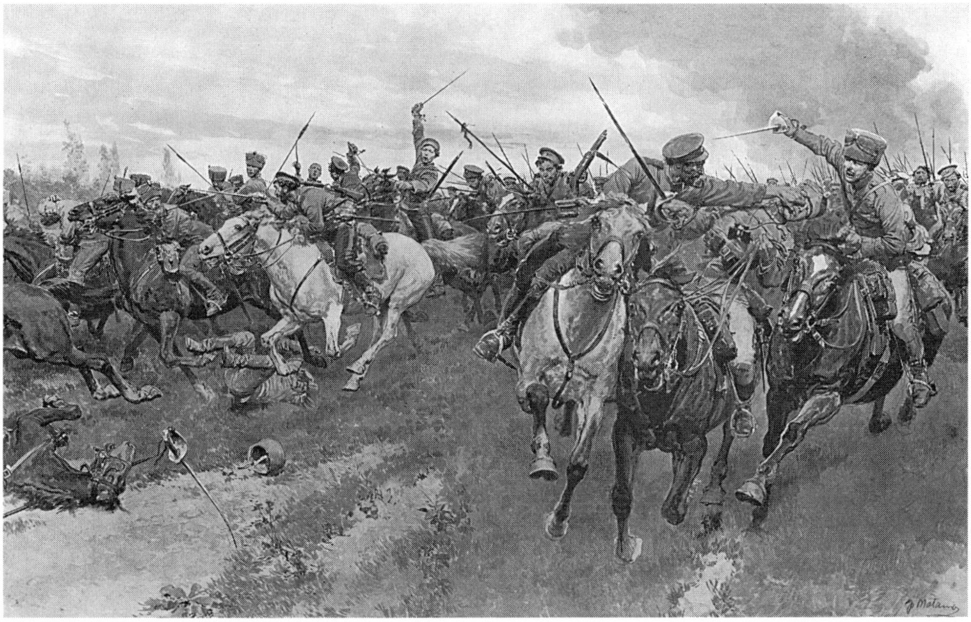

Figure 4.7 Fortunino Matania, 'Cossaks of the Russian Army Charging the German Death's Head Hussars between Korschen and Bartenstein in East Prussia', *The Sphere* (3 October 1914).

stirring compositions that showed British cavalry units, French cuirassiers or Russian Cossacks overwhelm German gunners. They employed a myriad of techniques to dramatize the scenes. Matania punctured the picture plane with action, using violent chiaroscuro, overwrought impasto and hyperbolized poses, gestures and facial expressions. His particular genius lay in the deployment of incidental detail: Matania used every single compositional element – agitated clouds, hats flying through the air, horrified expressions of onlookers and smaller confrontations within the whole (in Figure 4.7 a soldier reaches across to plunge his fingers into his rival's eyes) – to amplify the pictorial tension.

Popular war pictures were not simply there to entertain. They served political ends too, helping to sustain public support for the war as its toll grew ever heavier. Particularly valuable was their emphasis on the human drama at the heart of the conflict. The war is widely believed to have had dehumanizing effects. Those effects are today evidenced by the abundant visual record: war photographs show men homogenized, miniaturized or altogether absent, while modernist war pictures (by artists such as Nevinson) showed them incarcerated within mechanical faceting, transformed into little more than the machines they operate.[93] In contrast, popular illustrators depicted man as the emotional and dramatic nucleus of events – a protagonist who, with courage, strength and not a little bit of patriotism, could have a potentially decisive impact on the outcome of a battle. This had important consequences for the home front: humanistic war pictures gave civilians a focus for their attention, sympathy and admiration, and proved integral to the cultural construction of heroism.

Heroism indeed became an invaluable and profitable commodity during the war years. Numerous books were published to celebrate acts of valour in the field, and popular artists were frequently commissioned to illustrate them. The most ambitious of these volumes was *Deeds that Thrill the Empire*, published by Hutchinson in twenty fortnightly parts from early 1916. The publishers claimed that it was 'the greatest success in the book world since the commencement of the War', with its first part selling a staggering 120,000 copies in just one week. Each part contained extended accounts of Allied heroism in rich and patriotic language, all of which were 'made more vivid to the imagination by a series of magnificent illustrations, from paintings by artists each of whom is a master in his particular field of work'. It was a vast artistic undertaking. In total, the publishers commissioned almost a thousand original illustrations (some of which were coloured) and often gave away large presentation plates that could be framed and displayed by their owners.[94]

The artists behind *Deeds that Thrill the Empire* (who included J. H. Valda, A. Pearse and W. S. Bagdatopulos) depicted officers crossing no man's land to capture enemy flags, pipers rallying soldiers on amid gas attacks, infantrymen attacking machine-gun posts single-handedly and men carrying wounded comrades to safety as shells exploded behind them (Figure 4.8). They can perhaps be seen as the visual equivalents of what Paul Fussell has called 'high diction' in contemporaneous war literature. As high diction used archaic euphemisms ('comrade' instead of 'friend'; 'foe' instead of 'enemy'; 'the fallen' instead of 'the dead') to find glory in an inglorious war, so these artists used illustrations to transform the mundane or unpleasant reality of conflict into an uplifting theatre of heroism.[95] If this was what made them untrue, it was also what gave them their social value. One critic remarked that they provided 'a record dear to all hearts, an incentive to the boys and girls who come after us to keep the Flag flying, and a monument to our heroes which few will wish to be without'.[96]

The function and reception of popular war pictures reveals another capacity that artworks, unlike photographs, possessed: the ability to express an opinion. In a famous if disputed distinction between painting and photography, the philosopher Roger Scruton has argued that the former, unlike the latter, is inherently 'intentional'. Conceived and guided by an artist's mind, a painting represents thoughts and feelings about its subject where a photograph merely captures that subject's appearance.[97] If this is a rather uncharitable view of photography, it is undoubtedly the case that artists were able to exploit their subjectivity (the

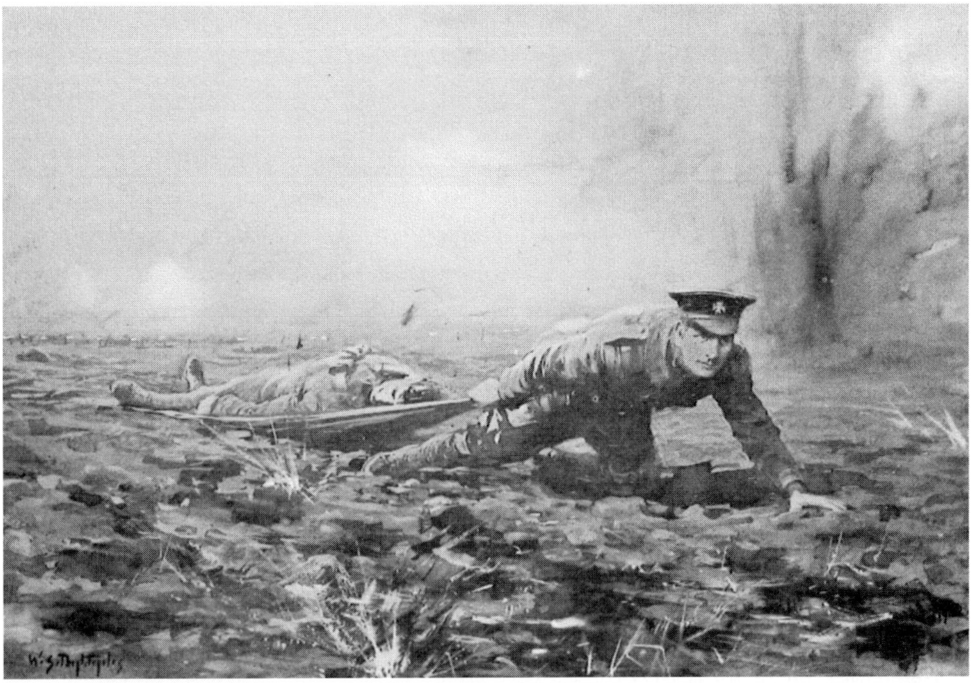

Figure 4.8 W. S. Bagdatopulos, 'Corporal James Upton Dragging a Wounded Comrade to the Trenches', reproduced in *Deeds that Thrill the Empire: True Stories of the Most Glorious Acts of Heroism of the Empire's Soldiers and Sailors during the Great War* (1917).

very subjectivity that was believed to have undermined the authenticity of their output) in extremely effective ways. Throughout the conflict artists employed metaphor and allegory, concentrated narrative and distorted form, and drew on references from the past in order to enhance the expressive power of their work. They thus articulated a viewpoint on the conflict that could be directly or indirectly absorbed by their audience.

These ambitions resulted in some of the most memorable images of the war. One of the most famous was Paul Nash's seminal *We Are Making a New World* (Plate 2). Nash's picture was inspired by his own experience of the front line, having travelled to Ypres as an official war artist at the end of the Battle of Passchendaele in October and November 1917.[98] It was based on a drawing he made one morning at Inverness Copse, where other official artists, photographers and cinematographers were working. At first sight it might not seem so different from its photographic equivalents. Like them, Nash focused on the aftermath of battle rather than the conflict itself. Moreover, his drawing's composition – a simple horizon line dividing mud from sky and punctuated by the staccato forms

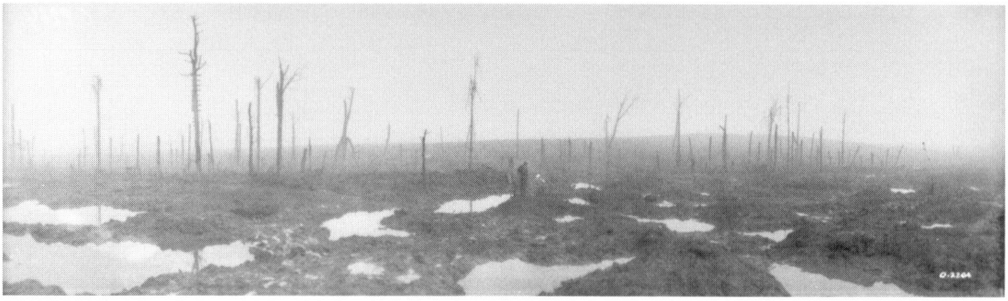

Figure 4.9 William Rider-Rider, *Passchendaele, Now a Field of Mud*, 1917. Photograph, dimensions unknown.

of broken trees – is very similar to photographs of the same site. It is in fact so similar to (the Canadian official war photographer) William Rider-Rider's panoramic photographs of Passchendaele (which were also made in November 1917) that it is hard not to conclude that one was somehow informed by the other, or at least that both were conceived together (Figure 4.9).[99]

When it came to his finished painting, however, Nash was able to manipulate his source material in ways that were unavailable to photographers like Rider-Rider. He compressed the picture space so that his motifs loom ominously and insistently. He played with perspective so that the viewer finds himself or herself looking up to and down on the subject at the same time. He distorted and exaggerated his forms for expressive effect: the ground becomes an ocean of writhing waves; the sky is painted bright red (an allusion, no doubt, to the blood that has been spilled); and the sun's rays extend across the picture surface like Futurist force-lines. Most revealing, though, is his treatment of the trees. Nash had long considered trees to be analogues of human beings, and had given them anthropomorphic qualities in much of his pre-war work. Here they are transformed into metaphors for the men who had suffered and perished around them: on the left, the branches resemble the sagging limbs of the dead; on the right, they form the unmistakable features of a hand imploring the heavens.

Nash's expressive deviation from reality is precisely what makes his picture so powerful, and it would surely have left even the most unobservant viewer in no doubt as to its meaning. *We Are Making a New World* was a jeremiad about violence and a condemnation of the conflict that necessitated it – one that when seen in tandem with its rhetorical title is a denunciation of the optimistic lies for which it was being fought. Hence the passage (from a letter that Nash wrote to his wife at the time) that is so often quoted alongside the picture: 'I am no longer an artist interested and curious, I am a messenger who will bring back word from the men who are fighting to those who want the war to go on for ever. Feeble, inarticulate, will be my message, but it will have a bitter truth, and may it burn their lousy souls.'[100] The irony of this pairing is that though Nash had claimed he was 'no longer an artist', only an artist could have produced an image that was so dense and evocative. And only the intentionality of painting, if we are to believe Roger Scruton, could have so clearly communicated a 'message' from artist to audience.

If there is any one reason for the enduring success of Nash's painting, it is its universality. Like Rider-Rider, Nash was inspired by a very specific place at a very specific time. But unlike Rider-Rider, Nash's image was not indexically bound to its referent: his landscape was thus free to become a landscape of anywhere and any time. By abstracting his forms and coupling them with an allegorical title, he turned his picture into a metaphor, or metonym, for the entire conflict. This has not been lost on scholars since. Sue Malvern described *We Are Making a New World* as a 'transcendent image, uncircumscribed by the historical conditions of its production, that can embody a universal truth, not just about the Great War, but all war, including the possibility of nuclear holocaust'.[101] Malvern is surely correct. Yet that 'universal truth', the 'bitter truth' to which Nash had so powerfully referred, was only made possible by his creative deviation from literal reality. It is here that it is perhaps instructive to recall Pablo Picasso's famous maxim: 'We all know that Art is not truth. Art is a lie that makes us realize the truth.'[102]

* * *

This chapter has shown how the First World War created a unique set of cultural opportunities in Britain. The need to obtain and control information about the war affected all spheres of culture, but it had a particularly powerful influence on those who produced images. This may have been partly attributable to the increasing visuality of British society in the decades before 1914, but it was also due to the fact that images were unusually well suited to the exigencies of war. Images had the ability to represent the conflict in vivid, varied and arresting ways; they could be distributed widely and inexpensively thanks to recent breakthroughs in printing technology; and they could immediately be understood by all social groups, including those who did not read English. Images were also believed to possess an authenticity that was largely absent in other media. Untarnished by the dubious and easily manipulated mechanisms of the written word, photographs, films, even paintings and illustrations were celebrated for embodying an uncorrupted indexical connection to the conflict itself. Those images were rarely as reliable as was often thought, but this did not stop them accumulating significant social currency.

These developments had a profound effect on the social status and position of art. As the first two chapters of this book have demonstrated, the art world had largely been marginalized and demonized by a society that was preoccupied by war. Yet paradoxically it was those very preoccupations that brought the country back to the art that it had otherwise rejected. The public demand for war pictures introduced vast new audiences to new kinds of artwork; the media's desire to profit from war fever led to the reproduction of unprecedented numbers of paintings and illustrations on the pages of newspapers and pictorial publications; and the government's need to control the way that its citizens saw and understood the conflict caused it to renege on its cuts to the cultural sector and instead embark on one of the most expansive projects of patronage in its history. What we are beginning to see here is the other side of a new wartime relationship between British art and society. If, as Chapter 3 has already shown, the art world was reaching out to the nation, this chapter has claimed that when it came to war pictures, the nation was more than willing to reach back.

5 PEACE PICTURES: ESCAPISM, CONSOLATION, CATHARSIS

The First World War created a set of unusual social demands that could be satisfied only by images. The public's desire to see the war, the press's determination to profit from the war and the government's need to manage the war made images of the front line an extremely useful currency on the home front. These demands had many cultural consequences, of which the proliferation and official endorsement of war art was one. This was only part of the story, for the simple reason that war art was not the only kind of art to be produced between 1914 and 1918. The conflict gave rise to another very different set of social needs, which in turn produced another set of artworks. These needs emerged later than those that provoked the nation's much-discussed war pictures, but they grew with every year of the conflict and by its end they were considerably more influential. The images that resulted from them could not have been more different from their bellicose counterparts, for their function was not to help Britons confront the hardships of war but rather to escape and overcome them.

Scholars have traditionally neglected the consolatory strands of wartime culture because they do not fit the narratives of despair, disillusionment and dissent that have long governed interpretations of the field.[1] In recent years, however, these cultural trends have finally started to receive the attention they deserve. The process began in 1995 with the publication of Jay Winter's cultural history of the war, *Sites of Memory, Sites of Mourning*. In that text Winter challenged the dominant view that artists' widespread determination to tell the 'bitter truth' about the front line led to an ascendancy of modern modes of expression. He claimed that though the conflict engendered a great deal of rebarbative war art, it also reinvigorated more traditional and reassuring cultural modes that helped grieving communities 'live with their losses'.[2] His persuasive argument has since rippled through other disciplines, as literary critics, archaeologists and military historians have begun to explore the ways that all kinds of cultural output – from diaries and mementoes to cinemas and singing groups – helped counteract rather than chronicle the disasters of war.[3]

This chapter explores the implications of Jay Winter's argument by reference to a wide and demotic range of visual material that was hugely popular with the British public during the war but has since been largely neglected. It will show how crowd-pleasing pastoral landscapes, mass-produced prints, private portrait commissions, amateur sketches and even an early iteration of art therapy proved integral to the ways in which soldiers and civilians endured the traumas of war. In the process, I will argue that the widespread need for escape, consolation and catharsis created a network of cultural exchange that in turn forged entirely new connections between the British people and their art. It gave rise to new artistic producers and consumers. It created novel channels through which art-works could be disseminated and experienced. It deepened the psychological resonances of pictures for nearly all who interacted with them. And, at the very end of the conflict, it even suggested a model for how the community as a whole might recover from the war.[4]

'Peace pictures'

Although the outbreak of war unleashed a voracious public appetite for images, reports and stories from the front, it was not long before this initial excitement was replaced with frustration or depression. From about 1915 many Britons increasingly craved diversions from the battlefields. These escapist urges had wide-ranging consequences for popular culture. In an otherwise lethargic literary market, fantasy and adventure novels saw their sales increase exponentially. In the West End, whimsical theatrical productions like *Peter Pan* and *Chu Chin Chow* attracted a seemingly interminable stream of crowds. And in the cinema, fantasies, romances and above all the comedies of Charlie Chaplin reached as many as 20 million British people every week.[5] As can be seen even from this brief survey, the public's demand for escape was made of, and supplied by, many different media. Indeed, it was so indiscriminate and so rapacious that the playwright George Bernard Shaw described it as a nationwide epidemic of 'hyperaesthesia'.[6]

This 'hyperaesthesia' gave rise to debates about which cultural medium was the most effective mode of escape. Publishers argued that the novel, with its extended narratives, could absorb consumers like no other art forms; composers claimed that music, being the most abstract art, was best able to draw its audiences away from reality; and cinema proprietors maintained that the carefree entertainment offered by films was more dynamic and democratic than any of their rivals. It might be thought that amid such company fine art was singularly unsuited to fulfilling these objectives. Yet this was not the case. In fact, pictures were extremely effective vehicles for escape. They could capture the human stories associated with the novel; they could gratify the senses like music; and unlike almost every other medium, they could function equally well both in public and in private. Thousands of people could enjoy diverting prints on streets or in periodicals, while a single person could lose himself in a painting in the most intimate corner of his home.[7]

The most ubiquitous form of escapist picture was the pastoral landscape. This is not, perhaps, a surprise. The pastoral mode is old and complex, but it has long been understood as a 'discourse of retreat'.[8] Its celebration of rural life has in particular been invoked as an escape from all things urban. This position was brilliantly elaborated by Raymond Williams in his 1973 book *The Country and the City*. By examining the development of English literature from the sixteenth century onwards, Williams contended that the pastoral was not merely a retreat from the country to the city; it was a retreat from 'the disturbance and disorder of the present' to 'an ordered and happier past'.[9] In August 1914 – a date that fell within the scope of Williams's study – millions of Britons were flung into an unusually disturbed and disordered present. In response, they attempted to mythologize and revisit the 'golden age' (to use Williams's term) that had flourished before it. As they did so, they produced and consumed a vast quantity of pastoral imagery whose explicit purpose was to help them return to their pre-war lives.

A representative example of this temporal escapism is a now-lost landscape by Benjamin Williams Leader, which was first exhibited at the Royal Academy in May 1915 (Figure 5.1). Leader's painting depicted a family picnic in a cornfield on a midsummer day. If it uncannily resembled the bucolic pictures he had been producing for years, this painting, however, was entitled *Peace*.[10] It was therefore instantly recognizable as an explicit visual counterpart to the conflict. And in case viewers still doubted his picture's meaning, Leader added an inscription to the frame that, (mis)quoting William Morris's *The Earthly Paradise*, read: 'Yellow the cornfields lay although as yet / Unto the stucks no sickle had been set'.[11] The metaphor was clear: the picture did not just represent any peaceful scene; it recreated a precise historical moment that preceded the August harvest, as well as its tragic equivalent – the human harvest of the August war. In other words, Leader's textual intervention ensured that when an audience of 1915 looked at his painting they would be looking back into the past, from war into peace.

Leader's longing for the summer of 1914 was not uncommon. Many artists and writers spent the war recreating the idyllic months before it. The most famous literary example is surely Edward Thomas's poem 'Adlestrop', which

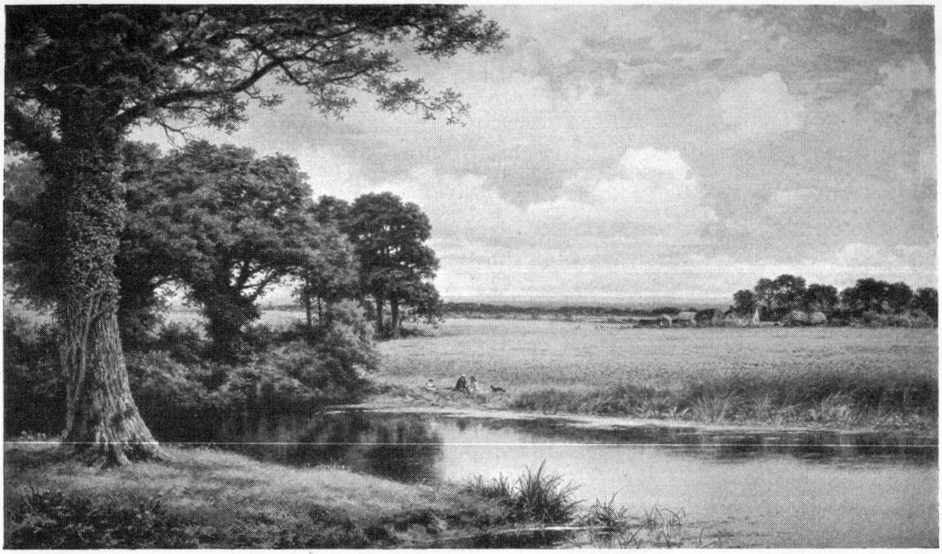

Peace.
"Yellow the cornfields lay although as yet
Unto the stucks no sickle had been set."—*Morris.*
B. W. LEADER, R.A.

Figure 5.1 B. W. Leader, *Peace*, 1915. Oil on canvas, dimensions unknown. Whereabouts unknown. Reproduced in *Royal Academy Pictures and Sculpture* (1915).

whisked its readers away from the worries of battle and deposited them deep in the English countryside in 'late June' 1914.[12] Artists nonetheless remained the most prolific manufacturers of *ante-bellum* escapism, and, more dependent than ever on securing sales, they started to produce images that were specifically targeted at the public's ever-growing nostalgia. In fact, they became so ubiquitous that they were soon classified as a genre in themselves: the 'Peace Picture'.[13] If artists' ambitions were to transport viewers back into a world before war, contemporary responses suggest that they very often succeeded: critics wrote that 'peace pictures' successfully 'recalled a time of peace that felt so far distant in the past'; convinced them that they had 'got back to the days before the war'; and reminded them of 'a past happiness which [they] never enjoyed as it deserved'.[14]

Not all peace pictures were portraits of the past, but increasing numbers of them took on lives outside their frames. Like Leader's summer landscape, Tom Mostyn's first peace painting debuted at the Royal Academy in 1915. But unlike the former's small elegiac offering, Mostyn served up a vast, exultant canvas called *The Garden of Peace* (Plate 3). It depicted a luxuriant garden at sunset, resplendent with blossoming flowers and inhabited by two embracing lovers in exotic robes. Far from depicting a real world that had subsequently been shattered by conflict, this was a fantasy realm that had never seen and would never see such hostilities. Mostyn's shamelessly saccharine painting was a huge commercial success: it was purchased instantly and then presented anonymously to the people of Liverpool through the Walker Art Gallery; it was distributed as a commercial lithograph for the modest price of a shilling; and it was reproduced in a range of magazines and newspapers throughout the war. Between 1915 and 1918 it was probably seen by tens if not hundreds of thousands of people.

In its mass-produced form, *The Garden of Peace* was packaged as an antidote to the ongoing conflict. When *Bibby's Annual* printed the picture in 1916 its editors wrote a caption to secure its meaning accordingly:

> This is an enchanted garden created by a painter-poet. He has filled it with rich and sensuous colour; the air is balmy with the scent of pines and sweet with flowers; all is quiet save the drowsy hum of insects and the soothing drip of fountains. Here it is always afternoon; within the cool depths of the woods are fragrant bowers inviting to seclusion and repose. We see a happy couple on the terrace deep in romantic converse; meet inhabitants they for this earthly Paradise; where no cries of pain and anguish disturb the calm, and only things that are lovely and true can come. From our world of strife and hatred, and base desire, and cruel hope, we look wistfully into this oasis of peace, and would fain escape awhile and enter in.[15]

The combination of image and text was not subtle, but it was effective. The latter presented the former as a quasi-musical experience – a wave of intoxicating oblivion that washed away the hardships of reality. The simplicity and directness of the appeal confirms that *The Garden of Peace* was being targeted at an audience that was unaccustomed to sophisticated aesthetic contemplation. Indeed, perhaps more than a few of its members had never scrutinized a painting so closely before.

The Garden of Peace was one symptom of a broader and more perplexing cultural trend. As the public was otherwise dismissing the art world, new social groups became increasingly – if not unprecedentedly – susceptible to the images that it was producing. Indeed, contemporary sources suggest that in the second half of the war an entirely new demographic of buyers entered the art market. This was largely due to the financial changes that the country itself was undergoing. While established art collectors from the aristocracy and the middle classes suffered from war taxation and the depreciation of their capital (as has been seen in Chapter 1), industrialists and the working classes benefited from lucrative war contracts, full employment and rising salaries. The latter groups grew determined to invest their new-found wealth. With the abiding instability of savings, stocks and shares, many of them decided, for the very first time, to invest their cash in art.[16]

The new buyers demanded pictures that, like *The Garden of Peace*, were straightforwardly reassuring. The *Fine Art Trade Journal* wrote that their taste inclined towards 'the art that is sentimental, the picture with a story, the literal landscape, especially if it recalls familiar scenes; the humble interior, especially if it recalls grandmother'.[17] Their particular predilection for the pastoral was soon felt at the very top of the market. At the war's first substantial non-charity sales in 1916 and 1917, this new group paid staggering sums – many of which exceeded even pre-war totals – for bucolic Victorian pictures: a 'novus homo from the north' paid a combined 11,500 guineas for John Constable's *Salisbury Cathedral* and a landscape by John Crome; an industrialist called 'Robson' purchased George Morland's *The Benevolent Sportsman* for 5,200 guineas;[18] and the whisky distiller Thomas Dewar paid 5,000 guineas for Edwin Landseer's *Monarch of the Glen* – an enduringly popular portrait of a stag in the Scottish highlands.[19] These are just a few representative examples of many hundreds of similar purchases.

The new collectors did not only buy expensive art. Less affluent men were also determined to acquire images that would beautify their homes, cheer their spirits and help them forget the war. From about 1916 these buyers started to demand affordable escapist prints like *The Garden of Peace*. At the same time, the art trade adjusted its output to supply the demand. In January 1916 the *Fine Art Trade Journal* issued the following advice to artists and illustrators: 'Anything which distracts our attention from scenes of sadness ought to be welcomed ... A special opportunity occurs here for the picture as well as for the picture postcard to assert its influence, and public gratitude is due to those ... who ... strive to show us the sunny side of things.'[20] The artistic result of this commercial conjunction was significant. Many in the art trade believed that peace pictures were the reason for a widespread 'revival of the print' in the second half of the war.[21] Indeed, this development was so enduring that when in 1924 one critic summarized the chief artistic changes that had taken place during the conflict, his list was headed by the boom in so-called 'lyrics for the small householder'.[22]

The miseries of war were evidently encouraging many British people to turn to art for the very first time. Indeed, anecdotal evidence suggests that in the latter years of the conflict the public started to visit exhibitions as though they were forms of popular entertainment. Critics observed that groups hitherto unseen in art galleries (particularly the working classes, women and the generally 'uncultured') now flocked to them in search of sheer unadulterated pleasure – as 'part of their daily penance'.[23] Exhibiting societies also noted a growing number of officers on leave at their shows. That particular trend was doubtless aided by the free admission that most had introduced for uniformed visitors, but many observers remarked that it was also due to a change in servicemen's cultural habits. They claimed that weeks or months on the front line had whetted soldiers' aesthetic sensibilities to such an extent that they now derived the same 'relief and solace' from peace pictures as they had done previously from the music halls.[24]

In fact, the escapist 'hyperaesthesia' was so intense on the front line that artists back in Britain were regularly asked to target peace pictures specifically at servicemen.[25] In one scheme, Frank Pick at the London Underground commissioned artists to produce images that would deliberately 'awaken thoughts of pleasant homely things' in the minds of those serving abroad.[26] The most successful of these was George Clausen's *A Wish* (Plate 4), which was sent in poster form to YMCA huts and other communal military spaces on the continent in 1916.[27] Clausen served up an irresistible pastoral fantasy that bore an uncanny resemblance to Leader's earlier *Peace*: it too represented a family relaxing in the English countryside on a summer's day, and it too enlisted a Romantic English poem (Samuel Rogers's 'A Wish') to reinforce its message.[28] But that is where the similarities ended. While Leader's painting was aimed at civilians who wished to return to the past, Clausen's picture was aimed at soldiers who wished to return home. The two artists thus hoped to incite altogether different modes of escapism, and closer examination of the latter reveals precisely why Clausen was so successful in doing so.

The most conspicuous components of Clausen's picture were two figures, sitting together in the foreground beneath a tree. They were generically delineated, but servicemen would instantly have understood that they were a mother and child, and they were without a man. These details had profound implications for their target audience. They suggested that the scene was not a vision of the past, but a vision of the present – or more precisely, of a wartime England depopulated of its young men. Moreover, they encouraged those very men, serving abroad away from their families, to replace the deliberately generic forms of 'wife' and 'child' with their own wives and their own children.[29] As soon as Clausen's viewers began to see their own families in his figures, his print provided them with two deeply reassuring messages: the first assured them that their loved ones at home were safe and happy; the second invited them to escape from the front, walk along the path that Clausen had so tantalizingly depicted and recomplete, at least temporarily, their broken family units.

A Wish, however, raised serving soldiers' morale in another, very different way. Surrounding the figures was an idyllic English scene, with village green, parish church and thatched cottages. This tableau of bucolic stereotypes was evidently not a representation of soldiers' real homes; it was an idealized symbol of the nation as a whole.[30] This was hardly a unique metaphor: scholars have since established that from the late nineteenth century the verdant, church-spired, field-folded villages of the 'south country' were regularly invoked as an 'essence of England' – an England that was pre-modern, agrarian, Christian and racially homogenous.[31] Furthermore, Alex Potts has argued that this conservative vision of 'Constable Country' was repeatedly 'mobilised at times of political tension' in order to reinforce awareness of the unique values of England and Englishness.[32] This, surely, is what Clausen and his patrons were hoping to achieve. For as soon as servicemen read his landscape this way, they would be reminded why they were fighting in the first place: their doubts would be dismissed, their resolve strengthened, their patriotism revived.

The ideological subtext of pastoral peace pictures was not lost on contemporaries. An observant reviewer in the right-wing *Morning Post* detected martial connotations in all wartime paintings of village greens and golden cornfields:

> These very pictures suggest war. For are our soldiers not fighting that all the people of these islands may enjoy as freemen the tranquillity, the charm, and the romance of the actual scenes so skilfully and feelingly represented? Therefore the Minister of Information's attention should be drawn to such pictures, which would far better serve propaganda purposes ... than misrepresentations of our heroic soldiers and of battle scenes on the Western Front.[33]

The author was preaching to the converted. The Parliamentary Recruiting Committee was so convinced by the morale-boosting potential of peace pictures that it used the genre for its posters. In one famous example a soldier gestures to a pristine landscape that looks like a scene painted by Leader or Clausen and exclaims: 'Isn't this worth dying for? Enlist now' (Plate 5).[34] As with Leader and Clausen, and with Mostyn too, the caption stabilized and clarified the message implicit in the image. But here that message had all but been reversed: the landscape was not a refuge from war; it was a reminder of war and an endorsement of it, too. For the peace to which the soldier gestured was a realm that could only be secured once the fighting – and winning – was concluded. It may not have been the most peaceful of peace pictures, but posters like this were printed in their millions, distributed throughout Britain and could apparently be seen 'on every hoarding, in most shop windows, in omnibuses, tramcars, and commercial vans'.[35] The peace picture had finally reached the public in its millions.

This section has demonstrated that pastoral imagery – so often thought to have perished in the mechanized wastelands of the western front – had actually experienced a renaissance on the home front.[36] Above all, it has argued that the

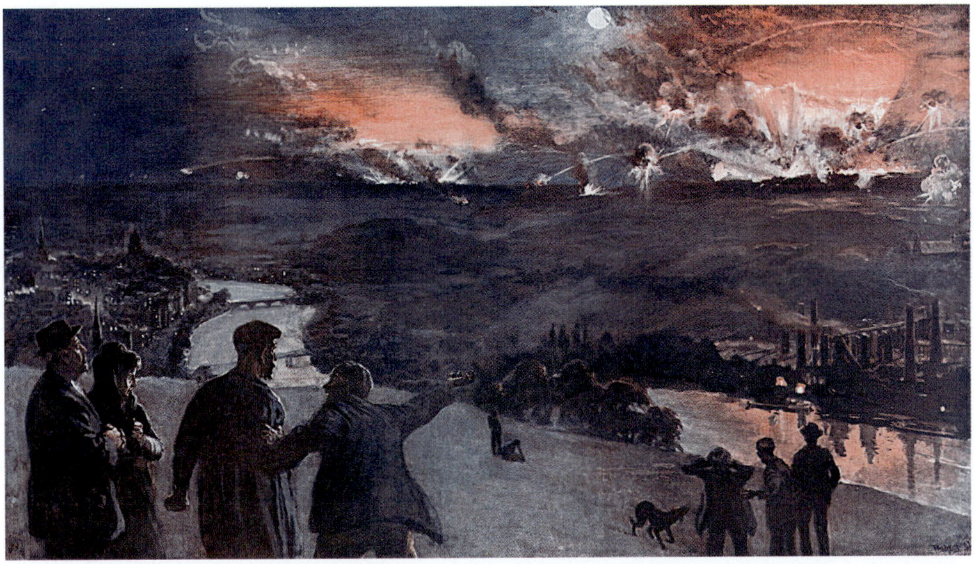

Plate 1 Philip Dadd, 'Bombardment of Fort Boncelles and Fort Barchon', *The Sphere* (7 December 1914).

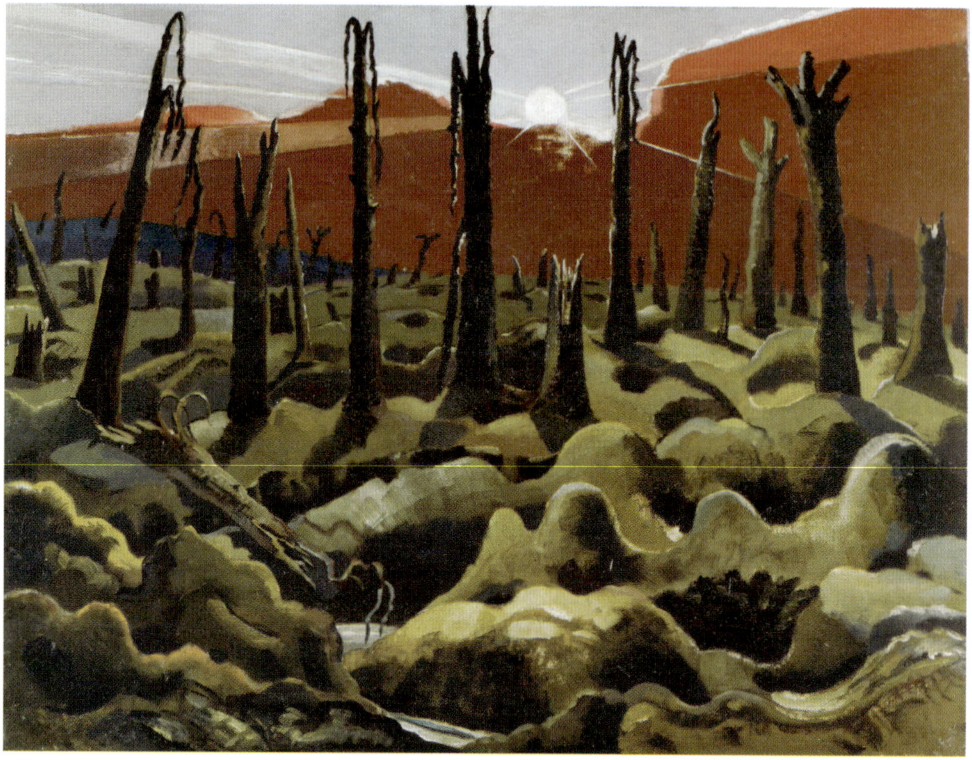

Plate 2 Paul Nash, *We Are Making a New World*, 1918. Oil on canvas, 71.1 × 91.4 cm. Imperial War Museum.

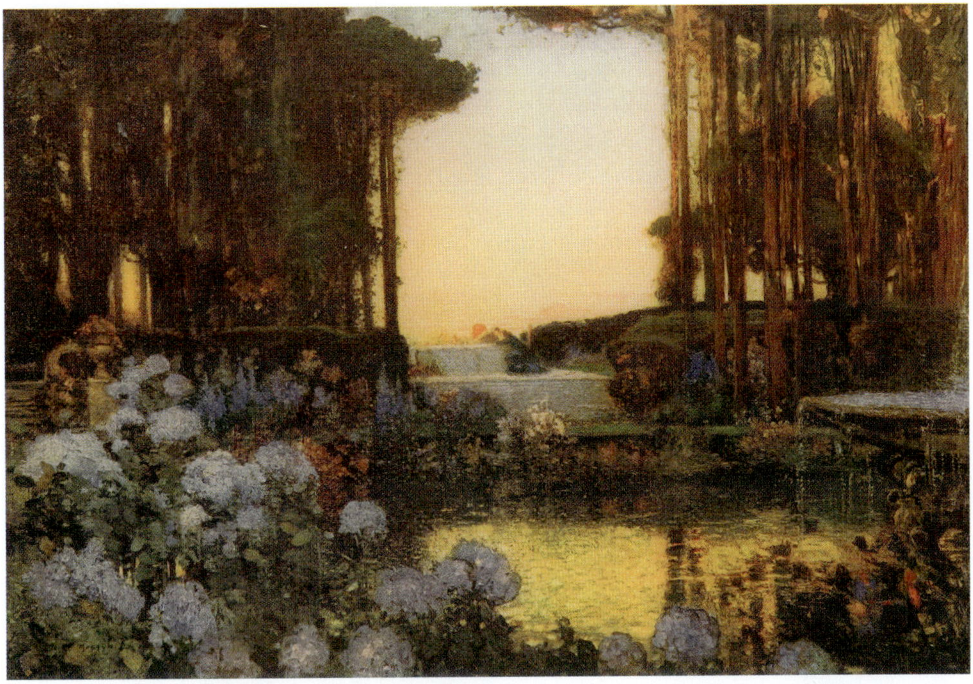

Plate 3 Tom Mostyn, *The Garden of Peace*, 1915. Oil on canvas, 172.5 × 233.7 cm. Walker Art Gallery.

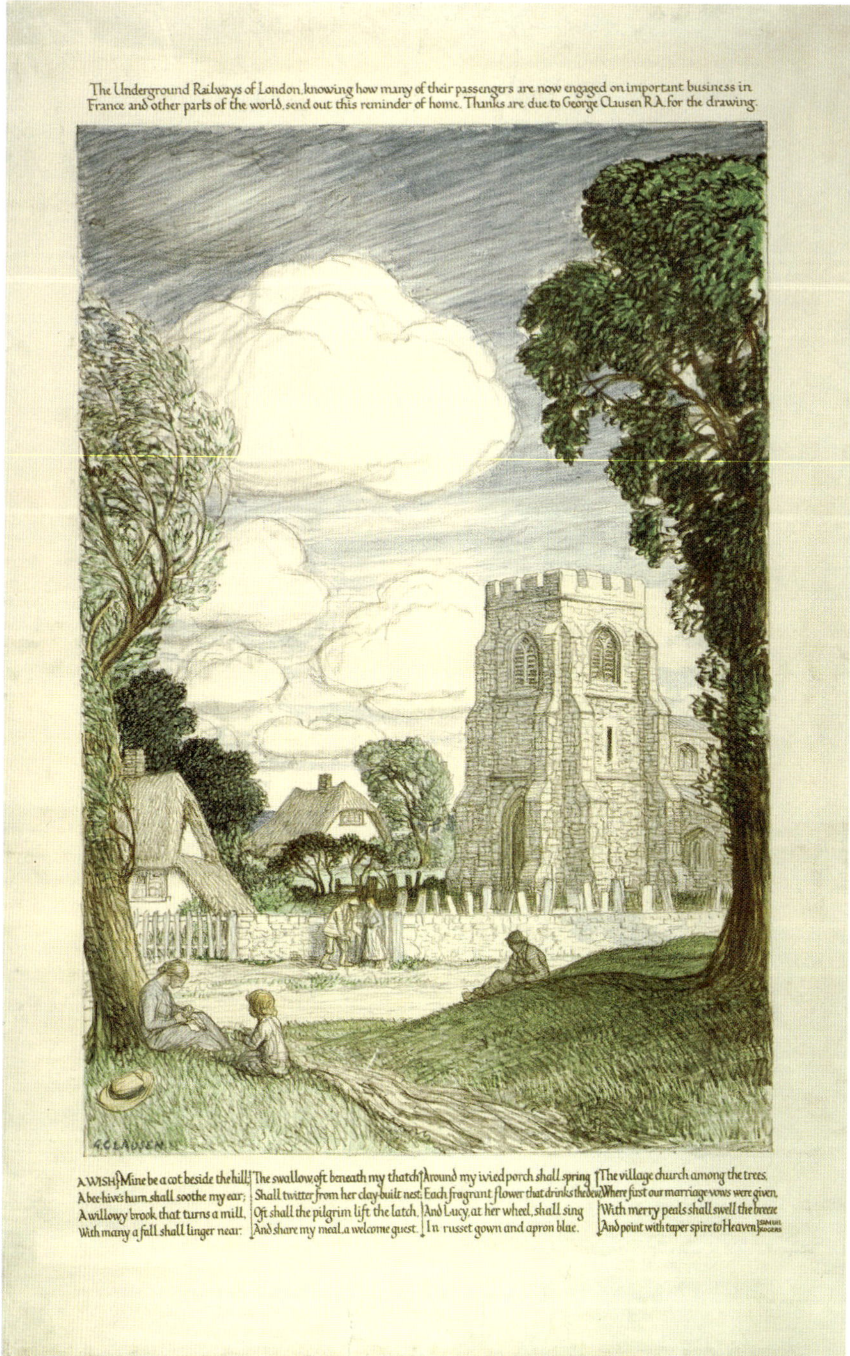

Plate 4 George Clausen, *A Wish*, 1916. Lithograph, 63.5 × 101.6 cm. Published by Underground Electric Railway Company Ltd. London Transport Museum.

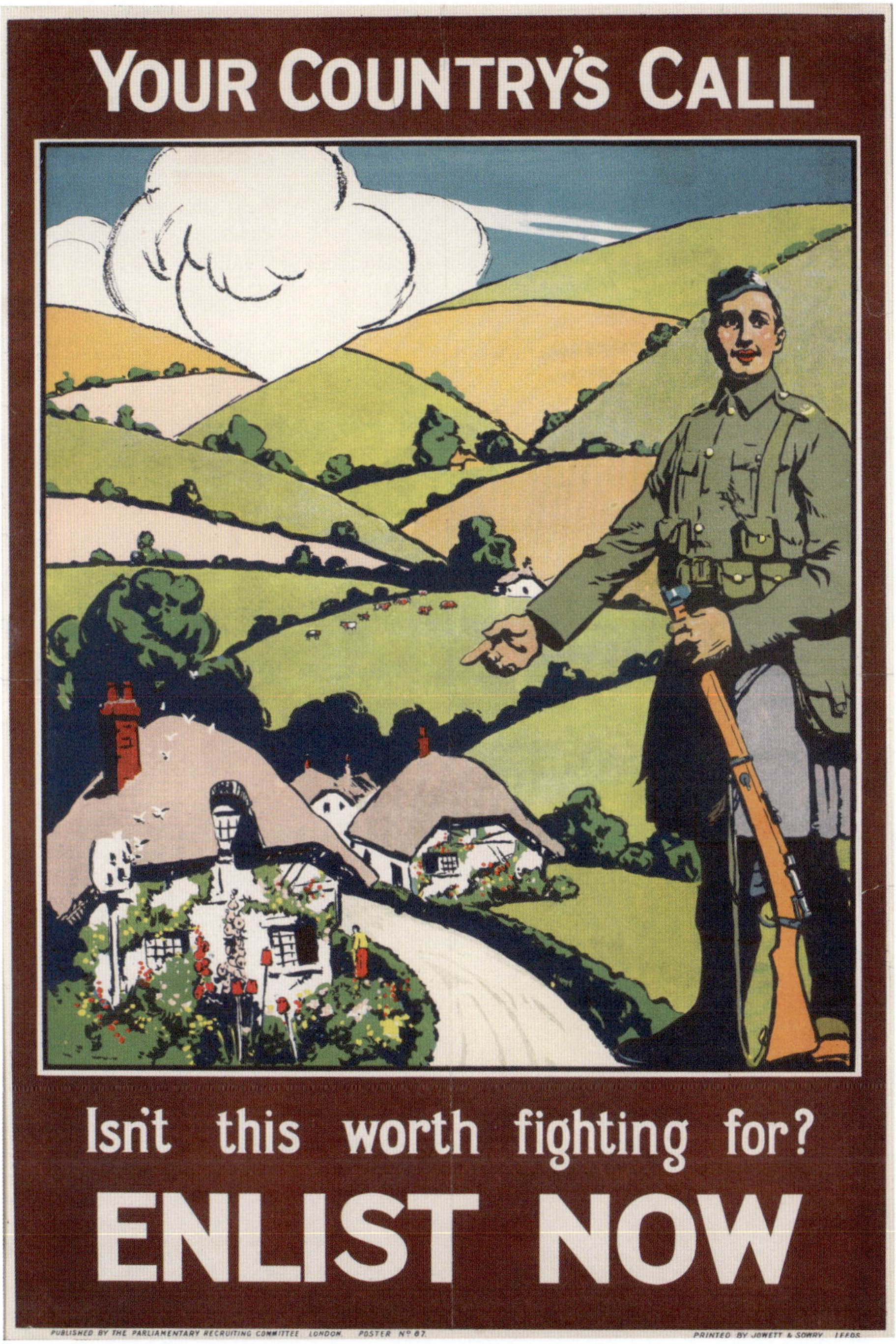

Plate 5 *Your Country's Call*, 1915. Parliamentary Recruiting Poster no. 87. Lithograph, 75.1 × 50 cm. Imperial War Museum.

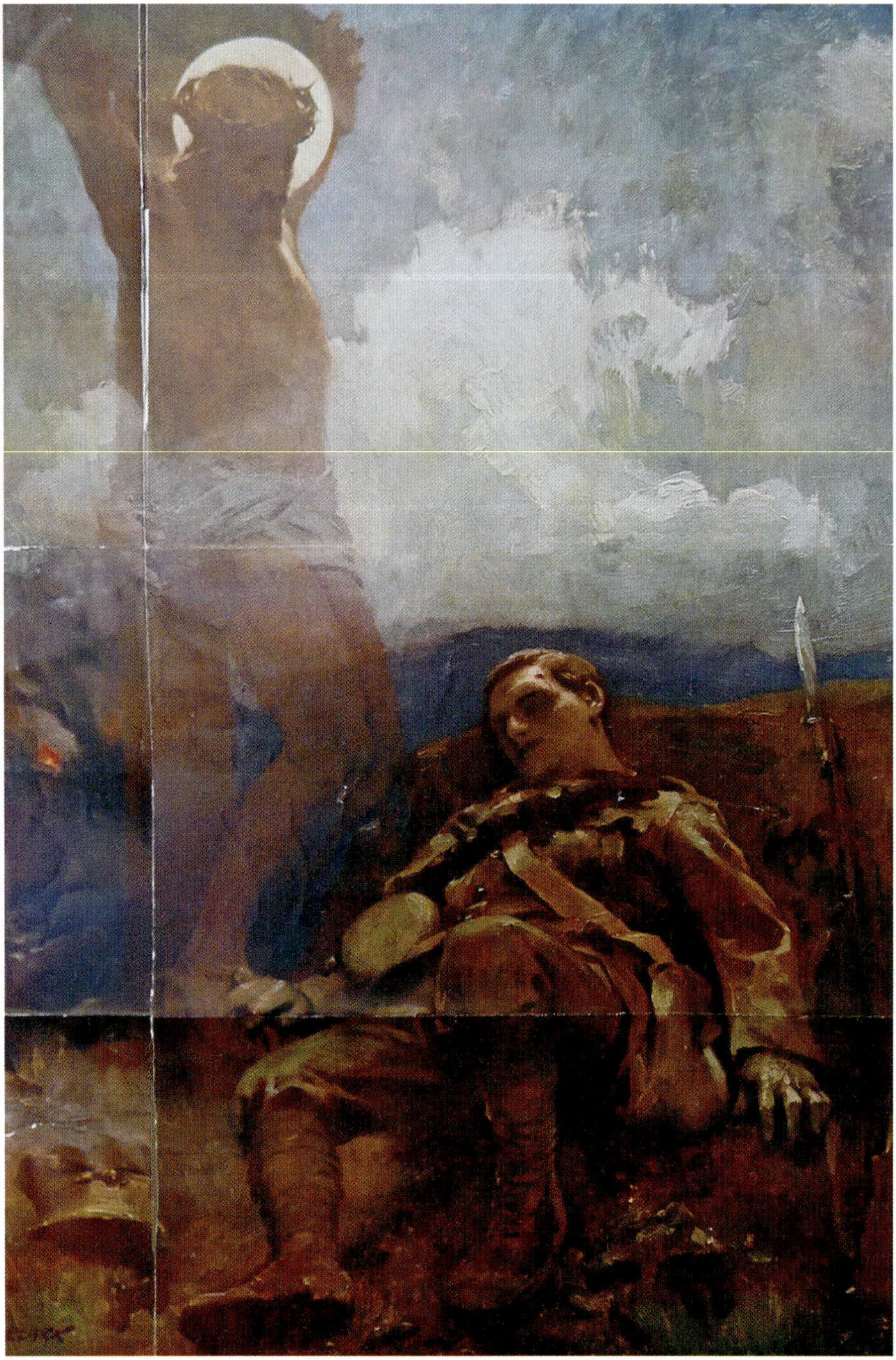

Plate 6 James Clark, *The Great Sacrifice*, 1914. Lithograph, 60.5 × 40 cm. Reproduced in *The Graphic* (23 November 1914).

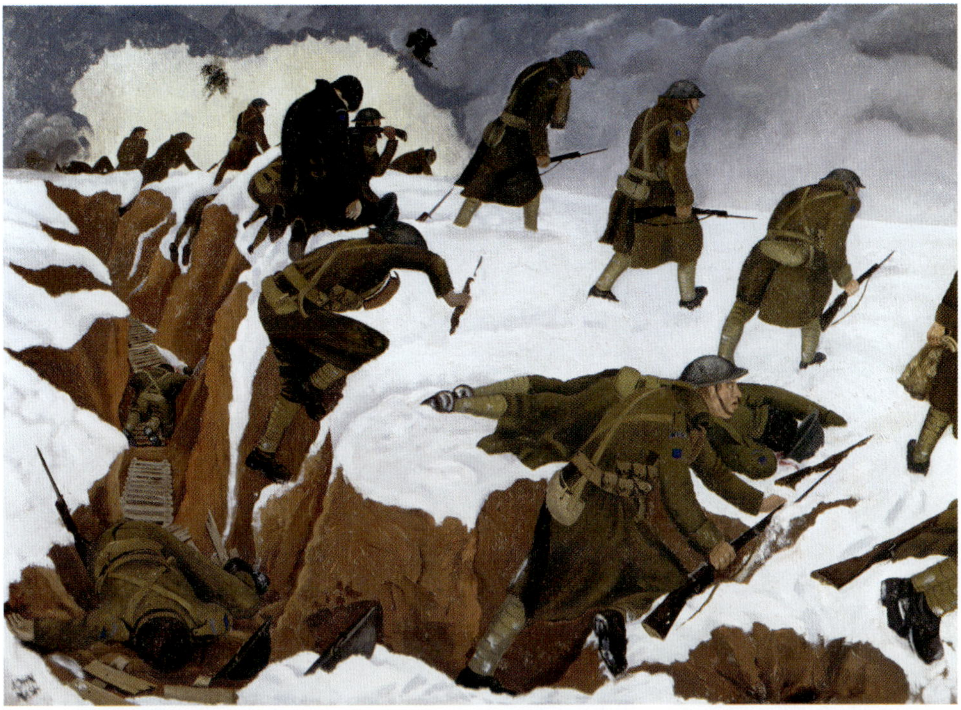

Plate 7 John Nash, *Over the Top: 1st Artists' Rifles at Marcoing, 30th December 1917*, 1918. Oil on canvas, 79.4 × 107.3 cm. Imperial War Museum.

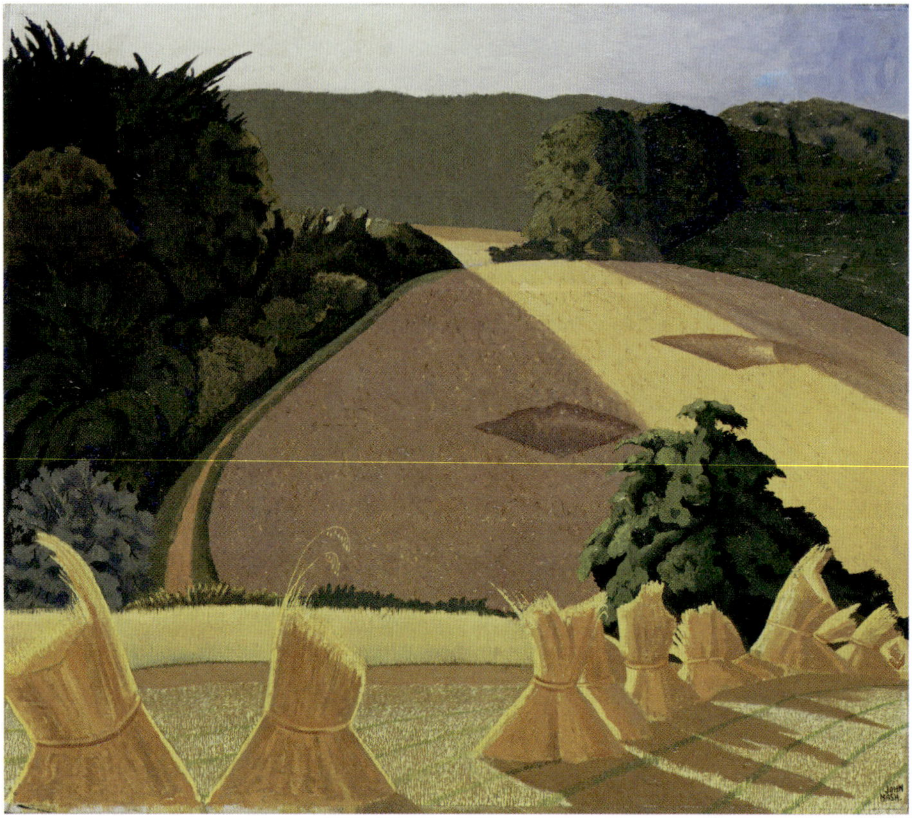

Plate 8 John Nash, *The Cornfield*, 1918. Oil on canvas, 68.6 × 67.2 cm. Tate Gallery.

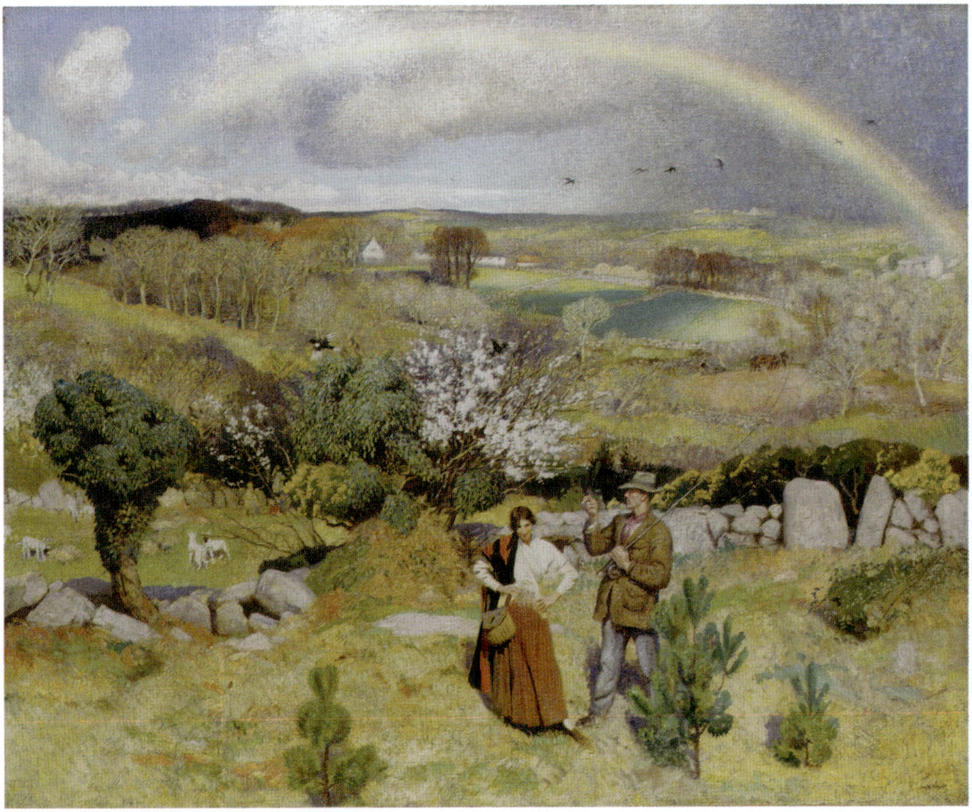

Plate 9 Laura Knight, *Spring*, 1916–20. Oil on canvas, 152.4 × 182.9 cm. Tate Gallery.

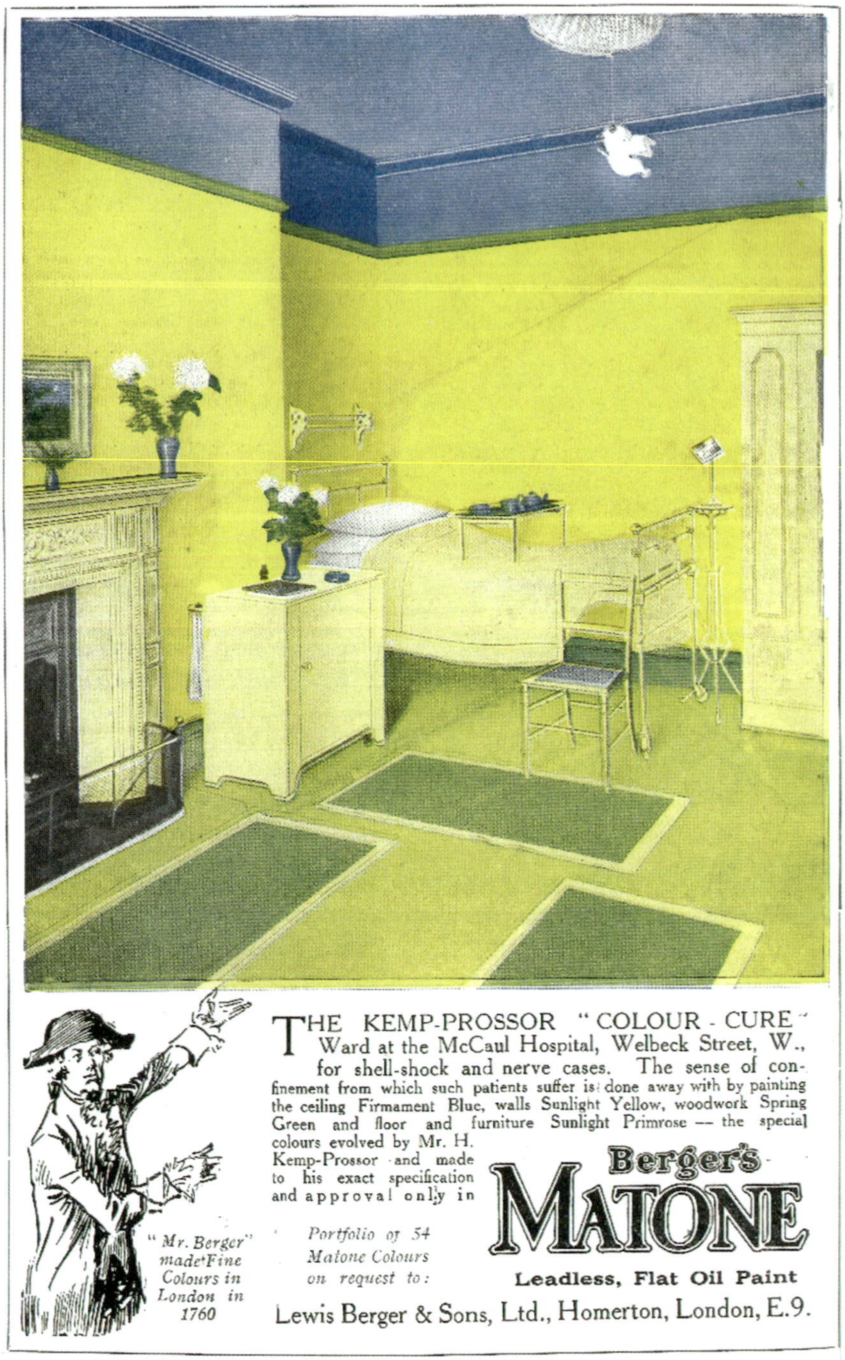

Plate 10 *The Kemp-Prossor 'Colour-Cure'*. Advertisement for Lewis Berger & Sons Ltd, 1918. Lithograph, 24 × 12 cm. Reproduced in *Colour* (March 1918).

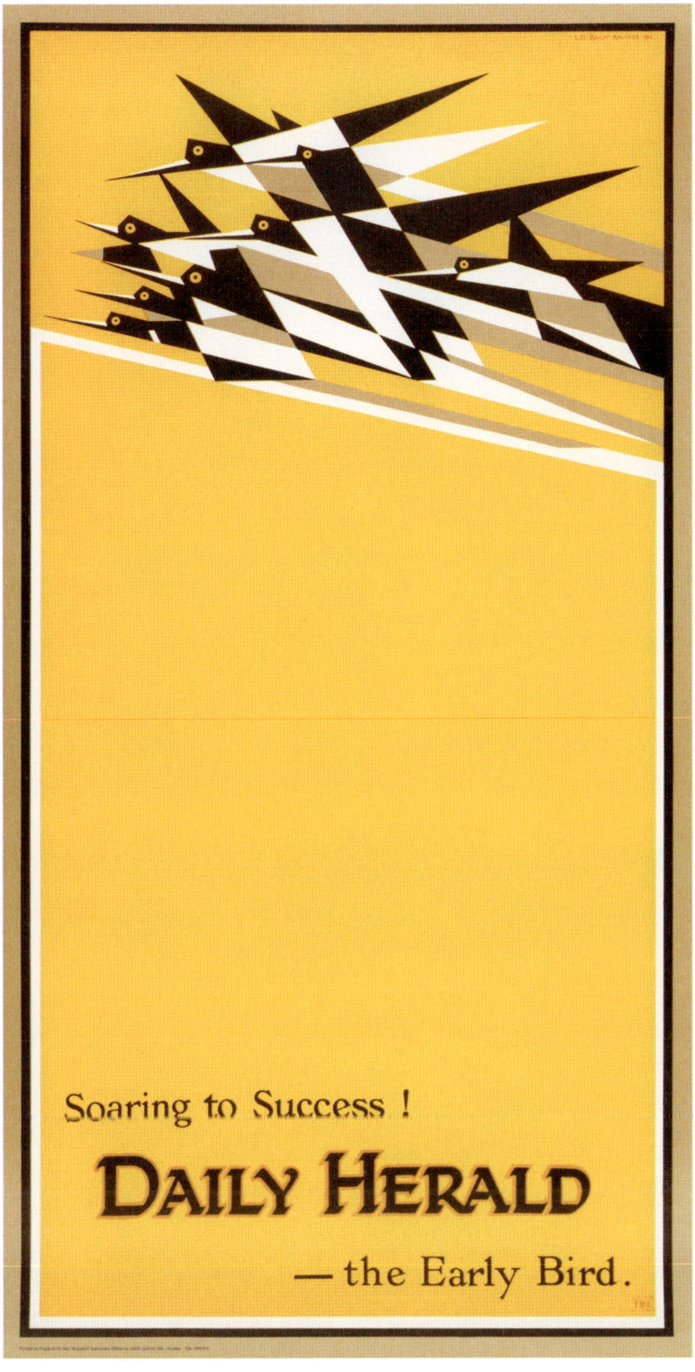

Plate 11 Edward McKnight Kauffer, 'Soaring to Success! – The Early Bird', 1919. Lithograph poster on paper, 297 × 152 cm. Victoria & Albert Museum.

conflict forged an unlikely alliance between the British people and pictorial art. The public's demand for distraction made new social groups unusually amenable to certain images just as financial hardship made artists unusually receptive to popular taste. The artworks that resulted from this correspondence may not have always been aesthetically distinguished, but they played an important role in British people's endurance of the war. They were not, however, the only images to do this. While the generalizing appeal of landscape was well suited to collective consumption, portraiture's genius for the particular enabled it to enter people's lives, respond to their unique circumstances and shepherd them through their own personal tragedies.

'A miracle of consolation'

For several decades cultural historians have described how the arts memorialized the disastrous events of the First World War. Much is therefore known about the history paintings that were commissioned to commemorate the conflict, the thousands of memorials that stand in villages, towns and cities across the country and the many rituals of remembrance that continue to accompany them today.[37] But not all memorials were monumental, and not all remembrance was public. Millions of men and women lost relatives between 1914 and 1918 and many of them preferred to confront their losses in private ways – or, in the words of one contemporary, 'from personal tributes to their dead, not from well drilled patterned-uniformity'.[38] In doing so, they too sought out cultural products that would help them in this task, and that would, as Jay Winter has put it, be able to 'mediate' their 'bereavement'.[39] To date, the remarkable imagery that arose from those needs has received little scholarly attention.[40] However, it was widespread during the war; it played an invaluable role in helping British families grieve, remember and recover; and it further entrenched the intimate new relationship that was being forged between wartime society and its art.

I have already shown how the outbreak of war suppressed the market for most kinds of art products. One of the few genres that benefited, however, was enlistment portraiture. This trend was motivated by the desire to celebrate husbands, brothers and sons before they went abroad on active service, but also by the need to secure permanent images of loved ones whom their patrons feared might never return. It was by no means a new practice. Portraiture had long been motivated by the prospect of absence. Indeed, Pliny the Elder claimed that it started when a girl traced the features of her lover onto a wall before he left her to go abroad.[41] Ancient though they were, these impulses offered a much-needed commercial boon to painters and photographers at the beginning of the conflict. The

Professional Classes War Relief Council, which was rarely optimistic about artists' wartime prospects, could at least report that in the first year of war 'hardly a day' passed without orders for 'portraits and miniatures, being done from photographs' by artists.[42] Moreover, trade papers stated that the 'ENORMOUS DEMAND' for 'portraits of those going abroad' had alone kept frame-makers in business through the penurious autumn of 1914.[43]

Established portraitists were among the many beneficiaries of this trend. Philip de László may have had numerous conventional commissions cancelled at the outbreak of war, but he was simultaneously inundated with requests to paint enlistees. The first was Viscount Castlereagh, whose portrait he made in just four hours the day before his sitter departed for France (Figure 5.2).[44] De László produced a number of similar likenesses for charity: in October he was one of ninety artists who agreed to paint portraits of 'any person serving the King' in exchange for donations to the Artists' General Benevolent Institution.[45] By the end of the war de László's various commitments had resulted in nearly eighty portraits of serving officers in different media – so many that his wife even suggested he don a khaki uniform himself for 'being the first portraitist to the Expeditionary Force'.[46] She was not being entirely serious, but a fascinating and often moving series of letters reveals that her husband was indeed providing an invaluable wartime service for the families of those fighting.

According to letters sent to de László, relatives repeatedly remarked how reassuring his pictures had been while their loved ones were abroad. One mother spoke for many when she confessed that his portrait of her son was 'a great comfort to me now as he is away & in danger'.[47] For most, the comfort was only needed temporarily, but some of de László's less fortunate sitters did not return from the front.[48] In such situations, his portraits became even more valuable to their relatives – and they acquired very different meanings. Pleasing mementoes became macabre memorials, and brisk likenesses ossified into icons of truncated lives. In some cases, de László's portraits ceased to be considered likenesses at all, and were instead invoked as relics, as surrogates for the men they represented, and as foci for rituals of mourning, remembering and recovering. One example will suffice here: the press baron Lord Rothermere had commissioned de László to paint two of his sons in 1916 before they were called up. Both were killed shortly afterwards. On hearing the news, Rothermere hung the two portraits above his bed and allegedly spoke to them every day for the remainder of his life.[49]

The Rothermere story may be apocryphal, but it is proof that portraiture did not only 'mediate bereavement'; it could act as a kind of intermediary between the living and the dead. The art historian Hans Belting has argued that portraits have done this throughout their history. Indeed, he has claimed that in all

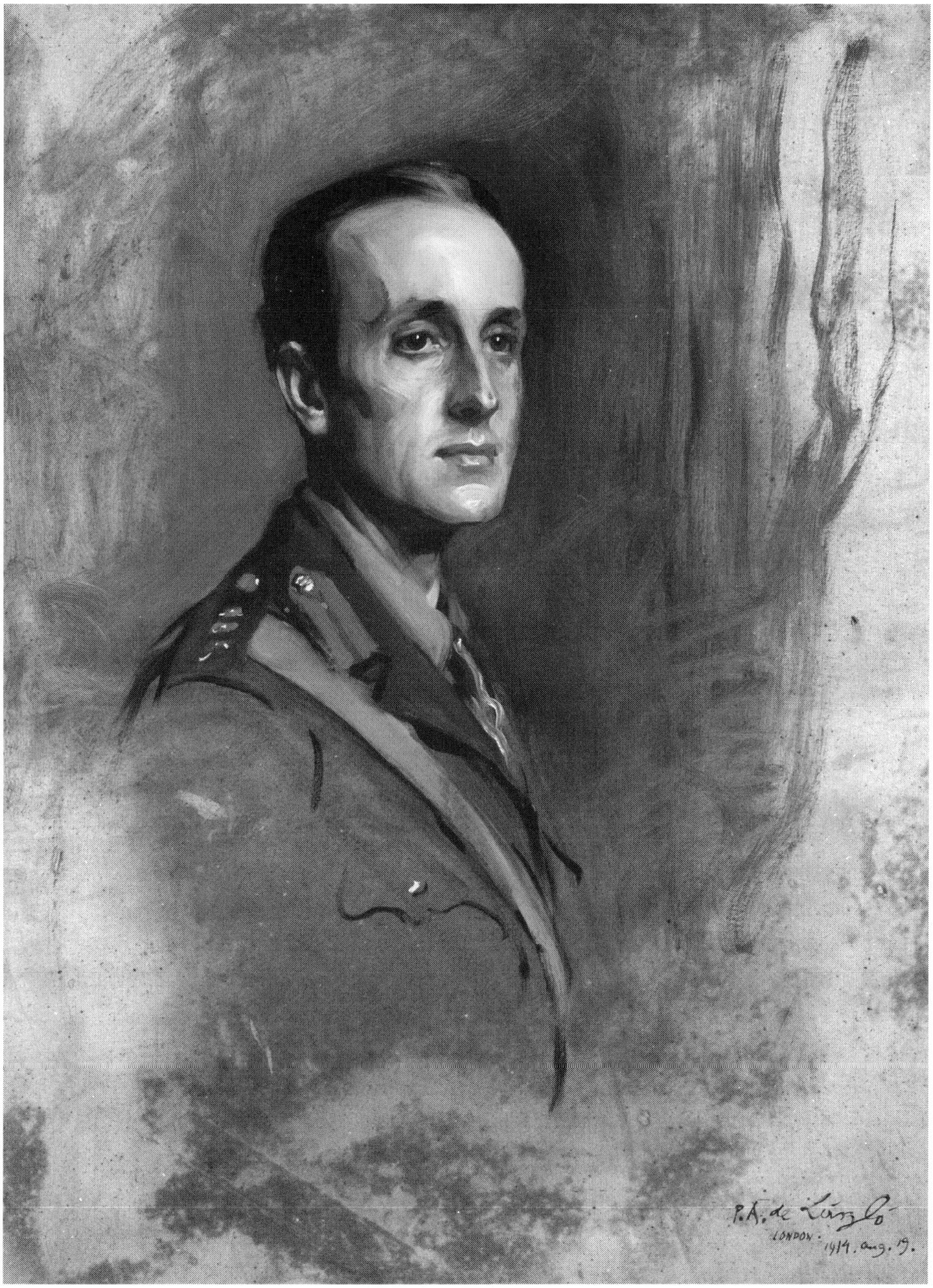

Figure 5.2 Philip de László, *Charles Stewart Henry Vane-Tempest-Stewart, Viscount Castlereagh*, 1914. Oil on board, 90.2 × 73.3 cm. Mount Stewart, Londonderry Collection, National Trust.

cultural traditions images possess a singular power to neutralize and invert the 'unbearable absence' of death, making the absent present, embodying the disembodied and producing a 'counter-meaning to that other image, the corpse'.[50] This deep-rooted belief was surely one of the reasons why so many wartime portraits were commissioned after the deaths of their subjects.[51] In fact, commissions of this kind were so plentiful that by the end of the war the Royal Academy pleaded with artists not to send posthumous portraits to its exhibitions for fear that they would overwhelm all other submissions.[52] Unfortunately, most of these pictures have since vanished from the public sphere, designed as they were for the most private corners of their owners' homes. This has made scholarly analysis of them difficult. Fortunately, Philip de László's meticulous paperwork offers an insight into why they were commissioned, how they were produced, what they cost and how effective they ultimately were.

De László made at least seven posthumous portraits, although the first had actually been commissioned before its sitter had died.[53] On 31 October 1914 Lord Leith of Fyvie wrote to de László to ask for a pencil portrait of his serving grandson Arthur Burn. He also asked that, because of Burn's inevitable unavailability, de László make the portrait from a photograph rather than from life. De László initially refused the request, but when it emerged that Burn had actually been killed in Ypres the day before his grandfather had first written to him, he had no choice but to agree to the demands and, further, to sympathetically reduce his honorarium to just fifty guineas.[54] Burn's grieving parents now took over the commission. His father informed de László that his wife would send him her favourite photograph of her son and would also instruct on colouring, before insisting that the finished picture (now in oil on canvas) arrive in time for Christmas 1914 – a request that suggests Burn's parents wanted to effect some form of family reunion at such an important time of year.[55] When it did arrive, Burn's mother wrote: 'I am so delighted to have it. Lord he looks just as he did before the war began ... Thank you again a thousand times.'[56]

In March 1916 de László received a similar commission from Lord and Lady Maxwell of Cardoness, whose only son had just been killed in the Dardanelles.[57] Following their initial request for a posthumous portrait in oils, de László once again agreed to a reduced honorarium (200 guineas), and Lady Maxwell subsequently sent him a set of photographs from which he could work, in addition to a tender description of her late son: 'He was good, & pure & true – brave and fearless with a deep earnestness which <u>shone in his eyes</u> ... Excuse these words, but I think ... the character of the person being painted, must be help'.[58] When the picture (whose location is now unknown) arrived five months later, she wrote to de László:

> Lord William is delighted with it ... Grateful thanks for giving us such a beautiful and truthful representation of our dear boy – the expression is so exactly his own ... It was more than skilful and wonderful, the way you have brought out the likeness when you had never seen him! Even when I saw your work from years ago, I have desired a Portrait, but never thought it wd. be a posthumous one! This is all we have of him to leave to our younger generations.[59]

Lady Maxwell's letters are extremely revealing. They not only indicate the importance that de László's portraits assumed for the families who commissioned them. They also reveal the decisive role that women played in the production and consumption of posthumous portraiture. With sons and husbands either dead or absent, mothers and widows typically proposed such commissions. They were responsible for providing artists with the photographs and pictorial instructions from which to work. And they also, it seems, became the principal custodians of the portraits once they were completed. Here, then, is yet another example of the war's unusual effects bringing a previously marginal demographic into the ambit of art.

Looking at Philip de László's posthumous pictures today, it can be difficult to comprehend the enthusiasm with which wives and mothers originally received them. Most were stilted, formulaic and painted without the bravura that characterized the rest of his *oeuvre*. Yet there were reasons for those deficiencies: de László's inevitable inability to work from life; his reliance on the photographic models that he was effectively expected to transcribe; and above all his patrons' unsurprisingly conservative demands: de László's grieving clients did not want distracting displays of painterly pyrotechnics; they wanted the most precise, sober and understated likenesses that money could buy. After all, they did not want to look *at* his paintings; they wanted to look *through* them, into the eyes of the sitters. In this context, de László's dependence on the photograph may not have been a disadvantage at all. If, as we have already seen, the indexicality of the photograph 'always carries its referent with itself', the photographic portrait by extension made its absent sitters, in one way, present.[60] When de László transcribed these photographs into paint he was, therefore, not simply copying their features; he was borrowing their indexicality. As a result, he was able to forge a direct connection between image and sitter that had never actually occurred, and in the process he too could render the absent subjects present.

If, then, the goal of painted posthumous portraits was simply to replicate the visual and ontological qualities of their photographic prototypes, why were they needed at all? There are, perhaps, a number of reasons: paintings were larger and more colourful than photographs, could be extravagantly framed and made the centrepieces of rooms; they were markers of wealth and status, particularly when commissioned from exclusive artists like de László; and it is certain that the very act of commissioning such pictures kept the dead alive in the minds of their relatives for at least the duration of the commission. Finally, posthumous portraits – by virtue of being made after death rather than before it – could respond much more directly to the consolatory functions now demanded of them. This subtle but profound difference can be seen by comparing de László's posthumous portrait of Robert Palmer, made in 1917, with the 1911 photograph on which it was based (Figures 5.3 and 5.4).

De László transcribed most of the photograph of Palmer almost exactly, refusing to alter even his clothes. But he made a number of small but suggestive changes that dramatically enriched the consolatory capacity of the image. He subtly modified the facial features, adding creases around the eyes and chin to update the portrait by the five years that had elapsed between the taking of the photograph and Palmer's final weeks alive; he added dots and dashes of pale violet in and beneath the eyes to bring the face to life and to capture a tender, fragile demeanour; and he subtly curled the red lips upwards to convert a stern and professional expression into a reassuringly warm smile. De László also included a barely perceptible silver crucifix on Palmer's watch-chain – a reminder to his relatives that its owner was in Heaven and his sacrifice had not been in vain. The painting was, in its own way, a masterpiece: it had combined the indexical legitimacy of the camera with the interpretive legitimacy of the artist. It should thus come as no surprise that Palmer's father considered the picture to be nothing less than a 'miracle of consolation'.[61]

Robert Palmer's father was not alone. Many other grieving patrons told de László that his portraits had done more than anything else to help them confront and overcome their losses. One correspondent wrote: 'Your wonderful talents and your sympathetic feeling … have helped the stricken hearts and homes more than ever you know.'[62] This was impressive praise indeed, but it must be remembered that de László's pictures were denied to all but the noblest and wealthiest families in Britain. Most Britons could not afford to commission artists to paint their dead relatives, let alone the most exclusive and expensive in the country. Nevertheless, consolatory imagery was so widely demanded and so singularly effective that – much like peace pictures – it made its reassuring presence felt at all levels of society. Cheap and 'sympathetical' prints – which sought to shepherd the bereaved through the mourning process – proliferated around the country throughout the conflict.[63] They showed religious figures comforting the mourners, soldiers returning to their wives and watching over their children and the dead ensconced happily in Heaven. But one of these images was more successful than any other.

In November 1914 *The Graphic* offered free with its Christmas number a large fold-out colour print of a painting by James Clark called *The Great Sacrifice* (Plate 6).[64] Described as 'the finest picture that the war has yet produced', it showed a dead British serviceman slumped peacefully next to the crucified Christ.[65] The picture was evidently aimed at those who had lost relatives in the opening months of the war: it was a flagrant idealization of death (a discreet spot of blood on the soldier's temple being the only indication of mortality), and a conspicuous justification of that death by likening the 'gallant young soldier sacrificed on the altar of duty' to Christ's own sacrifice.[66] In early 1915 *The Graphic* offered the picture for sale at a variety of prices so that people of all classes and institutions of all types could possess it.[67] Prints were soon 'in every shop window in the country' and subsequently entered homes, churches, schools and hospitals in Britain and abroad.[68] Moreover, the public response was overwhelming: *The Graphic* apparently received 15,000 letters of approval from around the world (whose authors, the periodical claimed, included thirteen bishops and one cardinal), while clergymen of all denominations preached sermons on it.[69]

The success of *The Great Sacrifice* was founded on an altogether different premise from de László's posthumous portraits. While the efficacy of the latter derived from the particular likeness, Clark's print deliberately obscured that individuality. The dead serviceman at the heart of his image was not an identifiable son or husband from a respectable family, but an unknown British Tommy with generic British features. This formulation had significant implications: it invited Clark's thousands of grieving viewers to see their own deceased relative in that one soldier's face; and at the same time to understand that he stood, synecdochically, for all of the fallen, sacrificing themselves for a cause that was bigger than any one individual. It may not have brought the dead back home quite like de László's portraits, but it certainly made their deaths more palatable. And in the end, Clark, de László and the many other artists who painted such portraits were united in one cause: they all, as one vicar observed, offered 'comfort to those who die and to those who mourn'.[70]

This section has described how the hardships of war generated public demand for portraits of the dead that artists endeavoured to supply. If it was a strikingly similar scenario to the concurrent boom in peace pictures, the two genres provided very different forms of consolation. Where peace pictures aimed to distract and delight the multitudes, posthumous portraits worked in more challenging, more private and perhaps more effective ways. It was through these images that parents, wives and siblings attempted to come to terms with their losses. Portraits not only became the focus for mourning, remembering and honouring the deceased; by enshrining their likenesses in real physical objects, they were able to make the absent present, and thus to effect some kind of resurrection.

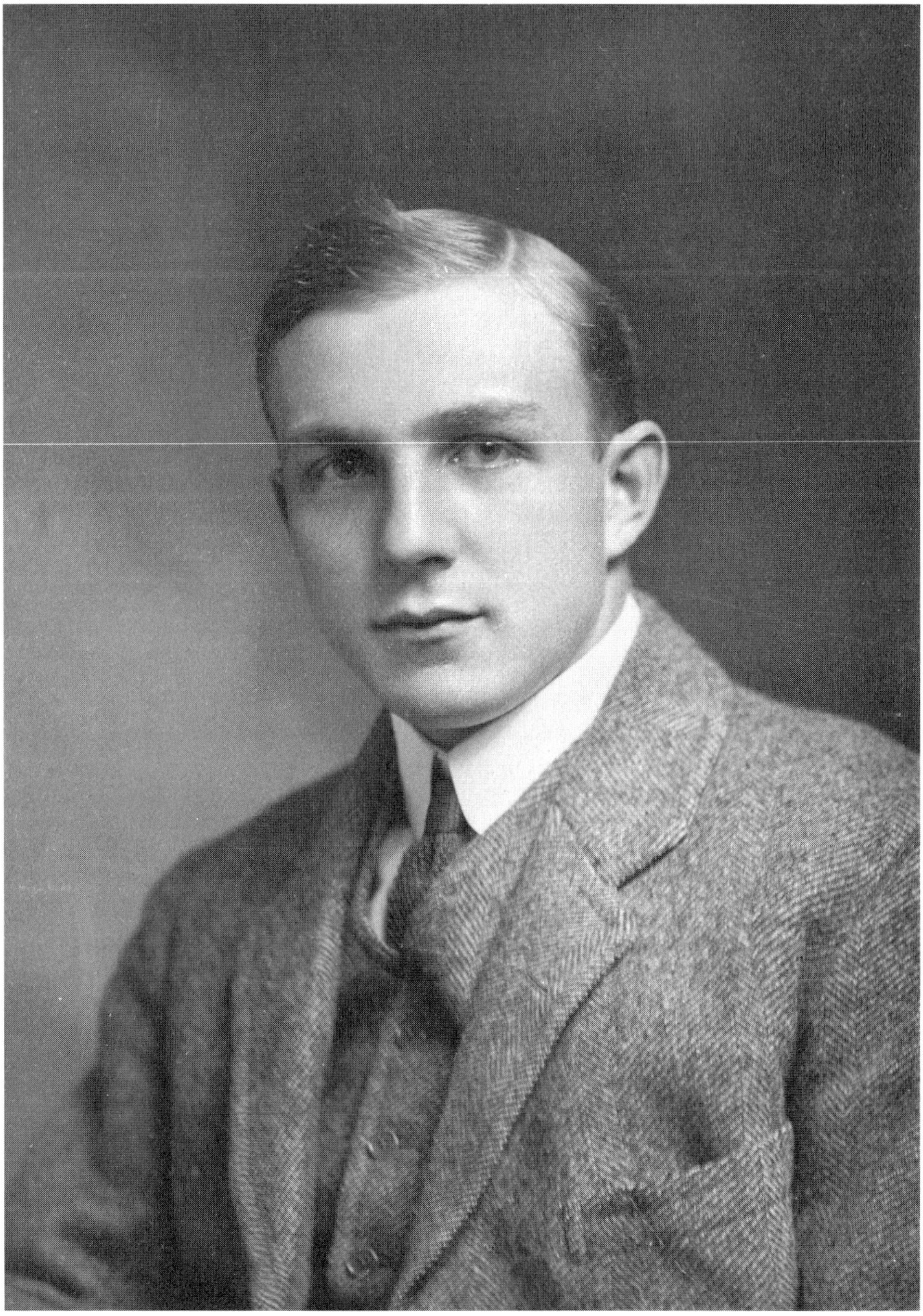

Figure 5.3 Elliott & Fry, *Robert Stafford Arthur Palmer*, 1911. Photograph, dimensions unknown. Private collection.

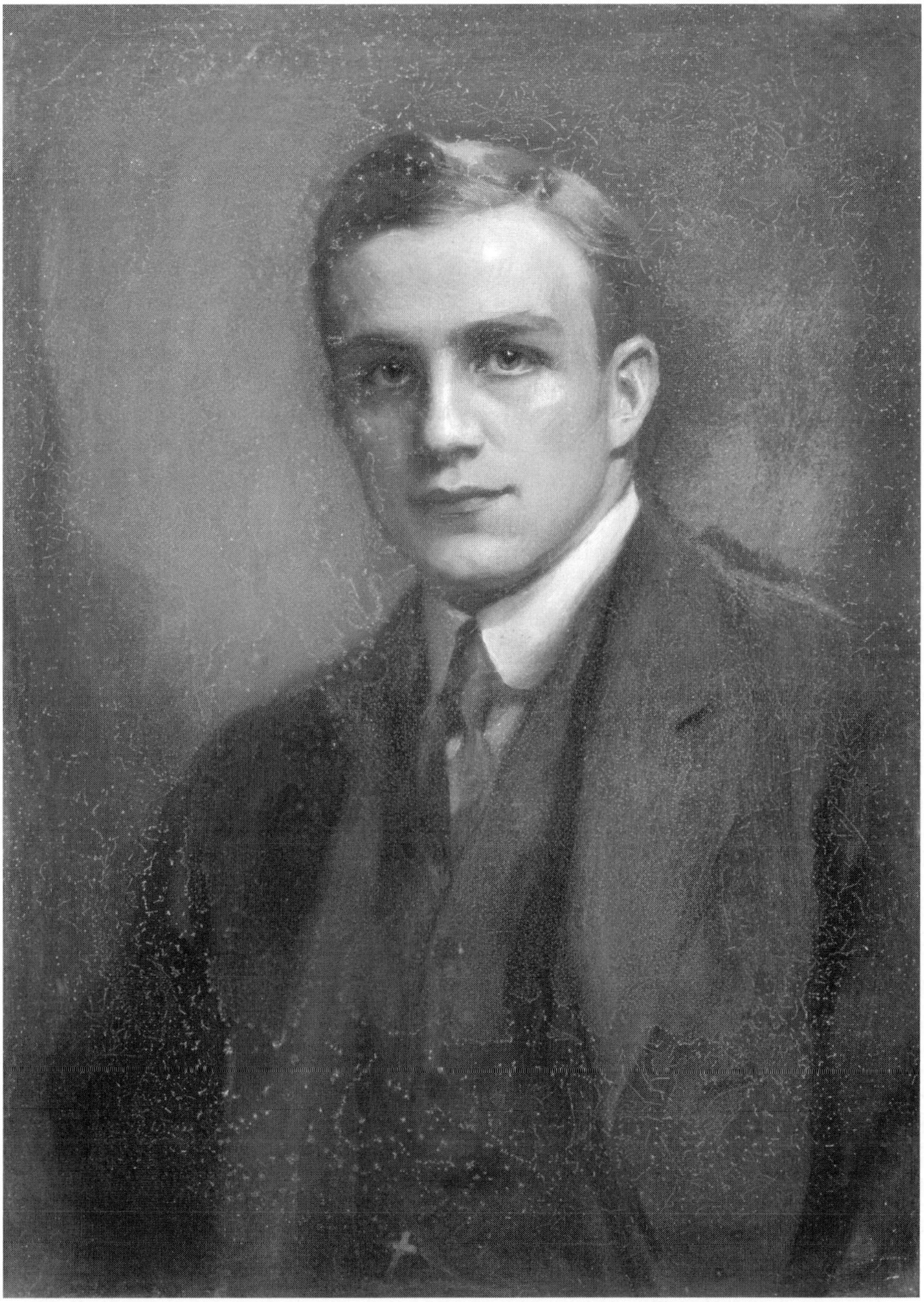

Figure 5.4 Philip de László, *Robert Stafford Arthur Palmer*, 1917. Oil on canvas, 70.5 × 50.8 cm. Private collection.

It is to this notion of resurrection that I will now turn, because many people in wartime Britain believed that art could not only comfort the war's victims; it could heal them, too.

'The mental branch of the Red Cross'

After more than a year serving in extreme danger on the front line, John Nash returned to England in 1918 to fulfill his obligations as an official war artist.[71] He acquired a studio in Buckinghamshire with his brother Paul, and there produced his celebrated war pictures *Over the Top* (Plate 7) and *Oppy Wood*. When the 'strain became too much doing nothing but war paintings', both men made a rule that every day after six o'clock they would explore the countryside and each make a 'peacetime landscape' for their own pleasure.[72] For John, the result was *The Cornfield* (Plate 8). For a period in late 1918, the picture sat next to *Over the Top* in Nash's studio, and it would seem that they were visual counterparts: midwinter is contrasted with midsummer; greys, whites and browns are juxtaposed with golds, greens and blues; and in what appears to be a cathartic act of expulsion, Nash's cornfield is cleared of those human figures who haunt and are haunted by the battlefield. Indeed, *The Cornfield*'s answer to *Over the Top*'s stumbling soldiers is a tranquil row of haystacks, swaying indifferently in the breeze. Here was a very different iteration of no man's land – one in which life defeats death, nature survives war and the human harvest is replaced by its regenerative pastoral equivalent.

The Cornfield was in some ways a conventional peace picture. After all, Benjamin Williams Leader had invoked similar harvest iconography three years earlier. But there was one crucial difference: where Leader's picture had been a straightforward retreat into the peace before the war, Nash's picture was an attempt to reconstruct the peace *after* the war. It was also an invaluable tool in Nash's own personal recovery from the battlefields: a 'thank-you' for surviving, and a means of exorcizing his traumatic memories so he could begin his life again.[73] Nash was not alone: in the second half of the war many artists tried to visualize a better future, and many of them did so by painting the reassuring cycle of the seasons. It was spring, however, with its associations of rebirth, that became the most popular subject, and Laura Knight's eponymous picture of the season (Plate 9) was perhaps its most accomplished representation. Her painting combined a dizzying array of symbols for peace, hope and renewal: under a rainbow and the passing of storm clouds, apple blossom, returning birds, newborn lambs and two of Knight's friends are brought together into a sacred union of nature and humankind.

Knight actually considered the work to possess therapeutic properties, and described it as her 'Nepenthe in a holocaust of hate that engulfed young, life and hope'.[74] Her choice of the word 'nepenthe' is revealing. Knight was referring to a medicine from ancient Greek mythology that was reputed to erase bad memories and combat despair in the minds of those afflicted with depression. By likening her own painting to such a drug, she was implying that art too could be a psychological cure. She was not the only person to make such claims: wartime discourses surrounding the function of the arts often employed explicitly remedial vocabulary. Artworks were described as 'antidotes' that could 'purge', 'purify', 'cleanse', 'soothe' and 'heal' their audiences, offering 'catharsis' to individuals who were 'heartsore', 'weary', 'shell-shocked' or whose nerves were 'a-gangle'.[75] This therapeutic interpretation of art was so widespread that it even traversed the Atlantic: in a 1918 speech the American collector Duncan Phillips declared without irony that painting was 'the mental branch of the Red Cross'.[76]

Phillips's claim was not as outlandish as it seemed. On the front line countless servicemen embraced art for its therapeutic properties. Wounded soldiers whiled away the hours with illustrated art books; prisoners of war filed requests for 'oil and water-colour painting, pastel, drawing and perspective printing' manuals; and thousands of serving officers took up sketching.[77] The Press Art School saw student numbers rise from 600 in 1913 to over 3,000 in 1916, twelve of whom were army generals. The director of the organization reported that art was a 'means of cheering, comforting and helping', and a 'positive God-send' to the men enrolled. Student letters supported his claims: a Canadian captain wrote that sketching had afforded him 'indescribable comfort', filled 'a gap which it is hard to describe' and kept him 'from going mad on several occasions'.[78] Back in Britain, 'the Muse of Painting' even came to the 'rescue' of Winston Churchill's spirits in May 1915 (and stayed with him for life) as he fought the frustration of being removed from the Admiralty.[79]

The most remarkable example of art's therapeutic capacities was the brainchild of the English artist, colour specialist and forgotten pioneer of art therapy, Howard Kemp-Prossor. As the war progressed, Kemp-Prossor became convinced that colour could prove 'beneficial to men whose nerves have become unstrung'. He offered to implement, at his own expense, an experimental scheme in any amenable ward: 'If there's anything in this theory', he wrote, 'here is a good opportunity to give it a real, practical trial.'[80] Kemp-Prossor debuted his project in 1917 at the McCaul ward for officers at St John's hospital in London. There he painted the ceiling 'firmament blue' to 'open it out', the walls yellow to simulate sunlight, and he chose violet (a 'powerful curative') for the curtains, primrose for the floor and 'spring green' for the woodwork.[81] Like Laura Knight, Kemp-Prossor deployed overwhelmingly vernal imagery: he believed that 'nerve patients do not want to be surrounded by autumn, they must be in the spring', and he even hung a painting of the season on the ward's wall.[82] The iconography, whose only extant illustration is a 1918 advertisement for oil paint (Plate 10), was not lost on observers. One nurse wrote:

> Mr. Kemp Prosser's [*sic*] wonderful idea of catching Spring in a sick room and keeping it there all the time is based on a sound physiological instinct of rare quality ... When we are ill, please surround us with Spring sunshine and its tender green and silver gleams – a canopy of Heavenly blue – and a primrose path.[83]

The scheme appears to have been effective. One newspaper reported that a patient with neurasthenia was cured of headaches by living in the purple room, that a man with hysteria recovered in the yellow room and that crime was noticeably lower on Kemp-Prossor's coloured wards.[84] Health professionals were suitably impressed. St John's hospital reported 'excellent results' and was 'fully convinced' of its efficacy,[85] and the *British Journal of Nursing* called for more like it to be implemented.[86]

For a brief period between 1917 and 1919, Kemp-Prossor's unusual work was widely known and discussed in Britain, and it even came to affect the way that artists thought about the wartime functions of their own work. Tom Mostyn, whose peace pictures were discussed at the beginning of this chapter, was particularly influenced by Kemp-Prossor's therapeutic aesthetics. In February 1919 he gave a number of his garden paintings to the nation 'for the benefit of those' who had 'become permanently injured' in the war. He stipulated that his pictures be distributed to hospitals and convalescent homes around the country so that they could, like Kemp-Prossor's colour wards, help cure the victims of the conflict.[87] Unfortunately, this was the extent of Kemp-Prossor's influence. His project failed to secure further support, and today it is one of the many curious but forgotten culs-de-sac of wartime invention.[88] Nevertheless, his belief that aesthetic experience was somehow connected to psychological recovery has been emphatically vindicated since.

In the decade after the First World War the psychoanalyst Melanie Klein (whose work went on to influence a number of art historians, including Adrian Stokes) posited that from as early as infancy, aesthetic impulses were bound to a concept called 'reparation'.[89] Typically following a regrettable, violent or destructive period of behaviour, the inherently (re)constructive nature of artistic experience had the capacity to neutralize, reverse or repair the damage that had previously been done. In recent years, Klein's ideas have been applied directly to adult individuals who have suffered acute physical or psychological trauma. In her 1985 book *The Body in Pain*, Elaine Scarry established an all but antithetical relationship between pain (which she called 'the unmaking of the world') and the creative imagination (which she called 'the making of the world').[90] In this theoretical context, Kemp-Prossor's patients were using the raw materials of art to 'remake' a world that had been 'unmade' through the traumas of war.

Nevertheless, the idea that an antithetical relationship existed between war and art had long been implicit in British aesthetic theory. Its origins dated back to the late nineteenth century, when aesthetes like Walter Pater and Oscar Wilde had insisted that 'Art' and 'Life' be discrete entities.[91] That view was most powerfully expressed only a few weeks before the outbreak of war, when Clive Bell's polemical text *Art* was published in the summer of 1914. In it Bell argued that art's value was principally derived from its 'absolute abstraction' from the world around it: 'The value of the greatest art', he wrote, 'consists not in its power of becoming a part of common existence but in its power of taking us out of it.'[92] His position would have doubtless met with approval from all wartime purveyors of cultural escapism, from music hall proprietors to peace picture producers. But Bell went further: he claimed that art could transport its participants into a 'world of aesthetic exaltation', and in the process 'leaven' and 'redeem' their lives.[93]

I have already shown in Chapter 2 how the war politicized the implications of this formulation, transforming Bell's notion of aesthetic autonomy into yet another argument against art's place in wartime Britain. Nevertheless, as the war continued and its casualties mounted, some aesthetes began to reclaim that position. The basis for their assertion was the cleavage between art and life on which Bell and his predecessors had long insisted. They argued that while most aspects of social life had been absorbed, corrupted or destroyed by the needs of total war, the purest constituents of the aesthetic realm had stubbornly ignored its existence. Thus insulated from the degrading consequences of the conflict, art and its values could emerge as an invaluable alternative to them – sustaining individuality in the face of mass opinion, spirituality in the face of materialism, beauty in the face of brutality and creation in the face of destruction.[94] These views – which prefigured Theodor Adorno's later belief in the political power of aesthetic autonomy – in turn convinced a number of thinkers that art's uncorrupted values were the only cures left for a world torn apart by war.[95]

From about 1916 – as news from the continent reached a nadir – aesthetes came to argue that art's 'reparative' capacities could inaugurate nothing less than a national renaissance. In an article called 'The Social Influence of Art' the artist, critic and Theosophist Jean Delville wrote:

> The time has come to penetrate Society with Art, with Ideal, with Beauty. Society to-day, that which has created the terrible moral chaos whence

> has proceeded the enormous and frightful war of this moment, tended too much to fall into instinct, it was saturated with materialism, with realism, with sensualism, and commercialism ... From the monstrous womb of this present war will be born a new era which will see develop a generation of men more accessible to the moral beauties of life as well as to the aesthetic ... Let us hope that, as with the heroes of Marathon and Salamine, the heroes of Liège, of the Yser, of Mons and the Marne, also will have fought for a purer social idea which will produce a generation of artists more capable of helping art in its great mission in the life of humanity.[96]

That Delville was a Theosophist is not as irrelevant as it might at first seem. The First World War energized all kinds of mystical world-views, from mainstream churchgoing to less orthodox forms of spiritualism and occultism. Jay Winter has argued that this process was part of a broader return to 'unmodern' cultural modes as men and women searched for 'languages of loss and consolation'.[97] In this search, spirituality was very often equated with the artistic imagination – both of them being romantic world-views that had been superseded or challenged by the modern materialism of war. Consequently, spiritual renewal was often taken to be interchangeable with imaginative or artistic renewal – the two operating together to repair a broken world. Such syntheses are implicit in much post-war art, the most famous example being Stanley Spencer's cycle of religious paintings in the 1920s, which culminated in an image (*Resurrection, Cookham*) that resurrected the dead and transformed his own village into an earthly paradise.

If such views were implicit in paintings, they were explicit in religious treatises. Ernest Newlandsmith's *The Temple of Life and the Mission of the Arts Therein* (1919) is particularly illuminating because it had first been published in 1911 and was then reissued with new material after the war. The most noticeable feature of the second edition was its frontispiece, which depicted a group of artists playing music to a crowd as the Lamb of God ushered in a new world. Its inscription read: 'We await the coming of the new Orphean Artists ... that the souls of thousands may be re-born in a day.'[98] Newlandsmith had established what he believed to be a powerful causal connection between religious faith, aesthetic liberation and social renewal. But the most memorable expression of that connection was *The Religion of Art*, written by the Arts and Crafts stained-glass designer Reginald Hallward in 1917. Taking Dostoevsky's maxim 'Beauty will save the World' as his credo, and repeatedly linking Art and Beauty to Truth and Faith, Hallward was convinced that man could be 'redeemed' and society 'restored' by Art.[99] In one of his final chapters, Hallward takes a morning walk and reaches the climax of his argument:

> Pitiless war-clouds, I saw them enveloping the world, and my heart crushed down, sank back within me. What if it all were but mockery and illusion? What trick had my sick brain played upon me, that I could believe in a world become so monstrous and horrible? ... We had accepted the alternative teaching of experience, and of the world, and had trod the whole length of that bitter pathway which had at last led us down to hell. Is it possible that the soul of a people may live again? And I looked, but not in vain; for I found redemption lying in the heart of the poet and the artist. In a world in which religion is dead they remain the believers![100]

Such rhapsodic writings may not seem like a practical set of instructions. Yet at precisely the same time, from the very middle of the war, practical men were beginning to put such principles into practice. In May 1915 the Design and Industries Association was established to make beauty a guiding force in the country's cultural, commercial and industrial future;[101] in 1916 a group of artists and designers (including George Clausen, John Lavery, William Rothenstein and William Lethaby) formed the Civic Arts Association to ensure that artists and craftsmen remade a post-war Britain in which war memorials, public parks and cities became 'beacons which will send from hill to hill heartening messages';[102] and in the same year the eleventh exhibition of the Arts and Crafts Exhibition Society opened at Burlington House, its catalogue promising that artists would once 'again take their place as guardians of humanity'.[103]

The extent to which these various initiatives helped Britain recover from the conflict will be discussed in the next chapter. What is important here is that they were being undertaken at all. They indicated that a previously abstract and idiosyncratic formulation – the conviction that art, imagination and beauty had something real and redemptive to offer the world – was now becoming something of a social reality. Indeed, this section has described the many ways that aesthetic experience was used to combat the traumas induced by war. Soldiers were taking up sketching at the front to diminish their anxiety; imagery was being deployed to treat shell-shocked officers in hospital; and cultural organizations were being formed to bring the reparative qualities of art to society as a whole. If at the start of the war the notion of the aesthetic had been rejected as a peacetime extravagance, now its value was being fundamentally reappraised. In the words of John Galsworthy, paraphrasing a great French sculptor: '"Beauty is useful", says Monsieur Rodin. Aye! It is useful!'[104]

* * *

This chapter has explored some of the ways that the war brought British art and the British public together. The 'hyperaesthesia' of conflict introduced vast audiences to the genre of landscape as they searched for novel forms of escapism; the hardships of estrangement and bereavement stimulated a mode of portraiture that genuinely helped families overcome their personal tragedies; and the widespread need for personal and collective recovery brought new kinds of aesthetic experience to new kinds of people. Yet this, as we have seen, was only one strand in art's developing wartime profile. The mobilization of the art world, as described in Chapter 3, and the concurrent rise in war pictures, as discussed in Chapter 4, had also contributed to its new social identity. Together, they had overturned virtually all of the initial criticisms that had initially been levelled at art. The results were remarkable. If in 1914 it was a dangerous distraction from the still nascent conflict, by 1918 it was an indispensible part of the nation's war effort.

6 ART AND SOCIETY AFTER THE WAR

At 11 a.m. on 11 November 1918 the Armistice between the Allies and Germany came into effect, and 1,560 days of conflict finally stuttered to a close. Much as in August 1914, many people felt that an entirely new world had been inaugurated. One of them was the Prime Minister. On the day after the Armistice, from his office in Downing Street, David Lloyd George declared that Britain stood on the threshold of a new era. The war had exposed the country's failings, tested its character and dismantled many of its traditions. Victory, therefore, was an invaluable 'impetus to reform' – a golden opportunity to rebuild the country better than it had been before. Lloyd George then outlined a vast housing programme, a raft of educational initiatives, reduced labour hours, a new minimum wage and a promise to bring 'light and beauty into the lives of the people'. All of this, he maintained, would be underpinned by the spirit of national unity, cooperation and self-sacrifice that had characterized British life during the war: 'If', he concluded, 'that spirit can be preserved for five years, the face of this country will be transformed.'[1]

If this was a pivotal moment for British society, it was also a pivotal moment for British art. The conflict, after all, had affected the latter as fundamentally as the former. War conditions may have initially marginalized art, but they had also created opportunities. The more ingenious members of the art world had established a new and more central place for themselves in national life, and the government as well as the public had embraced them accordingly. But now that the war was over conditions looked set to change again, and the art world was faced with a slew of pressing questions: what would happen to British artists' new, and hard-won, social position? Would art institutions take up as constructive a role in the Peace as they had done in the War? What kind of painting and sculpture would dominate the years ahead? And, perhaps most pressingly, would an exhausted and traumatized nation have any time for art at all?

This chapter seeks to answer those questions by examining the years 1919 to 1924 – the five-year period that Lloyd George believed was so crucial to

Britain's post-war recovery. Despite its social and political significance, the art of those years has traditionally been neglected, with art historians repeatedly dismissing it as a 'quiet' time of 'stagnation', 'uncertainty' and 'retreat'.[2] Indeed, in Charles Harrison's influential book *English Art and Modernism*, his chapter on the period was entitled simply 'Hiatus'.[3] In the following pages, however, I argue that those years were of profound art-historical importance. The guns may have fallen silent in November 1918, but it is only by scrutinizing the period after the Armistice that we can really ascertain the nature and extent of the war's cultural impact. Furthermore, study of these years' art reveals that the immediate post-war period was anything but an artistic hiatus. It was frenetic, productive, collaborative and socially engaged; an artistic era thoroughly commensurate with Reconstruction itself.

A new Renaissance

If there had been doubts about art's place in a world without war, the initial signs would have dispelled them. Driven by pent-up consumer demands and a high volume of liquidity, Britain's art market boomed with the rest of the economy in the immediate post-war period. Indeed, 1919 was widely considered to be the greatest year in the art market's history. In the auction rooms virtually every single record was broken, with an unprecedented 100 pictures fetching 1,400 guineas or more (the previous record of eighty-five having been set in 1913).[4] The consumer demand extended beyond the salerooms: reports suggested that living British artists were also benefiting from the post-war boom, with many receiving higher prices than they had ever commanded before.[5] Moreover, 1919 saw a 'constant succession of art exhibitions' as new dealerships sprung up around the country, intent on targeting the 'new rich'.[6] These market movements suggested that the public's appetite for images had never been more voracious. And at the end of 1919 it was confirmed that British artists were living up to their commercial success.

On 12 December 1919 – exactly one year, one month and one day after the Armistice had taken effect – a major exhibition opened at Burlington House in London. 'The Nation's War Paintings and Other Records' showcased some of the many artworks that had been commissioned, purchased or otherwise acquired by the state as a result of the war.[7] The exhibition consisted of 925 pictures and sculptures displayed across sixteen galleries, and though this represented less than a third of the 3,000 artworks owned by the newly formed Imperial War Museum, it nonetheless included virtually all of the images that have since entered the canon of twentieth-century British war art. Indeed, in just one room visitors would have seen John Singer Sargent's *Gassed*, Paul Nash's *The Menin Road*, John Nash's *Oppy Wood*, Stanley Spencer's *Travoys Arriving with the Wounded at a Dressing Station at Smol, Macedonia*, Henry Lamb's *Irish Troops in the Judean Hills Surprised by a Turkish Bombardment*, Henry Tonks's *An Advanced Dressing Station in France* and William Roberts's *A Shell Dump, France*.

The exhibition was a popular success. Indeed, it generated such intense public interest that the organizers kept it open for an extra week, from 31 January to 7 February 1920.[8] Moreover, the critical response was so rhapsodic that even the officials who commissioned the pictures were surprised.[9] The *Westminster Gazette* called the show 'a miracle'; the *Saturday Review* claimed that one had to 'go back to Italy in the 14th and 15th centuries to find painting of such communal interest'; and *The Times* declared that the ensemble offered something 'much richer, more interesting, more spiritual, than has been in English painting since the Middle Ages'.[10] Many writers even went as far as to claim that the exhibition marked the beginning of a golden age in British art. In the *Manchester Guardian*, C. J. Holmes concluded: 'It is no use blinking the facts. The present exhibition at Burlington House marks the arrival of a new artistic movement, as novel and startling as that which began some sixty years ago, when the first works by the Pre-Raphaelite Brotherhood stung a drowsy world into fury.'[11]

The lavishness of the praise was remarkable. British critics had long been in the habit of deploring the shortcomings of their nation's art, but now they were claiming that British art had been elevated 'to the highest place in the artistic hierarchy of Europe' and that it could 'hold its own against that of any other country in the world'.[12] In fact, the claims for British art were so widespread that some writers felt a salutary injection of sobriety was needed. In *The Athenaeum*, Clive Bell – whose Francophilia was admittedly legendary – concluded that everyone's heads had been 'swollen with hot air', and in an article called 'The False Dawn', another author supposed that it would not be long before British writers claimed 'that Herr Einstein is an Englishman'.[13] These voices, however, were largely ignored, because the majority of observers had reached an apparently incontestable conclusion: the cultural 'renaissance' that had been predicted back in August 1914 had finally arrived – and the war had brought it about.

What was the basis of this highly uncharacteristic self-promotion? The Nation's War Paintings appeared to anticipate several tendencies that would, according to optimists, underpin the post-war renaissance: it featured artworks that tackled subjects of great national importance, and thus suggested that modern artists were abandoning the so-called solipsistic trivialities that had occupied them before the war; its many exhibits had resulted from the greatest instance of state patronage in British history and therefore indicated that a profitable relationship between art and the state was just beginning; its admissions figures confirmed that contemporary art was reaching bigger, and more varied, audiences than it had ever reached before; and by bringing all kinds of artists – from old Academicians to young Vorticists – together in a single exhibition it suggested that a factional art world was finally ready to unite around a common cause. The remainder of this chapter will show how each of these issues indeed came to characterize the art of those years.

'A brotherhood of artists'

In the aftermath of the war British life was inflected with a mood of reconciliation. The tone had been set by Lloyd George's new consensus-driven coalition, but it filtered into all sectors of society, including, of course, the art world. At the 'Nation's War Paintings', visitors had seen the country's most radical artists share wall space with its most conservative – and in the Royal Academy of all places. The importance of such collaborations cannot be overestimated. The truce was so unlikely, and so much a result of the war, that critics could describe it only with the aid of military metaphors: the *Burlington Magazine* wrote that the Academicians, who had 'made the Hindenburg Line of the Academy their chief defence', now found 'their trenches occupied ... by their opponents';[14] the *Liverpool Post* observed that 'youth had rushed the gates and planted its standards in the very heart of the citadel';[15] and in a piece called 'Rebels in the Fortress', the *Daily Express* excitedly speculated on the scenes at varnishing day:

> 'By Jove, that chap is a perfect wonder!' said a mature painter of a minor but piercing light. 'Jiminy!' was the remark of a Cubist before the work of an A.R.A. It really was appreciation and not contempt ... Surely never before in the history of the Royal Academy were rebels like John, Wyndham Lewis and Nevinson hung in honour within the sacred provinces. The Great War and the Great Peace have assimilated strange colour schemes. Now life laughs and art laughs.[16]

The Royal Academy's inclusive approach at the Nation's War Paintings had been a long time coming. Condemned as reactionary and irrelevant, the organization had reassessed its identity during the difficult years of war. In May 1918 the architect and Academician Reginald Blomfield had submitted a confidential pamphlet to the council that argued for a complete overhaul.[17] It was only after the war that some of his proposals were put into effect.[18] In 1919 and 1920, under the presidency of Sir Aston Webb, the Academy made a raft of constitutional changes: a special committee was appointed to modernize the curriculum and character of training in its schools; more permissive figures like Charles Sims were brought in to run them; and it was controversially decided that Academicians and associates would cease to be acting members from the age of seventy-five in order to create vacancies for younger (and presumably more progressive) members.[19]

These were only the first steps. The success of the 'Nation's War Paintings' had confirmed that an important way for the Academy to renew its relevance in the post-war world was to reach out to the progressive artists who had suddenly become so popular. These inclinations were made all the more urgent by the mounting pressure to honour the many demobilized soldier-artists who had sacrificed so much more than their ageing academic counterparts. In a letter to the *Daily Telegraph*, an anonymous MP wrote:

> The original object of the foundation of the Academy was the encouragement and development of British art ... If we are to justify ourselves in the eyes of posterity, it is time the great corporate bodies in the country, whether they are trade unions, employers' federations, or a body like the Royal Academy, realised that they cannot efface the claims of the ex-Service man from their thoughts, or the knowledge of his sacrifices from their memories, without risking the creation of a great and enduring division in the ranks of the people of this country. Such a condition of affairs would do more to hinder real reconstruction than any other cause, for real reconstruction can only be achieved by a unity of effort from the whole nation. May I appeal to the council of the Royal Academy to look upon the plight of the ex-Service man, who was, and is, an artist, with a more sympathetic eye?[20]

The Academy dutifully obliged. In April 1921 it made Augustus John (who had been involved in numerous war schemes, was an honorary major in the Canadian army and also happened to be one of the most notoriously anti-establishment artists in Britain) an Associate of the Royal Academy. It was a decision that surprised almost everyone. On hearing the news, John wrote:

> Had I not been a Slade student? Was I not a member of the New English Art Club? Did I not march in the front ranks of the insurgents? The answer to these questions is 'yes'. But had I cultivated the Royal Academy in any way? Had I ever submitted a single work to the Selection Committee? ... History answers 'no'. Without even blowing my trumpet the walls of Jericho had fallen![21]

In the following year, 'Jericho' handed over what was left of its walls to John by offering him and like-minded artists an entire room in its summer exhibition. It was not quite as remarkable a decision as it seemed – the distinctly moderate exhibits that ended up there were 'isolated like lepers' in a sealed-off space – but it was unorthodox enough to draw fire from conservative critics.[22] Indeed, when Ebeneezer Wake Cook published *Retrogression in Art and the Suicide of the Royal Academy* (1924), his famously vituperative attack on modern art, he pinpointed the summer exhibition of 1922 as the moment when the 'great bulwark against the degradation of art' embarked on a path to suicide.[23] Cook's panic, though histrionic, is not difficult to understand: within a few years of the Armistice he had seen the most conservative institution in British art set about wooing the radicals.

Cook's concerns may have been intensified by knowledge that the process was being replicated throughout Britain. I have already described how the war laid the foundations for a greater public receptivity to modernism. Richard Nevinson's war pictures had been particularly successful in doing so, assuring contemporaries that moderate modernist methods were uniquely capable of recording the truth about the war.[24] It was, however, only in the post-war years that this appetite for modern art truly gripped the nation, with a surge of books, exhibitions and public policies. Yet even in the 1920s that receptivity continued to be framed by the discursive parameters of war. When Charles Marriott's *Modern Movements in Painting* (one of the first British surveys of modern art) was published in 1920, its frontispiece was not by Matisse, or Picasso, or even by Cézanne; it was Nevinson's war picture *La Mitrailleuse*. The conflict also shaped the decision to establish a National Gallery of Modern Foreign Art in London. Though plans for the institution had been afoot for some years, the political fallout of the war had only reinforced the desirability of a gallery that showcased the cultural achievements of Britain's allies: 'When we think of modern foreign art', a Tate Gallery statement announced, 'it is predominantly of the painting and sculpture of our Allies and above all the French that we are thinking.'[25]

If the war had encouraged institutions and publics to warm to modernism, it had also encouraged modern artists to warm to traditions. Earlier I argued that the most compelling reasons for this were pragmatic: traditional art was more commercially dependable than experimental art, so when faced with severe financial uncertainty normally experimental artists opted to produce for the market in order to guarantee sales. When the war ended, however, this strategy was not abandoned, but intensified. The reasons were similarly practical: the post-war art world was smaller, more integrated and more competitive than its rambling pre-war equivalent; and the 'new rich' – who had come to dominate art sales since the war – demanded more 'obvious' and 'pretty' pictures than their more educated *ante-bellum* counterparts.[26] If artists wanted to thrive, they had to make compromises.

No single artist's post-war realignment is more obvious, and better documented, than Richard Nevinson's – the man who had done more than anyone else to forge the terms on which traditional objectives and modern methods could meet.[27] In the aftermath of war, Nevinson did not return to his pre-war radicalism. On the contrary, in 1919 and 1920 he repeatedly asserted his traditionalist credentials. In a letter to the conservative magazine *The Connoisseur*, he wrote:

> My pictures are the result of continuous and constant hard work from nine to six each day, usually six days a week, but often seven, in addition to black-and-white work at night. Since the age of twelve, when John Fulleylove R.I., first grounded me and taught me the necessity of draughtmanship and technique, and with whom I first learnt a little of the glory of the old masters, I have constantly worked to overcome incompetence, worshipped at the shrine of nature, and steeped myself in the works of the past ... I hate all the freak stunting, the mad craze to do something different from anyone else, this mania for so-called individuality. I prefer to remember the Madonnas of the early Italians, or the absolute academic laws of the Chinese painters.[28]

Nevinson's testimony had been motivated by a desire to defend himself against the more reactionary elements in the press and to curry wider favour for his work in an increasingly competitive market. Nevertheless, in his emphasis on affinities over differences and old traditions over new rivalries, he was voicing a larger point about the future of British art. Indeed, in the 'Art in England' debate that ran in the *Morning Post* through January 1921, Nevinson made the remarkable suggestion that all artistic groups, movements and societies should be disbanded, and a single artists' organization be established in their place: 'Invariably', he wrote, 'English artists will realize that they have to amalgamate ... and to submerge their petty snobbery and jealousies.'[29]

If Nevinson's dream of amalgamation seemed implausible, it soon became a (somewhat modest) reality. In response to the 'Art in England' discussion to which Nevinson had contributed, Robert Tatlock at the *Burlington Magazine* mooted an unusual exhibition. The show would consist of pictures from three different 'schools' of British art: 'Academic', selected by Charles Sims of the Royal Academy; 'Intermediate', selected by Henry Tonks at the Slade; and 'Modernist', selected by the Bloomsbury critic Roger Fry. All three schools, Tatlock proposed, would then be hung together, 'with an eye solely directed to giving each picture the best possible opportunity to be advantageously seen'.[30] If this did not seem especially different from the 'Nation's War Paintings' exhibition a year earlier, Tatlock advanced one remarkable innovation: in his determination to banish the miasma of schools, movements, groupings, affiliations and names from his cultural coalition, he insisted that none of the pictures was to be labelled in any way.

The 'Nameless Exhibition', as it became known, opened at the Grosvenor Gallery (a deliberately neutral venue) on 20 May 1921. It featured work by ninety-seven artists who together represented virtually all of the tribes, tendencies and styles then thriving in British art. There were heavily abstracted efforts by Duncan Grant and David Bomberg; unorthodox figurative paintings by Walter Sickert and Stanley Spencer; and straightforward academic pictures by Oswald Birley and Sir David Murray. The exhibition was not an unqualified success: as Samuel Elmer has shown, most critics treated the enterprise as an amusing but ultimately frivolous guessing-game.[31] In retrospect, however, it confirms how much British art had changed. Before the war, Tatlock's undertaking would not have been possible: the selectors would have been unwilling to collaborate, most galleries would have been unwilling to cooperate and artists would have surely refused to exhibit anonymously, alongside their stylistic adversaries. Now, however, the British art world was prepared to put aside its 'cantankerous prejudices' and come together to celebrate the things that united it.

What is emerging here is a very different picture of the post-war *rappel à l'ordre*. This is not a story of modernism stagnating, collapsing or being altogether abandoned, but rather being adapted and incorporated into the existing art world. It is also a story in which a compromise between generations, groups, institutions and styles was negotiated, and a mutually habitable middle-ground established. This new collaborative spirit was absolutely a product of the war. And while it would be disingenuous to claim that the post-war peace was flawless, it was considerably more peaceful than the peace before the war. As one writer recollected:

> Previous to August 1914 … artists were, many of them, floundering hopelessly like owls in the light obsessed more with the jealousies of division and the propaganda of obscure groups and factions than by individual achievement … all running into blind alleys as their exponents were not expressing themselves but feasting, like cannibals, on each other; superficialities were noted and copied *ad nauseam* to the utter exclusion of all that is genuine, healthy and sane.[32]

Its author may have been exaggerating the extent of the cultural chaos before the war, but there is no doubt that British art – like British society – was riddled with fault lines in 1914, and the conflict had helped to neutralize them. The art world that emerged from the Armistice may not have been as excitingly divided as it was four years earlier, but it was arguably stronger, healthier and more sustainable. This, at least, was the conclusion drawn by William Orpen's *Outline of Art* in 1923:

> It now seems to us that [war], in a sense, was a very good thing for England's artistic future. If the war had not taken place, it is very plain that the work of disintegration of artistic creeds would have gone on, with disastrous results ... Not only did the War restore sanity to many of the most promising younger artists, it also prepared the public to accept and understand their works. Youthful artists, who in peacetime might have waited till middle age before their talent was recognised, became famous in a year or two. The wall of prejudice was broken down by the unparalleled upheaval of our normal world, so that even conservative minds were ready to consider impartially a new vision of new events.[33]

I have argued that the five-year period from 1919 to 1924 was marked by a series of new relationships within the British art world. Yet these years also changed the relationship between the art world and British society as a whole. I have previously shown that during the war years many artists and art institutions made a place for themselves at the heart of the nation's war effort. In the remainder of this chapter I will argue that artists' new-found civic consciousness not only continued into the post-war years; it was, if anything, emboldened. Between 1919 and 1924 a unique combination of conditions – relating principally to memorialization of the past and reconstruction for the future – offered artists and their representatives the opportunity to consolidate their positions at the centre of national life.

Memorials

If, after the war, any single issue could be said to have underpinned British art's renewed national importance, it was that of memorials. From the beginning of the conflict critics had discussed Britain's impending need to commemorate the fallen. Some had even predicted that it was the inevitable demand for commemorative monuments that would bring about the post-war renaissance.[34] None of these writers could ever have foreseen that the nation would ultimately need to mark the deaths of almost a million British servicemen, but they were right on one matter: as soon as the Armistice was signed, the country embarked on a vast and rambling project of memorial-making. Indeed, in the decade after the war so many memorials were constructed that, with more than 42,000 already catalogued, the National Inventory of War Memorials is still counting them.

Britain's memorials varied wildly. A number of them (typically village halls, civic facilities and scholarship funds) were ostensibly functional.[35] However, many contemporaries questioned the propriety of initiatives whose principal purpose was to serve the living rather than honour the dead.[36] For this reason, most patrons avoided commissioning 'useful' memorials, and opted instead for artworks. From as early as 1918 (if not indeed earlier), stained-glass windows, murals, figurative statues, obelisks, crosses, cenotaphs, arches, shrines and carved tablets started to be installed in Britain's cities, towns, villages, churches and civic buildings. Some of them were designed by the country's most eminent sculptors and architects; others were created by advanced young artists (many of whom had themselves served in the armed forces); and yet others were made by anonymous village artisans. The scale of the undertaking was unprecedented. Indeed, Nick Hewitt, the former coordinator of the National Inventory of War Memorials, has called it 'the largest public art project the country has ever seen'.[37]

It will come as no surprise, then, that scholars have devoted considerable attention to Britain's war memorials. Art historians have at length investigated the form, function and iconography of the finest examples of these objects, and cultural historians have examined how all of them – even those without particular aesthetic distinction – became foci for commemorative rituals and thus helped mediate memory, mourning and catharsis. Because this terrain is now so familiar, I do not intend to recount the history of memorials in exhaustive detail, and nor do I wish to plunge into the ocean of debate about art, memory and the war. I want merely to show how the patronage, production and reception of memorials helped reinforce the connection that the war had already forged between the British public and their art.

The first reason for memorials' unusually direct relationship with the public was that the public usually commissioned them. In his study of the subject, Alex King has shown that most monuments were selected by local committees that were meticulously representative of the communities they served. These committees consisted of MPs, councillors, clergymen, prominent private citizens, women of all ages, shopkeepers, trade union representatives and ex-servicemen. Moreover, committees held regular open meetings that everyone – even children – could attend. In a number of ways, then, the choice of a memorial in post-war Britain was significantly more democratic than the choice of a government. Yet the public did not just choose their memorials; they paid for them, too. The most common practice involved a voluntary subscription that was augmented by collections at cinemas, concerts, fund-raising balls and charity sporting events. As a result, virtually everyone in the community made some kind of contribution to the memorial fund, and virtually everyone, therefore, enjoyed some kind of ownership of the resulting memorial.

The public's proprietorial interest in memorials was so powerful that it even took ownership of monuments that were otherwise outside its ambit. Edwin Lutyens's Whitehall Cenotaph is a revealing, and famous, example of this process.[38] His original structure, which was made from wood and plaster, had been commissioned by the government as a centrepiece for its planned Peace Day parade in July 1919. Though initially intended as a temporary monument, it generated such intense public affection that the authorities were left with little choice but to make it permanent. A stone cenotaph was duly installed in time for Armistice Day of 1920, and, within just three days it was visited by 400,000 people.[39] Over the following months the public expressed its love of the Cenotaph in many other ways: people purchased miniature replicas of the monument (some of which stood on bases made from the wooden frame of the original) in their thousands;[40] they made pilgrimages to it from around the United Kingdom on Christmas Eve; and for many years afterwards, Londoners insisted on doffing their hats as they passed it in the street.[41]

The second way in which memorials brokered a connection between British art and the wider public was through the vast archipelago of committees, exhibitions, publications and consultations that emerged to educate the latter about the former. The first of these, the Civic Arts Association, had been established as early as 1915, with one of its principal objectives being to 'provide a consultative body on questions pertaining to memorials so that these may be worthy of their purpose'.[42] By 1922 it claimed to have given advice in hundreds of cases.[43] In 1917 the Royal Academy also formed an advisory body on memorials 'in response to requests for advice from various quarters'.[44] The committee, which included politicians, artists, architects and even two advisers from the armed forces, went public in 1918.[45] In its first year it apparently received a 'constant' stream of inquiries.[46]

The real significance of these organizations was the way by which they used war memorials to effect a nationwide educational programme in the arts. The Royal Academy was particularly proactive. It inaugurated its campaign in June 1918 with a major conference on the subject of memorials which was backed by, among others, Rudyard Kipling.[47] In the following year it coordinated two large exhibitions: the first, at the Victoria & Albert Museum, displayed great monuments from the past, including Greek gravestones, Roman urns, Celtic crosses and Plantagenet effigies; and the second, at Burlington House, selected proposals for contemporary monuments in order to show local committees 'the various forms which memorials might suitably take'.[48] At both exhibitions the Royal Academy also set up a bureau of information that offered books, photographs and even the contact details of artists and manufacturers to further aid the decision-making process.[49]

Most organizations did not possess the resources to stage major exhibitions, but all of them circulated books, pamphlets and guides in order to instruct the public on such pressing matters of taste. They informed local committees, for instance, that local stone was preferable to most other materials; that a bold Roman typeface was the most appropriate typeface; and that in all monuments, 'simplicity, scale, and proportion should be aimed at rather than profusion of detail or excessive costliness of material'.[50] At the same time, artists travelled around the country offering advice to committees, and (in its incessant coverage of memorial unveilings) the press set about explaining the history and meaning of crosses, cenotaphs, arches and obelisks. Moreover, the public was unusually receptive to these initiatives. Local committees knew that it was of great importance that they got their memorial right, and they were willing to listen to any expert advice in order to achieve it. The results of this collaboration were remarkable, for they did not only offer the art world a rare opportunity to teach a receptive public about taste; they also allowed it to 'diffuse broadcast a greater knowledge of the true intent and purposes' of art itself.[51]

The third reason for the blossoming connection between art, memorials and the public was the fact that, for almost the first time in the history of British art, such monuments were *about* the public. Most of Britain's war memorials were inscribed with the names of ordinary men; ordered not by rank or class but alphabetically – united as they were by their equality of sacrifice. When there were figurative elements, the figures depicted were not usually famous generals or leading politicians, but generic types, metonymic faces that stood, ultimately, for everyone. The logical conclusion of this idea was, of course, the Tomb of the Unknown Warrior. On 11 November 1920 an unidentified British soldier was buried in Westminster Abbey. The resulting tomb may not have been the most artistic of monuments, but it nonetheless reveals the way that the war had democratized memorials. It was not simply that an anonymous serviceman had been buried amid monarchs, aristocrats, clergymen and other eminent Britons; his very anonymity ensured that he could potentially be seen as anyone's relative. For the many bereaved men, women and children, the nation's monument had become their own monument.[52]

Today, most of Britain's war memorials are not considered to be major works of art. As a group, however, they are of great artistic importance, for they were the result of an unprecedented collaboration between British art and the British public. Indeed, it was through memorials that all sectors of the public finally participated in the artistic life of the nation. People who had traditionally been far removed from aesthetic matters now found themselves patrons as well as subjects of art. In return, artists and art institutions had actively established themselves in the heart of national, and local, life. However, a set of questions remained: outside the highly unusual business of memorialization, would this new state of affairs really translate into a world without war? Could artists' new public profile be consolidated in the 1920s? And as art had been central to Britain's rumination on the past, could it also prove integral to the country's future?

A state for the arts

At his speech after the Armistice, David Lloyd George had promised that the post-war years would bring 'light and beauty into the lives of the people'.[53] He may not have been referring directly to the arts, but the end of the war nevertheless offered the nation a rare opportunity to reconsider art's place in the world that lay ahead. This process had begun during the conflict itself: very early in the war many people came to believe that Britain's cultural sector was dangerously deficient. In March 1915 an exhibition of German and Austrian art at Goldsmiths' Hall appeared to confirm that British art education, product design and public taste were severely lagging behind their continental rivals.[54] Concerns of this sort had been voiced for many years, but there had not before been a widespread appetite for change. Now, however, officials, artists, industrialists and educationalists were so worried that Germany's cultural superiority would in turn produce commercial and military advantages that they set about trying to rectify the situation.

Some tried to diagnose the problem. In his influential 1916 book *The Ultimate Belief* the critic Arthur Clutton-Brock maintained that the war had exposed large gaps in British educations. Where Germany, he argued, derived its 'fanatical power' from the gestalt philosophy that underpinned the education of its youth, British schooling was patchy, brittle and myopically utilitarian. Its most glaring weakness was aesthetic. In Britain the arts had not only been marginalized; they had been condemned as 'an amusement too effeminate and enervating for manly English boys'.[55] In the subsequent years other critics, artists, theologians and educationalists joined Clutton-Brock in confronting the problems he had just outlined. Each tabled his or her own solution, but all were united in believing that national reconstruction had to be built in part on spiritual and aesthetic foundations.[56]

If few of these proposals were unprecedented (some had been regularly reissued from the mid nineteenth century), the novelty was that this time the government seemed to be listening. Indeed, after the Armistice the arts were considered to be so central to the nation's recovery that in 1919 the Ministry of Reconstruction published an entire pamphlet on the subject. 'Art and Industry' argued that the rebuilding of post-war Britain was an invaluable opportunity to rethink the position and function of the arts. This was not just a matter of cultural improvement; Britain had to ensure that it did not fall further behind Germany lest it lose the peacetime battle for export markets. The pamphlet's authors claimed that if their ideas were followed, British businesses would thrive and the 'great Renaissance' that so many critics had predicted would finally become a reality. First, however, a fundamental change of attitude was required:

> The great fact awaiting recognition is that art is indispensible in life, and therefore in education and in work. Art has become limited in meaning. It is generally understood to be a thing apart, the product of picture painters and craftsmen and similarly gifted and lucky persons. It is spelt with a big A. It is a decorative and purchasable luxury, to be hung up, stood about, and applied to things. It is 'applied' or 'fine' (two of the most ignorant and misleading terms ever invented) according as it is useful or not; but it concerns the people only so far as they can afford to buy some of it as a demonstration of the possession of taste – or money. We must work for the restoration of the broader meaning of art, for the reunion of the many subdivisions of Art into art – one and indivisible in its association with life and work. It must be recognised as a necessity to give us a truer appreciation and use of our country and ourselves.[57]

The Ministry of Reconstruction agreed with Clutton-Brock that the only way to effect this change was through education. In the autumn of 1919 its Adult Education Committee published an influential manifesto, written by the distinguished scholar R. H. Tawney. His '1919 Report' (as it was subsequently known) condemned the utilitarian approach hitherto favoured in British education, and argued for a new system that devoted more time to aesthetic and spiritual matters:

> A people which reserves its religion for Sundays is not religious, and it is not education if, while it multiplies schools, it takes pleasure in filling its evenings with bad plays, its houses with shoddy furniture, and its towns with municipal statuary. A conception of education which limits it to the training of intellect without seeking to humanise all social activities will lay no spell upon ordinary men.[58]

Tawney concluded that the arts were an integral component of this new model, and he hoped that educational reform would produce a genuinely popular culture that 'sprang from the soil and drew its inspiration from popular life'.[59] If his were not particularly original observations, they nonetheless confirmed that the authorities had finally absorbed some of the implications of non-governmental proposals, and were seriously thinking about the role of the arts in the broader task of reconstruction.

The government's increasingly sympathetic attitude towards the arts was largely due to the Minister of Education, Herbert Fisher. Fisher had been appointed to the role in 1916. As soon as he took office he pushed for the expansion of art education and for increased funding to institutions that provided it. His predilection for an inclusive model of the arts was first publicly revealed in 1917, when he helped William Rothenstein (a founder member of the Civic Arts Association) take up the newly founded chair of 'Civic Art' at the University of Sheffield. It was confirmed three years later when he made Rothenstein Principal of the Royal College of Art in London.[60] In the meantime, Fisher was trying to implement the wider initiatives outlined in his now famous 1918 Education Act. The legislation – which raised the school leaving age from twelve to fourteen, created a network of continuation schools for older children and abolished all fees in state elementary schools – also acknowledged the important educational work that museums had undertaken during the war, making it possible for them to play a future role in local schemes for educational development.[61]

Unfortunately, the transformative mood of the immediate post-war period soon evaporated. As the boom of 1919 degenerated into an economic slump that extended through the 1920s, most of Fisher's expensive proposals were curtailed, postponed or abandoned.[62] The dream of a new era of education, forged on the exciting uncertainty of the times, had been undermined by the very uncertainty that had produced it. But that dream still counted for something. The ideas of Clutton-Brock and his peers had been so ubiquitous in the years after 1916 that educational institutions could not fail to be influenced by them. Indeed, they came to inform even the most modest of policies. Here is one example: in the early 1920s numerous local authorities appointed committees to select, reproduce and distribute suitable artworks to schools so that they could be hung in classrooms in order to stimulate the aesthetic sensibilities of the young.[63] It was by no means a major reform, but it nonetheless reflected an increasing awareness of art's educational importance.

If the planned revolution in art education had ended up as a series of modest and superficial alterations, one major initiative did emerge from the war. In 1919 the government rolled out a series of grants for ex-servicemen whose educations (and indeed life plans) had been disrupted by the conflict. The bursaries enabled men to train for 'individual and commercial appointments, for the teaching professions and the ministry of religion, and for work in the field of art, medicine and law' so that they could re-establish themselves in the next stage of their lives.[64] The system was a success. In the first round of applications, some 26,500 ex-servicemen enrolled, and in the subsequent five years its beneficiaries numbered in excess of 100,000 – causing the country's universities, colleges and technical institutes to be temporarily 'filled to overflowing'.[65] The Board of Education estimated that a quarter of the recipients would not have considered taking up such training had it not been for the scheme.

The wider artistic consequences of ex-servicemen's grants remain a matter of speculation. However, the story surrounding one of their beneficiaries suggests that in the right hands they had the potential to be very significant indeed. In 1919 a young soldier, who had previously spent two months in hospital following a gas attack in Cambrai, applied for a grant to train as an artist. He had long harboured an interest in art, but as a Yorkshire miner's son had not been able to pursue it as a career. In September 1919, however, he received government funding to enrol in the Leeds School of Art, where an entire sculpture department was established solely for him. In 1921 he won a further scholarship to the Royal College of Art in London, where he received the loyal support of William Rothenstein. The young man was Henry Moore, and he would go on to become one of the most distinguished British artists of the century.

Henry Moore might never have become an artist had it not been for the unusual educational opportunities that had been created by the war. There were doubtless others like him about which the same could be said. And though the great ambitions of Clutton-Brock and the Ministry of Reconstruction perished in the economic decline of the 1920s, those ambitions had been enough in themselves to destabilize the status quo. The war had necessitated discussions about reconstruction, and reconstruction had necessitated discussions about all aspects of national life. As a result, the role of the arts in correcting and improving the nation was debated with a vigour and an urgency that had not been seen since the 1850s. And if between 1919 and 1924 central government had been incapable of turning these debates into realities, then another sector of society stepped forward to do so on its behalf.

Arts organizations

It is one of the many paradoxes of the First World War that though the conflict subjected cultural organizations to extreme, and often unendurable, pressures, it also convinced individuals of the virtues of collective action. As a consequence, the immediate aftermath of the war saw a proliferation of associations, societies, leagues and institutions devoted to the arts.[66] These groups represented virtually every aspect of cultural life: the British Music Society was established in 1918 to promote the appreciation of native classical music; the League of Arts for National and Civic Ceremony was created in 1919 to bring singing to 'the masses of the people';[67] in the same year, the British Drama League appeared, determined to unite the classes by encouraging the public to stage and perform their own plays;[68] and in 1922 the Faculty of Arts was formed with the intention of using conferences and exhibitions to 'irradiate the lives of the people' with art.[69] Despite their variety, nearly all of them shared two chief characteristics: they were consciously conceived as part of the larger project of reconstruction; and they were motivated by that persistent post-war desire to bring art to the people and the people to art.

The most influential of these post-war organizations – though one that has been virtually forgotten since the 1920s – was the Arts League of Service. Formed in May 1919 under the presidency of Lord Henry Cavendish-Bentinck, it reflected – perhaps more than any other group – the post-war determination to forge a permanent bond between British artists and the public. A few days after its foundation, Paul Nash wrote an article in praise of this ambition. Its pertinence is such that it is quoted at length:

> The time [has] come when artist and public should better understand one another. The public should realize the artist is not merely an idle, eccentric creature practically dependent upon the patronage of the rich, but an intelligent man fighting for his living like the rest of us, only under rather more adverse and unstable conditions. And the artist in his turn must grasp the fact that if the public does appear a fool to him, it is not wholly the public's fault, but rather the misfortune of its education and its lack of opportunity to appreciate what he, the artist, stands for. Up to now the artist and the public have had the same grievance about one another; the artist has accused the public of indifference to his work; and justly so, while the public has retorted to accusing the artist of indifference to its opinion, and not always so justly. This leads nowhere ... But times are changing ... people ... are beginning to think. It is proposed to bring the Arts into everyday life. 'Extravagant suggestion!' some will say. 'What will these Socialists do next? The country is going to the dogs! Muzzles! Bolshevism!' But it is unnecessary to be alarmed, the suggestion emanates from an apparently sound and serious movement, the roots of which, I hope, already grip the soil and strike down and whose growth is already evident. I refer to the Arts League of Service.[70]

Paul Nash's faith that the Arts League of Service could finally eradicate decades of mutual mistrust between artists and the public was not without foundation. After all, the organization's very nomenclature suggested as much, for the word 'service' referred to two reciprocal duties: the artist's duty to the public and the public's duty to the artist. The group's principal objective was to 'awaken public opinion to the importance of the Arts', to 'bring Art within the reach of all' and to eventually arouse a 'spirit of responsibility and civic pride in the culture of the nation'.[71] Like Clutton-Brock and the Ministry of Reconstruction, it envisioned a 'comprehensive and effective education programme' in order to achieve this.[72] Yet there was one telling difference: where the former had repeatedly struggled to put their ambitions into practice, the Arts League of Service did so without hesitation.

Within weeks of its foundation, the Arts League of Service unveiled a wide-ranging programme of events. At its core were regular talks that were aimed at as wide an audience as possible, with titles like 'How to Judge a Work of Art'. In the autumn of 1919 these talks were complemented by a series of high-profile lectures on 'Modern Tendencies in Art', in which T. S. Eliot discussed poetry, Eugene Goossens spoke about music, Margaret Morris reflected on dancing and Wyndham Lewis delivered a rambling lecture on modern painting.[73] In November the Arts League of Service staged its first major exhibition, at the XXI Gallery in London. Focusing on decorative art of an 'experimental nature', the show displayed work by major progressive figures like the one-time Vorticist Edward Wadsworth, the official war artist Paul Nash and the avant-garde designer Edward McKnight Kauffer. The choice of exhibitors and lecturers suggests that the Arts League of Service was not just trying to build bridges between the British people and art; it was trying to build bridges between the British people and *modern* art.

In the first half of the 1920s the Arts League of Service expanded its public outreach plans. It continued to stage art exhibitions; it created a small lending library of art books; it assembled portfolios of drawings and watercolours by modern artists that were distributed to buyers, schools and institutes for exhibition and purchase; and it set up a 'Service Bureau' that provided advice and assistance to writers and artists. More significantly, it extended its activities into the provinces: the introductory lectures that had originally been held in London were now given around the country; small exhibitions travelled as far as Edinburgh; and perhaps most successfully, a company of players was set up that toured the towns and villages of England performing amateur plays. These productions were great successes: excessively large crowds were repeatedly turned away from performances, and those that did attend wrote wildly appreciative letters to the organization. The *Manchester Guardian* was not exaggerating when it wrote: 'If the Arts League of Service does no more than keep this delightful group journeying around the counties of England, it cannot fail to make converts all the way.'[74]

The Arts League of Service's remarkable success was first confirmed two years after its foundation. In March 1921 the organization convened a major conference in Nottingham. It invited a range of other societies (including the British Drama League, the Nottingham Shakespeare Society, the Little Theatre Movement, the English Folk-Dance Society and the educational wing of the YMCA), and in doing so confirmed its place at the very centre of Britain's archipelago of post-war arts associations. However, its ambitions did not stop there.

The Arts League of Service also invited trade unions to its conference, and the Nottingham Trade Council, the Nottingham Postal Workers and the National Union of Railwaymen all duly sent speakers to the event.[75] At the end of the event, these groups unanimously passed the following resolution: 'This conference, realizing the need of art in everyday life and the urgent necessity for raising the standard of entertainments, pledges itself to exert every effort to bring the creative work of artists – in all the arts – into direct touch with the people in the various centres throughout the country.'[76] The resolution was only a speculative statement of intent, but it was remarkable for the collaboration that had produced it. After all, the Nottingham conference had united artists, performers, authors and arts administrators with postmen, railwaymen, miners and factory-workers; and together, all of these groups had agreed on the enduring importance of art. The Arts League of Service claimed that it had made the 'first definite move on the part of any society to come into direct touch with organised labour'.[77]

This section has shown how the collectivizing instincts of conflict, the need for reconstruction in its aftermath and the unstable financial conditions that characterized the post-war period together created unusually fertile terrain for the emergence of artists' groups. Many of these associations went on to achieve what the government was failing to do: to create the social conditions in which art and the people could regularly and productively meet. Nevertheless, their promising work would only be fully realized if the existing art world came to share their ambitions and was prepared to adjust its output accordingly. The final section of this chapter argues that this was very much the case. Although art historians have repeatedly claimed that post-war art was dominated by a mood of retreat and insularity, the evidence here indicates that between 1919 and 1924 artists, art institutions, art publishers and art dealers consciously set about producing an art for the people.

Art for the people

In many – but not all – ways, the First World War temporarily diminished class distinctions. On the front line, different social groups were forced to work, live and die together in often very cramped spaces, while on the home front civilians were expected to put aside their differences and concentrate on the things that united them. As Wilfred Trotter had argued in *Instincts of the Herd in Peace and War*, the subsequent 'establishment of homogeneity' was not only a by-product of the nation's war effort; it was a crucial component of its success.[78] Nevertheless, the early chapters of this book have shown how these 'herd instincts' were themselves divisive and served to undermine people (particularly artists) whose professional identities typically depended on singularity. Some artists, however, found this change to be salutary. The most famous of them was the French Cubist, Fernand Léger: 'I came out of a milieu of intellectuals', Léger wrote, but in the army 'I found myself on an equal footing with the whole French people.'[79]

British artists had similar experiences, and Wyndham Lewis – who proudly confessed that he was a 'masterpiece of conformity' during the war – realigned his artistic philosophy accordingly.[80] Before the conflict, Lewis could barely disguise his contempt for the British public: in *Blast* he had declared that his Vorticist movement had 'nothing to do with "The People"', maintaining that 'the Man in the Street and Gentleman [were] equally ignored'.[81] After the conflict he reversed this stance. In his 1919 book *The Caliph's Design* he repeatedly referred to releasing art into the 'general life of the community';[82] in his post-war journal *The Tyro* (1921–2) he made a concerted effort to explain his plans 'to the usual public';[83] and when in 1920 he formed the short-lived post-war movement Group X, he hoped its work could become widely accessible and even established a shop from which artworks could be sold, and through which the poster, film and other popular industries could be approached.[84]

Lewis's *volte-face* is often seen as emblematic of the failure of the British avant-garde. In reality, it was part of a broader attempt by all sectors of the art world to become more accessible. Indeed, at the same time even the Royal Academy was reinventing itself along popularist lines. In May 1920, after a speech given by Prince Albert at its annual banquet, the institution's president Sir Aston Webb initiated a nationwide competition to design a singularly vernacular work of art: the village sign.[85] The competition – which was open to all artists, professional and amateur alike – was to be promoted by the *Daily Mail* and judged by a panel of distinguished Academicians. By October, 617 designs had been submitted, and 250 of them went on display first at Australia House, then Selfridge's department store and finally the Royal Automobile Club. The competition – which was won by P. G. Matthews for a sign for St Peter's, Thanet – was a popular success.[86] Yet more importantly, it embodied the new cultural spirit of the 1920s: one in which artists, art institutions, the popular press and commercial outlets collaborated to promote, produce and disseminate an unmistakably civic brand of art.

This democratizing process was particularly apparent in the art market. From 1919 the highbrow hold of Bond Street was challenged in a number of ways: new galleries (such as the Hampstead Art Gallery on Finchley Road) opened in cheaper neighbourhoods, while established businesses (like the Redfern Gallery) started to exhibit the work of lesser-known artists at considerably lower prices.[87]

The most remarkable change, however, took place almost entirely outside the art world. In the second half of 1919 original pictures started to appear in drapers', milliners' and department stores. In fact, Heal & Son in Tottenham Court Road and Derry & Toms in Kensington had both decided to showcase the work of young, and often advanced, British artists in their furniture shops.[88] The purists may have been concerned that aesthetic experience was becoming overly commercialized, but the social benefits were significant: after all, there were many members of the public who might never have dared to step inside a Bond Street gallery, but could now see contemporary art in shops they regularly visited.

The ambition of making art more accessible to the wider public was similarly evident in the publishing world. In the early 1920s a number of books appeared that sought to introduce and explain art to a non-specialist audience.[89] The most notable of these initiatives was Hodder & Stoughton's 'The New Culture Library', which slotted neatly into the wider mood of self-improvement, educational reform and national reconstruction. The series was designed to appeal to most sectors of the public, although it was aimed specifically at 'those young people of both sexes who, as developing individuals, lost periods up to five years in the paramount service to their country and humanity during the Great War'.[90] Its initial run, in 1922, consisted of three conveniently sized and unpretentiously typeset volumes on 'Art', 'Practical Collecting' and 'Citizenship'. Together, they represented a brief and informal curriculum for post-war Britons, and offered further proof of the role that art would play in their everyday lives.

The most direct way by which post-war art entered the everyday lives of the people was through posters. The war had transformed British attitudes towards the medium: between 1914 and 1918, posters had been produced in their millions, had helped mould public opinion and had even begun to be appreciated as artworks in their own right.[91] Their new status had been recognized when they were finally admitted to the Arts and Crafts Exhibition in 1916. After the war, however, their reputation was if anything enhanced. In the 1920s posters were even discussed at the Royal Academy, where increasing numbers of Academicians were being employed to design commercial images. At the institution's annual banquet of 1923, the Prince of Wales made a well-received plea for what he called 'the Art of the Hoardings':

> Not so very long ago those dreary barricades of notices that marred the walls and waste places of our big cities were merely unsightly, and contained no pictorial art whatever. They might now be called, without exaggeration, the art galleries of the great public (Cheers) ... Many a man who has never given pictures a thought has had his interest in them stimulated by a casual study of the poster (Cheers) ... May I, with all

> deference, suggest to you that here is one possible channel for reaching and satisfying the elemental love of pictorial art which is hidden in the heart of practically every one? (Cheers).[92]

As the repeated cheers suggested, Prince Albert's request did not fall on deaf ears. In the aftermath of his speech a number of railway firms hired artists (including seventeen Academicians) to design posters for a large publicity initiative.[93] They were admittedly not the first to do so – Frank Pick of the London Underground had commissioned Frank Brangwyn, Charles Sims and others to design such posters during the war – but they nonetheless helped to usher in an era in which collaborations between established artists and advertisers became commonplace. As Michael Saler has shown, such collaborations were not just a pragmatic response to the economic crises of the interwar years; they were also part of a wider 'redefinition of art as design' that served to break down many of the remaining barriers between art, industry and the people.[94]

If in the post-war years many traditional British artists were turning to commercial art, the most popular image of the period was surprisingly radical. The young American-born artist Edward McKnight Kauffer had first shown *Flight* at the Arts and Crafts Exhibition in 1916 at Burlington House (Plate 11). Inspired by the geometrical abstractions of Vorticism, his design represented a flock of birds that, in its mesh of angular forms, better resembled the aircraft that had become such a feature of the war. In January 1917, the image was published in *Colour* magazine's 'Poster Gallery' and was subsequently purchased by the publisher Francis Meynell. In March 1919, Meynell used *Flight* to publicize the relaunch of the *Daily Herald*. The left-wing newspaper hoped to 'voice the aspirations of Labour' and to 'work unceasingly for a revolution, peaceful but complete'.[95] Meynell chose *Flight* (which he renamed 'Soaring to Success') because its depiction of a modern community ascending collectively into a radiant future seemed to correspond felicitously with his newspaper's political ambitions. His decision evidently worked: the *Daily Herald*'s advertising campaign was a success and helped establish McKnight Kauffer as a major figure in British art and design.

In some ways, *Flight* encapsulates all the major tendencies of post-war British art. It represented a new, accessible and commercial iteration of modernism: for though it was inspired by the uncompromising visual vocabulary of Vorticism, it had been stripped of that movement's divisive ideologies. It was instead an unashamedly inclusive form of art: one that sought out the many rather than the few, that bridged the gap between fine art and popular culture and that was at home both in Burlington House and on an average city street. But the most revealing feature of *Flight* was that it, more than any other image, captured the wider spirit of optimism that dominated this period of reconstruction: for while its mechanized forms were undoubtedly scarred by the memory of war, they had been transfigured into harbingers of the better world that could be forged in its aftermath.

***

In April 1924, more than five years after the war had ended and almost ten years after it had started, King George V opened a major event that sought to articulate Britain's sense of itself in the new world. The British Empire Exhibition embraced industry, engineering, commerce and sport, but one of its centrepieces was undoubtedly the Palace of Arts. The Palace itself was proof of the integral place that art had secured for itself in post-war Britain, and the display inside it revealed how much the country's attitudes had changed since 1914. Its most obvious characteristic was unity. The exhibition not only brought together Academicians and modernists; it united Old Masters like Gainsborough, Reynolds and Turner with young contemporary artists like the Nash brothers and Augustus John – confirmation, surely, that the war and its aftermath had helped integrate the new generation into a longer history of British art.[96] Moreover, these paintings and sculptures were displayed with parity alongside the applied arts, decorative interiors and, just outside the Palace, an avenue lined with hundreds of artist-designed posters.[97]

The British Empire Exhibition had, it seemed, fulfilled the dream expressed by the Ministry of Reconstruction in 1919: to reunite 'the many subdivisions of Art into art' and to heal the counterproductive rivalries that had flourished before 1914.[98] Yet it had done more than that. The exhibition was visited by some 17.5 million people – a not insignificant proportion of the British population; it distributed 550,000 of its posters around the country; and it made the visual arts a central component of an event that also included sporting fixtures and popular spectacles. In doing so, it enabled the whole spectrum of British art to reach the whole spectrum of the British public in inclusive and demotic ways, and thus to consolidate the social gains that the arts had made since the outbreak of war ten years earlier.

This chapter has examined the five and a half years between the signing of the Armistice and the opening of the British Empire Exhibition. It was a pivotal period in British history, as the nation made the difficult transition from war into peace, but it was also a pivotal period for British art. Between 1919 and 1924, the art world's previously warring factions reached an armistice of their own and together exploited the unusual conditions to secure a place for themselves in public life. As the government reconsidered the social possibilities of the arts in a reconstructed Britain, artists collaborated with countless local communities around the country to create fitting memorials to the dead. At the same time, organizations proliferated to promote the wider importance of the arts, while an increasingly frequent breakdown of the barriers between fine art and design made serious pictorial art more democratic than it had been before. These were remarkable developments, and they confirmed that, though the war was over, British art had by no means returned to the patterns of 1914; it had forged a new civic identity that would shape the nation's cultural life for the next two decades.

CONCLUSION

In his autobiography of 1965, the influential British arts administrator John Rothenstein – who had only the previous year retired from the Tate Gallery, where he had been director since 1938 – confessed that the First World War had made 'curiously little impact' on his life. Rothenstein had good reasons for making such a claim: he was only thirteen years old at the outbreak of war; he had not fought on the front line; and even the awful events he did recall had, he admitted, taken on a 'hideous normality' at the time.[1] Nevertheless, despite his almost complete absence of firsthand experience, Rothenstein's visual recollection of the conflict was extraordinarily vivid. He described his mental image of the western front as 'a long wide swathe of pestiferous mud, blasted tree-stumps and barbed wire, lit up at night by Verey lights and starshells'. And he added: 'Even for those of us who never saw it it was as familiar as our own back yards; it remains in my own memory more indelibly than any scene of bomb devastation inflicted on London during the Second World War, of which I was a continuous witness.'[2]

Rothenstein's passage is extremely revealing, for it gives some indication of the First World War's enduring visual resonance. Rothenstein, after all, was not remembering the conflict as a historical event, or a personal narrative or even as a human tragedy; he was remembering it as an *image*. Perhaps this was the natural expression of a man who had lived through a century in which visuality had become such a dominant cultural paradigm; or perhaps it betrayed the fact that, as Jay Winter has claimed, 'in wartime, images overwhelm words'.[3] Yet if these explanations are indeed the case, why would Rothenstein not have had a similarly vivid visual recollection of the Second World War, of which he had extensive experience? The reason, I suspect, is art. Britain's artists, after all, arguably played a more decisive role in the representation of the 1914–18 war than in any conflict before or since, producing a formidable set of images that were 'barely escapable' during the conflict and increasingly influential in its aftermath.[4]

The evidence for this argument is contained in the image that Rothenstein himself had recalled: 'A long wide swathe of pestiferous mud ... blasted tree-stumps and barbed wire ... Verey lights and starshells'. It is surely no coincidence that these forms also happen to be some of the distinguishing features of Britain's most famous war paintings. The mud dominates Nevinson's *The Road from Arras to Bapaume* and *The Harvest of Battle*; the broken trees and exploding starshells are immortalized in Paul Nash's *We Are Making a New World* and *The Ypres Salient at Night*; and barbed wire appears in so many British pictures of the western front that it sometimes seems difficult to find examples without it. Moreover, it is perhaps even tempting to think that by referring to the entire scene as a 'long wide swathe', Rothenstein had unconsciously been inspired by the broad landscape formats that were characteristic of so many official war pictures.[5] In short, it appears that when Rothenstein summoned up that mental image of war he was not visualizing the conflict itself; he was visualizing the artworks that represented the conflict.

Rothenstein was not alone. In the decades after the Armistice, Britain's paintings of war entrenched themselves in the country's collective imagination in much the same way as did the poems of Wilfred Owen and Rupert Brooke. They were exhibited many times and in many different places; they were reproduced in books and newspapers, on posters and postcards; they inspired novelists, playwrights and film directors; and in the process they became some of the most widely recognizable images in the history of British art.[6] As a result, those images – which were initially celebrated for rebutting the lies and myths about the war with their own 'bitter truth' – have themselves become myths.[7] Their constituent parts – the mud, the broken trees, the barbed wire, the blinding searchlights – have lost their connection to their specific historical contexts and have instead become wider symbols for the disasters of war.[8]

This is not only proof of what David Freedberg has famously called 'the power of images'; it is also evidence of the degree to which the fates of art, war and society became intertwined after 1914.[9] If total war had once conquered all sectors of British life and commandeered the arts to assist in its self-representation, now, as the conflict itself has receded into history, all that is left are its representations. Moreover, the countless paintings, poems, monuments, myths and rituals that resulted from the war, are, if anything, more resonant today than they were a century ago.[10] In the process, they have become integral to the meaning of the conflict that produced them: they have not only helped individuals, like Rothenstein, visualize events that cannot otherwise be remembered; they have shaped collective attitudes towards those events. In short, art's role in the social reception of the First World War has become so fundamental that the conflict might even be unimaginable without it.

Things had been so very different back in 1914. Before the war the British art world may have been large, but it had by no means been socially influential. This was partly because its members had possessed very few opportunities to forge a genuinely public profile, and partly because they were not particularly interested in doing so. Lacking official support and popular approval, the art world remained self-contained if not self-interested: its leading dealers catered only to the wealthiest members of society; its exhibiting societies attracted small and rarefied audiences; and its ageing Academicians continued to paint mythological subjects that had little to do with the realities of their time. Moreover, the emergence of modern cultural tendencies in the decades before the conflict had widened rather than narrowed this gulf. By 1914 the country's two most radical factions – the Bloomsbury Group and the Vorticists – possessed a barely disguised contempt for the social world from which they were trying to escape.

If some believed this policy of mutual disregard would survive the conflict, they were quickly proved wrong. As total war tightened its grip on all aspects of national life the discrete sphere that art had previously inhabited began to dissolve. With the country's mental and material resources not only limited but increasingly dominated by the conflict, the art world could no longer sustain itself independently and was instead forced to compete with the war effort for the same social terrain. This process was most apparent in the many debates about whether men should be artists or soldiers; whether museums should remain open or be occupied by war workers; whether the country's money should be spent on luxuries or saved for the nation; and whether the public's attention should be focused on aesthetic pleasure or national survival. In each case, art was understood as an adversary of the war effort and, by extension, of British society as a whole.

Nevertheless, this book has shown that despite those initial disruptions, the new conditions ultimately brought the art world into a more symbiotic union with national life than it had perhaps ever experienced before. Motivated in part by patriotism and in part by self-preservation, its members attempted to prove that they did indeed have significant social value. Art dealers exploited public interest in the conflict by staging topical or patriotic exhibitions whose profits were often devoted to war charities; artists' organizations were 'shaken out of the smug complacency' of the pre-war years and started to reform themselves along more democratic and socially responsible lines;[11] and museums gave up being refuges of 'cloistered learning' and endeavoured to become centres of 'energising force ... responsive to the pressing call of our country's danger'.[12] They staged public information displays, propagandistic exhibits and multimedia events – many of which attracted unprecedentedly large audiences.

Artists did not shirk from the wider cultural mobilization. The victims of extremely vicious criticisms throughout the conflict, they wished to prove that they too could contribute to the war effort. Many ceased to make images that appealed only to rarefied audiences and instead designed recruitment and National Savings posters that were printed in their millions and distributed around the country. Hundreds if not thousands of artists joined the armed forces and ended up fighting with the rest of the community. A number of these men deployed their artistic skills for explicitly military purposes: some made reconnaissance drawings that helped locate the positions of enemy troops and guns, while others worked in camouflage units that played a decisive role in the outcome of the conflict. Taken together, these were remarkable cultural developments and they were not lost on contemporaries. In 1918 one critic wrote that 'never since the Middle Ages, when the church taught its lessons by means of pictures … has art been called upon to serve in so many ways'.[13]

Before the war, one of the most enduring impediments to the art world's social aspirations had been apathy: the public, along with their government, was notoriously uninterested in visual art. This book, however, has argued that the conflict caused that long-running indifference not only to dissipate but to be replaced with something approaching enthusiasm. For one thing, the war's economic consequences introduced new audiences to art. Industrialists who had become wealthy from lucrative war contracts sought to confirm their new status (and to make secure investments in an otherwise unstable financial climate) by purchasing illustrious British paintings at high prices.[14] At the same time, the many workers who had benefited from full employment and increased wages began to spend some of their disposable income on modest artworks like watercolours, engravings and cheap prints. The purchases may have been very different but in both cases an entirely new demographic was developing a taste for art.

These social changes were augmented by a widespread wartime psychology that made rich and poor, soldiers and civilians, men and women unusually receptive to the appeal of images. On the one hand, the conflict created an insatiable curiosity which led the public to crave paintings and drawings (as well as films and photographs) that offered them an insight into the realities of the front line. On the other hand, it produced disorientation, distress and despair, for which other kinds of artworks became an invaluable cure. Disconsolate civilians hankered after pastoral landscapes in pursuit of nostalgic escapism; posthumous portraiture became a 'miracle of consolation' to many families who had lost loved ones in battle; traumatized soldiers took up sketching on the front line to distract themselves from their hardships; and those who were suffering from shellshock turned to aesthetic contemplation as a psychological restorative.

The war also encouraged the government to take a fresh interest in art. While the authorities had initially withdrawn funds from cultural institutions, increased taxation on aesthetic luxuries and commandeered the nation's museums as they recalibrated the country for conflict, they soon came to realize that art could be a very helpful ally in the war effort. Images were hugely popular and influential with all sectors of British society; if the government could control them, it could also exercise some kind of control over the public's attitude towards the ongoing war. In 1916, as popular support for the conflict reached its nadir, the government duly embarked on what may have been the largest act of artistic patronage in its history. Over the next three years, various official propaganda and memorial institutions employed, commissioned or bought work from more than 150 artists and amassed a collection of around 3,000 paintings, drawings and sculptures. The range and intelligence of its aesthetic choices continue to impress scholars today.

The war years, in short, had forged the conditions for a very different relationship between Britain and its art. And that relationship did not end with the ceasefire. Indeed, this new cultural fusion was not only sustained but enhanced in the five years after the Armistice. As the country transitioned from war to peace, the arts became a valuable part of the wider national reconstruction. Imbued with a civic consciousness that had been nourished by more than four years of war, Britain's artists advised on and designed memorials around the country; they set up regional organizations to bring the arts to the people; and they collaborated with industry to produce imagery that was more democratic and accessible than before. At the same time, the government began to rethink the role of the arts in the education of the next generation and in the beautification of the new Britain that it was in the process of building.

It is tempting to conclude that the unrealistic dream of 1914 – the hope that war would bring about a renaissance in British art – had, in some ways, been fulfilled. It was not of course that simple. The conflict had wreaked a significant amount of cultural damage, some of it irreparable, but it also left the art world in a considerably stronger social position. If in 1914 it had been a largely ignored entity that operated at the very margins of public life, half a decade of conflict had forced it to participate in one of the country's most decisive historical episodes. As a result, British art became more conscious of its public and the British public became more conscious of its art. But perhaps the final words should be those of John Rothenstein's father, William, who himself had been an official war artist. Looking back on the conflict in 1931, he concluded: 'While the War lasted ... and for the few years afterwards while the memory of it lingered, the gulf between life and art, which had widened steadily for more than a century, momentarily disappeared.'[15]

NOTES

Introduction

1 *The Times* (5 August 1914), p. 9.
2 For the symbolism of Trafalgar Square, see R. Mace, *Trafalgar Square: Emblem of Empire* (London: Lawrence & Wishart, 1976), pp. 15–22. For the establishment of the National Gallery there, see B. Taylor, *Art for the Nation: Exhibitions and the London Public 1747–2001* (Manchester University Press, 1999), pp. 29–66.
3 C. Playne, *Britain Holds On: 1917, 1918* (London: George Allen & Unwin, 1933), p. 241.
4 The institution had in fact been closed to the public all summer as a result of the ongoing threats posed by suffragettes. For more, see G. Kavanagh, *Museums and the First World War: A Social History* (London: Leicester University Press, 1994), pp. 22–4.
5 For the extent of the art world, see *The Year's Art*, a compendium published annually from 1880 (London: Macmillan & Co. *et al.*). Hereafter, *Year's Art*.
6 For a brief discussion of British 'philistinism', including Fry's quotation, see M. Saler, *The Avant-Garde in Interwar England: Medieval Modernism and the London Underground* (New York and Oxford: Oxford University Press, 2001), pp. 11–12. In 1914, however, the government neglect did seem ready to cease. On 29 July 1914 a Parliamentary Committee met to consider a root and branch overhaul of the government's arts policies. It proposed an increased grant to the National Gallery, a state-run school of fine art and even a Ministry of Art. The outbreak of war, however, caused these promising discussions to be abandoned before any of the proposals were implemented. *Year's Art* (1915), pp. 86–7.
7 In 1914 Clive Bell's seminal text in Bloomsbury aesthetics, *Art*, was targeted at 'educated persons of extraordinary sensibility' rather than 'the mass of mankind'. C. Bell, *Art* (London: Chatto & Windus, 1914), p. 261. In the same year, Wyndham Lewis declared that his Vorticist movement had absolutely 'nothing to do with "The People"'. 'Long Live the Vortex!', *Blast: Review of the Great English Vortex* 1 (1914), p. 7.
8 See R. Fry, 'Art and Life', in *Vision and Design* (London: Chatto & Windus, 1957), pp. 1–15.
9 'Special Notice', *Burlington Magazine* 25 (September 1914), p. 325.
10 'National Gallery Annual Report 1914' (1915), National Gallery Papers, NG17/7, p. 7, National Gallery Archive, London.
11 S. P. B. Mais, 'Literature and the War', *Journal of Education* 37 (April 1915), p. 208. For similar surveys, see H. Taylor, 'War and Art', *Colour* (September 1914), p. 46; and

P. Wyndham Lewis, 'Artists and the War', *Blast: Review of the Great English Vortex* 2 (1915), pp. 25–6.

12 G. Moore, *Modern Painting* (London: Walter Scott, 1893), p. 46. Contemporary knowledge of Moore is in C. R. Grundy, 'War and British Art', *The Connoisseur* 42 (August 1915), p. 195; and J. Delville, 'The Social Influence of Art', *Colour* 3 (January 1916), p. 229.

13 J. Ruskin, *The Crown of Wild Olive: Three Lectures on Work, Traffic, and War* (London: Smith, Elder & Co, 1866), pp. 70–1. Contemporary knowledge of Ruskin is evidenced in C. Gasquoine Hartley and A. Lewis, 'War and the Arts', *English Review* 23 (August 1916), p. 150; and H. Belloc, *A General Sketch of the European War* (London: Thomas Nelson & Sons, 1916), p. 17. The success of Ruskin's essay on 'War' necessitated *The Crown of Wild Olive*'s republication in 1915.

14 C. R. W. Nevinson, 'War Notes and Queries. Comments and Suggestions in Brief from our Readers', *The Graphic* (11 March 1915), p. 51.

15 'Artists and the War', *The Times* (5 May 1916), p. 9. The idea of art as a muse was one of the most ubiquitous tropes in the early cultural discourses of the war. Dora Marsden, editor of *The Egoist*, wrote: 'Security in life has a deadening effect on art. The absence of risk, this monotony of service in our fat, rich, and peaceful civilisation, cannot even enforce itself under such advantageous conditions ... Science prospers in peace, but knowledge of images which are furnished by heightened heart-beats must needs wait until thinkers' own hearts beat high. Great philosophies can come only from lives greatly lived.' D. Marsden, 'Culture', *The Egoist* 1 (1 September 1914), p. 323. See also A. Clutton-Brock, 'War and Poetry', *Times Literary Supplement* (8 October 1914), p. 448; and C. H. Collins Baker, 'A Painter's Confession', *Saturday Review* (22 August 1914), p. 220.

16 *Year's Art* (1915), p. 8.

17 *Daily Express* (25 February 1915). For more on Futurism and war, see M. Perloff, *The Futurist Moment: Avant-Garde, Avant-Guerre, and the Language of Rupture* (University of Chicago Press, 2003).

18 E. Gosse, 'War and Literature', *Edinburgh Review* 220 (October 1914), p. 313; S. Image, *Art, Morals, and the War* (London: Oxford University Press, 1914), p. 19; and W. K. Colton, 'The Effects of War on Art', *Architect* 45 (17 March 1916), p. 200.

19 'War Notes', *Poetry Review* 3 (September 1914), p. 140. For more on artists' and intellectuals' belligerent reception of war, see R. N. Stromberg, *Redemption by War: The Intellectuals and 1914* (Lawrence: Regents Press of Kansas, 1982), pp. 1–13.

20 C. J. Holmes, 'Notes', *Burlington Magazine* 25 (September 1914), p. 366.

21 The Hague Convention declared that: 'In sieges and bombardments all necessary steps must be taken to spare, as far as possible, buildings dedicated to religion, art, science, or charitable purposes, historic monuments, hospitals ... provided they are not being used at the time for military purposes.' 'Peace Conference of 1907', Section II, chapter I, article 27, in J. Brown Scott (ed.), *Texts of the Peace Conferences at the Hague, 1899 and 1907* (Boston and London: Ginn & Co, 1908), pp. 220–1.

22 See M. Derez, 'The Flames of Louvain: The War Experience of an Academic Community', in H. Cecil and P. Liddle (eds.), *Facing Armageddon: The First World War Experienced* (London: Leo Cooper, 1996); pp. 617–29; A. Kramer, *Dynamic of Destruction: Culture and Mass Killing in the First World War* (Oxford University Press, 2007), pp. 6–30; and J. Horne and A. Kramer, *German Atrocities, 1914: A History of Denial* (New Haven and London: Yale University Press, 2001).

23 Anon., *The Real Crown Prince: A Record and an Indictment* (London: George Newnes, 1915), pp. 174–5.

24 'Art after Armageddon', *The Athenaeum* (12 September 1914), p. 269.

25 L. Haward, *The Effect of War upon Art and Literature* (Manchester University Press, 1916), pp. 15, 30.

26 For two useful summaries of the historiography, see the introduction to A. Roshwald and R. Stites (eds.), *European Culture in the Great War: Arts, Entertainment and Propaganda 1914–18* (Cambridge University Press, 1999); and J. Winter, 'Catastrophe and Culture: Recent Trends in the Historiography of the First World War', *Journal of Modern History* 64 (September 1992), pp. 525–32.

27 See R. Cork, *A Bitter Truth: Avant-Garde Art and the Great War* (New Haven and London: Yale University Press, 1994); P. Dagen, *Le silence des peintres: les artistes face à la Grande Guerre* (Paris: Fayard, 1996); and, more recently, D. Boyd Haycock, *A Crisis of Brilliance: Five Young British Artists and the Great War* (London: Old Street Publishing, 2010).

28 B. Buchloh, 'Figures of Authority, Ciphers of Regression: Notes on the Return of Representation in European Painting', *October* 16 (Spring 1981), p. 41. For more on the European 'call to order', see C. Green, *Léger and the Avant-Garde* (London: Yale University Press, 1976), pp. 119–35; and E. Cowling and J. Mundy, *On Classic Ground: Picasso, Léger, de Chirico and the New Classicism 1910–30* (London: Tate, 1990).

29 For two discussions, see R. Cork, 'The Vorticist Circle, Bomberg and the First World War', in S. Compton (ed.), *British Art in the Twentieth Century: The Modern Movement* (Munich: Prestel, 1987), pp. 138–41; V. Sherry, *The Great War and the Language of Modernism* (Oxford University Press, 2003); and K. Silver, *Esprit de Corps: The Art of the Parisian Avant-Garde and the First World War, 1914–1925* (London: Thames and Hudson, 1989).

30 D. Farr, *English Art 1870–1940* (Oxford University Press, 1978), pp. 231, 248. See also C. Harrison, *English Art and Modernism 1900–1939* (London: Allen Lane, 1981), pp. 145–66; F. Spalding, *British Art since 1900* (London: Thames & Hudson, 1986) pp. 57–61; and R. Cork, 'Machine Age, Apocalypse and Pastoral', in S. Compton (ed.), *British Art in the Twentieth Century: The Modern Movement* (Munich: Prestel, 1987), pp. 63–72.

31 G. Brockington, *Above the Battlefield: Modernism and the Peace Movement in Britain, 1900–1918* (New Haven and London: Yale University Press, 2010); D. Peters Corbett, *The Modernity of English Art 1914–30* (Manchester University Press, 1997), p. 73.

32 For two recent discussions of British war art, see S. Malvern, *Modern Art, Britain and the Great War: Witnessing, Testimony and Remembrance* (New Haven and London: Yale University Press, 2004); and P. Gough, *'A Terrible Beauty': War, Art and Imagination, 1914–1918* (Bristol: Samson & Co., 2009).

33 W. Lipke, *David Bomberg: A Critical Study of his Life and Work* (London: Evelyn Adams & Mackay, 1967), p. 45.

34 J. Winter and A. Prost, *The Great War in History: Debates and Controversies, 1914 to the Present* (Cambridge University Press, 2005), p. 30.

35 *Ibid.*, p. 164. For major cultural histories of the war, see J. Winter, *Sites of Memory, Sites of Mourning: The Great War in European Cultural History* (Cambridge University Press, 1995); G. Mosse, *Fallen Soldiers: Reshaping the Memory of the World Wars* (New York and Oxford: Oxford University Press, 1990); and J. Winter and J.-L. Robert (eds.), *Capital Cities at War: Paris, London, Berlin 1914–1919*,

2 vols. (Cambridge University Press, 2007), vol. II. For graffiti, see A. Becker, 'Graffiti et sculptures des soldats', *14/18 Aujourd'hui –Today – Heute* 2 (1999), special issue: *L'Archéologie et la Grande Guerre*, pp. 117–27; for toys see, S. Audoin-Rouzeau, *La guerre des enfants, 1914–1918: essai d'histoire culturelle* (Paris: A. Colin, 1993); for postcards, see J. Laffin, *World War I in Post-Cards* (Gloucester: Alan Sutton, 1988); for photographs, see M. Huss, *Histoires de famille: cartes postales et culture de guerre* (Paris: Noesis, 2000); for memorials, see A. King, *Memorials of the Great War in Britain: The Symbolism and Politics of Remembrance* (Oxford: Berg, 1998).

36 See H. Becker, *Art Worlds* (Berkeley, Los Angeles and London: University of California Press, 1982), pp. 35–9, and G. Dickie, *Art and the Aesthetic: An Institutional Analysis* (Ithaca, NY: Cornell University Press, 1974). The term 'artworld' was coined somewhat earlier by Arthur Danto. See A. Danto, 'The Artworld', *Journal of Philosophy* 61 (1964), pp. 571–84.

37 For my earlier discussion of these themes, see J. Fox, '"Traitor Painters": Artists and Espionage in the First World War, 1914–1918', *British Art Journal* 10 (Spring 2009), pp. 62–8; and J. Fox, '"Fiddling While Rome is Burning": Hostility to Art during the First World War, 1914–1918', *Visual Culture in Britain* 11 (Spring 2010), pp. 49–65.

38 For my earlier discussion of these themes, see J. Fox, 'Conflict and Consolation: British Art and the First World War, 1914–1919', *Art History* 36 (September 2013), pp. 810–33.

1 The outbreak of war and the business of art

1 See L. Chiozza Money, 'British Trade and the War', *Contemporary Review* 106 (July–December 1914), p. 482.

2 For 'business as usual', see J. Lawrence, M. Dean and J.-L. Robert, 'The Outbreak of War and the Urban Economy: Paris, Berlin and London in 1914', *Economic History Review* 45 (August 1992), pp. 564–93; D. French, 'The Rise and Fall of "Business as Usual"', in K. Burke (ed.), *War and the State: The transformation of British Government, 1914–1919* (London: George Allen & Unwin, 1982), pp. 7–32; J. McDermott, '"A Needless Sacrifice": British Businessmen and Business As Usual in the First World War', *Albion* 21 (Spring 1989), pp. 263–82; and S. Broadberry and P. Howlett, 'The United Kingdom during World War I: Business as Usual?', in S. Broadberry and M. Harrison (eds.), *The Economics of World War I* (Cambridge University Press, 2005), pp. 206–34.

3 Local Government Board, 'Report on the Causes of Depression in Various Trades, August 1914–July 1915', London Intelligence Committee Papers, vol. II, pp. 25–39, British Library of Political and Economic Science, London.

4 Becker, *Art Worlds*, p. 36.

5 *Year's Art* (1915), p. 387.

6 Lady Gregory, *Sir Hugh Lane: His Life and Legacy* (Gerrards Cross: Colin Smythe, 1973), pp. 14–15, 152–3.

7 *Year's Art* (1916), p. 387.

8 H. C. Marillier, *Christie's: 1766–1925* (London: Constable, 1926), p. 160.

9 *Burlington Magazine* 27 (April 1915), p. 42.

10 Marillier, *Christie's*, p. 150.

11 R. Lacey, *Sotheby's: Bidding for Class* (London: Warner Books, 1999), p. 59.
12 *Year's Art* (1918), p. 294.
13 *Punch* (22 September 1915), p. 255
14 *Blast: Review of the Great English Vortex* 2 (1915), p. 11.
15 A. L. Bowley, *Some Economic Consequences of the War* (London: Thornton Butterworth, 1930), p. 77.
16 For a survey, see F. M. L. Thomson, *English Landed Society in the Nineteenth Century* (London: Routledge & Kegan Paul, 1963), pp. 269–345.
17 See D. Cannadine, D, *The Decline and Fall of the British Aristocracy* (New Haven and London: Yale University Press, 1990), pp. 97–102.
18 *The Times* (14 June 1918), p. 10.
19 *The Times* (19 July 1917), p. 9. The first was the liquidation of Sir Walter Gilbey's 8,000-acre estate at Elsenham Hall, Essex, in June 1915. Of the many sales that followed, the most famous were of Lord Sydney's estate at Chislehurst, the possessions of Sir Francis Montefiore at Worth Park and the Wigan, Baker, Barratt, Hope, Joseph, Jardine and Poynter sales in the years that followed.
20 M. Daunton, *Just Taxes: The Politics of Taxation in Britain, 1914–1979* (Cambridge University Press, 2002), p. 47.
21 H. Strachan, *Financing the First World War* (Oxford University Press, 2004), p. 75.
22 For a good discussion, see C. Masterman, *England after War: A Study* (London: Hodder & Stoughton, 1922).
23 See 'Report of the Committee of the Trustees of the National Gallery appointed to enquire into the Retention of Important Pictures in this Country and Other Matters Connected with the National Art Collections', 1915 (Cd. 7878/9), in *Reports from Commissioners, Inspectors and Others* 29 (London, HMSO, 1914–16), pp. 317–489.
24 See Kavanagh, *Museums and the First World War*, pp. 97–9.
25 For the complete figures, see the *Annual Reports of the National Art-Collections Fund* (London, 1914–20).
26 D'Abernon, *Parliamentary Debates, Lords* 23 (21 November 1916), pp. 539–41. D'Abernon proposed selling some of the thousands of Turners that dominated the national collection in order to raise funds for works by artists who were not so well represented.
27 Weardale, *Parliamentary Debates, Lords* 23 (21 November 1916), p. 545; Burnham, *Parliamentary Debates, Lords* 23 (28 November 1916), p. 701. For the abandonment of the bill, see Bonar-Law, *Parliamentary Debates, Commons* 88 (18 December 1916), p. 1135. See also R. Fry, 'The National Gallery Bill', *Burlington Magazine* 30 (January 1917), pp. 21–3.
28 'War and the Fine Art Trade', *Fine Art Trade Journal* 11 (February 1915), pp. 42–3.
29 Entry (2 February 1915), Francis Howard Letter Book 3, TGA 737/12, p. 203, Tate Archives, London.
30 Entries (14 October 1915 and 3 January 1916), Francis Howard Letter Book 3, TGA 737/12, pp. 326, 378.
31 Entries (16 July 1915 and 14 October 1915), Francis Howard Letter Book 3, TGA 737/12, pp. 303, 327.
32 Entry (29 February 1916), Francis Howard Letter Book 3, TGA 737/12, pp. 399–400.
33 *The Times* (6 November 1919), p. 8.
34 *Daily Mirror* (23 November 1914), p. 12.

35 For Bialogowski's bankruptcy, see *Fine Art Trade Journal* 10 (December 1914), p. 360. For the Tooth bankruptcy, see *Fine Art Trade Journal* 11 (March 1915), p. 64. For Airey and Milley, see *Fine Art Trade Journal* 10 (September 1914), p. 268.
36 *Fine Art Trade Journal* 12 (February 1916), p. 42.
37 *Art News* (24 August 1914), p. 236.
38 For more, see A. Gruetzner Robins, *Modern Art in Britain 1910–14* (London: Merrell Holberton, 1997).
39 See *Art News* (31 October 1914), pp. 271–3; and *Art News* (30 November 1914), p. 10.
40 *Fine Art Trade Journal* 11 (December 1915), p. 304.
41 'Fine Art Trade Guild Roll of Honour', *Year's Art* (1915), pp. 430–44.
42 *Fine Art Trade Journal* 11 (May 1915), p. 132.
43 *Fine Art Trade Journal* 12 (January 1916), p. 12.
44 Walter Crane described the pre-war period as 'the age of societies'. Cited in J. Codell, 'Artists' Professional Societies: Production, Consumption, and Aesthetics', in B. Allen (ed.), *Towards a Modern Art World* (New Haven and London: Yale University Press, 1995), p. 169.
45 Lists of Britain's art societies were published annually in the *Year's Art*.
46 Pound to Lewis (24 June 1916), in T. Materer (ed.), *Pound/Lewis: The Letters of Ezra Pound and Wyndham Lewis* (London: Faber & Faber, 1985), p. 39.
47 *Year's Art* (1919), pp. 75–6. The Allied Artists' Association was established in 1908 along the lines of the French Salon des Indépendants. Its first exhibition, at the Royal Albert Hall, displayed 3,000 items, including work by Kandinsky and Brancusi.
48 Committee Meeting (2 October 1915), Junior Art-Workers' Guild Council Meetings Minute Book 1914–18, Art-Workers' Guild, London.
49 'Average Age of Members 1806–1986', Royal Watercolour Society, London. 'Council Meetings' (17 October 1914 and 3 January 1917), Minutes of Council Meetings 1905–20, A26, Royal Watercolour Society.
50 General Meeting (30 November 1914), General Meetings Minutes 1904–42, A10, Royal Watercolour Society.
51 '33rd Annual Report' (1916), Annual Reports 3, 1913–33, p. 5, Art-Workers' Guild; General Meeting (15 June 1917), General Minute Book 3, AAD/2000/5/3, Archive of Art and Design, Victoria & Albert Museum, London.
52 Parsons to Royal Watercolour Society (30 November 1918), in General Meetings Minutes 1904–42, A10, Royal Watercolour Society.
53 *Western Press* (7 November 1914), p. 3.
54 Royal Institute of Oil Painters Council Meetings (13 August and 21 August 1914), Council Meetings Minute Book 3, AAD/2000/5/10, Archive of Art and Design.
55 *The Times* (16 April 1915), p. 11.
56 *Allied Artists' Association Catalogue to the 8th Salon* (London, 1916), p. 7.
57 For a review, see *Sunday Times* (26 November 1916), p. 3.
58 *British Journal of Photography* (6 November 1915), p. 58.
59 See Annual Reports 1913–18, B163–7, Royal Watercolour Society.
60 *Imperial Arts League Journal* (June 1915), p. 70.
61 General Assembly (19 March 1915), General Assembly Minutes Book 10, 1913–32, p. 48, Royal Academy.

62 'Minutes of a Committee to consider ways and means for securing a satisfactory balance between income and expenditure' (8 July 1915), Council Records of Committees 1851–1948, RAA/PC/6/8, p. 4, Royal Academy.
63 'Deputation' (28 April 1916), Papers Relating to Entertainments Tax, 1916–26, Minutes of Deputation, RAA/SEC/17/14, pp. 8–9, Royal Academy.
64 Council Meeting (29 October 1914), Minutes of Council Meetings 1905–20, A26, Royal Watercolour Society; Council Meeting (22 October 1914), Council Minutes 23, 1913–18, RAA/PC/1/23, Royal Academy.
65 Council Meeting (27 May 1918), Council Minutes 24, 1918–23, RAA/PC/1/24, Royal Academy.
66 '32nd Annual Report' (1915), Annual Reports 3, 1913–33, p. 15, Art-Workers' Guild; Entry, Letter Book (1 November 1917), Letter Book 1906–19, AC6, Royal Watercolour Society.
67 De Cruchy to Royal Academy (5 October 1917), Council Minutes 23, 1913–18, RAA/PC/1/23, Royal Academy.
68 Council Meeting (8 October 1914), Council Minutes 23, 1913–18, RAA/PC/1/23; Wilkinson to Poynter (28 June 1917), Correspondence from Non-Members 1879–1963, RAA/SEC/6/52, Royal Academy.
69 National Portrait Gallery, *Reports for the Years 1914–1916*, Cd. 8290 (1916), vol. XIV, p. 7.
70 Committee on Public Retrenchment, 'Third Report of the Committee on Retrenchment in the Public Expenditure', Cd. 8180 (1916), in *Reports from Commissioners, Inspectors and Others, 1916*, vol. XV, pp. 177–80.
71 *Ibid.*
72 *Ibid.*
73 'Deputation to the Prime Minister on Museum Closure', 10 February 1916, *Museums' Journal* 15 (April 1916), p. 319.
74 Quoted in the *Museum's Journal* 15 (April 1916), p. 338.
75 Master's Address (12 January 1917), '33rd Annual Report' (1916), Annual Reports 3, 1913–33, p. 17, Art-Workers' Guild.
76 Quoted from the back cover of Becker, *Art Worlds*, n.p.
77 'Art after Armageddon', *The Athenaeum* (12 September 1914), p. 269.
78 *Sunday Times* (15 November 1914), p. 5; *Scotsman* (22 October 1914), p. 5; *Art News* (24 August 1914), p. 241.
79 'Chairman's Note' (May 1917), Arts in War Time Committee Annual Report 1917, p. 3, Professional Classes Aid Council, London, 1918. See also *Charity Organisation Review* 39 (February 1916), p. 85.
80 Quoted in the *Scotsman* (19 January 1915), p. 9.
81 'Various Entries', Applicants' Book 5, Artists' General Benevolent Institution, London.
82 *Ibid.*, pp. 14, 17, 23, 94, 14, 87, 46.
83 The first statement is from Benson to de László (20 October 1914), DLA 053-0122, De László Archive, Heinz Archive and Library, National Portrait Gallery, London. The second and third are respectively from Winfield Sifton and Beryl Stanhope. Quoted in S. Bailey, 'De László's Relationships with his Patrons and Sitters', in S. Bailey and S. de Laszlo (eds.), *A Brush with Grandeur: Philip de László 1869–1937* (London: Paul Holberton, 2004), p. 56. Two further cancellations were made by the Earl of Shaftesbury, and the Countess of Kerry.
84 B. Arnold, *Orpen: Mirror to an Age* (London: Jonathan Cape, 1981), p. 422.

85 J. Salis, 'Reward of the Patriot', *New Witness* (11 May 1916), p. 45.
86 'Exhibition Figures 1913–1918', Annual Reports 1913–18, B163–7, Royal Watercolour Society.
87 Epstein to Quinn (19 August 1914), in J. Rose, *Daemons and Angels: A Life of Jacob Epstein* (London: Constable, 2002), p. 92.
88 Gertler to Brett (autumn 1914), in J. Woodeson, *Mark Gertler: Biography of a Painter, 1891–1939* (London: Sidgwick & Jackson, 1972), pp. 149–50.
89 Quoted in J. Hone, *The Life of Henry Tonks* (London: William Heinemann, 1939), p. 111.
90 John to Quinn (10 October 1914), in B. L. Reid, *The Man from New York: John Quinn and his Friends* (Oxford and New York: Oxford University Press, 1968), p. 205.
91 Pound to Quinn (18 April 1915), in T. Materer (ed.), *The Selected Letters of Ezra Pound to John Quinn, 1915–1924* (Durham, NC: Duke University Press, 1991), p. 26; Pound to Quinn (17 December 1915), in Reid, *The Man from New York*, p. 204; W. Roberts, *Memories of the War to End War, 1914–1918* (London: Lund Humphries, 1974), p. 1.
92 Council Meeting (24 November 1915), Minute Book 1907–16, p. 367, Artists' General Benevolent Institution.
93 Annual Report, 1914–15, pp. 20–1, Professional Classes Aid Council.
94 Council Meeting (9 November 1914), Minute Book 1907–16, pp. 374–5, Artists' General Benevolent Institution.
95 Council Meeting (7 October 1914), Minute Book 1907–16, p. 290, Artists' General Benevolent Institution.
96 Spalding, *British Art*, pp. 57–61.
97 Gertler to Strachey (May 1916), in Woodeson, *Mark Gertler*, pp. 223–4.
98 'War and the Artists', *Manchester Guardian* (8 March 1915), p. 4. See also J. Courtney, 'The War and Women's Employment', *Fortnightly Review* (February 1915), p. 243.
99 England imported £750,000 of German painters' colours in 1912 and £180,000 of picture-frame materials in 1914. The British printing industry imported 50 per cent of all its materials from Germany alone in 1914. *Journal of Royal Society of Arts* 63 (30 April 1915), p. 566; *British Printer* 27 (October-November 1914), pp. 196–204; *Fine Art Trade Journal* 10 (November 1914), p. 315.
100 *British Printer* 28 (December–January 1915–16), p. 195.
101 *Fine Art Trade Journal* 10 (September 1914), pp. 274–6.
102 Orpen to Roberson (29 November 1914), ROB MS 529-1993, Hamilton Kerr Institute, Whittlesford. See also W. Orpen, *An Onlooker in France 1917–1919* (London: Williams & Norgate, 1921), p. 66.
103 *British Printer* 28 (December–January 1915–16), p. 195. See also 'Art by Weight', *Burlington Magazine* 32 (June 1918), p. 243.
104 Quoted in *British Printer* 27 (October-November 1914), p. 204.
105 *Imperial Arts League Journal* (November 1919), pp. 187–8.
106 Paper Restriction legislation from 1917 controlled the 'purchase, sale, distribution, supply, transport or storage' of paper. It also prohibited excessive paper use, such as posters larger than a specified size. *British Printer* 30 (April-May 1917), p. 40.
107 Aluminium became controlled in December 1915, copper in December 1916 and tin in April 1918. *The History of the Ministry of Munitions*, 12 vols. (London, 1922), vol. VII, pp. 106–13.

108 *Ibid.*, p. 45.
109 K. Grieves, *The Politics of Manpower, 1914–1918* (Manchester University Press, 1988), p. 1.
110 See E. Potton (ed.), *A Record of the United Arts Rifles, 1914–1919* (London: Alexander Moring Ltd., 1920).
111 C. J. Blomfield, *Once an Artist Always an Artist* (London: Page & Co., 1921), p. 105; A. Hill, 'Imperial War Museum Interview' (1975), from *Artists in an Age of Conflict*, IWM 561, Reel 1, Imperial War Museum, London.
112 *The Studio* 63 (December 1914), p. 239; *The Studio* 65 (August 1915), p. 217; *Imperial Arts League Journal* (January 1915), pp. 23–6; *Imperial Arts League Journal* (April 1915), pp. 51–4; *Imperial Arts League Journal* (July 1915), pp. 80–2; *Imperial Arts League Journal* (November 1915), pp. 88–90.
113 'Occupations of persons, males and females, aged 10 years and upwards, distinguishing for females the unmarried, married, and widowed, 1911: Painters, Sculptors, Artists', General Register Office, *Census of England and Wales 1911: General Report with Appendices* (Cd. 8591), London: HMSO (1917), p. 2.
114 See the *Slade School of Art Reports 1915–16*, pp. 13–14, and *1917–18*, p. 13, UCLGB0103-UCLCA/SS, University College London Archive, London.
115 Gough, *'A Terrible Beauty'*, pp. 35–40. See also P. Gough, 'The Experience of British Artists in the Great War', in H. Cecil and P. Liddle (eds.), *Facing Armageddon: The First World War Experienced* (London: Leo Cooper, 1996, pp. 841–53.
116 D. Cuppleditch, *The London Sketch Club* (Stroud: Alan Sutton, 1994), p. 91; L. Gosling, *Brushes and Bayonets: Cartoons, Sketches and Paintings of World War I* (London: Osprey, 2008), p. 146.
117 M. Chamot, D. Farr and M. Butlin, *The Tate Gallery Catalogues: The Modern British Paintings, Drawings and Sculpture*, 2 vols. (London: Tate, 1964), vol. I, p. 25.
118 *Year's Art* (1918), p. 142; various entries, Register of Admission of Students 1890–1922, RAA/KEE/1/1/4, Royal Academy.
119 Paramore to Royal Academy (20 September 1914), Correspondence from Members' Files 1867–1986, RAA/SEC/10/74/1, Royal Academy.
120 F. Rutter, *Art in My Time* (London: Rich & Cowan, 1933), p. 161.

2 Perceptions of art

1 R. Chartier, 'Intellectual History or Sociocultural History?', in D. LaCapra and S. L. Kaplan (eds.), *Modern European Intellectual History: Reappraisals and New Perspectives* (Ithaca, NY and London: Cornell University Press, 1982, pp. 40–1. French scholars have broadly described this as *l'histoire des mentalités* – an approach pioneered in the 1960s. For all its weaknesses – indeed many scholars now prefer to avoid its original term and use *répresentation or l'imaginaire social* – it is a fruitful way to connect the history of ideas with social history. For a discussion, see P. Burke, *Varieties of Cultural History* (Cambridge: Polity, 1997), pp. 162–82.
2 M. Healy, *Vienna and the Fall of the Habsburg Empire: Total War and Everyday Life in World War I* (Cambridge University Press, 2004), p. 3.
3 See A. Gregory, *The Last Great War: British Society and the First World War* (Cambridge University Press, 2008), pp. 9–39. See also A. Gregory, 'British "War Enthusiasm"

in 1914: A Reassessment', in G. Braybon (ed.), *Evidence, History and the Great War: Historians and the Impact of 1914–1918* (Oxford and New York: Berghahn, 2003), pp. 67–85.
4 C. Playne, *Society at War: 1914–1916* (London: George Allen & Unwin, 1931), p. 29.
5 For its impact on writers, see S. Hynes, *A War Imagined: The First World War and English Culture* (London: Bodley Head, 1990), pp. 10–11.
6 The fall of Namur was reported by the Press Bureau on 24 August 1914 and in *The Times* on 25 August 1914.
7 C. H. Collins Baker, 'A Painter's Confession', *Saturday Review* 118 (28 November 1914), p. 556.
8 Fry to Vildrac (17 February 1916), in D. Sutton (ed.), *Letters of Roger Fry*, 2 vols. (London: Chatto & Windus, 1972), vol. II, p. 393; A. Mayes, 'The Young Bomberg 1914–1922', unpublished memoir, TGA 7312 (1972), pp. 5–6, Tate Archives; Spencer, quoted in R. Carline, *Stanley Spencer at War* (London: Faber & Faber, 1978), pp. 40–1.
9 Milner to Brumfit (13 August 1914), Fredrick Milner Papers, TGA 9511/17, Tate Archives.
10 Milner to Brumfit (9 February 1915), Fredrick Milner Papers, TGA 9511/24; Milner to Brumfit (14 March 1915), Fredrick Milner Papers, TGA 9511/25, Tate Archives.
11 W. Trotter, *Instincts of the Herd in Peace and War* (London: Fisher & Unwin, 1916), pp. 142–4. For similar ideas, see G. Murray, 'Herd Instinct and the War', in E. Sidgwick *et al.*, *The International Crisis in its Ethical and Psychological Aspects* (London: Oxford University Press, 1915), pp. 22–45.
12 'On Art and the National Spirit', *The Studio* 65 (August 1915), p. 218.
13 *Newspaper Press Directory* (1916), p. 3; *Newspaper Press Directory* (1917), p. 16; *Newspaper Press Directory* (1918), p. 9.
14 'The New Weekly', *New Weekly* (22 August 1914), p. 292.
15 *Arts and Letters* 1 (July 1917), p. 1.
16 E. Newman, 'The Artist and the People', *Musical Times* 55 (1 October 1914), p. 605.
17 A. Palmer, 'Beauty and the Beast', *New Weekly* (22 August 1914), p. 290.
18 J. D. Symon, 'War and Creative Art', *English Review* 21 (December 1915), p. 519; Taylor, 'War and Art', p. 46; M. Anderson, 'Note', *Little Review* 1 (October 1914), p. 3; F. A. Bather, 'Museums and National Service', *Museums' Journal* 14 (October 1914), p. 121; A. Bennett, 'Officialism and War Painting', *New Statesman* 14 (20 December 1919), p. 847. See also W. Rothenstein, 'Help for Artists', *The Times* (23 February 1915), p. 9; R. Ross, 'Notes', *Burlington Magazine* 27 (September 1914), p. 367; E. Evans, 'Music and the War', *New Weekly* (15 August 1914), p. 272; and E. Storer, 'Art in War Time', *New Witness* (22 October 1914), p. 615.
19 Image, *Art, Morals, and the War*, pp. 18–19.
20 See Peters Corbett, *The Modernity of English Art*, pp. 43–51.
21 C. H. Collins Baker, 'Dry Bones', *Saturday Review* 119 (20 March 1915), p. 44.
22 L. De Fonseca, 'War and the Aesthete', *New Age* 16 (31 December 1914), p. 216.
23 S. G. Ervine, 'The War and Literature', *North American Review* 202 (July 1915), p. 98; E. Gosse, 'War and Literature', *Edinburgh Review* 220 (October 1914), p. 330; *The Studio* 68 (June 1916), p. 70; *The Times* (15 January 1916), p. 9.
24 R. McKenna, *Parliamentary Debates, Commons* 81 (4 April 1916), p. 1058.
25 *Ibid.* (17 April 1916), p. 2088.

26 Rimbault Dibdin to Royal Academy (20 November 1916), Papers Relating to Entertainments Tax, 1916–26, RAA/SEC/17/14, Royal Academy.
27 'Suggestion for a Memorandum to H.M. Commissioners of Customs and Excise on The Educational Value of the Royal Academy Exhibition', RAA/SEC/17/25, pp. 4–5, Royal Academy.
28 Mr Young to RA (25 October 1916), Papers Relating to Entertainments Tax, RAA/SEC/17/14, Royal Academy.
29 A. Baldry, 'The Entertainments Tax', *Imperial Arts League Journal* (June 1916), p. 31.
30 See 'War and Play', *Saturday Review* (5 September 1914), p. 262.
31 Newman, 'The Artist and the People', p. 605.
32 'War and Play', *Saturday Review* (5 September 1914), p. 262. For a defence of amusement, see J. Palmer, 'Patriotism and Amusement', *Saturday Review* (22 August 1914), pp. 218–19; and G. Du Maurier, 'The Case for Amusements', *The Times* (23 March 1915), p. 13. For more on entertainment, see J. Rüger, 'Entertainments', in J. Winter and J.-L Robert (eds.), *Capital Cities at War: Paris, London, Berlin 1914–1919*, 2 vols. (Cambridge University Press, 2007), vol. II, pp. 112–14.
33 W. Schooling, 'National Saving in the United Kingdom', *Annals of the American Academy of Political and Social Science* 87 (January 1920), pp. 201–2. See also Strachan, *Financing the First World War*, pp. 115–60.
34 'Pamphlet 14', National Savings Committee Papers, British Library.
35 'Pamphlet 21', in *War Savings Handbook* (London: National Savings Committee, 1916), pp. 55–60.
36 Various unnumbered National War Savings Committee pamphlets, British Library. For similar arguments, see H. Withers, 'The War-Saving Idea', *Cornhill Magazine* 42 (1917), p. 626.
37 Quoted in *The Connoisseur* 40 (October 1914), p. 113.
38 'The Report from the Select Committee on Luxury Duty', HC 101, in *Reports from Committees* 4 (1918), p. 46.
39 *Ibid.*, pp. 45, 60.
40 For a comparison of the three, see R. Lennard, 'The Taxation of Luxury', *Economic Journal* 28 (September 1918), pp. 287–90.
41 R. Grundy, 'The Luxury Tax', *The Connoisseur* 52 (September 1918), p. 3.
42 'Report from the Select Committee on Luxury Duty', pp. 67–9. For a response, see J. Quinn, 'Why Art Should Not Be Taxed', *Metropolitan Museum of Art Bulletin* 13 (September 1918), pp. 198–9.
43 See B. Waites, *A Class Society at War: England 1914–1918* (Leamington Spa: Berg, 1987).
44 *John Bull* (5 July 1919), p. 10; *Star* (26 May 1917), p. 4.
45 For the representation of wartime profiteers, see J.-L. Robert, 'The Image of the Profiteer', in Winter and Robert, *Capital Cities at War*, vol. I, pp. 104–32.
46 'Business as Usual: Shocking Taste of London Tombstone Sculptors', *John Bull* (10 October 1914), p. 8.
47 *Charity Organisation Review* 39 (February 1916), p. 59.
48 *Fine Art Trade Journal* 13 (March 1917), p. 66.
49 For the 'feminization' of art, see L. Tickner, 'Men's Work? Masculinity and Modernism', in N. Bryson, M. A. Holly and K. Moxey (eds.), *Visual Culture: Images and Interpretations* (Hanover, NH: Wesleyan University Press, 1994), p. 47.
50 Brockington, *Above the Battlefield*, p. 121.

51 P. Wyndham Lewis, *Blasting and Bombardiering* (London: Eyre & Spottiswoode, 1937), pp. 184–5.
52 S. Gardiner, *Epstein: Artist against the Establishment* (London: M. Joseph, 1992), p. 159.
53 P. Burne-Jones, 'Art and War: Sir Philip Burne-Jones on Sculptor's Exemption – Mr. Epstein's Case – Distinguished Men's Views on "Fame"', *Evening Standard* (7 June 1917), p. 5.
54 G. K. Chesterton, 'Art and War – Noted Sculptor's Exemption', *Sunday Herald* (10 June 1917), p. 4.
55 'The Artist and the War', *Pall Mall Gazette* (7 June 1916), p. 4. See also *Daily Mail* (11 June 1917), p. 4, and *Daily Express* (7 June 1917), p. 3.
56 C. H . Collins Baker, 'Art in Tin Shoes', *Saturday Review* 123 (21 July 1917), p. 44.
57 See A. Stephenson, 'Refashioning Modern Masculinity: Whistler, Aestheticism and National Identity', in D. Peters Corbett and L. Perry (eds.), *English Art 1860–1914: Modern Artists and Identity* (Manchester University Press, 2000), pp. 133–49.
58 Bell, *Art*, p. 241.
59 For criticisms of 'art for art's sake', see 'On Art and Affectation', *The Studio* 63 (July 1916), p. 130, and *Colour* (May 1915), p. 156.
60 See L. Merrill, *A Pot of Paint: Aesthetics on Trial in Whistler vs Ruskin* (Washington, DC and London: Smithsonian Institution Press, 1992); and T. Barringer, *Men at Work: Art and Labour in Victorian Britain* (New Haven and London: Yale University Press, 2005), pp. 313–322.
61 B. Anderson, *Imagined Communities: Reflections on the Origin and Spread of Nationalism* (London: Verso, 1983).
62 See J. Winter, 'British National Identity and the First World War', in S. Green and R. Whiting (eds.), *The Boundaries of the State in Modern Britain* (Cambridge University Press, 1996), pp. 261–77.
63 P. Panayi, *The Enemy in Our Midst: Germans in Britain during the First World War* (New York and Oxford: Berg, 1991).
64 *Fine Art Trade Journal* 10 (August 1914), p. 236. Firms include A. W. Faber, L. C. Hardtmuth, William Müller, H. L. Sterkel and Günther Wagner.
65 Albert and Charles Rothenstein were other Jewish-named artists. They anglicized their name to Rutherston in 1916. Only William, at the very last moment, retained his original name. M. Lago, 'Rothenstein, Sir William (1872–1945)', *Oxford Dictionary of National Biography* (Oxford University Press), www.oxforddnb.com/view/article/35842 (accessed 27 May 2012).
66 Silver, *Esprit de Corps*.
67 See P. Peppis, *Literature, Politics, and the English Avant-Garde: Nation and Empire, 1901–1918* (Cambridge University Press, 2000), pp. 96–130; and B. Taylor, 'Foreigners and Fascists: Patterns of Hostility to Modern Art in Britain before and after the First World War', in D. Peters Corbett, Y. Holt and F. Russell (eds.), *The Geographies of Englishness: Landscape and the National Past 1880–1940* (New Haven and London: Yale University Press, 2002), pp. 169–98.
68 *The Times* (10 March 1915), p. 8.
69 Woodeson, *Mark Gertler*, p. 186.
70 See D. French, 'Spy Fever in Britain, 1900–1915', *Historical Journal* 21 (June 1978), pp. 355–70; and S. T. Felstead, *German Spies at Bay: Being an Actual Record of the German Espionage in Great Britain during the Years 1914–1918, Compiled from*

Official Sources (London: Hutchinson, 1920). For spy literature, see D. Trotter, *The English Novel in History, 1895–1920* (London: Routledge, 1993).

71 W. Le Queux, *German Spies in England: An Exposure* (London: Stanley Paul, 1915), p. 72.

72 R. Baden-Powell, *My Adventures as a Spy* (London: C. Arthur Pearson, 1915), pp. 62–5.

73 Le Queux, *German Spies in England*, p. 66, pp. 69–70.

74 'The Spy at Work: An Apparently Innocent Landscape that is Really a Plan of a Harbour', *Illustrated War News* (7 October 1914), pp. 28–9. The *Illustrated London News* ran a similar feature (3 October 1914), p. 477.

75 'Defence of the Realm (no. 2) Act, 1914; a Bill to Amend the Defence of the Realm Act, 1914' (Bill 383), in *Bills, Public* 1 (1914), p. 937.

76 For a discussion, see Hynes, *A War Imagined*, pp. 78–81. This edict was famously enforced against the official war artist C. R. W. Nevinson when, at a 1918 exhibition, one of his paintings was refused public display because its contents were deemed inimical to the country's morale. 'When the Censor Censored "Censored"', *British Legion Journal* (October 1932), pp. 114–15.

77 Reprinted in 'Sketching and Painting in War-Time', Imperial Arts League Papers, LMA/4054/A/06/001, London Metropolitan Archive, London.

78 Mackintosh to Davidson (29 July 1915), Imperial Arts League Papers, LMA/4054/A/06/001, London Metropolitan Archive.

79 'St Ives Petition' (3 September 1915), Imperial Arts League Papers, LMA/4054/A/06/001, London Metropolitan Archive.

80 Royal Academy to Imperial Arts League (2 February 1916), Imperial Arts League Papers, LMA/4054/A/06/001, London Metropolitan Archive.

81 *Parliamentary Debates, Commons* 66 (9 September 1914), p. 564.

82 A. W. Rimington, 'Painting Out of Doors in War Time', *Imperial Arts League Journal* (January 1916), p. 6.

83 *The Studio* 63 (January 1915), p. 240; *Imperial Arts League Journal* (November 1914), p. 3; Playne, *Society at War*, p. 267.

84 '"German Spy" Craze in Galloway', *Scotsman* (10 September 1914), p. 7.

85 'On the Risks which Artists Run', *The Studio* 63 (January 1915), p. 240.

86 In the United States, a German spy was arrested when dynamite was found in his home. He had been posing as a landscapist and had 'carefully drawn plans of the Pacific Coast defences and the municipal works of the chief towns of California'. *The Times* (5 April 1917), p. 5. An artist in Switzerland was imprisoned for two months, *New York Times* (1 April 1916), p. 3; and another expelled from Newfoundland, Canada, for similar acts. *New York Times* (28 October 1918), p. 5.

87 Felstead, *German Spies at Bay*, pp. 256–63.

88 Le Queux, *German Spies in England*, p. 181.

89 O. Rutter, *Portrait of a Painter: The Authorized Life of Philip de László* (London: Hodder & Stoughton, 1939), pp. 297–305, 328–9.

90 Lucy de László, 'Notes' (15 August 1917), uncatalogued, De László Archive.

91 Rutter, *Philip de László*, pp. 310–18.

92 See, for instance, the *Weekly Dispatch* (23 September 1917), p. 1.

93 Wagner to de László (25 February 1918), uncatalogued, De László Archive.

94 Jerome to Solomon (17 and 21 March 1918), De László Archive.

95 See *Daily Express* (12 October 1917), p. 2; *National News* (7 October 1917), p. 2. Sir Richard Cooper MP spoke of a 'mysterious influence protecting this particular man'

and asked: 'Why is he not tried for high treason, and if found guilty shot?' Cooper, *Parliamentary Debates, Commons* 98 (30 October 1917), p. 1579. See also Beresford, *Parliamentary Debates, Lords* 27 (17 January 1918), pp. 774–5.

96 *The Times* (24 September 1917), p. 8.

97 *People* (4 November 1917), p. 2; *Evening Standard* (1 November 1917), p. 3.

98 'László and the Liars: The Traitor Painter and a Public Inquiry', *John Bull* (7 June 1919), p. 6; *John Bull* (3 August 1918), p. 7.

99 Rutter, *Philip de László*, p. 333.

100 *Bristol Times* (28 September 1917), p. 2.

101 'That Traitor László', *John Bull* (17 May 1919), p. 6.

102 *Evening Standard* (27 September 1917), p. 4. See also *Evening Standard* (28 September 1917). p. 3.

103 *The Times* (24 June 1919), p. 7; *The Times* (25 June 1919), p. 7.

104 All referees (who included the Earl of Selborne, the Duke of Portland and Lord Devonport) rejected the suspicions. Naturalization (Revocation) Committee, 'Character Witness Statements' (1919), Internment Papers, uncatalogued, De László Archive.

105 Typed translation of Geneva letter (14 June 1917), with notes by de László (*c.* 1919), De László Archive.

106 Further Instructions, Legal Papers for Counsel (1919), De László Archive.

107 *John Bull* (5 July 1919), p. 10.

108 *Pall Mall Gazette* (2 November 1917), p. 6.

109 'On the Practical Value of Art', *The Studio* 66 (November 1915), p. 148.

3 The arts mobilize

1 C. Bell, 'Art and War', *International Journal of Ethics* 26 (October 1915), pp. 1–10.

2 J. Horne (ed.), *State, Society and Mobilization in Europe during the First World War* (Cambridge University Press, 1997), p. 6.

3 Hynes, *A War Imagined*, pp. 26–7.

4 'Britain's Destiny and Duty: Declaration by Authors', *The Times* (18 September 1914), p. 3.

5 For more on this, see Peppis, *Literature, Politics and the English Avant-Garde.*

6 J. Cowper Powys, *The War and Culture* (New York: G. Arnold Shaw, 1914).

7 For another revealing example, see A. Rawlinson, 'The War and Culture', *English Review* 20 (April 1915), pp. 77–87.

8 J. Winter, 'Popular Culture in Wartime Britain', in Roshwald and Stites, *European Culture in the Great War*, p. 345.

9 *Dundee Advertiser* (11 February 1898), p. 3.

10 Council Meeting (24 September 1914), Minute Book of Council Meetings, TGA 738.3.156, International Society Papers, Tate Archives.

11 Frampton to Royal Society of British Artists (9 January 1915), Council Meeting (11 January 1915), Council Minute Book 1910–16, AAD/1997/8/13, Archive of Art and Design.

12 Frampton to Royal Society of British Artists (6 February 1915), Council Meeting (8 February 1915), Council Minute Book 1910–16, AAD/1997/8/13, Archive of Art and Design.

13 'Council Meeting' (5 February 1916), Council Minute Book 1910–16, AAD/1997/8/13, Archive of Art and Design. The Royal Academy sent out similar letters to twenty-five of its members that held suspiciously exotic names. Secretary's Letter Book 20 November 1914–18 June 1915, RAA/SEC 9/1/21, Royal Academy.
14 Council Meeting (2 August 1916), Council Meetings Minute Book 1914–18, Art-Workers' Guild.
15 Frampton to Art-Workers' Guild (3 August 1916), Council Meetings Minute Book 1914–18, Art-Workers' Guild.
16 Krall to Art-Workers' Guild (16 October 1916), Council Meetings Minute Book 1914–18, Art-Workers' Guild.
17 Quoted in Woodeson, *Mark Gertler*, p. 228.
18 Hunt to London Salon of Photography (9 September 1914), Letter Book 1912–20, L8, Royal Watercolour Society.
19 'Mr Rodin's Gift', *The Times* (11 November 1914), p. 9.
20 'Rodin's Gift to the Nation', *Burlington Magazine* 26 (December 1914), p. 122.
21 *The Times* (13 November 1914), p. 9. In August 1915 the art world purchased, for £800, the Belgian sculptor Égide Rombaux's *Le premier matin* and presented it to the nation. It was, said Sir Edward Poynter, President of the Royal Academy, 'an act of homage to the nation which … has stood single-handed in the path of our common enemy and saved Europe from disaster'. *Year's Art* (1916), pp. 2–3. The sculpture is now in the Tate.
22 E. Clegg, 'Meštrović, England and the Great War', *Burlington Magazine* 144 (December 2002), p. 747.
23 W. G. Blaikie-Murdock 'The Serbian National Sculptor', *Art and Progress* (December 1915), p. 59.
24 *Manchester Guardian* (25 June 1915), p. 5.
25 *The Times* (1 July 1915), p. 9.
26 R. W. Seton-Watson, 'Meštrović and the Jugoslav Idea', in *Exhibition of the Works of Ivan Meštrović* (London: Victoria & Albert Museum 1915), np.
27 The only notable exception was Robert Ross, who wrote that 'the nationalism of Meštrović's art has been overstated'. *Burlington Magazine* 149 (August 1915), p. 211.
28 The most notable critic of Meštrović's work was Selwyn Image. In a letter to *The Times*, he called the sculptures 'wilful, inchoate, amorphous, even monstrous; and at least one work as morally offensive'. *The Times* (30 June 1915), p. 9.
29 *The Times* (1 July 1915), p. 9.
30 *Year's Art* (1916), p. 1.
31 *Catalogue of an Exhibition of Modern Spanish Art* (London: Grafton Galleries, 1914).
32 *The Studio*, 63 (January 1915), p. 296.
33 *British Architect* (1 January 1915), p. 9.
34 *Year's Art* (1916), pp. 85–6.
35 *The Times* (20 March 1915), p. 7.
36 See J. Bowyer Nichols, 'Two Exhibitions in Aid of National Funds', *Burlington Magazine* 26 (January 1915), pp. 163–9.
37 *Observer* (18 April 1915), p. 4.
38 *Sunday Times* (15 November 1914), p. 5.
39 *Reports by the Joint War Committee and the Joint Finance Committee of the British Red Cross and the Order of St. John of Jerusalem in England on the Voluntary Aid*

Rendered to the Sick and Wounded at Home and Abroad and to the British Prisoners of War, 1914–1919 (London: HMSO, 1921), p. 31.

40 *Ibid.*, p. 32.

41 *Daily Telegraph* (28 April 1915), p. 6. Lane eventually died with the sinking of the *Lusitania*. His executors asked Sargent to paint Woodrow Wilson.

42 *Year's Art* (1917), p. 5.

43 *Daily Telegraph* (26 March 1917), p. 7.

44 *Year's Art* (1919), p. 158.

45 'The Red Cross Sale', *Saturday Review* (8 April 1916), pp. 346–7.

46 See Kavanagh, *Museums and the First World War*, p. 8.

47 Bather, 'Museums and National Service', pp. 126–7.

48 F. A. Bather, 'Museums and the War', *Museums' Journal* 15 (July 1915), p. 3.

49 *Ibid.*

50 *Ibid.*, p. 6.

51 *Ibid.*, p. 4.

52 *Ibid.*, p. 9.

53 *Ibid.*, p. 8.

54 *Ibid.*, p. 10.

55 *Museums' Journal* 15 (September 1915), pp. 106–7.

56 *Museums' Journal* 15 (August 1915), p. 76.

57 Kavanagh, *Museums and the First World War*, p. 77.

58 Malvern, *Modern Art, Britain and the Great War*, p. 41.

59 Kavanagh, *Museums and the First World War*, p. 114.

60 *Ibid.*, p. 130.

61 For a recent discussion, see P. James (ed.), *Picture This: World War I Posters and Visual Culture* (Lincoln and London: University of Nebraska Press, 2010).

62 H. R. C., 'The Appeal of the Poster', *Manchester Guardian* (5 April 1915), p. 10.

63 N. Hiley, '"Kitchener Wants You" and "Daddy, what did YOU do in the Great War?": The Myth of British Recruiting Posters', *Imperial War Museum Review* 11 (1997), p. 40.

64 P. Dutton, 'Moving Images? The Parliamentary Recruiting Committee's Poster Campaign, 1914–1916', *Imperial War Museum Review* 4 (1989), pp. 43–58.

65 For further discussion, see C. Ginzburg, '"Your Country Needs You": A Case Study in Political Iconography', *History Workshop Journal* 42 (Autumn 2001), pp. 1–22.

66 M. Hardie and A. Sabin (eds.), *War Posters Issued by Belligerent and Neutral Nations 1914–1919* (London: A. & C. Black, 1920), p. 12.

67 *Ibid.*, p. 10.

68 See *A Catalogue of War Auto Lithographs Designed by Frank Brangwyn* (London: Avenue Press, 1918).

69 Hardie and Sabin, *War Posters*, p. 14.

70 P. Bradshaw, *The Art of the Illustrator: Bert Thomas* (London: Press Art School, 1918), pp. 3–4.

71 H. Shaw, 'Bert Thomas and His Work', *Strand Magazine* 77 (1929), p. 134.

72 See 'Mr. Bert Thomas: Obituary', *The Times* (7 September 1966), p. 16.

73 Shaw, 'Bert Thomas', p. 136.

74 See Hiley, '"Kitchener Wants You"', pp. 48–9.

75 V. Branford, 'Art and Life', *The Athenaeum* (May 1918), p. 226.

76 For an extended discussion of the invisibility of the war, see Dagen, *Le silence des peintres*, pp. 81–139.

77 P. Virilio, *War and Cinema: The Logistics of Military Perception*, trans. Patrick Camillier (London: Verso, 1989), p. 1.
78 Gough, *'A Terrible Beauty'*, pp. 79–80.
79 B. C. Lake, *Knowledge for War: Every Officer's Handbook for the Front* (London: Harrison & Sons, 1916), pp. 38–44. See also R. F. C., 'Topographical Sketching in the Army', *The Studio* 62 (February 1916), pp. 44–5.
80 Adrian Hill became a scout and sniper, and made almost 200 observation drawings of the front line. Horace Gaffron, Sydney Jones and Warwick Lendon were among the other artists who produced these images.
81 L. Smith, *Drawing Fire: The Diary of a Great War Soldier and Artist* (London: Collins, 2009), p. 367.
82 JHM, 'Lieut. Colonel Harold Wyllie' (unpublished biography), Private Papers of H. Wyllie, RAF 84/5/1, Imperial War Museum.
83 Entry (31 January 1915), 'Private Log Book', Private Papers of H. Wyllie, RAF 84/5/1, p. 20, Imperial War Museum.
84 Entry (23 January 1915), 'Private Log Book', Private Papers of H. Wyllie, RAF 84/5/1, p. 19, Imperial War Museum.
85 P. Maze, *A Frenchman in Khaki* (London and Toronto: W. Heinemann Ltd., 1934), p. 114; pp. 210–11.
86 *Ibid.*, p. 130.
87 See E. Kahn, *The Neglected Majority: 'Les Camoufleurs', Art History, and World War I* (Lanham, MD: University Press of America, 1984).
88 *The Times* (27 January 1915), p. 9.
89 R. Behrens, 'The Role of Artists in Ship Camouflage during World War I', *Leonardo* 32 (1999), pp. 53–9. For more on dazzle camouflage, see P. Atterbury, 'Dazzle Painting', *Antique Collector* 47 (1975), pp. 25–9.
90 The letter is reproduced in H. Blechman and A. Newman (eds.), *DPM – Disruptive Pattern Material: An Encyclopedia of Camouflage*, 2 vols. (London: DPM, 2004), vol. I, n.p.
91 Behrens, 'The Role of Artists', p. 58.
92 D. Williams, *Naval Camouflage 1914–1945: A Complete Visual Reference* (London: Chatham Publishing, 2001), p. 37.
93 S. Solomon, *Strategic Camouflage* (London: John Murray, 1920), p. vi.
94 *Ibid.*, pp. 453–4.
95 *Ibid.*, p. 62.
96 *Ibid.*, p. 51.
97 See Blechman and Newman, *DPM*, p. 171; and 'A Dazzle Advertisement of a Dazzling Discovery', *Illustrated London News* (28 June 1919), p. 962.
98 'The Art of Naval "Camouflage" Applied to Fancy Dress: The Chelsea Arts Club "Dazzle" Ball', *Illustrated London News* (22 March 1919), pp. 414–15.
99 Kahn, *Neglected Majority*.
100 N. Wilkinson, *A Brush with Life* (London: Seeley, 1969), p. 26.

4 War pictures: truth, fiction, function

1 Perhaps the most striking evidence for this trend is the trebling of national expenditure on newspapers between 1914 and 1918. A. Prest and A. Adams, *Consumers'*

Expenditure in the United Kingdom 1900–1919 (Cambridge University Press, 1954), p. 133. For more on the conflict's impact on the press, see B. Clarke, 'How the Progress of the War was Chronicled by Pen and Camera', in H. Wilson and J. Hammerton (eds.), *The Great War: The Standard History of the All-Europe Conflict* (London: London Amalgamated Press, 1918), vol. X, pp. 413–28; and E. Cook, *The Press in War-Time* (London: Macmillan, 1920).

2 M. Jay, 'Scopic Regimes of Modernity', in H. Foster (ed.), *Vision and Visuality: Discussions in Contemporary Culture* (Seattle: Bay View Press, 1988), p. 3.

3 C. L. Moore, 'Pictures and Words', *The Dial* (September 1914), p. 127.

4 For a broader discussion, see J. Crary, *Techniques of the Observer: On Vision and Modernity in the Nineteenth Century* (Cambridge, MA: MIT Press, 1990).

5 The most powerful expression of this was Pictorialism. For a discussion, see J. Taylor, *Pictorial Photography in Britain 1900–1920* (London: Arts Council of Great Britain, 1978); and M. Weaver (ed.), *British Photography in the Nineteenth Century: The Fine Art Tradition* (Cambridge University Press, 1989).

6 For a concise discussion of these developments, see R. Flukinger, *The Formative Decades: Photography in Great Britain, 1839–1920* (Austin: University of Texas Press, 1985), pp. 13–16.

7 See F. Beeson and A. Williams, *Amateur Photography* (London: Thomas Nelson & Sons, 1913).

8 For a discussion, see N. Harris, 'Iconography and Intellectual History: The Halftone Effect', in *Cultural Excursions: Marketing Appetites and Cultural Tastes in Modern America* (Chicago and London: University of Chicago Press, 1990), pp. 304–17.

9 *Colour* magazine was the most famous of these. It was first published in 1914.

10 For the debate, see G. Beegan, *The Mass Image: A Social History of Photomechanical Reproduction in Victorian London* (Basingstoke: Palgrave Macmillan, 2008), pp. 188–9.

11 For an analysis of the *Illustrated London News*, see P. Sinnema, *Dynamics of the Printed Page: Representing the Nation in the Illustrated London News* (Aldershot: Ashgate, 1998).

12 N. Hiley, '"Nothing More than a 'Craze'": Cinema Building in Britain from 1909 to 1914', in A. Higson (ed.), *Young and Innocent? The Cinema in Britain, 1896–1930* (University of Exeter Press, 2002), p. 119; and N. Hiley, '"Let's go to the pictures": The British Cinema Audience in the 1920s and 1930s', *Journal of Popular British Cinema* 2 (1999), p. 40.

13 N. Reeves, *The Power of Film Propaganda: Myth or Reality?* (London: Cassell, 1999), p. 22.

14 This process was not entirely new. In 1900 *The Sphere* was established at the height of – and partly in response to – the public's hunger for images of the Boer War.

15 *Newspaper Press Directory* (1916), p. 20.

16 For a discussion, see Kavanagh, *Museums and the First World War*, pp. 65–81.

17 *Museums' Journal* 15 (March 1916), p. 308.

18 *The Times* (20 March 1916), p. 10.

19 *The Times* (14 April 1916), p. 5.

20 *Fine Art Trade Journal* 10 (September 1914), pp. 265–6. See also 'A Trade Opportunity during the War', *Fine Art Trade Journal* 10 (August 1914), pp. 250–2.

21 Many dealers reported that their initial war losses were often compensated by this kind of war business. See, for instance, *Fine Art Trade Journal* 11 (February 1915), pp. 42–3.

22 *Fine Art Trade Journal* 10 (September 1914), p. 263.
23 M. Paris (ed.), *The First World War and Popular Cinema: 1914 to the Present* (Edinburgh University Press, 1999), pp. 1–2.
24 *The Cinema: Its Present Position and Future Possibilities, Being the Report of and Chief Evidence taken by the Cinema Commission of Inquiry instituted by the National Council of Public Morals* (London: Williams & Norgate, 1917), p. xxi.
25 R. Niemi, *History in the Media: Film and Television* (Santa Barbara, CA: ABC-Clio, 2006), p. 45.
26 See Malvern, *Modern Art, Britain and the Great War*, pp. 17–24.
27 M. Sanders and P. Taylor, *British Propaganda during the First World War* (London: Macmillan, 1982), p. 40.
28 N. Hiley, *Making War: British Propaganda* (Cambridge University Press, 2000), p. 400.
29 I. Nicholson, 'An Aspect of British Official Wartime Propaganda', *Cornhill Magazine* 70 (May 1931), p. 595.
30 Sanders and Taylor, *British Propaganda*, pp. 119–21.
31 Nicholson, 'British Official Wartime Propaganda', p. 597.
32 *Ibid.*, p. 596.
33 The most thorough account is Malvern, *Modern Art, Britain and the Great War.*
34 M. Bone, *The Western Front: Drawings by Muirhead Bone* (New York: G. H. Doran, 1917).
35 In the end, Lavery was unable to travel, and instead painted scenes of war around the British Isles.
36 The image had initially been commissioned for another government publication: a series of lithographs called *Britain's Efforts and Ideals*, which was first published in 1917.
37 For a superb discussion, see M. Jay, *Downcast Eyes: The Denigration of Vision in Twentieth-Century French Thought* (Berkeley and London: University of California Press, 1993).
38 *A Lantern Lecture on Heroic Actions and Daring Deeds of the Great War* (London: Newton & Co., 1916), n.p. For a concurrent loss of faith in print correspondents, see M. Farish, 'Modern Witnesses: Foreign Correspondents, Geopolitical Vision, and the First World War', *Transactions of the Institute of British Geographers* 26 (2001), pp. 273–87; and P. Knightley, *The First Casualty: The War Correspondent as Hero, Propagandist, and Myth Maker from the Crimea to Vietnam* (London: Deutsch, 1975).
39 H. Gower, L. Jast and W. Topley, *The Camera as Historian* (London: Sampson Low Marston, 1916), pp. 2–3. See also J. Salis, 'Art and the Camera', *New Witness* (21 December 1916), pp. 236–7.
40 C. Hartshorne, P. Weiss and A. Burks (eds.), *The Collected Papers of Charles Sanders Peirce*, 8 vols. (Cambridge, MA: Harvard University Press, 1933), vol. IV, p. 447.
41 R. Barthes, *Camera Lucida: Reflections on Photography* (London: Hill & Wang, 1981), pp. 80, 87.
42 A. Bazin, *What is Cinema?*, trans. H. Gray, 2 vols. (Berkeley and Los Angeles: University of California Press, 1967), vol. I, pp. 12–13.
43 See T. Gunning, 'What's the Point of an Index? or, Faking Photographs', *Nordicom Review* 24 (2004), pp. 39–49.
44 'Photographers and Pictures', *Saturday Review* 126 (28 September 1918), pp. 885–6.

45 *Manchester Guardian* (11 August 1916), p. 4; *Daily Express* (11 August 1916), p. 2; *Daily Mirror* (11 August 1916), p. 10.
46 *Star* (6 September 1916), p. 2.
47 *The Times* (11 August 1916), p. 3. See also Dagen, *Le silence des peintres*, pp. 12–13.
48 R. Smither, '"A Wonderful Idea of the Fighting": The Question of Fakes in "The Battle of the Somme"', *Historical Journal of Film, Radio and Television* 13 (1993), special issue: *Britain and the Cinema in the First World War*, pp. 149–68.
49 See Malvern, *Modern Art, Britain and the Great War*, pp. 37–49. For more on this 'contest of images', see D. Apel, *War Culture and the Contest of Images* (New Brunswick, NJ and London: Rutgers University Press, 2012).
50 'On the Record of Passing Events', *The Studio* 64 (February 1915), p. 330.
51 K. Walton, 'Transparent Pictures: On the Nature of Photographic Realism', *Critical Inquiry* 11 (December 1984), pp. 246–77.
52 C. Montague, *British Artists at the Front*, 4 vols. (London: Country Life and George Newnes, 1918), vol. I.
53 *The Graphic* (17 October 1914), p. 543.
54 *The Graphic* (17 October 1914), p. 546; *War Illustrated* (12 September 1914), p. 75; and *Illustrated War News* (26 August 1914), p. 7.
55 *Illustrated War News* (2 September 1914), p. 11; *The Sphere* (29 August 1914), p. 3; *The Graphic* (28 November 1914), p. 743; *The Graphic* (22 August 1914), p. 315.
56 *The Sphere* (19 September 1914), p. 314–15.
57 P. Bradshaw, *The Art of the Illustrator: Fortunino Matania* (London: Press Art School, 1917), p. 6.
58 G. Norman, 'History in Pictures', *The Times* (22 October 1977), p. 9.
59 Bradshaw, *Matania*, pp. 4–5.
60 C. Prigg (ed.), *The War Dispatches* (London: Times Press, 1964), p. i.
61 *The Graphic* (31 October 1914), p. 620.
62 F. Villiers, *His Five Decades of Adventure*, 2 vols. (London: Hutchinson, 1921), vol. II, pp. 308–19.
63 R. Graves, 'The British Soldier', in *The British Soldier: An Exhibition of Pictures by Eric H. Kennington, an Official War Artist on the Western Front* (London: Ernest Brown & Phillips, 1918), pp. 3–8. See also 'Lord Beaverbrook on Art in Propaganda', *The Times* (2 March 1918), p. 3.
64 J. Crawford Flitch, *The Great War: Fourth Year* (London: Grant Richards, 1918), p. 9.
65 S. Malvern, '"War as it Is": The Art of Muirhead Bone, C. R. W. Nevinson, and Paul Nash, 1916–17', *Art History* 9 (December 1986), p. 510. Nevinson's independence was most clearly dramatized in the censorship controversy he ignited in 1918. For his own response to it, see C. R. W. Nevinson, 'When the Censor Censored "Censored"', *British Legion Journal* (October 1932), pp. 114–15.
66 C. H. Collins Baker, 'War Paintings', *Saturday Review* 122 (7 October 1916), pp. 342–3.
67 Crawford Flitch, *The Great War*, p. 7.
68 Montague, *British Artists at the Front*, vol. III.
69 Quoted in the *Saturday Review* 126 (25 May 1918), p. 510.
70 Hynes, *A War Imagined*, p. 159, 166.
71 The comments were reproduced in C. R. W. Nevinson, *Paint and Prejudice* (London: Methuen, 1937), p. 86.
72 A. Clutton-Brock, 'Personality or Process. Mr Nevinson's Pictures of Men as War Machines', *The Times* (29 September 1916), p. 9.

73 O. R. D., 'Mr Nevinson's War Pictures', *Westminster Gazette* (2 October 1916), p. 2.
74 Hynes, *A War Imagined*, p. 159, 166; Cork, *A Bitter Truth*, p. 125.
75 It was reported that 'snapshooters taking pictures of battlefields run more risks than soldiers'. 'Perils of War Photography', *Washington Post* (15 November 1914), p. 45.
76 For an extended discussion of the 'invisibility' of the war, see Dagen, *Le silence des peintres*, pp. 81–139.
77 See B. Hüppauf, 'Experiences of Modern Warfare and the Crisis of Representation', *New German Critique* 59 (Spring 1993), pp. 41–76.
78 For a criticism, see F. Tilney, 'Photographs as Illustrations', *British Journal of Photography* (4 December 1914), pp. 885–7.
79 The best example of this is the production and reception of the Australian photographer Frank Hurley's composite photographs of Passchendaele. See M. Jolly, 'Australian First-World-War Photography: Frank Hurley and Charles Bean', *History of Photography* 23 (Summer 1999), pp. 141–8.
80 S. Sontag, *On Photography* (New York: Farrar, Straus & Giroux, 1977), p. 86.
81 *The Times* (5 April 1918), p. 8.
82 Sontag, *On Photography*, pp. 22–3.
83 *The Sphere* (7 December 1914), pp. 20–1. Dadd was killed in action in France on 2 August 1916.
84 *Illustrated London News* (3 October 1914), p. i.
85 *Illustrated London News*, supplement (3 October 1914), pp. ii-iii.
86 P. Gibbs, *Realities of War* (London: Hutchinson & Co., 1929), pp. 242–3.
87 For more on this issue, see Apel, *War Culture and the Contest of Images*, p. 3.
88 P. Konody, 'On War Memorials', in Canadian War Records Office, *Art and War: Canadian War Memorials* (London: Colour, 1919), p. 5.
89 P. Hogarth, *The Artist as Reporter* (London: Gordon Fraser, 1986), p. 110.
90 Tilney, 'Photographs as Illustrations', pp. 886–7.
91 'War and the Imagination', *New Statesman* 3 (8 August 1914), p. 554.
92 For cavalry in the war, see S. Badsey, 'Cavalry and the Development of Breakthrough Doctrine', in P. Griffith (ed.), *British Fighting Methods in the Great War* (London: F. Cass, 1996), pp. 138–74.
93 For war, the body and the machine, see J. Bourke, *Dismembering the Male: Men's Bodies, Britain and the Great War* (London: Reaktion, 1996); and H. Foster, 'Prosthetic Gods', *Modernism/Modernity* 4 (April 1997), pp. 5–38.
94 Advertisement in *The Times* (10 February 1916), p. 3.
95 P. Fussell, *The Great War and Modern Memory* (Oxford University Press, 1975), pp. 21–3.
96 *Review of Reviews* (March 1916), p. 265.
97 R. Scruton, 'Photography and Representation', *Critical Inquiry* 7 (Spring 1981), p. 581.
98 See R. Cork, 'Images of Extinction: Paul Nash at the Western Front', in J. Howlett and R. Mengham (eds.), *The Violent Muse: Violence and the Artistic Imagination in Europe, 1910–1939* (Manchester University Press, 1994), pp. 56–64.
99 For more on Rider-Rider, see J. Carmichael, *First World War Photographers* (London and New York: Routledge, 1999).
100 Quoted in Cork, 'Images of Extinction', pp. 59–60.

101 Malvern, *Modern Art, Britain and the Great War*, p. 18.
102 M. de Zayas, 'Picasso Speaks', *The Arts* 7 (May 1923), p. 315.

5 Peace pictures: escapism, consolation, catharsis

1 For the most influential architect of this paradigm, see Fussell, *The Great War and Modern Memory*.
2 Winter, Sites of Memory, p. 5.
3 For examples in these respective fields, see S. Das, *Touch and Intimacy in First World War Literature* (Cambridge University Press, 2006); N. Saunders, *Trench Art: Materialities and Memories of War* (Oxford: Berg, 2003); and A. Watson, *Enduring the Great War: Combat, Morale and Collapse in the German and British Armies, 1914–1918* (Cambridge University Press, 2008).
4 For more, see Fox, 'Conflict and Consolation'.
5 For a discussion, see G. DeGroot, *Blighty: British Society in the Era of the Great War* (London: Longman, 1996), ch. 11.
6 G. Bernard Shaw, *Heartbreak House, Great Catherine, and Playlets of War* (London: Constable, 1919), p. xxxvii.
7 For more on these debates, see 'The Popular Art', *The Times* (16 June 1915), p. 9.
8 T. Gifford, *Pastoral* (London: Routledge, 1999), p. 46. See also D. Kalstone, 'Conjuring with Nature: Some Twentieth-Century Readings of Pastoral', in R. A. Brower (ed.), *Twentieth-Century Literature in Retrospect* (Cambridge, MA: Harvard University Press, 1971), p. 249.
9 R. Williams, *The Country and the City* (London: Chatto & Windus, 1973), p. 45.
10 For another almost identical picture called *A Woodland Pool*, also from 1915, see F. Lewis, *Benjamin Williams Leader RA, 1831–1923* (Leigh-on-Sea: F. Lewis, 1971), cat. 663.
11 It should read: 'The yellow cornfields lay, although as yet / Unto the stalks no sickle had been set.' W. Morris, *The Earthly Paradise*, ed. F. Boos (New York and London: Routledge, 2002), p. 430.
12 G. Thomas (ed.), *Collected Poems of Edward Thomas* (Oxford University Press, 1978), pp. 71–3.
13 For a typical use of the term 'peace picture', see the *Daily Chronicle* (29 October 1918), p. 4.
14 *Morning Post* (13 November 1914), p. 4; *Yorkshire Post* (4 November 1914), p. 6; *The Times* (7 May 1918), p. 9.
15 *Bibby's Annual* (1916), p. 33
16 Waites, *A Class Society at War*, p. 100.
17 'The New Collector', *Fine Art Trade Journal* 14 (April 1918), p. 76.
18 *Year's Art* (1918), p. 291.
19 *Daily Telegraph* (12 May 1916), p. 7.
20 *Fine Art Trade Journal* 12 (January 1916), p. 30.
21 *Fine Art Trade Journal* 11 (August 1915), p. 196.
22 C. L. Hind, *Landscape Painting from Giotto to the Present Day*, 2 vols. (London: Chapman & Hall, 1924), vol. II, p. 323.
23 *Lady's Pictorial* (2 December 1916), in 'Press Cuttings Book', P8, Royal Watercolour Society.

24 *Queen* (13 February 1915), in 'Press Cuttings Book', P8, Royal Watercolour Society.
25 Representative examples are those produced for E. Rhys (ed.), *The Old Country: A Book of Love and Praise of England* (London: YMCA, 1917). The book was marketed as a 'golden remembrancer' for homesick servicemen.
26 O. Green and S. Taylor, *The Moving Metropolis: A History of London's Transport since 1800* (London: Lawrence King, 2003), p. 167.
27 The other artists commissioned to produce such images were Francis Ernest Jackson, Joseph Walter West and Charles Sims. See also Hardie and Sabin, *War Posters*.
28 The poem, which ran along the bottom of the poster, read: 'Mine be a cot beside the hill, / A bee-hive's hum shall soothe my ear; / A willowy brook, that turns a mill, / With many a fall shall linger near. / The swallow, oft, beneath my thatch, / Shall twitter from her clay-built nest; / Oft shall the pilgrim lift the latch, / And share my meal, a welcome guest. / Around my ivy'd porch shall spring / Each fragrant flower that drinks the dew; / And Lucy, at her wheel, shall sing / In russet gown and apron blue. / The village church among the trees, / Where first our marriage-vows were given, / With merry peals shall swell the breeze, / And point with taper spire to Heaven.' S. Rogers, *The Pleasures of Memory, with Other Poems* (Oxford: T. Cadell, 1799), pp. 180–1.
29 This reading was reinforced by the final stanza of Rogers's poem, included above, which made direct reference to an earlier marriage.
30 See S. Sillars, 'Icons of Englishness: Tradition and Development in the Arts of the Great War', *Critical Quarterly* 23 (June 1981), pp. 51–9.
31 A. Howkins, 'The Discovery of Rural England', in R. Colls and P. Dodd (eds.), *Englishness: Politics and Culture 1880–1920* (London: Croom Helm, 1976), p. 69.
32 A. Potts, '"Constable Country" between the Wars', in R. Samuel (ed.), *Patriotism: The Making and Unmaking of British National Identity*, 3 vols. (London: Routledge, 1989), vol. III, p. 162.
33 *Morning Post* (22 April 1918), p. 6.
34 For a discussion, see Mosse, *Fallen Soldiers*, pp. 108–9. For more on recruiting posters, see Dutton, 'Moving Images'.
35 Quoted in C. Haste, *Keep the Home Fires Burning: Propaganda in the First World War* (London: Allen Lane, 1977), p. 55.
36 Samuel Hynes devoted a whole chapter to 'The Death of Landscape' in his *A War Imagined*, pp. 189–202.
37 For two excellent studies, see A. Gregory, *The Silence of Memory: Armistice Day, 1919–1946* (Oxford: Berg, 1994); and A. King, *Memorials of the Great War in Britain: The Symbolism and Politics of Remembrance* (Oxford: Berg, 1998).
38 *The Times* (23 December 1919), p. 4.
39 Winter, *Sites of Memory*, p. 5.
40 For a brief account, see C. Moriarty, '"Though in a Picture Only": Portrait Photography and the Commemoration of the First World War', in Braybon, *Evidence, History and the Great War*, pp. 30–47.
41 Pliny the Elder, *Natural History: A Selection*, ed. J. F. Healey (London: Penguin Books, 1991), p. 151.
42 'Professional Classes Aid Council Report, 1 November 1914–16 October 1915', Arts in War Time Committee Annual Report 1915, pp. 43–4. Professional Classes Aid Council, 1916.
43 *Fine Art Trade Journal* 10 (September 1914), pp. 275, 278. See also *The Studio* 67 (April 1916), p. 188.

44 The portrait was made on Wednesday, 19 August. Rutter, *Philip de László*, p. 277.
45 *Burlington Magazine* 26 (November 1914), p. 88.
46 Quoted in Bailey, 'De László's Relationships, p. 56.
47 Dunsterville to de László (22 January 1916), DLA 044-0095. See also Buxton to de László (10 May 1917), DLA 055-0138; and Buxton to de László (25 January 1917), DLA 055-0142. All at the De László Archive.
48 Several of his sitters were killed in action after he had painted them: James McEwen died at the Somme on 12 October 1916, a year after his portrait; Bryan Guinness died two years after his 1915 portrait; and Cecil Molyneux was killed (aged sixteen) near Jutland (in May 1916) ten months after his portrait.
49 R. Bourne, *Lords of Fleet Street: The Harmsworth Dynasty* (London: Unwin Hyman, 1990), pp. 83–4.
50 H. Belting, *Anthropology of Images: Picture, Medium, Body*, trans. T. Dunlop (Princeton University Press, 2011), p. 86.
51 Walter Sickert, Alfred Munnings, Frank Salisbury and Allan Stewart were just some of the many distinguished artists to produce posthumous portraits in the war years, though few enjoyed the work: Stewart called it a 'rather lugubrious job', and Sickert complained that it was the '*pompes funèbres* department' of his output. Stewart, quoted in P. Harrington, *British Artists and War: The Face of Battle in Paintings and Prints, 1700–1914* (London: Greenhill Books, 1993), p. 304. Sickert, quoted in W. Baron, *Sickert: Paintings and Drawings* (New Haven and London: Yale University Press, 2006), p. 102. For Salisbury's posthumous pictures, see F. Salisbury, *Portrait and Pageant: Kings, Presidents and People* (London: John Murray, 1944), pp. 31–7.
52 General Assembly (25 April 1919), General Assembly Minutes 1913–32, RAA/GA/1/10, Royal Academy.
53 De László made posthumous portraits of Arthur Burn; Prince Maurice of Battenberg (commissioned by Princess Beatrice after he was killed on 28 October 1914 near Mons); Baron Bruni von Schröder (who was painted shortly after being declared missing on the Eastern Front in 1915); Geoffrey Gunnis; Robert Palmer; and Charles Nairne (who had been killed in October 1914 near Ypres).
54 Lord Leith of Fyvie to de László (28 and 31 October 1914), DLA 075-0003-4, De László Archive.
55 Burn to de László (1 December 1914), DLA 075-0118, De László Archive.
56 Burn to de László (no date), DLA 054-0116, De László Archive.
57 Maxwell to de László (7 March 1916), DLA 047-0002, De László Archive.
58 Maxwell to de László (14 March 1916), DLA 047-0004, De László Archive.
59 Maxwell to de László (20 August 1916), DLA 047-0003, De László Archive.
60 R. Barthes, *Camera Lucida: Reflections on Photography*, trans. R. Howard (London: Vintage, 2000), p. 5.
61 Quoted in Rutter, *Philip de László*, p. 307.
62 Quoted in Rutter, *Philip de László*, pp. 304–5.
63 *Fine Art Trade Journal* 12 (January 1916), p. 19.
64 *The Graphic* (23 November 1914), p. i.
65 *The Graphic* (21 November 1914), p. iii.
66 The original was donated to the mourning Princess Beatrice (who had also commissioned de László to paint her dead son, Prince Maurice), and it still hangs in a chapel devoted to his memory, the Battenberg Chapel in St Mildred's Church, Whippingham, on the Isle of Wight.

67 Prices ranged from a simple unframed colour print at 1s to a framed facsimile oil print at £1 11s 6d). *The Graphic* (6 February 1915), p. 183.
68 T. Pym and J. Gordon, *Papers from Picardy, by Two Chaplains, the Rev. T. W. Pym and the Rev. Geoffrey Gordon* (London: Constable, 1917), pp. 175–6. For the print's influence in Canada, see J. Vance, *Death So Noble: Memory, Meaning and the First World War* (Vancouver: UBC Press, 1997), pp. 40–1.
69 *The Graphic* (21 August 1915), p. iii.
70 Quoted in *The Graphic* (17 April 1915), p. iii.
71 In a particularly dangerous manoeuvre on 30 December 1917, Nash was one of only twelve soldiers to survive an eighty-man offensive. A. Freer, *John Nash: 'The Delighted Eye'* (Aldershot: Ashgate, 1993), pp. 14–15.
72 John Nash, 'Interview' (1974), in *Artists in an Age of Conflict*, IWM 323, Reel 2, Imperial War Museum.
73 *Ibid.*
74 L. Knight, *Autobiography: Oil Paint and Grease Paint* (London: Ivor Nicholson & Watson, 1936), pp. 205–6.
75 *Daily Telegraph* (3 April 1916), p. 7; *Lady's Pictorial* (2 June 1917), p. 4. See also A. Marwick, *The Deluge: British Society and the First World War* (London: Macmillan, 1965), p. 185; and G. Clarke (ed.), *A Treasury of War Poetry: British and American Poets of the World War, 1914–1919* (London: Hodder & Stoughton, 1919, p. 36, 40. For more quotations, see *Yorkshire Post* (2 November 1916), p. 3; *Lady's Pictorial* (24 November 1915), p. 4; *Lady's Pictorial* (14 December 1917), p. 4.
76 D. Phillips, 'Art and War', *Bulletin of the College Art Association of America* 1 (September 1918), p. 35.
77 T. W. Koch, *Books in Camp, Trench and Hospital* (London: J. M. Dent & Sons, 1917), p. 36.
78 P. Bradshaw, *Drawn from Memory* (London: Chapman & Hall, 1943), pp. 47–8.
79 W. Churchill, *Painting as a Pastime* (London: Ernest Benn, 1948), pp. 16–17.
80 *Flight* (7 March 1918), p. 258.
81 F. Rutter, 'Art and Healing: The Colour Cure of Shell Shock', *Sunday Times* (16 September 1917), p. 10.
82 H. Carrington, *Psychical Phenomena and the War* (London: T. Werner Laurie, 1919), pp. 91–3.
83 E. G. F., 'Sunshine for Shell Shock', *British Journal of Nursing* (6 October 1917), p. 224.
84 'Kemp Prosser "Cure by Colour"', *Times of India* (7 May 1919), p. 10.
85 *Flight* (14 February 1918), p. 166.
86 *British Journal of Nursing* (4 October 1919), p. 212.
87 'Mr. Tom Mostyn's "Gardens of Romance"', *Observer* (2 February 1919), p. 7.
88 Kemp-Prossor's project represents a forgotten early stage in the development of art therapy – a practice developed for traumatized soldiers in the Second World War by another artist of the First, Adrian Hill. See S. Hogan, *Healing Arts: The History of Art Therapy* (London: Jessica Kingsley, 2001), pp. 132–59.
89 M. Klein, 'Infantile Anxiety Situations Reflected in a Work of Art and in the Creative Impulse' (1929), in *The Writings of Melanie Klein*, 4 vols. (London: Hogarth Press, 1975), vol. IV, pp. 210–18.
90 E. Scarry, *The Body in Pain: The Making and Unmaking of the World* (New York and Oxford: Oxford University Press, 1985).

91 For canonical examples of this view, see W. Pater, *The Renaissance: Studies in Art and Poetry* (London: Macmillan, 1877); and J. Whistler, *Mr Whistler's Ten O'Clock* (London: Chatto & Windus, 1888).
92 Bell, *Art*, p. 266.
93 *Ibid.*, pp. 25, 276.
94 For an excellent study of these discourses, see J. Atkin, *A War of Individuals: Bloomsbury Attitudes to the Great War* (Manchester University Press, 2002).
95 See T. Adorno, *Aesthetic Theory*, trans. G. Adorno and R. Tiedemann (London: Athlone, 1999).
96 J. Delville, 'The Social Influence of Art', *Colour* (January 1916), pp. 228–9.
97 Winter, *Sites of Memory*, p. 54, 76.
98 E. Newlandsmith, *The Temple of Life and the Mission of the Arts Therein* (London, New York and Bombay: Longmans, Green & Co., 1919).
99 R. Hallward, *The Religion of Art* (London: Heath Cranton, 1917), p. 56.
100 *Ibid.*, p. 113.
101 For a study of the Design and Industries Association, see Saler, *The Avant-Garde in Interwar England*.
102 W. Rothenstein, *A Plea for a Wider Use of Artists and Craftsmen* (London: Constable, 1916), p. 15.
103 *Arts and Crafts Exhibition Society: Catalogue of the Eleventh Exhibition* (London: Chiswick Press, 1916), p. 22.
104 J. Galsworthy, 'Art and the War', *Fortnightly Review* 98 (1 November 1915), p. 927.

6 Art and society after the war

1 *The Times* (13 November 1918), p. 9.
2 Cork, 'Machine Age, Apocalypse and Pastoral', p. 71; Farr, *English Art*, p. 231, 248.
3 Harrison, *English Art and Modernism*, pp. 145–66.
4 *Year's Art* (1920), p. 274. George Romney's portrait of the Beckford sisters raised £52,000 – the highest price ever paid for a picture in the open market, at the Hamilton Palace sale. *Year's Art* (1920), p. 282. In May £1,600 was paid for a watercolour by Myles Birket Foster, which doubled the highest sum paid for a work by a 'contemporary British painter'. *Year's Art* (1920), p. 4.
5 *Year's Art* (1920), p. 4.
6 *Colour* (November 1919), p. xiv.
7 It was not the first such exhibition. In February, Burlington House had shown pictures acquired by the Canadian government. This exhibition too received rapturous responses: one critic called it 'the most important art exhibition ever held in London'. *Colour* (February 1919), p. xiv.
8 *The Times* (29 January 1920), p. 12.
9 *Parliamentary Debates, Commons* 125 (24 February 1920), pp. 1497–9.
10 *Westminster Gazette* (18 December 1919), p. 10; *Saturday Review* (3 January 1920), pp. 6–7; *The Times* (12 December 1919), p. 15.
11 *Manchester Guardian* (12 December 1919), p. 8.
12 *Morning Post* (3 January 1920), p. 7; *Colour* (March 1920), p. xiv.
13 C. Bell, 'Wilcoxism', *The Athenaeum* (5 March 1920), p. x; 'The False Dawn', *The Athenaeum* (9 January 1920), p. x.

14 X., 'The Imperial War Museum – Exhibition of War Paintings and Other Records', *Burlington Magazine* 36 (February 1920), pp. 94–5.
15 'The Nation's War Paintings: Youth at the Academy', *Liverpool Post* (12 December 1919), p. 7.
16 J. L. McQ., 'Rebels in the Fortress', *Daily Express* (3 January 1919), p. 4.
17 R. Blomfield, 'Considerations on the Policy and Position of the Royal Academy 1918' (May 1918), in General Assembly Minutes Book 10: 1913–32, RAA/GA/1/10, Royal Academy.
18 For more on the Royal Academy's post-war realignment, see Peters Corbett, *The Modernity of English Art*, pp. 192–200; M. A. Stevens, *The Edwardians and After: The Royal Academy, 1900–1950* (London: Royal Academy, 1988, pp. 15–21); and T. Cowdell, 'The Role of the Royal Academy in English Art, 1918–1930', unpublished PhD thesis, University of London (1980).
19 S. Hutchison, *The History of the Royal Academy 1768–1986* (London: Robert Royce, 1987), p. 162.
20 'The Young British Artist', *Daily Telegraph* (28 December 1920), p. 12.
21 Quoted in M. Holroyd, *Augustus John: The New Biography* (London: Heinemann, 1996), p. 475.
22 *The Times* (29 April 1922), p. 13.
23 E. Wake Cook, *Retrogression in Art and the Suicide of the Royal Academy. Part the second, Coming Renaissance with an Outline of a New Philosophy of Life and of Art* (London: Hutchinson, 1924), pp. 25–6.
24 See Hynes, *A War Imagined*, pp. 161–5.
25 Quoted in Taylor, *Art for the Nation*, p. 144.
26 *The Times* (11 August 1919), p. 8.
27 For a thorough study, see M. Walsh, *C. R. W. Nevinson: This Cult of Violence* (New Haven and London: Yale University Press, 2002).
28 *The Connoisseur* 57 (June 1920), p. 110. He expressed similar sentiments in 'Bolshevism in Art', *Daily Express* (10 March 1919), p. 6.
29 'Art in England', *Morning Post* (4 January 1921), p. 8
30 R. Tatlock, 'Modern British Painting – A Proposal', *Burlington Magazine* 38 (April 1921), pp. 155–6.
31 S. Elmer, 'The "Nameless Exhibition", London, 1921', *Burlington Magazine* 153 (September 2011), pp. 583–90.
32 *Arts and Letters* 1 (1917), p. 25.
33 W. Orpen (ed.), *Outline of Art* (London: Newnes, 1923), p. 369.
34 See 'Art after Armageddon', *The Athenaeum* (12 September 1914), pp. 268–9.
35 For a compelling argument in favour of functional memorials, see W. Lethaby, 'Memorials of the Fallen: Service or Sacrifice?', in *Form in Civilization: Collected Papers on Art and Labour* (London: Oxford University Press, 1922), pp. 56–65.
36 See *The Times* (9 April 1919), p. 8.
37 N. Hewitt, 'The National Inventory of War Memorials', in J.-M. Teutonico and J. Fidler (eds.), *Monuments and the Millennium: Proceedings of a Joint Conference Organised by English Heritage and the United Kingdom Institute for Conservation* (London: James & James, 2001), p. 13.
38 See E. Homberger, 'The Story of the Cenotaph', *Times Literary Supplement* (12 November 1976), pp. 1429–30; and A. Greenberg, 'Lutyens's Cenotaph', *Journal of the Society of Architectural Historians* 48 (March 1989), pp. 5–23.

39 Greenberg, 'Lutyens's Cenotaph', p. 11.
40 *New York Times* (16 May 1920), p. 6.
41 *Manchester Guardian* (27 December 1919), p. 7.
42 Cecil Harcourt Smith, chairman of the Civic Arts Association, quoted in *Year's Art* (1919), p. 113.
43 *Ibid*., p. 111.
44 *The Times* (6 April 1918), p. 3.
45 *The Times* (7 December 1918), p. 11.
46 *The Times* (6 June 1919), p. 7.
47 *Manchester Guardian* (8 July 1918), p. 8.
48 Royal Academy of Arts, *War Memorials Exhibition, 1919* (London: William Clowes & Sons, 1919), p. B2.
49 *The Times* (13 May 1919), p. 6.
50 *The Times* (6 April 1918), p. 3.
51 *Year's Art* (1919), p. 110.
52 One story circulated in November 1920 that deliberately exploited this ambiguity on behalf of its readers. See *To my 'Unknown' Warrior* (London: Hodder & Stoughton, 1920).
53 *The Times* (13 November 1918), p. 9.
54 See D. Thistlewood, 'The Early History of the NSEAD', *Journal of Art and Design Education* 7 (1988), pp. 37–64.
55 A. Clutton-Brock, *The Ultimate Belief* (London: Constable, 1916), p. 79.
56 F. Hayward and A. Freeman, *The Spiritual Foundations of Reconstruction: A Plea for New Educational Methods* (London: P. S. King & Son, 1919).
57 Ministry of Reconstruction, *Art and Industry* (London: HMSO, 1919), p. 6.
58 *A Design for Democracy: An Abridgement of a Report of the Adult Education Committee of the British Ministry of Reconstruction, commonly called the 1919 Report* (London: M. Parrish, 1956), p. 103.
59 *Ibid*., p. 104.
60 For the response to the appointment, see W. Rothenstein, *Men and Memories: Recollections, 1872–1938* (London: Chatto & Windus, 1978), pp. 365–6.
61 Kavanagh, *Museums and the First World War*, p. 87.
62 *Report of the Board of Education for the Year 1921–2* (London: HMSO, 1923), p. 1.
63 *Parliamentary Debates, Commons 127* (24 March 1920), pp. 433–4.
64 *Report of the Board of Education for the Year 1921–2*, p. 5.
65 *Ibid*., p. 7.
66 For a discussion, see A. H. H. 'The Organization of Art', *The Athenaeum* (18 July 1919), p. 1.
67 'The League of Arts', *Musical Times* (1 July 1920), p. 477.
68 'The British Drama League', *Observer* (1 June 1919), p. 16.
69 'Necessity of Art', *Observer* (13 May 1923), p. 14.
70 P. Nash, 'The Arts League of Service', *New Witness* (23 May 1919), p. 72.
71 *Arts League of Service Annual* (1921–2), p. 9.
72 *Ibid*.
73 P. O'Keeffe, *Some Sort of Genius: A Life of Wyndham Lewis* (London: Pimlico, 2001), pp. 214–15.
74 For an account of the Arts League of Service travelling players, see E. Elder, *Travelling Players: The Story of the Arts League of Service* (London: F. Muller, 1939).

75 'Bringing the Arts to the People: A Nottingham Conference', *Manchester Guardian* (21 March 1921), p. 6.
76 *Arts League of Service Annual* (1921–2), p. 19.
77 *Ibid.*
78 Trotter, *Instincts of the Herd*, p. 144.
79 Quoted in Cork, *A Bitter Truth*, p. 163.
80 Wyndham Lewis, *Blasting and Bombardiering*, p. 186.
81 *Blast: Review of the Great English Vortex* 1(1914), pp. 6–7.
82 P. Wyndham Lewis, *The Caliph's Design: Architects! Where is Your Vortex?* (London: Egoist Press, 1919), p. 7.
83 P. Wyndham Lewis (ed.), *The Tyro: A Review of the Arts of Painting, Sculpture and Design* 2 (1922), p. 3.
84 P. Edwards, *Wyndham Lewis: Art and War* (London: Wyndham Lewis Memorial Trust in association with Lund Humphries, 1992), p. 218.
85 *The Times* (3 May 1920), p. 9.
86 *The Times* (19 October 1920), p. 19; *The Times* (25 October 1920), p. 13; *The Times* (5 November 1920), p. 9.
87 P. Konody, 'The Glut of Art Shows', *Observer* (4 November 1923), p.10. See also O. Brown, *Exhibition: The Memoirs of Oliver Brown* (London: Evelyn, Adams & Mackay, 1968), p. 62.
88 'Fine Art in the Stores', *The Athenaeum* (22 August 1919), p. 788. See also *Colour* (November 1919), p. xiv.
89 See N. Catty (ed.), *Training in Appreciation: Art, Literature, Music* (London: Sidgwick & Jackson, 1921).
90 Quoted from the back cover of *Art* (London: Hodder & Stoughton, 1922).
91 'On the Possibilities of the Poster', *The Studio* 70 (February 1917), p. 52.
92 *The Times* (7 May 1923), p. 17.
93 *Year's Art* (1924), pp. 6–7.
94 For more on this process, see Saler, *The Avant-Garde in Interwar England*.
95 See M. Haworth-Booth, *E. McKnight Kauffer: A Designer and His Public* (London: Gordon Fraser Gallery, 1979), p. 24.
96 M. Cook, *The British Empire Exhibition 1924: Designed to Display the Natural Resources of the Various Countries within the Empire, and the Activities, Industrial and Social, of their Peoples (Official Guide)* (London: Fleetway, 1924), n.p.
97 See J. Woodham, 'Design and Empire: British Design in the 1920s', *Art History* 3 (June 1980), pp. 229–40.
98 Ministry of Reconstruction, *Art and Industry*, p. 6.

Conclusion

1 J. Rothenstein, *Summer's Lease: Autobiography 1901–1938* (London: Hamish Hamilton, 1965), p. 38.
2 *Ibid.*, p. 40.
3 J. Winter, 'Imaginings of War: Posters and the Shadow of the Lost Generation', in James (ed.), *Picture This*, p. 37.
4 Rothenstein, *Summer's Lease*, p. 40.

5 The British War Memorials Committee's larger pictures were 184 × 317 cm. John Singer Sargent's *Gassed*, the largest of them all, was more than six metres wide. For more on the formats and dimensions of these canvases, see Malvern, *Modern Art, Britain and the Great War*, pp. 69–107.
6 Mark Gertler's satirical war painting *Merry-Go-Round* inspired a scene in Joan Littlewood's 1963 musical *Oh, What a Lovely War!* and subsequently a scene in its cinematic adaptation directed by Richard Attenborough in 1969. For a broader discussion of this process, see D. Reynolds, *The Long Shadow: The Great War and the Twentieth Century* (London: Simon & Schuster, 2013).
7 See Cork, *Bitter Truth*. The phrase is Paul Nash's.
8 See R. Barthes, *Mythologies*, trans. A. Lavers (London: Vintage, 1993), p. 129.
9 D. Freedberg, *The Power of Images: Studies in the History and Theory of Response* (University of Chicago Press, 1989).
10 One way of quantifying this is looking at the ritual involving the recent success of the Royal British Legion's annual poppy appeal. At the beginning of the new millennium, its appeal income remained relatively static at between £20 and £21 million; in the second half of its first decade, that figure virtually doubled, to £40 million in 2011. For a more detailed rumination on this, see J. Fox, 'Poppy Politics: Remembrance of Things Present', in C. Sandis (ed.), *Cultural Heritage Ethics* (Cambridge: Open Book Publishers, 2014), pp. 21–30.
11 Master's Address (12 January 1917), in Annual Reports 3, 1913–33, p. 13, Art-Workers' Guild.
12 Bather, 'Museums and the War', p. 10.
13 'French, Russian, and American Paintings', *New York Times* (7 April 1918), p. 85.
14 William Schooling of the War Savings Committee remarked that a 'number of people who were making large profits out of war contracts' were spending them 'with ostentatious extravagance'. He concluded: 'The best shops in the west end of London and elsewhere experienced a great change in the character of their customers and gradually began to cater for the extravagant and vulgar tastes of the *nouveaux riches*.' W. Schooling, 'National Saving in the United Kingdom', *Annals of the American Academy of Political and Social Science* 87 (January 1920), p. 197.
15 W. Rothenstein, *British Artists and the War* (London: Peter Davies, 1931), p. 21.

BIBLIOGRAPHY

Unpublished sources

Archive of Art and Design (AAD)

Victoria & Albert Museum, London

Royal Institute of Oil Painters (AAD/2000/5)
General Meeting Minute Book 2 (AAD/2000/5/2)
Council Meetings Minute Book 3 (AAD/2000/5/10)
General Minute Book 3 (AAD/2000/5/3)

Royal Society of British Artists (AAD/1997/8)
Council Minute Book 1910–16 (AAD/1997/8/13)
Council Minute Book 1916–23 (AAD/1997/8/14)
Minutes of General Meetings (AAD 1997/8/4)

Society of Women Artists (AAD/1996/7)
Exhibition Catalogues 1914–19 (AAD/1996/7/60–65)

Artists' General Benevolent Institution

London (uncatalogued)

Applicants Book 5
Minute Book: July 1907–October 1916
Minute Book: November 1916–November 1926

Art-Workers' Guild (AWG)

London (uncatalogued)

Art-Workers' Guild
Annual Reports 3, 1913–33
Council Meetings Minute Book 1914–18

Civic Arts Association
Papers pertaining to the formation of the Civic Arts Association

Junior Art-Workers' Guild
Council Meetings Minute Book 1914–18

British Library of Political and Economic Science

London

London Intelligence Committee Papers (LIC), 9 vols., vol. II.
Local Government Board, 'Report on the Causes of Depression in Various Trades' (August 1914–July 1915)

De László Archive (DLA)

Heinz Archive and Library, National Portrait Gallery, London

Internment Papers (loose items cited individually in footnotes; all uncatalogued)
Letters Database (letters are cited individually in footnotes; most are catalogued under DLA 044, 047, 053, 054, 055, 075)
Lucy de László, 'Notes' (uncatalogued)

Hamilton Kerr Institute

Whittlesford

Roberson Archive (ROB)
Letters (ROB/MS 529)

Imperial War Museum (IWM)

London

Boydell, P. (1977). 'We Spend our Years as a Tale that is Told' (TS memoir), in Private Papers of P. Boydell (IWM 3642 85/28/1)
Carline, R. (1975). 'IWM Interview', from *Artists in an Age of Conflict* (IWM 671)
Hill, A. (1975). 'IWM Interview', from *Artists in an Age of Conflict* (IWM 561)
Nash, J. (1974). 'IWM Interview', from *Artists in an Age of Conflict* (IWM 323)
Wyllie, H. Private Papers of H. Wyllie (RAF 84/5/1)

London Metropolitan Archive (LMA)

London

Imperial Arts League Papers (LMA/4054)
AGM Reports and Supplementary Minutes 1911–20 (LMA/4054/A/01/002)
Minute Book, Annual General Meetings, Balance Sheets and Council Reports 1911–20 (LMA/4054/A/01/003)
Minute Book, Committee Meetings and War Emergency Fund Committee 1910–27 (LMA/4054/A/02/001)
'Sketching and Painting in War-Time' (LMA/4054/A/06/001)

London Transport Museum

London

Poster collection

National Gallery Archive (NG)

London

National Gallery Papers
National Gallery Annual Report 1914 (NG17/7)

Professional Classes Aid Council (PCAC)

London (uncatalogued)

Annual Reports 1914–18
  Arts in War Time Committee Annual Report 1915 (1916)
  Arts in War Time Committee Annual Report 1917 (1918)
'Professional Classes War Relief Council: Aims and Objects'

Royal Academy of Arts Archive (RAA)

London

Correspondence from Members' Files 1867–1986 (RAA/SEC/10/74/1)
Correspondence from Non-Members 1879–1963 (RAA/SEC/6/52)
Council Minutes 23, 14 January 1913–2 May 1918 (RAA/PC/1/23)
Council Minutes 24, 9 May 1918–31 July 1923 (RAA/PC/1/24)
Council Records of Committees 1851–1948 (RAA/PC/6/8)
General Assembly Minutes Book 10, 1913–32 (RAA/GA/1/10)
Papers Relating to Entertainments Tax, 1916–26 (RAA/SEC/17/14)
Records of the Secretary (RAA/SEC/8/35)
Register of Admission of Students 1890–1922 (RAA/KEE/1/1/4)
Secretary's Letter Book, 20 November 1914–18 June 1915 (RAA/SEC 9/1/21)

Royal Society of British Sculptors

London (uncatalogued)

Minutes of Council Meetings 2

Royal Watercolour Society

London

Royal Society for Painter-Etchers & Engravers (RE)
  Council Minute Book (RE 3)
  Exhibition Register (RE 7)

Letters (RE 167)
Papers Pertaining to Entertainments Tax (RE 197b)

Royal Watercolour Society Papers (RWS)
Annual Reports (B163–7)
'Average Age of Members 1806–1986' (uncatalogued)
Council Minute Book 1905–20 (A26)
Leases of Pall Mall Buildings (B215)
Letter Book 1906–19 (AC6)
Letter Books (L7 and L8)
Letters with Regard to Paper Manufacturers (B228)
Minutes Book 1904–42 (A10)
Miscellaneous Correspondence (B237)
Press Cuttings (P8)
Sales Books (S67)

Tate Archives (TGA)

London

Bomberg Papers (TGA 7312)
Mayes, A. (1972). 'The Young Bomberg 1914–1922' (TS memoir) (TGA 7312)

Frederick Milner Papers (TGA 9511)
Letters to Mrs Brumfit (TGA 9511/17–37)

Grosvenor Gallery Papers (TGA 737)
Francis Howard Letter Book 3 (TGA 737/12)

International Society Papers (TGA 738)
Minute Book of Council Meetings (TGA 738.3.156)

Stanhope Forbes Papers (TGA 9015)
Diary, 1916 (TGA 9015.1.2)
Letters (TGA 9015.4.1)

Tate Closures during War (TG 2/7/1)
Requests to View the Gallery when Closed during War-Time (TG 2/7/1/1–11)

University College London Archive (UCL)

London

Reynolds, M. (1974). 'The Slade: The Story of an Art School, 1871–1971' (MS ADD 250)

Slade School of Art Papers (SS)
UCL Annual Records (UCLCS/SS)
UCL Slade School Records (UCLGB0103-UCLCA/SS)

Winsor & Newton

Harrow & Wealdstone (uncatalogued)

Company Records
Master Catalogue (1914)

Published sources

Contemporary journals, newspapers and reviews

Art Annual
Art News
Art Prices Current
Arts League of Service Annual
The Athenaeum
Blast: Review of the Great English Vortex
British Journal of Photography
British Printer
Burlington Magazine for Connoisseurs
The Bystander
Colour
The Connoisseur
Daily Mirror
Daily Sketch
Daily Telegraph
The Egoist
English Review

Fine Art Trade Journal
Fortnightly Review
The Graphic
Illustrated London News
Illustrated Sunday Herald
Illustrated War News
Imperial Arts League Journal
John Bull
Lady's Pictorial
Little Review
Museums' Journal
Musical Times
New Age
New Witness
New York Times
Newspaper Press Directory
Parliamentary Debates, Commons
Parliamentary Debates, Lords
Print Prices Current
Punch
Royal Academy Illustrated
Royal Academy Pictures and Sculpture
Saturday Review
The Sphere
Star
The Studio
Sunday Pictorial
The Times
The Tyro: A Review of the Arts of Painting, Sculpture and Design
War Illustrated
War Pictorial
The Year's Art

Primary printed sources

'£6,930 For a Portrait: Lusitania Survivor's Purchase', *The Times* (8 June 1915), p. 11.
A. H. H., 'The Organization of Art', *The Athenaeum* (18 July 1919), pp. 1–3.
Aldington, R., *Life for Life's Sake: A Book of Reminiscences* (London: Cassell, 1968).
'Notes on the Present Situation', *The Egoist* (1 September 1914), pp. 326–7.

Allen Browne, L., 'Is Your Business Essential?', *Forum* (February 1918), pp. 165–80.
Allied Artists' Association Catalogue to the 8th Salon (London, 1916).
Anderson, M., 'Note', *Little Review* 1 (October 1914), p. 3.
Anon., *The Real Crown Prince: A Record and an Indictment* (London: George Newnes, 1915).
Art (London: Hodder & Stoughton, 1922).
'Art after Armageddon', *The Athenaeum* (12 September 1914), pp. 268–9.
'Art and War – Noted Sculptor's Exemption', *Sunday Herald* (10 June 1917), p. 4.
'Art by Weight', *Burlington Magazine* 32 (June 1918), p. 243.
'The Art of Naval "Camouflage" Applied to Fancy Dress: The Chelsea Arts Club "Dazzle" Ball', *Illustrated London News* (22 March 1919), pp. 414–15.
'Art Sales of 1915: A Lean Year', *Scotsman* (25 December 1915), p. 5.
'The Artist and the War', *Pall Mall Gazette* (7 June 1916), p. 4.
'Artists and the War', *The Times* (5 May 1916), p. 9.
'Artists "Targets" Train Troops' Eyes', *New York Times* (5 March 1918), p. 9.
Arts and Crafts Exhibition Society: Catalogue of the Eleventh Exhibition (London: Chiswick Press, 1916).
Axe, E. C., *Military Panorama Sketching* (London: Forster & Groom, 1916).
Baden-Powell, R., *My Adventures as a Spy* (London: C. Arthur Pearson, 1915).
Balderston, J. L., 'The Dusk of the Gods: A Conversation on Art with George Moore', *Atlantic Monthly* (August 1916), pp. 165–75.
Baldry, A. L., 'The Entertainments Tax', *Imperial Arts League Journal* (June 1916), p. 31.
Bather, F. A., 'Museums and National Service', *Museums' Journal* 14 (October 1914), pp. 121–7.
'Museums and the War', *Museums' Journal* 15 (July 1915), pp. 2–10.
Beeson, F. and Williams, A., *Amateur Photography* (London: Thomas Nelson & Sons, 1913).
Bell, C., *Art* (London: Chatto & Windus, 1914).
'Art and War', *International Journal of Ethics* 26 (October 1915), pp. 1–10.
'Wilcoxism', *The Athenaeum* (5 March 1920), pp. 311–12.
Belloc, H., *A General Sketch of the European War* (London: Thomas Nelson & Sons, 1916).
Bennett, A., 'Officialism and War Painting', *New Statesman* 14 (20 December 1919), pp. 847–8.
Binyon, L., 'Art and Life', *Saturday Review* (20 August 1910), pp. 229–30.
English Poetry in its Relation to Painting and the other Arts (London: Oxford University Press, 1918).
The Vision of Painters', *New Statesman* (13 July 1918), pp. 292–3.
Blaikie-Murdock, W. G., 'The Serbian National Sculptor', *Art and Progress* (December 1915), p. 59.
Blomfield, C. J., *Once an Artist Always an Artist* (London: Page & Co, 1921).
Blomfield, R., 'The Tangled Skein: Art in England, 1800–1920', in *Proceedings of the British Academy 1919–1920* (London: Oxford University Press, 1920), pp. 375–88.
Blumenfeld, R. D., *All in a Lifetime* (London: Ernest Benn Ltd, 1931).
Blythe, R. (ed.), *First Friends: Paul and Bunty, John and Christine – and Carrington* (London: Viking, 1999).
'Bolshevist Art and Jew Control', *Hidden Hand* 5 (April 1924), p. 57.

Bone, M., *The Western Front: Drawings by Muirhead Bone* (New York: G. H. Doran, 1917).
'Boom in Modern Art', *Fine Art Trade Journal* 14 (April 1918), p. 66.
Bosanquet, B., *Three Lectures on Aesthetic* (London: Macmillan, 1915).
Bowyer Nichols, J., 'Two Exhibitions in Aid of National Funds' *Burlington Magazine* 26 (January 1915), pp. 163–9.
Bradshaw, M., *Royal Society of British Artists: Members Exhibiting 1911–1930* (Leigh-on-Sea: F. Lewis, 1975).
Bradshaw, P., *The Art of the Illustrator*, 20 vols.(London: Press Art School, 1917–).
Drawn from Memory (London: Chapman & Hall, 1943).
Branford, V., 'Art and Life', *The Athenaeum* (May 1918), p. 226.
'Bringing the Arts to the People: A Nottingham Conference', *Manchester Guardian* (21 March 1921), p. 6.
Brinton, C., 'War Pictures by British Artists', *Vanity Fair* (February 1919), pp. 29–31.
'Britain's Destiny and Duty: Declaration by Authors', *The Times* (18 September 1914), p. 3.
'The British Drama League', *Observer* (1 June 1919), p. 16.
Brown, O., *Exhibition: The Memoirs of Oliver Brown* (London: Evelyn, Adams & Mackay, 1968).
Brown Scott, J. (ed.), *Texts of the Peace Conferences at the Hague, 1899 and 1907* (Boston and London: Ginn & Co., 1908).
Bull, P., *Our Duty at Home in Time of War* (Oxford: A. R. Mowbray, 1915).
Bullard, F. L., *Famous War Correspondents* (London: Pitman, 1914).
Burne-Jones, P., 'Art and War: Sir Philip Burne-Jones on Sculptor's Exemption – Mr. Epstein's Case – Distinguished Men's Views on "Fame"', *Evening Standard* (7 June 1917), p. 5.
Buschmann, P., 'Belgian Artists in England', *The Studio* 63 (December 1914), pp. 183–210.
'Business as Usual: Shocking Taste of London Tombstone Sculptors', *John Bull* (10 October 1914), p. 8.
Carrington, H., *Psychical Phenomena and the War* (London: T. Werner Laurie, 1919).
Carrington, N. (ed.), *Mark Gertler: Selected Letters* (London: Rupert-Hart-Davies, 1965).
Catalogue of an Exhibition of Modern Spanish Art (London: Grafton Galleries, 1914).
A Catalogue of War Auto Lithographs Designed by Frank Brangwyn (London: Avenue Press, 1918).
Catty, N. (ed.), *Training in Appreciation: Art, Literature, Music* (London: Sidgwick & Jackson, 1921).
Courtney, J., 'The War and Women's Employment', *Fortnightly Review* (February 1915), p. 243.
'Chaplin and Patients', *Kinematograph Weekly* (20 April 1917), p. 61.
Chesterton, G. K., 'Art and War – Noted Sculptor's Exemption', *Sunday Herald* (10 June 1917), p. 4.
Chiozza Money, L., 'British Trade and the War', *Contemporary Review* 106 (July–December 1914), pp. 482–7.
Churchill, W., *Painting as a Pastime* (London: Ernest Benn, 1948).
Cinema Commission, *The Cinema: Its Present Position and Future Possibilities, Being the Report of and Chief Evidence taken by the Cinema Commission of Inquiry instituted by the National Council of Public Morals* (London: Williams & Norgate, 1917).

'Cinematograph: What It May Become', *The Times* (30 August 1917), p. 9.
Clarke, B., 'How the Progress of the War was Chronicled by Pen and Camera', in H. Wilson and J. Hammerton (eds.), *The Great War: The Standard History of the All-Europe Conflict* (London: London Amalgamated Press, 1918), vol. X, pp. 413–28.
Clarke, G. H. (ed.), *A Treasury of War Poetry. British and American Poets of the World War, 1914–1919* (London: Hodder & Stoughton, 1919).
'Closure of Museums', *The Nation* (29 January 1916), pp. 628–9.
Clutton-Brock, A., 'Personality or Process. Mr Nevinson's Pictures of Men as War Machines', *The Times* (29 September 1916), p. 9.
'War and Poetry', *Times Literary Supplement* (8 October 1914), p. 448.
The Ultimate Belief (London: Constable, 1916).
Collier, J., 'Soldiers and War Plays', *The Times* (29 May 1915), p. 7.
Collins Baker, C., 'Art in Tin Shoes', *Saturday Review* 123 (21 July 1917), p. 44.
'Dry Bones', *Saturday Review* 119 (20 March 1915), p. 44.
'A Painter's Confession', *Saturday Review* 118 (28 November 1914), p. 556.
'The Royal Academy', *Saturday Review* 119 (1 May 1915), p. 450.
'Royal Academy Again', *Saturday Review* 123 (12 May 1917), p. 429.
'War Paintings', *Saturday Review* 122 (7 October 1916), pp. 342–3.
Colton, W. K., 'The Effects of War on Art', *Architect* 45 (17 March 1916), pp. 199–201.
Committee on Public Retrenchment, 'Final Report of the Committee on Retrenchment in the Public Expenditure', 1916', Cd. 8200, in *Reports from Commissioners, Inspectors and Others* 15 (1914–16), pp. 181–206.
'Third Report of the Committee on Retrenchment in the Public Expenditure, 1916', Cd. 8180, in *Reports from Commissioners, Inspectors and Others* 15 (1914–16), pp. 177–80.
Committee of the Trustees of the National Gallery, 'Report of the Committee of the Trustees of the National Gallery appointed to enquire into the Retention of Important Pictures in this Country and Other Matters Connected with the National Art Collections, 1915', Cd. 7878/9, in *Reports from Commissioners, Inspectors and Others* 29 (1914–16), pp. 317–489.
Cook, M., *The British Empire Exhibition 1924: Designed to Display the Natural Resources of the Various Countries within the Empire, and the Activities, Industrial and Social, of their Peoples (Official Guide)* (London: Fleetway, 1924).
Cornelius, J., 'The Value of Landscape Targets', *Scribner's* 65 (October 1918), pp. 433–40.
Cowper Powys, J. *The War and Culture* (New York: G. Arnold Shaw, 1914).
Crawford Flitch, J. E., *The Great War: Fourth Year* (London: Grant Richards, 1918).
'The Cure for Luxury', *Saturday Review* 120 (20 November 1915), pp. 485–6.
Cust, L., 'The National Gallery', *Burlington Magazine* 27 (June 1915), pp. 110–13.
Darwin, L., 'Distress among the Professional Classes', *Charity Organisation Review* 61 (May 1917), pp. 180–92.
'A Dazzle Advertisement of a Dazzling Discovery', *Illustrated London News* (28 June 1919), p. 962.
'Death of a Well-Known Artist', *Scotsman* (28 September 1914), p. 6.
Deeds that Thrill the Empire: True Stories of the Most Glorious Acts of Heroism of the Empire's Soldiers and Sailors during the Great War, 2 vols. (London: Hutchinson & Co., 1917).

'Defence of the Realm (no. 2) Act, 1914; a Bill to Amend the Defence of the Realm Act, 1914' (Bill 383), in *Bills, Public* 1 (1914), p. 937.
De Fonseca, L., 'War and the Aesthete', *New Age* 16 (31 December 1914), pp. 216–17.
Delville, J., 'The Social Influence of Art', *Colour* 3 (January 1916), pp. 228–9.
De Maetzu, R., 'On Art and Luxury', *New Age* 16 (15 April 1915), pp. 640–2.
'On Luxury and Waste', *New Age* 17 (13 May 1915), pp. 34–5.
'Deputation to the Prime Minister on Museum Closure', *Museums' Journal* 15 (April 1916), p. 319.
Derwent Wood, F., 'Masks for Facial Wounds', *The Lancet* (23 June 1917), pp. 949–51.
A Design for Democracy: An Abridgement of a Report of the Adult Education Committee of the British Ministry of Reconstruction, commonly called the 1919 Report (London: M. Parrish, 1956).
'The Detachment of the Painter', *The Times* (20 March 1915), p. 3.
Dibdin, E., 'Presidential Address', *Museums' Journal* 16 (August 1916), pp. 29–40.
Du Maurier, G., 'The Case for Amusements', *The Times* (23 March 1915), p. 13.
E. G. F., 'Sunshine for Shell Shock', *British Journal of Nursing* (6 October 1917), p. 224.
Ervine, S. G., 'The War and Literature', *North American Review* 202 (July 1915), p. 98.
Evans, E., 'Music and the War', *New Weekly* (15 August 1914), p. 272.
'The False Dawn', *The Athenaeum* (9 January 1920).
'Fine Art in the Stores', *The Athenaeum* (22 August 1919) p. 788.
'Fine Art Trade Guild Roll of Honour', *Year's Art* (1915), pp. 430–44.
'French, Russian, and American Paintings', *New York Times* (7 April 1918), p. 85.
Fry, R., 'The National Gallery Bill', *Burlington Magazine* 30 (January 1917), pp. 21–3.
'The New Movement in Art in Its Relation to Life. A Lecture Given at the Fabian Society Summer School', *Burlington Magazine* 31 (October 1917), pp. 162–8.
'Notes', *Burlington Magazine* 26 (October 1914), pp. 40–1.
Vision and Design (London: Chatto & Windus, 1957).
Galsworthy, J., 'Art and the War', *Fortnightly Review* 98 (1 November 1915), pp. 924–9.
A Sheaf (New York: Scribner's, 1916).
Garnett, D. (ed.), *Carrington: Letters and Extracts from her Diaries* (London: Cape, 1970).
Gasquoine Hartley, C. and Lewis, A., 'War and the Arts', *English Review* 23 (August 1916), pp. 150–8.
General Register Office, *Census of England and Wales 1911: General Report with Appendices* (London: HMSO, 1917).
Census of England and Wales 1921: General Report with Appendices (London: HMSO, 1927).
'German Destruction: Protest of British Art-Lovers', *Museums' Journal* 14 (November 1914), pp. 76–7.
'"German Spy" Craze in Galloway', *Scotsman* (10 September 1914), p. 7.
Gibbs, P., *Realities of War* (London: Hutchinson & Co., 1929).
Glew, A. (ed.), *Stanley Spencer: Letters and Writings* (London: Tate, 2001).
Gosse, E., 'War and Literature', *Edinburgh Review* 220 (October 1914), pp. 313–32.
Gower, H., Jast, L. and Topley, W., *The Camera as Historian* (London: Sampson Low Marston, 1916).
Graves, R., 'The British Soldier', in *The British Soldier: An Exhibition of Pictures by Eric H. Kennington, an Official Artist on the Western Front* (London: Ernest Brown & Phillips, 1918), pp. 3–8.
Grundy, C. R., 'Art and National Economy', *The Connoisseur* 43 (September 1915), pp. 54–8.

'Art and the Budget: An Essay on Artistic Economy', *The Connoisseur* 43 (November 1915), pp. 129–34.
'The Luxury Tax', *The Connoisseur* 52 (September 1918), p. 3.
'War and British Art', *The Connoisseur* 42 (August 1915), pp. 195–201.
Hallward, R., *The Religion of Art* (London: Heath Cranton, 1917).
Harper, G., 'New Faces for Mutilated Soldiers', *Red Cross Magazine* (November 1918), pp. 44–5.
Hartrick, A. S., *A Painter's Progress through Fifty Years* (Cambridge University Press, 1939).
Haward, L., *The Effect of War upon Art and Literature* (Manchester University Press, 1916).
Hayward, F. and Freeman, A., *The Spiritual Foundations of Reconstruction: A Plea for New Educational Methods* (London: P. S. King & Son, 1919).
Hind, C. L., 'What Armageddon did to Art', *The Graphic* (12 January 1924), p. 43.
Holmes, C. J., 'Notes', *Burlington Magazine* 25 (September 1914), pp. 366–7.
Self and Partners (Mostly Self) (London: Constable, 1936).
H. R. C., 'The Appeal of the Poster', *Manchester Guardian* (5 April 1915), p. 10.
Huish, M. B., 'Whence Comes this Great Multitude of Painters?', *Nineteenth Century* 32 (November 1892), pp. 720–32.
Image, S., *Art, Morals, and the War* (London: Oxford University Press, 1914).
'In the Royal Academy Private View', *Illustrated London News* (May 1918), p. 121.
Jacks, L. P., 'The Changing Mind of a Nation at War', in E. Sidgwick *et al.*, *The International Crisis in its Ethical and Psychological Aspects* (London: Oxford University Press, 1915), pp. 78–102.
J. C. E., *Carry On: Your Duty in War Time* (London: Electrical Press, 1914).
John, A., *Chiaroscuro* (London: Jonathan Cape, 1952).
'Kemp Prosser "Cure by Colour"', *Times of India* (7 May 1919), p. 10.
Kenyon, F. G., *The British Museum in War Time* (Glasgow: Jackson, Wylie & Co, 1934).
Knight, L., *Autobiography: Oil Paint and Grease Paint* (London: Ivor Nicholson & Watson, 1936).
Koch, T. W., *Books in Camp, Trench and Hospital* (London: J. M. Dent & Sons, 1917).
Konody, P., 'The Glut of Art Shows', *Observer* (4 November 1923), p. 10.
Modern War Paintings by C. R. W. Nevinson (London: Grant Richards, 1917).
'On War Memorials', in Canadian War Records Office, *Art and War: Canadian War Memorials* (London: Colour Ltd, 1919).
Lake, B. C., *Knowledge for War: Every Officer's Handbook for the Front* (London: Harrison & Sons, 1916).
Langfeld, H., *The Aesthetic Attitude* (New York: Harcourt, Brace & Howe, 1920).
A Lantern Lecture on Heroic Actions and Daring Deeds of the Great War (London: Newton & Co., 1916).
'László and the Liars: The Traitor Painter and a Public Inquiry', *John Bull* (7 June 1919), p. 6.
Lavery, J., *The Life of a Painter* (London: Cassell, 1940).
'The League of Arts', *Musical Times* (1 July 1920), p. 477.
Legge, R., *Military Sketching and Map Reading for Non-Coms. and Men* (Aldershot: Gale & Polden, 1915).
Lennard, R., 'The Taxation of Luxury', *Economic Journal* 28 (September 1918), pp. 287–99.

Lennard, W., 'What It Means to the Artist', *Fortnightly Review* 98 (October 1915), pp. 765–72.
Le Queux, W., *German Spies in England: An Exposure* (London: Stanley Paul, 1915).
Lethaby, W., 'Memorials of the Fallen: Service or Sacrifice?', in *Form in Civilization: Collected Papers on Art and Labour* (London: Oxford University Press, 1922), pp. 56–65.
'Lord Beaverbrook on Art in Propaganda', *The Times* (2 March 1918), p. 3.
'Lost Masterpieces', *The Times* (30 April 1915), p. 11.
McClandish Smith, B., 'The War as Seen by Camera', *The Graphic* (11 May 1918), p. 576.
MacDonagh, M., *In London during the Great War: The Diary of a Journalist* (London: Eyre & Spottiswoode, 1935).
McQ., J. L., 'Rebels in the Fortress', *Daily Express* (3 January 1919), p. 4.
Mais, S., 'Literature and the War', *Journal of Education* 37 (April 1915), pp. 207–9.
Marler, R. (ed.), *Selected Letters of Vanessa Bell* (London: Bloomsbury, 1993).
Marriott, C. and 'Tis', *Modern Art* (London: Colour Ltd, 1919).
Marsden, D., 'Culture', *The Egoist* 1 (1 September 1914), pp. 321–3.
Martin Wood, T., 'The International Society of Painters, Sculptors and Gravers', *Burlington Magazine* 29 (November 1916), p. 343.
Masterman, C., *England after War: A Study* (London: Hodder & Stoughton, 1923).
Materer, T. (ed.), *Pound/Lewis: The Letters of Ezra Pound and Wyndham Lewis* (London: Faber & Faber, 1985).
The Selected Letters of Ezra Pound to John Quinn, 1915–1924 (Durham, NC: Duke University Press, 1991).
Maxwell, D., *Adventures with a Sketch Book* (London: Bodley Head, 1914).
Maze, P., *A Frenchman in Khaki* (London and Toronto: W. Heinemann Ltd, 1934).
Ministry of Munitions, *The History of the Ministry of Munitions*, 12 vols. (London: HMSO, 1922).
Ministry of Reconstruction, *Art and Industry* (London: HMSO, 1919).
'Mr Rodin's Gift', *The Times* (11 November 1914), p. 9.
'Mr. Tom Mostyn's "Gardens of Romance"', *Observer* (2 February 1919), p. 7.
Montague, C., *British Artists at the Front*, 4 vols. [on C. R. W. Nevinson, Sir John Lavery, John Nash and Eric Kennington] (London: Country Life and George Newnes, 1918).
Moore, C. L., 'Pictures and Words', *The Dial* (September 1914), pp. 127–35.
Munnings, A., *An Artist's Life* (London: Museum Press, 1950).
Murray, G., 'Herd Instinct and the War', in E. Sidgwick *et al.*, *The International Crisis in its Ethical and Psychological Aspects* (London: Oxford University Press, 1915), pp. 22–45.
'Music in War-Time', *Musical Times* 55 (1 December 1914), p. 707.
Nash, P., 'The Arts League of Service', *New Witness* (23 May 1919), pp. 72–5.
Outline: An Autobiography (London: Faber & Faber, 1949).
National Art-Collections Fund, *Annual Reports of the National Art-Collections Fund* (London, 1914–20).
National Portrait Gallery, *Reports for the Years 1914–1916*, cd. 8290, vol. XIV (London, 1916).
'A National Treasure! Epstein the Sculptor too Precious to Fight', *Daily Express* (7 June 1917), p. 3.

'The Nation's War Paintings: Youth at the Academy', *Liverpool Post* (12 December 1919), p. 7.
'Necessity of Art', *Observer* (14 May 1923), p. 14.
Nevinson, C. R. W., 'Bolshevism in Art', *Daily Express* (10 March 1919), p. 6.
Paint and Prejudice (London: Methuen, 1937).
'War Notes and Queries. Comments and Suggestions in Brief from our Readers', *The Graphic* (11 March 1915), p. 51.
'When the Censor Censored "Censored"', *British Legion Journal* (October 1932), pp. 114–15.
'The New Collector', *Fine Art Trade Journal* 14 (April 1918), p. 76.
'The New Weekly', *New Weekly* (22 August 1914), p. 292.
Newlandsmith, E., *The Temple of Life and the Mission of the Arts Therein* (London, New York and Bombay: Longmans, Green & Co, 1919).
Newman, E., 'The Artist and the People', *Musical Times* 55 (1 October 1914), pp. 605–7.
Newton, W., *Military Landscape Sketching and Target Indication* (London: Hugh Rees, 1916).
Nicholson, I., 'An Aspect of British Official Wartime Propaganda', *Cornhill Magazine* 70 (May 1931), pp. 593–606.
'On Art and Affectation', *The Studio* 63 (July 1916), p. 130.
'On Art and the National Spirit', *The Studio* 65 (August 1915), p. 218.
'On Art and War', *The Studio* 63 (October 1914), p. 80.
'On Art in Daily Life', *The Studio* 67 (April 1916), p. 210.
'On the Artistic Inspiration of the War', *The Studio* 63 (September 1914), p. 76.
'On the Possibilities of the Poster', *The Studio* 70 (February 1917), p. 52.
'On the Practical Value of Art', *The Studio* 66 (November 1915), p. 148.
'On the Record of Passing Events', *The Studio* 64 (February 1915), p. 330.
'On the Risks which Artists Run', *The Studio* 63 (January 1915), p. 240.
O. R. D., 'Mr Nevinson's War Pictures', *Westminster Gazette* (2 October 1916), p. 2
Orpen, W., *An Onlooker in France 1917–1919* (London: Williams & Norgate, 1921).
Orpen, W. (ed.), *Outline of Art* (London: Newnes, 1923).
'Our Duty Towards the Cinema: Woodbine or Havana', *The Times* (6 April 1916), p. 11.
'The Outlook for British Musicians', *Musical Times* 55 (1 November 1914), pp. 645–6.
Palmer, A., 'Beauty and the Beast', *New Weekly* (22 August 1914), p. 290.
Palmer, J., 'The Deserted Theatre', *Saturday Review* (8 August 1914), pp. 172–3.
'Patriotism and Amusement', *Saturday Review* (22 August 1914), pp. 218–19.
'The Pleasures of London – I', *Saturday Review* (24 July 1915), pp. 84–5.
Parliamentary War Savings Committee, *The National Savings Movement: Its Origin, Aims and Development* (London: HMSO, 1931).
War Savings Handbook (London: HMSO, 1916).
Why We Must Save and How (London: HMSO, 1915).
Pater, W., *Appreciations: With an Essay on Style* (London: Macmillan, 1889).
The Renaissance: Studies in Art and Poetry (London: Macmillan, 1877).
Peixotto, E., 'Special Service for Artists in War Time', *Scribner's* 62 (July 1917), pp. 1–10.
Pender, H., 'Studies in Contemporary Literature', *The Egoist* 3 (1 January 1916), pp. 13–14.
'Perils of War Photography', *Washington Post* (15 November 1914), p. 45.
Phillips, D., 'Art and War', *Bulletin of the College Art Association of America* 1 (September 1918), pp. 24–37.

'Photographers and Pictures', *Saturday Review* 126 (28 September 1918), pp. 885–6.
Pickard, J., 'Art's Counter-Offensive', *Bulletin of the College Art Association of America* 1 (September 1918), pp. 19–24.
'Pictures and Real Drama', *Saturday Review* 122 (23 September 1916), p. 290.
'The Popular Art', *The Times* (16 June 1915), p. 9.
'The Position of British Musicians', *Musical Times* 55 (1 November 1914), pp. 657–9.
'The Position of the Art Societies: Why they Should be Assisted', *Birmingham Post* (9 August 1921), p. 3.
Potton, E. (ed.), *A Record of the United Arts Rifles, 1914–1919* (London: Alexander Moring Ltd, 1920).
Price, J., *On the Path of Adventure: A War-Correspondent's Experiences at the French Front in 1914* (London: John Lane, 1919).
'Primary Trades', *The Times* (22 February 1917), p. 7.
Pulbrook, E., *The English Countryside* (London: Batsford, 1915).
Pym, T. and Gordon, J., *Papers from Picardy, by Two Chaplains, the Rev. T. W. Pym and the Rev. Geoffrey Gordon* (London: Constable, 1917).
Quinn, J., 'Why Art Should Not Be Taxed', *Metropolitan Museum of Art Bulletin* 13 (September 1918), pp. 198–9.
'Raphael Tuck and Paper', *Fine Art Trade Journal* 13 (September 1917), pp. 218–19.
Rawlinson, A., 'The War and Culture', *English Review* 20 (April 1915), pp. 77–87.
'The Red Cross Sale', *Saturday Review* (8 April 1916), pp. 346–7.
Repington, C., *The First World War, 1914–1918: Personal Experiences of Lieut.-Col. C. à Court Repington* (London: Houghton Miffin, 1920).
Report of the Board of Education for the Year 1921–2 (London: HMSO, 1923).
Reports by the Joint War Committee and the Joint Finance Committee of the British Red Cross and the Order of St. John of Jerusalem in England on the Voluntary Aid Rendered to the Sick and Wounded at Home and Abroad and to the British Prisoners of War, 1914–1919 (London: HMSO, 1921).
'Restricted Industries/Occupations Order', *The Times* (2 March 1917), p. 3.
R. F. C., 'Topographical Sketching in the Army', *The Studio* 62 (February 1916), pp. 44–5.
Rhys, E. (ed.), *The Old Country: A Book of Love and Praise of England* (London: YMCA, 1917).
Rimington, A., 'Painting Out of Doors in War Time', *Imperial Arts League Journal* (January 1916), p. 6.
Roberts, W., *Memories of the War to End War, 1914–1918* (London: Lund Humphries, 1974).
'Rodin's Gift to the Nation', *Burlington Magazine* 26 (December 1914), p. 122.
Rogers, S., *The Pleasures of Memory, with Other Poems* (Oxford: T. Cadell, 1799).
Ross, R., 'Notes', *Burlington Magazine* 27 (September 1914), p. 367.
Rothenstein, W., 'Help for Artists', *The Times* (23 February 1915), p. 9.
Men and Memories: Recollections, 1872–1938 (London: Chatto & Windus, 1978).
A Plea for a Wider Use of Artists and Craftsmen (London: Constable, 1916).
Summer's Lease: Autobiography, 1901–38 (London: Hamish Hamilton, 1965).
Royal Academy of Arts, *War Memorials Exhibition, 1919* (London: William Clowes & Sons, 1919).
Runciman, J., 'German Music and the Prussian Spirit', *Saturday Review* (10 October 1914), pp. 390–3.
'In Support of Music', *Saturday Review* (7 November 1914), p. 484.

Ruskin, J., *The Crown of Wild Olive: Three Lectures on Work, Traffic, and War* (London: Smith, Elder & Co., 1866).
Rutter, F., 'Art and Healing: The Colour Cure of Shell Shock', *Sunday Times* (16 September 1917), p. 10.
Art in My Time (London: Rich & Cowan, 1933).
Since I was Twenty-Five (London: Constable, 1927).
Sadleir, M., *Michael Ernest Sadler: A Memoir by his Son* (London: Constable, 1949).
'Sales of Antiquities Increased by War', *New York Times* (21 August 1916), p. 11.
Salis, J., 'Art and the Camera', *New Witness* (21 December 1916), pp. 236–7.
'The Art of the Boudoir', *New Witness* (23 November 1916), pp. 108–9.
'No Genius Need Apply', *New Witness* (4 May 1916), p. 13.
'Reward of the Patriot', *New Witness* (11 May 1916), p. 45.
'The War Artist', *New Witness* (6 September 1917), p. 447.
Salisbury, F., *Portrait and Pageant: Kings, Presidents and People* (London: John Murray, 1944).
Salmon, A., 'Effect on Art of Present War', *New York Times* (11 July 1915), p. 8.
Sanderson, R., 'Winter Conference', *Charity Organisation Review* 39 (February 1916), pp. 62–93.
Sassoon, S., *Selected Poems* (London: Heinemann, 1925).
Select Committee on Luxury Duty, 'The Report from the Select Committee on Luxury Duty', white paper no. 101, in *Reports from Committees* 4 (1918), pp. 45–70.
'Selling Subjects for War Time', *Fine Art Trade Journal* 10 (August 1914), pp. 254–5.
Seton-Watson, R. W., 'Meštrović and the Jugoslav Idea', in *Exhibition of Works by Ivan Meštrović* (London: Victoria & Albert Museum, 1915).
Shaw, G. Bernard, *Heartbreak House, Great Catherine, and Playlets of War* (London: Constable, 1919).
Sidgwick, E. *et al.*, *The International Crisis in its Ethical and Psychological Aspects* (London: Oxford University Press, 1915).
'Signals from the Shore', *Scotsman* (27 February 1915), p. 13.
Sims, C., *Picture Making: Technique and Inspiration* (London: Seeley Service, 1934).
'The Slade Professorship of Art at Oxford', *Saturday Review* 122 (22 July 1916), p. 78.
Smith, L., *Drawing Fire: The Diary of a Great War Soldier and Artist* (London: Collins, 2009).
Snedden, D., 'The Waning Powers of Art', *American Journal of Sociology* 22 (May 1917), pp. 801–21.
Solomon, S., *Strategic Camouflage* (London: John Murray, 1920).
Spencer, S., *Stanley Spencer: Letters and Writings* (ed. A. Glew) (London: Tate, 2001).
'The Spy at Work: An Apparently Innocent Landscape that is Really a Plan of a Harbour and its Forts', *Illustrated London News* (3 October 1914), p. 477.
'The Spy at Work: An Apparently Innocent Landscape that is Really a Plan of a Harbour and its Forts', *Illustrated War News* (7 October 1914), pp. 28–9.
Storer, E., 'Art in War Time', *New Witness* (22 October 1914), p. 615.
Sutton, D. (ed.), *Letters of Roger Fry*, vol. II, *1913–34* (London: Chatto & Windus, 1972).
Symon, J., 'War and Creative Art', *English Review* 21 (December 1915), pp. 512–20.
Tatlock, R., 'Modern British Painting – A Proposal', *Burlington Magazine* 38 (April 1921), pp. 155–6.
Taylor, H., 'War and Art', *Colour* (September 1914), p. 46.
'That Traitor László', *John Bull* (17 May 1919), p. 6.

Thomas, G. (ed.), *Collected Poems of Edward Thomas* (Oxford University Press, 1978).
Tilney, F., *The Appeal of the Picture: An Examination of the Principles of Picture-Making* (London and Toronto: J. M. Dent, 1915).
'Photographs as Illustrations', *British Journal of Photography* (4 December 1914), pp. 885–7.
To my 'Unknown' Warrior (London: Hodder & Stoughton, 1920).
'A Trade Opportunity during the War', *Fine Art Trade Journal* 10 (August 1914), pp. 250–2.
Trustees of the National Portrait Gallery, '60th Annual Report of the Trustees of the National Portrait Gallery, 1916–1917', 1918 (cd. 8644), in *Reports from Commissioners, Inspectors and Others* 17 (1917–18), pp. 6–20.
Trystan Edwards, A., *The Things Which Are Seen: A Revaluation of the Visual Arts* (London: Philip Allan & Co., 1921).
Villiers, F., *His Five Decades of Adventure*, 2 vols. (London: Hutchinson, 1921).
Wake Cook, E., *Retrogression in Art and the Suicide of the Royal Academy. Part the second, Coming Renaissance with an Outline of a New Philosophy of Life and of Art* (London: Hutchinson, 1924).
'War and Play', *Saturday Review* 118 (5 September 1914), p. 262.
'War and the Artists', *Manchester Guardian* (8 March 1915), p. 4.
'War and the Fine Art Trade', *Fine Art Trade Journal* 11 (February 1915), pp. 42–3.
'War and the Imagination', *New Statesman* 3 (8 August 1914), p. 554.
'War Has Stopped European Letters and Art', *New York Times* (5 November 1916), p. 8.
'War Helps Sales Here of Diamonds and Art', *New York Times* (4 January 1917), p. 5.
'War Map Posters: A Timely and Practical Suggestion, from one of Mr. Chas. E. Dawson's Recent Lessons to his Students', *Art News* (28 September 1914), pp. 261–2.
'War Notes', *Poetry Review* 3 (September 1914), p. 140.
'The War Time Collector: Some Sacrifices', *The Times* (6 October 1916), p. 9.
Warren, H., 'The Appeal of Poetry at the Present Hour' (address given at annual meeting of Poetry Society, 25 May 1916), *Fortnightly Review* 100 (1 July 1916), pp. 110–23.
Weirter, L., *A Few Hints on Military Sketching with the 'Whirter Retractor'* (Aldershot: Gale & Polden, 1915).
'What the Public Want', *Fine Art Trade Journal* 10 (September 1914), p. 266.
Whistler, J., *Mr Whistler's Ten O'Clock* (London: Chatto & Windus, 1888).
Whitley, W., 'A General View', *Burlington Magazine* 27 (April 1915), pp. 41–3.
Wilkinson, N., *A Brush with Life* (London: Seeley, 1969).
Wilson, H. and Hammerton, J. (eds.), *The Great War: The Standard History of the All-Europe Conflict*, 10 vols. (London: London Amalgamated Press, 1914–20).
Withers, H., 'The War-Saving Idea', *Cornhill Magazine* 42 (1917), pp. 623–30.
Witt, R., 'The Trustees' Report on the National Gallery', *Quarterly Review* 224 (October 1915), pp. 344–55.
Wyndham Lewis, P., 'Artists and the War', *Blast: Review of the Great English Vortex* 2 (1915), pp. 23–6.
Blasting and Bombardiering (London: Eyre & Spottiswoode, 1937).
The Caliph's Design: Architects! Where is Your Vortex? (London: Egoist Press, 1919).
'Long Live the Vortex!', *Blast: Review of the Great English Vortex* 1 (1914), pp. 7–8.
X., 'The Imperial War Museum – Exhibition of War Paintings and Other Records', *Burlington Magazine* 36 (February 1920), pp. 94–5.

X. B., 'The Export of Art Treasures', *Saturday Review* 123 (20 January 1917), pp. 57–8.
'The Young British Artist', *Daily Telegraph* (28 December 1920), p. 12.

Secondary sources

Adorno, T., *Aesthetic Theory*, trans. G. Adorno and R. Tiedemann (London: Athlone, 1999).
Allen, B. (ed.), *Towards a Modern Art World* (New Haven and London: Yale University Press, 1995).
Anderson, B., *Imagined Communities: Reflections on the Origin and Spread of Nationalism* (London: Verso, 1983).
Apel, D., *War Culture and the Contest of Images* (New Brunswick, NJ and London: Rutgers University Press, 2012).
Arnold, B., *Orpen: Mirror to an Age* (London: Jonathan Cape, 1981).
Ashcroft T., *English Art and English Society* (London: Peter Davies, 1936).
Atkin, J., *A War of Individuals: Bloomsbury Attitudes to the Great War* (Manchester University Press, 2002).
Atterbury, P., 'Dazzle Painting', *Antique Collector* 47 (1975), pp. 25–9.
Audoin-Rouzeau, S., *La guerre des enfants, 1914–1918: essai d'histoire culturelle* (Paris: A. Colin, 1993).
Badsey, S., 'Cavalry and the Development of Breakthrough Doctrine', in P. Griffith (ed.), *British Fighting Methods in the Great War* (London: F. Cass, 1996), pp. 138–74.
Bailey, S., 'De László's Relationships with his Patrons and Sitters', in S. Bailey and S. de Laszlo (eds.), *A Brush with Grandeur: Philip de László (1869–1937)* (London: Paul Holberton, 2004), pp. 51–64.
Barker, E., 'The Primitive Within: The Question of Race in Epstein's Career, 1917–1929', in E. Silber (ed.), *Jacob Epstein: Sculpture and Drawings* (Leeds: Maney, in association with the Henry Moore Centre for the Study of Sculpture, 1989), pp. 45–8.
Baron, W., *Perfect Moderns: A History of the Camden Town Group* (Aldershot: Ashgate, 2000).
Sickert (London: Phaidon, 1973).
Sickert: Paintings and Drawings (New Haven and London: Yale University Press, 2006).
Barringer, T., *Men at Work: Art and Labour in Victorian Britain* (New Haven and London: Yale University Press, 2005).
Barthes, R., *Camera Lucida: Reflections on Photography*, trans. R. Howard (London: Hill & Wang, 1981).
Mythologies, trans. A. Lavers (London: Vintage, 1993).
Bazin, A., *What is Cinema?*, trans. H. Gray, 2 vols. (Berkeley and Los Angeles: University of California Press, 1967).
Becker, A., 'Graffiti et sculptures des soldats', *14/18 Aujourd'hui –Today – Heute* 2 (1999), special issue: L'Archéologie et la Grande Guerre, pp. 117–27.
Becker, H., *Art Worlds* (Berkeley, Los Angeles and London: University of California Press, 1982).
Beckett, I., *The First World War: Essential Guide to Sources in the UK National Archives* (London: Public Record Office, 2002).
The Great War 1914–1918 (Harlow: Pearson Education, 2001).
Home Front: 1914–1918 (Kew: National Archives, 2006).

Beckett, J., '(Is)land Narratives: Englishness, Visuality and Vanguard Culture 1914–1918', in D. Peters Corbett and L. Perry (eds.), *English Art, 1860–1914: Modern Artists and Identity* (Manchester University Press, 2000), pp. 195–212.
Beckett, J. and Cherry, D., 'Reconceptualizing Vorticism: Women, Modernity, Modernism', in P. Edwards (ed.), *Blast: Vorticism 1914–18* (Aldershot: Ashgate, 2000), pp. 59–73.
Beegan, G., *The Mass Image: A Social History of Photomechanical Reproduction in Victorian London* (Basingstoke: Palgrave Macmillan, 2008).
Behrens, R., 'The Role of Artists in Ship Camouflage during World War I', *Leonardo* 32 (1999), pp. 53–9.
Belting, H., *Anthropology of Images: Picture, Medium, Body*, trans. T. Dunlop (Princeton University Press, 2011).
Bickel, L., *In Search of Frank Hurley* (Melbourne: Macmillan, 1980).
Black, J., '"The Real Thing": Eric Kennington's 24th Infantry Division Memorial in Battersea Park, London (1921–24)', *Burlington Magazine* 145 (December 2003), pp. 854–9.
Black, J. *et al.*, *Blasting the Future! Vorticism in Britain 1910–20* (London: Philip Wilson, 2004).
Blechman, H. and Newman, A. (eds.), *DPM – Disruptive Pattern Material: An Encyclopedia of Camouflage*, 2 vols. (London: DPM, 2004).
Boswell, J. and Johns, B., 'Patriots or Profiteers? British Businessmen and the First World War', *Journal of European Economic History* 11 (1982), pp. 423–45.
Bourdieu, P., *Distinction: A Social Critique of the Judgement of Taste*, trans. R. Nice (London: Routledge & Kegan Paul, 1984).
Bourke, J., *Dismembering the Male: Men's Bodies, Britain and the Great War* (London: Reaktion, 1996).
Bourne, J., *Britain and the Great War 1914–18* (London: Edward Arnold, 1989).
Bourne, R., *Lords of Fleet Street: The Harmsworth Dynasty* (London: Unwin Hyman, 1990).
Bowley, A., *Some Economic Consequences of the War* (London: Thornton Butterworth, 1930).
Bowley, A. and Stamp, J., *The National Income, 1924. A Comparative Study of the Income of the United Kingdom in 1911 and 1924* (Oxford: Clarendon Press, 1927).
Boyd Haycock, D., *A Crisis of Brilliance: Five Young British Artists and the Great War* (London: Old Street Publishing, 2010).
Brandon, L., *Art and War* (London: I. B. Tauris, 2007).
Broadberry, S. and Howlett, P., 'The United Kingdom during World War I: Business as Usual?', in S. Broadberry and M. Harrison (eds.), *The Economics of World War I* (Cambridge University Press, 2005), pp. 206–34.
Brockington, G., *Above the Battlefield: Modernism and the Peace Movement in Britain, 1900–1918* (New Haven and London: Yale University Press, 2010).
'"Tending the Lamp" or "Minding Their Own Business"? Bloomsbury Art and Pacifism in the First World War', *Immediations* 1 (Spring 2004), pp. 6–19.
Brook, D., 'Painting, Photography and Representation', *Journal of Aesthetics and Art Criticism* 42 (Winter 1983), pp. 171–80.
Brothers, C., *War and Photography: A Cultural History* (London: Routledge, 1997).
Brownlow, K., *The War, the West and the Wilderness* (London: Secker & Warburg, 1979).

Bryant, B., 'Thomas, Herbert Samuel (1883–1966)', *Oxford Dictionary of National Biography* (Oxford University Press), www.oxforddnb.com/view/article/66126 (accessed 29 June 2013).

Buchloh, B., 'Figures of Authority, Ciphers of Regression: Notes on the Return of Representation in European Painting', *October* 16 (Spring 1981), pp. 39–68.

Burden, R. and Kohl, S. (eds.), *Landscape and Englishness* (Amsterdam and New York: Rodopi, 2006).

Burke, K. (ed.), *War and the State: The Transformation of British Government, 1914–1919* (London: George Allen & Unwin, 1982).

Burke, P., *Varieties of Cultural History* (Cambridge: Polity, 1997).

Cannadine, D., *The Decline and Fall of the British Aristocracy* (New Haven and London: Yale University Press, 1990).

Carey, J., *The Intellectuals and the Masses: Pride and Prejudice among the Literary Intelligentsia, 1880–1939* (London: Faber & Faber, 1992).

Carline, R., *Stanley Spencer at War* (London: Faber & Faber, 1978).

Carmichael, J., *First World War Photographers* (London and New York: Routledge, 1999).

Causey, A., *Paul Nash* (Oxford: Clarendon Press, 1980).

Cecil, H., 'Herbert Read and the Great War', in D. Goodway (ed.), *Herbert Read Reassessed* (Liverpool University Press, 1998), pp. 30–45.

Chamot, M., Farr, D. and Butlin, M., *The Tate Gallery Catalogues: The Modern British Paintings, Drawings and Sculpture*, 2 vols. (London: Tate, 1964).

Chaplin, S., *A Slade School of Art Archive Reader* (London: University College London, 1998).

Charteris, E., *Life and Letters of Sir Edmund Gosse* (New York and London: Harper & Bros, 1931).

Chartier, R., *Cultural History: Between Practices and Representations*, trans. L. G. Cochrane (Cambridge: Polity, in association with Blackwell, 1988).

'Intellectual History or Sociocultural History?', in D. LaCapra and S. L. Kaplan (eds.), *Modern European Intellectual History: Reappraisals and New Perspectives* (Ithaca, NY and London: Cornell University Press, 1982), pp. 13–47.

Chickering, R. and Förster, S. (eds.), *Great War, Total War: Combat and Mobilization on the Western Front, 1914–1918* (Cambridge University Press, 2000).

Clegg, E., 'Meštrović, England and the Great War', *Burlington Magazine* 144 (December 2002), pp. 740–51

Cobley, E., *Representing War: Form and Ideology in First World War Narratives* (London and Toronto: University of Toronto Press, 1993).

Codell, J., 'Artists' Professional Societies: Production, Consumption, and Aesthetics', in B. Allen (ed.), *Towards a Modern Art World* (New Haven and London: Yale University Press, 1995), pp. 169–87.

Cohen, A., *Imagining the Unimaginable: World War, Modern Art, and the Politics of Public Culture in Russia, 1914–1917* (Lincoln: University of Nebraska Press, 2008).

Comentale, E., *Modernism, Cultural Production, and the British Avant-Garde* (Cambridge University Press, 2004).

Cook, E., *The Press in War-Time* (London: Macmillan, 1920).

Cork, R., 'Allies of the Avant-Garde: Patrons of Advanced Art in Britain, 1910–1920', in A. Bowness (ed.), *British Contemporary Art 1910–90: Eighty Years of Collecting by the Contemporary Art Society* (London: Herbert Press, 1991), pp. 23–53.

Art beyond the Gallery in Early Twentieth-Century England (New Haven and London: Yale University Press, 1985).
A Bitter Truth: Avant-Garde Art and the Great War (New Haven and London: Yale University Press, 1994).
'Images of Extinction: Paul Nash at the Western Front', in J. Howlett and R. Mengham (eds.), *The Violent Muse: Violence and the Artistic Imagination in Europe, 1910–1939* (Manchester University Press, 1994), pp. 56–64.
'Innovation, Retrenchment and Renewal', in B. Ford (ed.) *The Cambridge Guide to the Arts in Britain*, vol. VIII, *The Edwardian Age and the Inter-war Years* (Cambridge University Press, 1989), pp. 157–80.
'Machine Age, Apocalypse and Pastoral', in S. Compton (ed.), *British Art in the Twentieth Century: The Modern Movement* (Munich: Prestel, 1987), pp. 63–72.
Vorticism and Abstract Art in the First Machine Age, 2 vols. (London: G. Fraser, 1976).
'The Vorticist Circle, Bomberg and the First World War', in S. Compton (ed.), *British Art in the Twentieth Century: The Modern Movement* (Munich: Prestel, 1987), pp. 138–41.
Cowling, E. and Mundy, J., *On Classic Ground: Picasso, Léger, de Chirico and the New Classicism 1910–30* (London: Tate, 1990).
Crary, J., *Techniques of the Observer: On Vision and Modernity in the Nineteenth Century* (Cambridge, MA: MIT Press, 1990).
Crellin, S., 'Hollow Men: Francis Derwent Wood's Masks and Memorials, 1915–1925', *Sculpture Journal* 6 (2001), pp. 75–88.
Cross, T., *Artists and Bohemians: 100 Years with the Chelsea Arts Club* (London: Quiller Press, 1992).
Cumming, R., *Artists at War, 1914–18* (Cambridge: Kettle's Yard Gallery, 1974).
Cuppleditch, D., *The London Sketch Club* (Stroud: Alan Sutton, 1994).
Dagen, P., *Le silence des peintres: les artistes face à la Grande Guerre* (Paris: Fayard, 1996).
Dakers, C., *The Countryside at War 1914–1918* (London: Constable, 1986).
Danto, A., 'The Artworld', *Journal of Philosophy* 61 (1964), pp. 571–84.
Das, S., *Touch and Intimacy in First World War Literature* (Cambridge University Press, 2006).
Daunton, M., *Just Taxes: The Politics of Taxation in Britain, 1914–1979* (Cambridge University Press, 2002).
De Groot, G., *Blighty: British Society in the Era of the Great War* (London: Longman, 1996).
Delaney, J., *Charles Ricketts: A Biography* (Oxford: Clarendon Press, 1990).
Derez, M., 'The Flames of Louvain: The War Experience of an Academic Community', in H. Cecil and P. Liddle (eds.), *Facing Armageddon: The First World War Experienced* (London: Leo Cooper, 1996), pp. 617–29.
De Zayas, M., 'Picasso Speaks', *The Arts* 7 (May 1923).
Dibbets, K. and Hogenkamp, B. (eds.), *Film and the First World War* (Amsterdam University Press, 1995).
Dickie, G., *Art and the Aesthetic: An Institutional Analysis* (Ithaca, NY: Cornell University Press, 1974).
Dixon, R., '"Where are the dead?" Spiritualism, Photography and the Great War', *History of Photography* 28 (Autumn 2004), pp. 247–60.
Dowling, L., *The Vulgarization of Art: The Victorians and Aesthetic Democracy* (Charlottesville and London: University Press of Virginia, 1996).
Dunbar, J., *Laura Knight* (London: Collins, 1975).

Dutton, P., 'Moving Images? The Parliamentary Recruiting Committee's Poster Campaign, 1914–1916', *Imperial War Museum Review* 4 (1989), pp. 43–58.

Duveen, J., *The Rise of the House of Duveen* (London: Longmans, Green & Co., 1957).

Thirty Years of British Art (London: The Studio, 1930).

Edwards, P., *Wyndham Lewis: Art and War* (London: Wyndham Lewis Memorial Trust, in association with Lund Humphries, 1992).

Wyndham Lewis: Painter and Writer (New Haven and London: Yale University Press, 2000).

Edwards, P. (ed.), *Blast 1914–18* (Aldershot: Ashgate, 2000).

Eksteins, M., *Rites of Spring: The Great War and the Birth of the Modern Age* (New York: Bantam Press, 1989).

Elder, E., *Travelling Players: The Story of the Arts League of Service* (London: F. Muller, 1939).

Elmer, S., 'The "Nameless Exhibition", London, 1921', *Burlington Magazine* 153 (September 2011), pp. 583–90.

Faith, N., *Sold: The Revolution in the Art Market* (London: Hamish Hamilton, 1985).

Farish, M., 'Modern Witnesses: Foreign Correspondents, Geopolitical Vision, and the First World War', *Transactions of the Institute of British Geographers* 26 (2001), pp. 273–87.

Farr, D., *English Art 1870–1940* (Oxford University Press, 1978).

Felstead, S., *German Spies at Bay: Being an Actual Record of the German Espionage in Great Britain during the Years 1914–1918, Compiled from Official Sources* (London: Hutchinson, 1920).

Fer, B., Batchelor, D. and Wood, P., *Realism, Rationalism, Surrealism: Art between the Wars* (New Haven and London: Yale University Press, in association with the Open University, 1993).

Ferguson, J., *The Arts in Britain in World War I* (London: Macmillan, 1980).

Ferguson, N., *The Pity of War* (London: Penguin Books, 1998).

Flukinger, R., *The Formative Decades: Photography in Great Britain, 1839–1920* (Austin: University of Texas Press, 1985).

Foot, M., *Art and War: Twentieth Century Warfare as Depicted by War Artists* (London: Imperial War Museum, 1990).

Forge, A., 'The Slade' (part III), *Motif* 6 (Spring 1961).

Foss, B., *War Paint: Art, War, State and Identity in Britain, 1939–1945* (New Haven and London: Yale University Press, 2007).

Foster, H., 'Prosthetic Gods', *Modernism/Modernity* 4 (April 1997), pp. 5–38.

Fox, J., 'Conflict and Consolation: British Art and the First World War, 1914–1919', *Art History* 36 (September 2013), pp. 810–33.

'"Fiddling While Rome is Burning": Hostility to Art during the First World War, 1914–1918', *Visual Culture in Britain* 11 (Spring 2010), pp. 49–65.

'Poppy Politics: Remembrance of Things Present', in C. Sandis (ed.), *Cultural Heritage Ethics* (Cambridge: Open Book Publishers, 2014), pp. 21–30.

'"Peace Pictures": Optimistic Art in the First World War', in A. Murrin and B. Eastham (eds.), *Optimism* (London: Hannah Barry Publishing, 2008), pp. 12–16.

'"Traitor Painters": Artists and Espionage in the First World War, 1914–1918', *British Art Journal* 10 (Spring 2009), pp. 62–8.

Fraser Jenkins, D., 'Art in Exile: Flanders, Wales and the First World War', *Apollo* 157 (April 2003), pp. 56–7.

Frayling, C., *The Royal College of Art: One Hundred and Fifty Years of Art and Design* (London: Barrie & Jenkins, 1987).
Freedberg, D., *The Power of Images: Studies in the History and Theory of Response* (University of Chicago Press, 1989).
Freer, A., *John Nash: 'The Delighted Eye'* (Aldershot: Scolar Press, 1993).
French, D., 'The Rise and Fall of "Business as Usual"', in K. Burke (ed.), *War and the State: The Transformation of British Government, 1914–1919* (London: George Allen & Unwin, 1982), pp. 7–32.
'Spy Fever in Britain, 1900–1915', *Historical Journal* 21 (June 1978), pp. 355–70.
Fuller, J., *Troop Morale and Popular Culture in the British and Dominion Armies 1914–1918* (Oxford: Clarendon, 1990).
Fussell, P., *The Great War and Modern Memory* (Oxford University Press, 1975).
Gallatin, A., *Art and the Great War* (New York: E. P. Dutton, 1919).
Gardiner, S., *Epstein: Artist against the Establishment* (London: M. Joseph, 1992).
Gee, M., 'The Avant-Garde, Order and the Art Market, 1916–23', *Art History* 2 (March 1979), pp. 96–8.
Getsy, D., 'Locating Modern Art in Britain', *Art Journal* 60 (Winter 2001), pp. 98–102.
Gifford, T., *Pastoral* (London: Routledge, 1999).
Ginzburg, C., '"Your Country Needs You": A Case Study in Political Iconography', *History Workshop Journal* 42 (Autumn 2001), pp. 1–22.
Gledhill, J., 'Matthew Smith's Experience of War and its Effect on his Cornish Landscapes of 1920', *British Art Journal* 4 (Spring 2003), pp. 97–101.
Glew, A., '"Blue Spiritual Sounds": Kandinsky and the Sadlers 1911–16', *Burlington Magazine* 139 (September 1997), pp. 600–15.
Goebel, S., 'Exhibitions', in J. Winter and J.-L. Robert (eds.), *Capital Cities at War: Paris, London Berlin 1914–1919*, 2 vols. (Cambridge University Press, 2007), vol. II, pp. 143–87.
The Great War and Medieval Memory: War, Remembrance and Medievalism in Britain and Germany, 1914–1940 (Cambridge University Press, 2006).
Gosling, L., *Brushes and Bayonets: Cartoons, Sketches and Paintings of World War I* (London: Osprey, 2008).
Gough, P., 'The Empty Battlefield', *Imperial War Museum Review* 8 (1993), pp. 38–47.
'The Experience of British Artists in the Great War', in H. Cecil and P. Liddle (eds.), *Facing Armageddon: The First World War Experienced* (London: Leo Cooper, 1996), pp. 841–53.
'A Terrible Beauty': War, Art and Imagination, 1914–1918 (Bristol: Samson & Co., 2009).
Green, C., *Léger and the Avant-Garde* (London: Yale University Press, 1976).
Green, O. and Taylor, S., *The Moving Metropolis: A History of London's Transport since 1800* (London: Lawrence King, 2003).
Greenberg, A., 'Lutyens's Cenotaph', *Journal of the Society of Architectural Historians* 48 (March 1989), pp. 5–23.
Gregory, A., 'British "War Enthusiasm" in 1914: A Reassessment', in G. Braybon (ed.), *Evidence, History and the Great War: Historians and the Impact of 1914–1918* (Oxford and New York: Berghahn, 2003), pp. 67–85.
The Last Great War: British Society and the First World War (Cambridge University Press, 2008).
The Silence of Memory: Armistice Day, 1919–1946 (Oxford: Berg, 1994).

Gregory, [Isabella] Augusta, Lady, *Sir Hugh Lane: His Life and Legacy* (Gerrards Cross: Colin Smythe, 1973).
Grieves, K., *The Politics of Manpower, 1914–1918* (Manchester University Press, 1988).
Gruetzner Robins, A., *Modern Art in Britain 1910–14* (London: Merrell Holberton, 1997).
Gunning, T., 'What's the Point of an Index? or, Faking Photographs', *Nordicom Review* 25 (2004), pp. 39–49.
Hardie, M. and Sabin, A. (eds.), *War Posters Issued by Belligerent and Neutral Nations 1914–1919* (London: A. & C. Black, 1920).
Harries, M. and S., *The War Artists: British Official Art of the Twentieth Century* (London: Michael Joseph, 1983).
Harrington, P., *British Artists and War: The Face of Battle in Paintings and Prints, 1700–1914* (London: Greenhill Books, 1993).
'Early Paintings of the Great War', *Imperial War Museum Review* 7 (1992), pp. 46–54.
Harris, N., 'Iconography and Intellectual History: The Halftone Effect', in *Cultural Excursions: Marketing Appetites and Cultural Tastes in Modern America* (Chicago and London: University of Chicago Press, 1990), pp. 304–17.
Harrison, C., *English Art and Modernism 1900–1939* (London: Allen Lane, 1981).
'"Englishness" and "Modernism" Revisited', *Modernism/Modernity* 6 (1999), pp. 75–90.
Hartshorne, C., Weiss, P. and Burks, A. (eds.),*The Collected Papers of Charles Sanders Peirce*, vol. IV. (Cambridge, MA: Harvard University Press, 1933).
Harvey, A., *A Muse of Fire: Literature, Art and War* (London: Hambledon Press, 1998).
Hassall, C., *Edward Marsh: Patron of the Arts* (London: Longmans, 1959).
Haste, C., *Keep the Home Fires Burning: Propaganda in the First World War* (London: Allen Lane, 1977).
Haworth Booth, M., *E. McKnight Kauffer: A Designer and His Public* (London: Gordon Fraser Gallery, 1979).
Healy, M., *Vienna and the Fall of the Habsburg Empire: Total War and Everyday Life in World War I* (Cambridge University Press, 2004).
Herrmann, F., *Sotheby's: Portrait of an Auction House* (London: Chatto & Windus, 1980).
Hewitt, N., 'The National Inventory of War Memorials', in J.-M. Teutonico and J. Fidler (eds.), *Monuments and the Millennium: Proceedings of a Joint Conference Organised by English Heritage and the United Kingdom Institute for Conservation* (London: James & James, 2001).
Hiley, N., '"Kitchener Wants You" and "Daddy, what did YOU do in the Great War?": The Myth of British Recruiting Posters', *Imperial War Museum Review* 11 (1997), pp. 40–58.
'"Let's go to the pictures": The British Cinema Audience in the 1920s and 1930s', *Journal of Popular British Cinema* 2 (1999), pp. 39–53.
Making War: British Propaganda (Cambridge University Press, 2000).
'"Nothing More than a 'Craze'": Cinema Building in Britain from 1909 to 1914', in A. Higson (ed.), *Young and Innocent? The Cinema in Britain, 1896–1930* (University of Exeter Press, 2002), pp. 111–27.
Hind, C. L., *Landscape Painting from Giotto to the Present Day*, vol. II, *From Constable to the Present Day* (London: Chapman & Hall, 1924).
Hodgson, P., *The War Illustrators* (London: Osprey, 1977).
Hogan, S., *Healing Arts: The History of Art Therapy* (London: Jessica Kingsley, 2001).
Hogarth, P., *The Artist as Reporter* (London: Gordon Fraser, 1986).

Holroyd, M., *Augustus John: The New Biography* (London: Heinemann, 1996).
Holt, Y., *British Artists and the Modernist Landscape* (Aldershot: Ashgate, 2003).
'Nature and Nostalgia: Philip Wilson Steer and Edwardian Landscapes', *Oxford Art Journal* 19 (1996), pp. 28–45.
Philip Wilson Steer (Cardiff: Seren Books, 1992).
Homberger, E., 'The Story of the Cenotaph', *Times Literary Supplement* (12 November 1976), pp. 1429–30.
Hone, J., *The Life of Henry Tonks* (London: William Heinemann, 1939).
Horne, J., *State, Society and Mobilization in Europe during the First World War* (Cambridge University Press, 1997).
Horne, J. and Kramer, A., *German Atrocities, 1914: A History of Denial* (New Haven and London: Yale University Press, 2001).
Howkins, A., 'The Discovery of Rural England', in R. Colls and P. Dodd (eds.), *Englishness: Politics and Culture 1880–1920* (London: Croom Helm, 1976).
Humphrey, J. (ed.), *The London Group* (London: London Group Publishing, 2003).
Hüppauf, B., 'Experiences of Modern Warfare and the Crisis of Representation', *New German Critique* 59 (Spring 1993), pp. 41–76.
Huss, M., *Histoires de famille: cartes postales et culture de guerre* (Paris: Noesis, 2000)
Hutchison, H., *London Transport Posters* (London: London Transport Board, 1963).
Hutchison, S., *The History of the Royal Academy 1768–1986* (London: Robert Royce, 1987).
Hyman, T. and Wright, P. (eds.), *Stanley Spencer* (London: Tate, 2001).
Hyne, A. (ed.), *David Jones: A Fusilier at the Front* (Bridgend: Seren, 1995).
Hynes, S., *A War Imagined: The First World War and English Culture* (London: Bodley Head, 1990).
Inglis, F., 'Landscape as Popular Culture', *Landscape Research* 12 (1987), pp. 20–4.
James, P. (ed.), *Picture This: World War I Posters and Visual Culture* (Lincoln and London: University of Nebraska Press, 2010).
Jay, M., *Downcast Eyes: The Denigration of Vision in Twentieth-Century French Thought* (Berkeley and London: University of California Press, 1993).
'Scopic Regimes of Modernity', in H. Foster (ed.), *Vision and Visuality: Discussions in Contemporary Culture* (Seattle: Bay View Press, 1988).
Johnson, J. and Gruetzer, A. (eds.)., *Dictionary of British Artists 1880–1940* (London: Antique Collectors Club, 1980).
Johnson, P., *Front Line Artists* (London: Cassell, 1978).
Jolly, M., 'Australian First-World-War Photography: Frank Hurley and Charles Bean', *History of Photography* 23 (Summer 1999), pp. 141–8.
'Composite Propaganda Photographs during the First World War', *History of Photography* 27 (Summer 2003), pp. 154–65.
Jones, B., 'Denying the "Foe-to-graphic": C. R. W. Nevinson and Photography', in M. J. K. Walsh (ed.), *A Dilemma of English Modernism: Visual and Verbal Politics in the Life and Work of C. R. W. Nevinson 1889–1946* (Newark: University of Delaware Press, 2007), pp. 134–81.
Kahn, E., *The Neglected Majority: 'Les Camoufleurs', Art History and World War I* (Lanham, MD: University Press of America, 1984).
Kalstone, D., 'Conjuring with Nature: Some Twentieth-Century Readings of Pastoral', in R. A. Brower (ed.), *Twentieth-Century Literature in Retrospect* (Cambridge, MA: Harvard University Press, 1971).

Kavanagh, G., *Museums and the First World War: A Social History* (London: Leicester University Press, 1994).
Kern, S., *The Culture of Time and Space, 1880–1918* (Cambridge, MA and London: Harvard University Press, 2003).
King, A., *Memorials of the Great War in Britain: The Symbolism and Politics of Remembrance* (Oxford: Berg, 1998).
Klein, M., *The Writings of Melanie Klein*, 4 vols. (London: Hogarth Press, 1975).
Knightley, P., *The First Casualty: The War Correspondent as Hero, Propagandist, and Myth Maker from the Crimea to Vietnam* (London: Deutsch, 1975).
Kramer, A., *Dynamic of Destruction: Culture and Mass Killing in the First World War* (Oxford University Press, 2007).
Lacey, R., *Sotheby's: Bidding for Class* (London: Warner Books, 1999).
Laffin, J., *The Western Front Illustrated, 1914–1918* (Stroud: Sutton, 1991).
World War I in Post-Cards (Gloucester: Alan Sutton, 1988).
Lago, M., 'Rothenstein, Sir William (1872–1945)', in *Oxford Dictionary of National Biography* (Oxford University Press), www.oxforddnb.com/view/article/35842 (accessed 27 May 2012).
Lasswell, H., *Propaganda Technique and Identity in the World War* (London: Kegan Paul, 1927).
Lawrence, J., 'Material Pressures on the Middle Classes', in J. Winter and J.-L. Robert (eds.), *Capital Cities at War: Paris, London, Berlin 1914–1919*, 2 vols. (Cambridge University Press, 1997), vol. I, pp. 229–54.
'Public Space, Political Space', in J. Winter and J.-L. Robert, *Capital Cities at War: Paris, London, Berlin 1914–1919*, 2 vols. (Cambridge University Press, 2007), vol. II, pp. 280–312.
Lawrence, J., Dean, M. and Robert, J.-L., 'The Outbreak of War and the Urban Economy: Paris, Berlin and London in 1914', *Economic History Review* 45 (August 1992), pp. 564–93.
Leed, E., *No Man's Land: Combat and Identity in World War I* (Cambridge University Press, 1979).
Lewis, F., *Benjamin Williams Leader RA, 1831–1923* (Leigh-on-Sea: F. Lewis, 1971).
Lipke, W., *David Bomberg: A Critical Study of his Life and Work* (London: Evelyn, Adams & Mackay, 1967).
Low, R., *The History of the British Film*, vol. III, *1914–1918* (New York: R. R. Bowker, 1973).
Luhmann, N., *Art as a Social System*, trans. E. Knodt (Stanford University Press, 2000).
McConkey, K., 'Haunts of Ancient Peace', in D. Peters Corbett, Y. Holt and F. Russell (eds.), *The Geographies of Englishness: Landscape and the National Past, 1880–1940* (New Haven and London: Yale University Press, 2002), pp. 65–89.
McDermott, J., '"A Needless Sacrifice": British Businessmen and Business as Usual in the First World War', *Albion* 21 (Spring 1989), pp. 263–82.
Mace, R., *Trafalgar Square: Emblem of Empire* (London: Lawrence & Wishart, 1976).
Malvern, S., 'Art and War: Truth or Fiction?', *Art History* 19 (1996), pp. 307–12.
'Memorizing the Great War: Stanley Spencer at Burghclere', *Art History* 23 (2000), pp. 182–204.
Modern Art, Britain and the Great War: Witnessing, Testimony and Remembrance (New Haven and London: Yale University Press, 2004).

'"War as it Is": The Art of Muirhead Bone, C. R. W. Nevinson, and Paul Nash, 1916–17', *Art History* 9 (December 1986), pp. 487–515.
'War Tourisms: "Englishness", Art and the First World War', *Oxford Art Journal* 24 (2001), pp. 45–66.
Marillier, H., *Christie's: 1766–1925* (London: Constable, 1926).
Martin, W., *'The New Age' under Orage: Chapters in English Cultural History* (Manchester University Press, 1967).
Marwick, A., *The Deluge: British Society and the First World War* (London: Macmillan, 1965).
Marwick, A. (ed.), *Total War and Social Change* (London: Macmillan, 1988).
Masterman, C., *England after War: A Study* (London: Hodder & Stoughton, 1922).
Materer, T., *Vortex: Pound, Eliot and Lewis* (London: Cornell University Press, 1979).
Matless, D., *Landscape and Englishness* (London: Reaktion, 1988).
Merrill, L., *A Pot of Paint: Aesthetics on Trial in Whistler vs Ruskin* (Washington, DC and London: Smithsonian Institution Press, 1992).
Mitchell, W. J. T. (ed.), *Landscape and Power* (Chicago and London: University of Chicago Press, 1994).
Moore, G., *Modern Painting* (London: Walter Scott, 1893).
Moriarty, C., '"Through a Picture Only": Portrait Photography and the Commemoration of the First World War', in G. Braybon (ed.) *Evidence, History, and the Great War: Historians and the Impact of 1914–18* (Oxford: Berghahn, 2005), pp. 31–47.
Morris, W., *The Earthly Paradise*, ed. F. Boos (New York and London: Routledge, 2002).
Mosse, G., *Fallen Soldiers: Reshaping the Memory of the World Wars* (New York and Oxford: Oxford University Press, 1990).
'Mr. Bert Thomas: Obituary', The Times (7 September 1966), p. 16.
Niemi, R., *History in the Media: Film and Television* (Santa Barbara, CA: ABC-Clio, 2006).
Norman, G., 'History in Pictures', *The Times* (22 October 1977), p. 9.
O'Keeffe, P., *Some Sort of Genius: A Life of Wyndham Lewis* (London: Pimlico, 2001).
Orchard, K., '"A Laugh like a Bomb": The History and Ideas of the Vorticists', in P. Edwards and J. Beckett (eds.), *Blast: Vorticism 1914–1918* (Aldershot: Ashgate, 2000), pp. 14–26.
Panayi, P., *The Enemy in Our Midst: Germans in Britain during the First World War* (New York and Oxford: Berg, 1991).
Pankhurst, E., *The Home Front* (London: Hutchinson & Co., 1932).
Paret, P., *Imagined Battles: Reflections of War in European Art* (Chapel Hill and London: University of North Carolina Press, 1997).
Paris, M., *Over the Top: The Great War and Juvenile Literature in Britain* (London: Greenwood Publishing Group, 2004).
Paris, M. (ed.), *The First World War and Popular Cinema: 1914 to the Present* (Edinburgh University Press, 1999).
Parker, J., *Great Art Sales of the Century* (London: Pitman Publishing, 1975).
Penny, N., 'English Sculpture and the First World War', *Oxford Art Journal* 4 (November 1981), pp. 36–42.
Peppis, P., *Literature, Politics, and the English Avant-Garde: Nation and Empire, 1901–1918* (Cambridge University Press, 2000).
Perloff, M., *The Futurist Moment: Avant-Garde, Avant-Guerre, and the Language of Rupture* (University of Chicago Press, 2003).

Peters Corbett, D., 'The Geography of *Blast*: Landscape, Modernity and English Painting, 1914–30', in D. Peters Corbett, Y. Holt and F. Russell (eds.), *The Geographies of Englishness: Landscape and the National Past, 1880–1940* (New Haven and London: Yale University Press, 2002), pp. 115–38.

'Laurence Binyon, and the Aesthetic of Modern Art', *Visual Culture in Britain* 6 (2005), special issue: *Civilised Painting*, pp. 101–19.

The Modernity of English Art 1914–30 (Manchester University Press, 1997).

Peters Corbett, D. (ed.). *Wyndham Lewis and the Art of Modern War* (Cambridge University Press, 1998).

Peters Corbett, D. and Perry, L. (eds.), *English Art, 1860–1914: Modern Artists and Identity* (Manchester University Press, 2000).

Playne, C., *Britain Holds On: 1917, 1918* (London: George Allen & Unwin, 1933).

Society at War: 1914–1916 (London: George Allen & Unwin, 1931).

Pliny the Elder, *Natural History: A Selection*, ed. J. F. Healey (London: Penguin Books, 1991).

Potts, A., '"Constable Country" between the Wars', in R. Samuel (ed.), *Patriotism: The Making and Unmaking of British National Identity*, 3 vols. (London: Routledge, 1989), vol. III, pp. 160–86.

Powers, A., 'Murals of the Arts and Crafts Movement at the 1916 Exhibition', *Craft History* 1 (October 1988), pp. 23–30.

Prendeville, B., *Realism in Twentieth-Century Painting* (London: Thames & Hudson, 2000).

Prest, A. and Adams, A., *Consumers' Expenditure in the United Kingdom 1900–1919* (Cambridge University Press, 1954).

Prigg, C. (ed.), *The War Dispatches* (London: Times Press, 1964).

Read, H., *The Contrary Experience* (London: Secker & Warburg, 1973).

Reeves, N., *Official British Film Propaganda during the First World War* (London: Croom Helm, 1986).

'Official War Propaganda', in M. Paris (ed.), *The First World War and Popular Cinema: 1914 to the Present* (Edinburgh University Press, 1999), pp. 27–50.

The Power of Film Propaganda: Myth or Reality? (London: Cassell, 1999).

'Through the Eyes of the Camera: Contemporary Cinema Audiences and their "Experience" of War in the film, *Battle of the Somme*', in C. Cecil and P. Liddle (eds.), *Facing Armageddon: The First World War Experienced* (London: Leo Cooper, 1996), pp. 781–92.

Reid, B., *The Man from New York: John Quinn and his Friends* (Oxford and New York: Oxford University Press, 1968).

Reynolds, D., *The Long Shadow: The Great War and the Twentieth Century* (London: Simon & Schuster, 2013).

Robb, G., *British Culture and the First World War* (London: Palgrave, 2002).

Robert, J.-L., 'The Image of the Profiteer', in J. Winter and J.-L. Robert (eds.), *Capital Cities at War: Paris, London, Berlin 1914–1919*, 2 vols. (Cambridge University Press, 1997), vol. I, pp. 104–32.

Rose, J., *Daemons and Angels: A Life of Jacob Epstein* (London: Constable, 2002).

Rose, P., '"It Must Be Done Now": The Arts and Crafts Exhibition at Burlington House, 1916', *Journal of the Decorative Arts Society* 17 (1992), pp. 3–12.

Roshwald, A. and Stites, R. (eds.), *European Culture in the Great War: Arts, Entertainment and Propaganda 1914–18* (Cambridge University Press, 1999).

Rothenstein, W., *British Artists and the War* (London: Peter Davies, 1931).
Rüger, J., 'Entertainments', in J. Winter and J.-L. Robert, *Capital Cities at War: Paris, London, Berlin 1914–1919*, 2 vols. (Cambridge University Press, 2007), vol. II, pp. 105–40.
Rutter, O., *Portrait of a Painter: The Authorized Life of Philip de László* (London: Hodder & Stoughton, 1939).
Saler, M., *The Avant-Garde in Interwar England: Medieval Modernism and the London Underground* (New York and Oxford: Oxford University Press, 2001).
'Making It New: Visual Modernism and the "Myth of the North" in Interwar England', *Journal of British Studies* 37 (October 1998), pp. 419–40.
Sanders, M. and Taylor, P., *British Propaganda during the First World War* (London: Macmillan, 1982).
Saunders, N., *Matters of Conflict: Material Culture, Memory and the First World War* (London: Routledge, 2004).
Trench Art: Materialities and Memories of War (Oxford: Berg, 2003).
Scarry, E., *The Body in Pain: The Making and Unmaking of the World* (New York and Oxford: Oxford University Press, 1985).
Schooling, W., 'National Saving in the United Kingdom', *Annals of the American Academy of Political and Social Science* 87 (January 1920), pp. 199–204.
Scruton, R., 'Photography and Representation', *Critical Inquiry* 7 (Spring 1981), pp. 577–603.
Shaw, H., 'Bert Thomas and his Work', *Strand Magazine* 77 (1929), p. 134.
Sherry, V., *The Great War and the Language of Modernism* (Oxford University Press, 2003).
Sillars, S., *Art and Survival in First World War Britain* (London: Macmillan, 1987).
'Icons of Englishness: Tradition and Development in the Arts of the Great War', *Critical Quarterly* 23 (June 1981), pp. 51–9.
Silver, K., *Esprit de Corps: The Art of the Parisian Avant-Garde and the First World War, 1914–1925* (London: Thames & Hudson, 1989).
Sinnema, P., *Dynamics of the Printed Page: Representing the Nation in the Illustrated London News* (Aldershot: Ashgate, 1998).
Smither, R., '"A Wonderful Idea of the Fighting": The Question of Fakes in "The Battle of the Somme"', *Historical Journal of Film, Radio and Television* 13 (1993), special issue: *Britain and the Cinema in the First World War*, pp. 149–68.
Snyder, J. and Allen, N., 'Photography, Vision, and Representation', *Critical Inquiry* 2 (Autumn 1975), pp. 143–69.
Sontag, S., *On Photography* (New York: Farrar, Straus & Giroux, 1977).
Spalding, F., *British Art since 1900* (London: Thames & Hudson, 1986).
Roger Fry: Art and Life (Norwich: Black Dog Books, 1999).
Vanessa Bell (London: Weidenfeld & Nicolson, 1983).
Stephenson, A., 'Refashioning Modern Masculinity: Whistler, Aestheticism and National Identity', in D. Peters Corbett and L. Perry (eds.), *English Art 1860–1914: Modern Artists and Identity* (Manchester University Press, 2000), pp. 133–49.
Stevens, M. A., *The Edwardians and After: The Royal Academy, 1900–1950* (London: Royal Academy, 1988, pp. 15–21).
Strachan, H., *Financing the First World War* (Oxford University Press, 2004).
Stromberg, R., *Redemption by War: The Intellectuals and 1914* (Lawrence: Regents Press of Kansas, 1982).

Taylor, B., *Art for the Nation: Exhibitions and the London Public 1747–2001* (Manchester University Press, 1999).

'Foreigners and Fascists: Patterns of Hostility to Modern Art in Britain before and after the First World War', in D. Peters Corbett, Y. Holt and F. Russell (eds.), *The Geographies of Englishness: Landscape and the National Past 1880–1940* (New Haven and London: Yale University Press, 2002), pp. 169–98.

Taylor, G., *Orage and 'The New Age'* (Sheffield Hallam University Press, 2000).

Taylor, J., *A Dream of England: Landscape, Photography and the Tourist's Imagination* (Manchester University Press, 1994).

Pictorial Photography in Britain 1900–1920 (London: Arts Council of Great Britain, 1978).

Thistlewood, D., 'The Early History of the NSEAD', *Journal of Art and Design Education* 7 (1988), pp. 37–64.

Thomson, F., *English Landed Society in the Nineteenth Century* (London: Routledge & Kegan Paul, 1963).

Tickner, L., 'Men's Work? Masculinity and Modernism', in N. Bryson, M. A. Holly and K. Moxey (eds.), *Visual Culture: Images and Interpretations* (Hanover, NH: Wesleyan University Press, 1994), pp. 42–82.

Modern life and Modern Subjects: British Art in the Early Twentieth Century (New Haven and London: Yale University Press, 2000).

Tillyard, S., *The Impact of Modernism 1900–1920: Early Modernism and the Arts and Crafts Movement in Edwardian England* (London: Routledge, 1988).

Tippett, M., *Art at the Service of War* (London: University of Toronto Press, 1984).

Trotter, D., *The English Novel in History, 1895–1920* (London: Routledge, 1993).

Trotter, W., *Instincts of the Herd in Peace and War* (London: Fisher & Unwin, 1916).

Vance, J., *Death So Noble: Memory, Meaning and the First World War* (Vancouver: UBC Press, 1997).

Verhey, J., *The Spirit of 1914: Militarism, Myth and Mobilization in Germany* (Cambridge University Press, 2000).

Viney, N., *Images of Wartime: British Art and Artists of World War I* (Newton Abbot: David & Charles, 1991).

Virilio, P., *War and Cinema: The Logistics of Perception*, trans. Patrick Camillier (London: Verso, 1989).

Waites, B., *A Class Society at War: England 1914–1918* (Leamington Spa: Berg, 1987).

Wallace, S., *War and the Image of Germany: British Academics 1914–1918* (Edinburgh: John Donald, 1988).

Walsh, M. J. K., *C. R. W. Nevinson: This Cult of Violence* (New Haven and London: Yale University Press, 2002).

Walsh, M. J. K. (ed.), *A Dilemma of English Modernism: Visual and Verbal Politics in the Life and Work of C. R. W. Nevinson 1889–1949* (Newark: University of Delaware Press, 2007).

London, Modernism, and 1914 (Cambridge University Press, 2010).

Walton, K., 'Transparent Pictures: On the Nature of Photographic Realism', *Critical Inquiry* 11 (December 1984), pp. 246–77.

Watson, A., *Enduring the Great War: Combat, Morale and Collapse in the German and British Armies, 1914–1918* (Cambridge University Press, 2008).

Weaver, M. (ed.), *British Photography in the Nineteenth Century: The Fine Art Tradition* (Cambridge University Press, 1989).

Wees, W., *Vorticism and the English Avant-Garde* (University of Toronto Press, 1972).
Wilcox, D., *The London Group 1913–39* (Aldershot: Scolar Press, 1995).
Williams, D., *Naval Camouflage 1914–1945: A Complete Visual Reference* (London: Chatham Publishing, 2001).
Williams, J., *The Home Fronts: Britain, France and Germany 1914–1918* (London: Constable, 1972).
Williams, R., *The Country and the City* (London: Chatto & Windus, 1973).
Willsdon, C., *Mural Painting in Britain 1840–1940: Image and Meaning* (Oxford University Press, 2000).
Winter, J., 'British National Identity and the First World War', in S. J. D. Green and R. C. Whiting (eds.), *The Boundaries of the State in Modern Britain* (Cambridge University Press, 1996), pp. 261–77.
'Catastrophe and Culture: Recent Trends in the Historiography of the First World War', *Journal of Modern History* 64 (September 1992), pp. 525–32.
The Great War and the British People (London: Macmillan, 1986).
'Imaginings of War: Posters and the Shadow of the Lost Generation', in P. James (ed.), *Picture This: World War I Posters and Visual Culture* (Lincoln and London: University of Nebraska Press, 2009).
'Popular Culture in Wartime Britain', in A. Roshwald and R. Stites (eds.), *European Culture in the Great War: Arts, Entertainment and Propaganda 1914–18* (Cambridge University Press, 1999), pp. 330–48.
Sites of Memory, Sites of Mourning: The Great War in European Cultural History (Cambridge University Press, 1995).
Winter, J. and Prost, A., *The Great War in History: Debates and Controversies, 1914 to the Present* (Cambridge University Press, 2005).
Winter, J. and Robert, J.-L. (eds.), *Capital Cities at War: Paris, London, Berlin 1914–1919*, vol. I (Cambridge University Press, 1997).
Capital Cities at War: Paris, London, Berlin 1914–1919, vol. II (Cambridge University Press, 2007).
Wohl, R., *The Generation of 1914* (Cambridge, MA: Harvard University Press, 1979).
Wood, R., *Benjamin Williams Leader RA, 1831–1923: His Life and Paintings* (Woodbridge: Antique Collectors' Club, 1998).
Woodeson, J., *Mark Gertler: Biography of a Painter, 1891–1939* (London: Sidgwick & Jackson, 1972).
Woodham, J., 'Design and Empire: British Design in the 1920s', *Art History* 3 (June 1980), pp. 229–40.
Zilczer, J., *The Noble Buyer: John Quinn, Patron of the Avant-Garde* (Washington, DC: Smithsonian Institution, 1978).

Unpublished dissertations

Brockington, G., '"Above the Battlefield": Art for Art's Sake and Pacifism in the First World War', unpublished DPhil thesis, University of Oxford (2003).
Cowdell, T., 'The Role of the Royal Academy in English Art, 1918–1930', unpublished PhD thesis, University of London (1980).
Elmer, S., 'Democratic Modernism: Promoting Modern Art in England, *c.* 1908–1934', unpublished PhD thesis, Courtauld Institute (2012).

Fox, J., '"Business Unusual": Art in Britain during the First World War, 1914–1918', unpublished PhD thesis, University of Cambridge (2009).

'From Vortex to Vacuum: The First World War and the British Artworld, 1914–1918', unpublished MPhil thesis, University of Cambridge (2005).

Gassert, I., 'Collaborators and Dissidents: Aspects of British Literary Publishing in the First World War, 1914–1919', unpublished DPhil thesis, University of Oxford (2001).

Holmes, C., '"A bright memory to remain": The Life and Work of Charles Sims RA (1873–1928)', unpublished PhD thesis, University of Northumbria at Newcastle (2005).

Potter, J., 'Boys in Khaki, Girls in Print: Women's Literary Responses to the Great War 1914–18', unpublished DPhil thesis, University of Oxford (2001).

Wright, B., 'Modern Art and the Professionalisation of Culture: The Development of Modern Painting in England at the Beginning of the Twentieth Century', unpublished PhD thesis, Courtauld Institute (2004).

INDEX

Page numbers in *italics* refer to figures; *pl.* denotes plate number.